AF443268

SOFT COMPUTING AGENTS

Frontiers in Artificial Intelligence and Applications

Volume 83

Published in the subseries
Knowledge-Based Intelligent Engineering Systems
Editors: L.C. Jain and R.J. Howlett

Recently published in KBIES:

Recently published in FAIA:

ISSN: 0922-6389

Soft Computing Agents

A New Perspective for Dynamic Information Systems

Edited by

Vincenzo Loia

*Department of Mathematics and Informatics, University of Salerno,
Baronissi (Salerno), Italy*

IOS

Press

Ohmsha

Amsterdam • Berlin • Oxford • Tokyo • Washington, DC

ISBN 1 58603 283 6 (IOS Press)
ISBN 4 274 90544 6 C3055 (Ohmsha)
Library of Congress Control Number: 2002112410

Publisher
IOS Press
Nieuwe Hemweg 6B
1013 BG Amsterdam
The Netherlands
fax: +31 20 620 3419
e-mail: order@iospress.nl

Distributor in the UK and Ireland
IOS Press/Lavis Marketing
73 Lime Walk
Headington
Oxford OX3 7AD
England
fax: +44 1865 75 0079

Distributor in the USA and Canada
IOS Press, Inc.
5795-G Burke Centre Parkway
Burke, VA 22015
USA
fax: +1 703 323 3668
e-mail: iosbooks@iospress.com

Distributor in Germany, Austria and Switzerland
IOS Press/LSL.de
Gerichtsweg 28
D-04103 Leipzig
Germany
fax: +49 341 995 4255

Distributor in Japan
Ohmsha, Ltd.
3-1 Kanda Nishiki-cho
Chiyoda-ku, Tokyo 101-8460
Japan
fax: +81 3 3233 2426

Foreword

Researchers in the field of information systems, whose aim is to integrate innovation and ensure highest quality results particularly in the field of soft computing agents, need to acknowledge first that being 'wired' does not necessarily mean 'interconnected'. It is important to really reach a 'cognitive interconnectivity', which is the real ability of sharing meaning as to make sure that those deliverable, which are passed around, are based upon commonly shared knowledge.

An enthusiastic approach to soft computing agents has lead researchers in the field to think of integrating different amounts of intelligence into embedded devices as a really winning strategy to implement the vision of ubiquitous computing. The idea is to transfer cognitive load from individuals to machines in ways, which make the process somewhat invisible to users.

It should never be forgotten that the very idea of intelligent systems started out of a major dream of full awareness, where individuals empowered by the result of their own thinking processes would be able to broaden the reach and realm of their expectations as for their reasoning capacities and understanding and consistent acting.

The very same dream which first inspired the pioneers in the field of information systems, should never be left behind as innovative research, which looses its first reasons to exist and primary aims, is definitely meant to loose its identity and finally dissolve.

We wish to congratulate Professor Loia, the authors and the publisher for this wonderful piece of work.

Dr Graziella Tonfoni
Professor
The George Washington University

Dr Lakhmi Jain
Professor of Knowledge-Based Engineering
University of South Australia

Soft Computing Agents

A New Perspective for Dynamic Information Systems

Preface

In the last thirty years researchers involved in the design of intelligent systems have continuously experimented with methodologies and technologies which deal with human and artificial behaviors. The study of intelligent machines is documented by an enormous and growing literature. There is a remarkable spin-off in wide range of innovative projects. In spite of this effort, intelligent-based systems design remains an open problem. Recent advances in networking technology and the ubiquity of the Internet open new perspectives in software application improvement. This new scenario demands new paradigms to cope with computational models which are characterized by unceasing dynamism, strong decentralization, and high unpredictability.

Agents or Multi-Agent Systems sketch intelligent behaviors by describing and managing computational activities shared over communities of large-grain entities. Thanks to its large potential. Agent technology has been adopted during the last years as a winning strategy to capture the essence of today's information-intensive systems

The appealing agent-based approach to problem solving arises from the development of methods which distribute groups of smart entities. Each one of these actively committed to perform independent or semi-independent tasks and to exchange asynchronous messages by means of suitable communication protocols. Agents which act on behalf of humans, machines, or other agents, in trying to solve the final goal by means of interaction-oriented mechanisms. In the last years agents have acquired growing importance due to the explosion of the WWW. The availability of a global communication infrastructure imposes the need for truely distributed computations.

This evolution has lead to a radical change of the traditional approach in conceiving software systems only from the action-based algorithmic systems to interaction-based systems. The rationale behind, is not only to capitalize on the opportunities offered by an underlying distributed, concurrent environment but to also explore new paradigms. There are able to model real or virtual worlds and to overcome the fracture between the power of natural expressions (such as linguistic acts, social behaviors, *communityware* systems) and the illusory assumption of a realistic model.

The quantity and the quality of agent-oriented books is so impressive that I do not try to undertake a complete discussion in this short informal preface but in this volume the reader will find a new perspective in the plethora of the agent works. The chapters of the volume describe interesting experiences, views, proposals stemming in different areas. Web systems play an important role as a complex arena where soft computing methodologies are employed to model agent behaviors.

Soft Computing, and in particular Fuzzy Technology, may greatly contribute to the design of smart. agents. Promising benefits derive from well founded soft computing-oriented approaches when used to better manage the behavioral models of the agents, especially when the interactions occur in an environment characterized by imprecision, uncertainty, and partial truth.

All the contributions represent well-described, self descriptive discussions. We acknowledge that as a result of the continuously increasing complexity of systems that need to be modeled there is a genuine need for a new modeling paradigm. This is referred to by the name of *"Soft Computing Agents"*.

Soft Computing Agents embody but are not limited to the following facets:

- (a) a plausible level of abstraction for building complex models,
- (b) mechanisms of approximate reasoning power which can naturally handle the uncertainty present in their environment or in their intra/extra communication activities,
- (c) an adaptive control mechanism to better cope with the evolution of the underlying environment, and
- (d) a distributed and concurrent processing of knowledge and information.

This book focuses on recent results of outstanding research projects framed within this new discipline, in particular:

- it presents the state-of-the-art in the development of soft computing -based agents;
- it examines the role of soft computing-based technology in various facets of agent design (problem-solving, autonomy, adaptivity, reactivity, communication, interaction, …);
- it cross-fertilizes ideas on the soft computing perspective to the development of agent-based intelligent information systems.

I wish to thank all the contributors for their research interests in this new field !

Vincenzo Loia

About the Editor

Dr. Vincenzo Loia is an Associate Professor at the Department of Mathematics and Computer Science at University of Salerno. He is co-founder of the Soft Computing Laboratory and founder of the Multi Agent Systems Laboratory, both at the Department of Mathematics and Computer Science.

He received the PhD in Computer Science from the University of Paris VI, France in 1989, and the bachelor's degree in Computer Science from the University of Salerno in 1984. His current research interests focus on merging Soft Computing and Agent Technology to implement intelligent systems. He is Managing Editor of the *Soft Computing* journal, and co-editor of the books "Soft Computing Agents: New Trends for Designing Autonomous Systems", 2001, and "Fuzzy Logic and the Internet", in press.

Vincenzo Loia can be contacted at:

Dipartimento di Matematica e Informatica
Università di Salerno
via S. Allende - 84081 Baronissi (Salerno) ITALY
Tel   +39-089-965212
Fax   +39-089-965438
Email loia@unisa.it

Contents

Soft Computing Agents
V. Loia (Ed.)
IOS Press, 2002

Chapter 1

Soft Computing Agents Based Distributed Intelligent Systems

Rafik A. Aliev
Bijan Fazlollahi

1.1 Introduction

Complex systems such as industry, economy, finance, marketing, ecology are composed of a number of agents interacting in distributed mode. Advances in distributed artificial intelligence (DAI), intelligent agent theory and soft computing technology make it possible for these agents as components of complex system to interact, cooperate, contend and coordinate in order to form global behavior. Therefore the use of multi-agent distributed intelligence technology has been growing in planning, control, decision making and solving other problems of complex systems. Recently, there has been great interest in development of Intelligent Agents (IA) and Multi-agent systems (Franklin and Graesser 1997, Luck and D'Inverno 1995/a-b, Aliev and Aliev 2001, Whinston 1997). The theory of Intelligent Agents and Multi-Agent Systems originates from the research in Distributed Artificial Intelligence (Nwana and Ndumu 1997, Wooldridge and Jennings 1995/b). The field of Distributed Artificial Intelligence (DAI) has been rapidly growing over the last couple of decades (Bond and Gasser 1988). In Distributed Artificial Intelligence the overall intelligence of the system is distributed among multiple nodes for cooperative problem solving. Some of the rationale for distribution of intelligence includes: better adaptability; cost efficiency; ease of development and management; greater efficiency/speed; autonomy; naturalness; reliability due to redundancy; "width" of expertise; openness; and possibility of having multiple conflicting goals (Bond and Gasser 1988, Maes 1995). Many publications are devoted to general problems of creating DAI (Aliev and Aliev 1997, Bond and Gasser 1992, Stephen and Wong 1989, Werner 1989). (Bond and Gasser 1992) refers to over 500 works in the area of cooperation, coordination, distributed control, distributed knowledge, knowledge representation, multi-agent planning, etc.
Bond and Gasser point that there are two directions of research originating from DAI: Distributed Problem Solving, and Multi-Agent Systems (Bond and Gasser 1988). Generally, agents are assumed to have their own goals that may be in conflict. The key question in Multi-Agent systems is: can cooperation among intelligent agents achieve better performance than each component separately (Denzinger 1995, Tokoro 1996).
The important design-related issues with multi-agent systems include how agents coordinate, and how they solve problems. Gasser & Bond define coordination as "a property of interaction among some set of agents performing some collective activity (Bond and Gasser 1988). Cooperation can be viewed as a special case of coordination when the participating agents are not antagonistic (Bond and Gasser 1988, Rosenschein and Genesereth 1985). Competition is a form of coordination when antagonistic agents are involved (Nwana and Ndumu 1997). Coordination may take place without communication among agents if they have each other's models in their possession (Singh 1994). In this case coordination may be achieved through organization (Nwana and Ndumu 1997). Nwana et al. categorized different types of coordination schemes in multi-agent environments

(Nwana and Ndumu 1997). These include: organizational structuring; contracting; multi-agent planning; and negotiation. In organizational structuring each node of a distributed system has its own "role" in an overall organizational structure (Nwana and Ndumu 1997, Bond and Gasser 1988). Durfee suggested that there is a priori defined long-term relationships among agents (Durfee and Lesser 1987). The coordination in this setup is mainly viewed in a client-server fashion. Blackboard architecture is often used for coordination of agents (Corkill *et al.* 1986, Hayes-Roth 1985, Corkill *et al.* 1987). In blackboard architecture, agents communicate via writing messages to and reading from the system component called blackboard.

Contract-based coordination stems from the work by Smith and Davis in the late seventies/early eighties (Davis and Smith 1983). In a contract-based setup, the system uses contract-net protocol for coordinating agents. In this market-like structure, an agent-manager announces a job and a number of contractor agents submit their bids to the agent-manager, which evaluates the bids and awards the contract to the agent with the lowest bid. The contract-net protocol is a coordinating strategy that provides means of distributing tasks and self organizing a group of agents (Singh 1994). Examples of use of contract net protocol include: allocation of jobs among multiple CPUs (Chavez *et al.* 1997); transportation scheduling (Fischer *et al.* 1995). Another coordination strategy is to utilize multi-agent planning mechanisms which can be either centralized, or decentralized (Nwana and Ndumu 1997, Bond and Gasser 1988). The necessity for coordination here is dictated by the fact that multiple agents may develop their own plans that could be inconsistent or conflicting with each other. One approach to detect the conflicts and inconsistencies would be to use central coordinating agent (Georgeff and Ingrand 1989, Georgeff and Lansky 1987). Another approach is to have agents exchange their individual plans to avoid conflicts and inconsistencies (Corkill *et al.* 1987). One example of implementing such an approach is through use of partial global planning and general partial global planning, where agents receive the commitments of other agents and plan their actions to avoid conflicts (Durfee and Lesser 1987, Decker and Lesser 1995). Negotiation is another important basis for coordination in a community of autonomous agents (Nwana and Ndumu 1997). Negotiation is initiated by agents in order to reach certain agreement on some issue (Miller 1986).

(Moulin and Cloutier 1994) presents multi-agent scenario-based methods involving human and artificial agents using different approaches to describe scenarios. The authors do not intend to propose general method for designing multi-agent systems. They illustrate the usefulness of the developed technique for supporting cooperative work between autonomous artificial and human agents.

An attempt to create the coordination theory in DAI is shown in (Kamel and Chenniwa 1994). The authors attempted to determine the concept of coordination on the basis of quantitative representation of components, structure and parameters, as well as performance measures. They considered both centralized and decentralized coordination structures of DAI. The proposed coordination theory and technique are illustrated in a real-world domain. The general problems and practical application of DAI for industrial plants are considered in (Kusiak 1988). It is shown that instead of using centralized artificial intelligence with a single agent carrying the global knowledge (which is usually implemented on computers with monolith programs), it is preferable to use the DAI with a proper distribution of functions, knowledge, and resources of the "center" among intelligent agents.

It should be noted that intelligent agents often deal with incomplete, contradictory, missing and inaccurate data and knowledge (Aliev and Aliev 1997, Aliev et al. 1997). Furthermore, the agents have to make decision in uncertain situations, i.e. in the real world DAI functions within an environment of uncertainty and imprecision. Obviously, emerging technologies, especially fuzzy logic and soft computing are adequate approaches to deal with real application areas with such properties (Aliev and Aliev 1997, Jamshidi 1997, Zadeh 1988). However, there are only few published works (Aliev *et al.* 1993, Nakamati *et al.* 1994, Vojdani 1997) devoted to fuzzy and soft computing based multi-agent distributed intelligent systems. Aliev et al. in (1997, 1993) introduce the concept of fuzzy distributed multi-agent intelligent system (FDIS). They describe the problem of coordination of intelligent cooperative autonomous agents, namely, fuzzy planning, fuzzy scheduling, dispatching, and local online dynamic systems. They consider rules and conventions, protocol of interactions, unique internode language of information representation among intelligent agents, models of transferring and processing distributed data and knowledge in FDIS. Experimental results of working of the FDIS on industry plant are given. In (Vojdani 1997) fuzzy contract net responsible for planning and controlling the associated machines, service staff, and resources is presented. The cooperation and coordination of the fuzzy contract nets are considered. (Nakamati *et al* 1994) presents fuzzy DAI system which consists of a network of processing nodes. These nodes cooperate to achieve global goals as a community. Nodes communicate by sending high level fuzzy-structured messages, allowing the representation of uncertainties throughout the system. It discusses applications of fuzzy traffic light control system.

Some application areas of Intelligent Agent based systems include: World Wide Web agents for finding useful information on WWW (Davies *et al.* 1997, Moukas and Giorgos 1997); recommending webpages (Balabanowic 1997); electronic shopping (Doorenbos *et al.* 1997); advertising on the web (Yager 1997); electronic marketplace agents for buying and selling decisions (Chavez *et al.* 1997); trading on the stock market (Munday *et al.* 1995); assistant agents for meeting scheduling (Haynes *et al.* 1997, Maes 1994); document classification (Clack *et al.* 1997); entertainment agents (Grand *et al.* 1997, Hayes-Roth and Van Gent 1997); scheduling tasks in computer networks (Chavez *et al.* 1997, Malone et al. 1988); manufacturing and robotics (Arlabosse 1994, Bonarini 1993, Bonarini 1994, Bonarini and Basso 1997, Neves and Oliveira 1997); different expert agents, for example for medical diagnosis (Das *et al.* 1997); business process management (O'Brien and Wiegand 1997) and many others. The above list is a sample of applications of agent-based systems and is by no means complete.

As it is seen from the review of the most important works mentioned above and (Bond and Gasser 1988, Gasser and Huhns 1989) it is reasonable to conclude that in conventional concept of multi-agent distributed intelligent systems the main idea is granulation of functions and powers from a central authority to local authorities. In these terms, DAI is composed of several agents, which can perform their own functions independently, and, therefore, have information, authority and power necessary to perform only their own function. These intelligent agents can communicate together to work, cooperate and be coordinated in order to reach a common goal.

This chapter is mainly based on (Aliev *et al.* 2000) and introduces an alternative concept of a multi-agent distributed intelligent system (MADIS) with cooperation and competition among agents, distinguished from the conventional approach by the following: each intelligent agent acts fully autonomously; each intelligent agent proposes full solution of the problem (not only for own partial problem); each agent has access to full available input information; total solution of the problem is determined as proposal of one of the parallel functioning agents on the basis of a competition procedure (not by coordinating and integrating partial solutions of agents, often performed iteratively); agents' cooperation produces desired behavior of the system; cooperation and competition acts in the systems are performed simultaneously (not sequentially).

The effectiveness of the proposed concept is illustrated by a multi-agent distributed intelligent marketing DSS.

It should be noted that a similar idea of decomposition of the overall system into subsystems with cooperation and competition among subsystems for approximation of nonlinear functions is implemented in (Jong *et al.* 1997). Distributed trajectory generation for multi-arm robots through cooperation and competition among subsystems is considered in (Tsuji *et al.* 1997/a-b).

Zhang proposed a way to synthesize final solutions in systems where different agents use different inexact reasoning models to solve a problem (Zhang 1992). In this approach a number of expert systems propose solutions to a given problem. These solutions are then synthesized using ego-altruistic approach (Khan and Jain 1985). In this approach the agents either cooperate (by "moving" their solutions closer to each other) or compete depending on the extent to which their proposals are different. The final solution generated using the mean and uniformity of solutions. Zhang & Zhang also reported the set of neural networks for the synthesis of solutions in a simulated medical diagnosis example (Zhang and Zhang 1995). A special case of synthesis is competitive synthesis, where the best proposed solution is selected (Sikora and Shaw 1998).

1.2 Architecture of the Proposed MADIS

Fig. 1 shows the basic structure of the proposed MADIS. The MADIS is composed of N agents. All agents receive the same input information $x_1, x_2, ..., x_m$. Each agent performs inference and produces its own solution to the full problem:

$$U_j = [u_{j1}, u_{j2}, ..., u_{jl}]^T, j = \overline{1, N}$$

The estimator uses the agents' current solutions $U_1, U_2, ..., U_N$, input information $x_1, x_2, ..., x_m$, and any other necessary information to determine system outcomes for each agent's proposal (e.g. production volume in industry plant, expected profit in marketing mix, etc). These outcome values are the basis for competition among agents Ag1,....., AgN. The evaluator compares the outcome values and determines a "winner" (for example, ith) agent, with the best outcome value. The winner's solution is accepted as the total solution of the full system:

$$Ui = [u_{i1}, u_{i2}, ..., u_{iN}]^T.$$

Below we describe the components of the proposed MADIS.

1.2.1 Agent's Solution Estimator

This component estimates the expected values of outcome of the system on the basis of proposed solutions of each contending agent. Agents' solutions estimator is implemented as fuzzy neural network with crisp and fuzzy inputs and fuzzy weights ($\widetilde{W}$ and $\widetilde{V}$) represented as fuzzy numbers.

Inputs to the fuzzy neural network consist of the current total input of the system and solution produced by agents. Fuzzy neural network transforms these data into the value of the outcome of the system. The number of input neurons is determined by the number of total inputs and agent's solution variables.

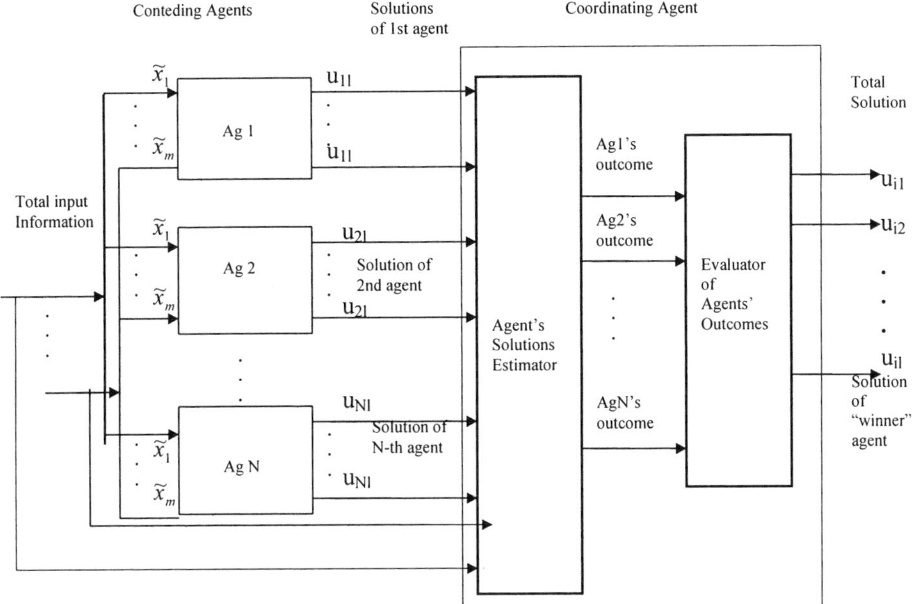

Figure 1. The architecture of MADIS

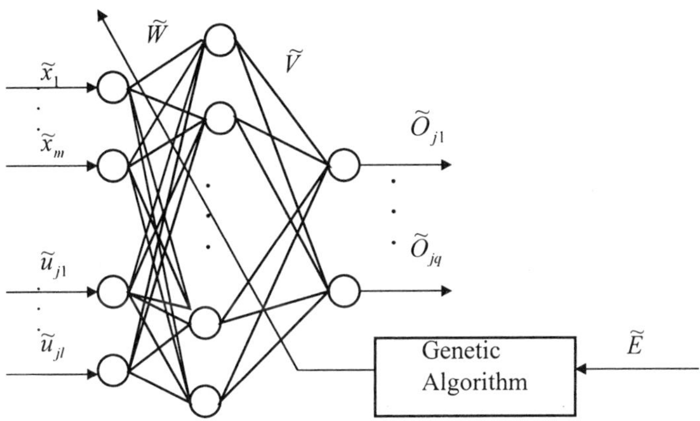

Figure 2. Structure of estimator of agent's solution

The number of hidden layers and the number of neurons in hidden layers are determined by the required accuracy. The number of output neurons is equal to the number of system's outcomes. Learning of fuzzy weights, which are expressed by triangular membership functions is performed by genetic algorithm using experimental training set and fuzzy distance $\widetilde{E}$ between actual and desired outputs of agent. The fuzzy-neural genetic estimator in testing mode produces set of fuzzy values of the system's outcomes $\widetilde{O}_{j1}, \widetilde{O}_{j2}, ..., \widetilde{O}_{jq}$ for each agent proposal. The structure of the neuro-fuzzy genetic estimator is shown in Figure 2.

1.2.2 Evaluation of Contending Agent's Solutions

The outputs of the estimator are fuzzy numbers $\tilde{O}_{j1},\tilde{O}_{j2},...,\tilde{O}_{jq}, j=1,N$ which describe system outcome values for each agent solution. The fuzzy solutions $\tilde{O}_{j1},\tilde{O}_{j2},...,\tilde{O}_{jq}$ must be ranked to determine the best solution. The agent with the best solution will be the "winner" and its solution will be taken as the total solution of the system. The evaluator receives the fuzzy numbers, associated with the agent solutions and performs fuzzy ranking to obtain the ordering for the fuzzy numbers. Output of the evaluator, corresponding to the highest fuzzy value outcome determines the solution. The structure of the evaluator is shown in Figure 3.

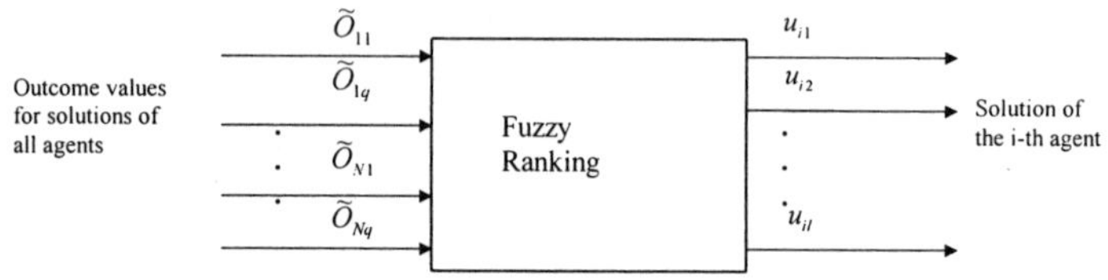

Figure 3. Structure of the evaluator of contending agent

1.3 Architecture of Soft Computing Intelligent Agent

It is very difficult to precisely define a term like agent (Franklin and Graesser 1997, Luck and D'lnverno 1995, Nwana and Ndumu 1997, Wooldridge and Jennings 1995b). Very often the works on Multi-Agent Systems are criticized for inadequate expression by authors of what the agent is. That is why we give a detailed description of this matter below.

Authors in (Smith *et al.* 1994) define an agent as "persistent software entity dedicated to a specific purpose". Here, persistency and purposefulness are emphasized.

In (Selker 1994) agents are defined as "computer programs that simulate a human relationship by doing something that another person could do for you". Implicitly, an idea of delegation is viewed as central to the concept of agency here.

In definition given in (Shoham 1993) an agent is any entity to which mental state can be ascribed. Shoham sees mental states (consisting of beliefs, capabilities, and commitments) as the key to defining agents. The Beliefs, Desires, and Intentions model of agents specify that agents have their mental attitudes in terms of what they believe is true, what their desires are, and what they intend to do (Jennings 1992, Kinny and Georgeff 1996, Rao and Georgeff 1995).

In Russel and Norvig's definition an agent is anything that can be viewed as perceiving its environment through sensors and acting upon that environment through effectors (Russel and Norvig 1995). Here the idea of agent actively involved in interaction with the environment is emphasized.

In (Maes 1995/a-b) an agent is defined as a "system that tries to fulfill a set of goals in a complex, dynamic environment. Maes realizes that agents need to have goals to fulfill. Also, the agent environments are complex and dynamic.

Definition given in (Brustoloni 1991) is similar to the above: "Autonomous agents are systems capable of autonomous, purposeful action in the real world". The author emphasizes autonomy and real world environment for the agents.

In (Hayes-Roth 1995) a definition is proposed according to which intelligent agents continuously perform three functions: perception of dynamic conditions in the environment; actions to affect conditions in the environment; and reasoning to interpret perceptions, solve problems, draw inferences, and determine actions. Here the reasoning capability is introduced in order for an agent to be intelligent.

In (Franklin and Graesser 1997) it is stated that "an autonomous agent is a system situated within and a part of an environment that senses that environment and acts on it, over time, in pursuit of its own agenda and so as to affect what it senses in the future". In this definition the authors point that affecting the environment in the future is an important part of notion of agency.

Along the dimensions of autonomy, learning and cooperation dimensions the autonomous agents that have learning capability are classified as interface agents; those that combine autonomy and cooperation are collaborative agents. The agents that possess all of these characteristics are smart agents (Nwana and Ndumu 1997, Wooldridge and Jennings 1995/a).

A definition similar to (Nwana and Ndumu 1997, Wooldridge and Jennings 1995/a, Hayes-Roth 1995) was suggested by us in 1986 (Aliev and Tsercovny 1988) and we will use this definition in this work which embraces the following features: autonomy; interaction with an environment and other agents; perception capability; learning; reasoning capability. In (Aliev and Tsercovny 1988) a system with the mentioned characteristics was called a smart system.

The architecture of Soft Computing intelligent agent in accordance with this definition is given in Figure 4. It is a prototype system of intelligent (smart) agents which will be used in the investigated MADIS.

Note that granulation fine, i.e. number of agents in MADIS is determined by the system designer (in our case using genetic algorithm).

The mathematical description of knowledge in the KB of agent is based on fuzzy interpretation of antecedents and consequents in production rules.

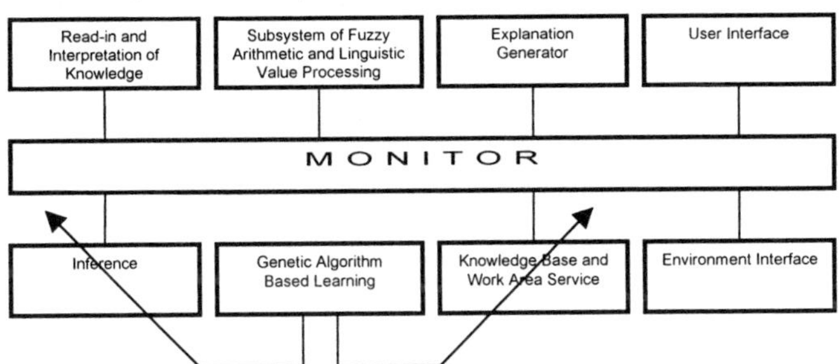

Figure 4. Structure of intelligent agent

For the knowledge representation the antecedent of each rule contains a conjunction of logical connectives like (Figure 5) <name of object> $\begin{Bmatrix} = \\ \neq \end{Bmatrix}$ <linguistic value> named elementary antecedent.

The consequent of the rule is a list of imperatives, among which may be some operator-functions (i.e. input and output of objects' values, operations with segments of a knowledge base, etc). Each rule may be complemented with a confidence degree $cf \in [0,100]$ and with the author's comments on the rule. Each linguistic value has a corresponding membership function which is built using parametric LR-representation.

The subsystem of fuzzy arithmetic and linguistic values processing (see Figure 4) provides automatic interpretation of linguistic values like "high", "low", "OK", "near...", "from ... to

..." and so on; i.e. for each linguistic value this subsystem automatically computes parameters of membership functions using universes of corresponding variable. The user of the system may define new linguistic values, modify built-in ones and explicitly prescribe a membership function in any place where linguistic values are useful.

Learning of agents is based on genetic algorithms which includes adjusting of agent's KB and choosing appropriate inference mechanism (see Figure 4).

The agents knowledge-base includes certain number of fuzzy rules related through "ALSO":

$$R^k : IF\, x_1\, is\, A_{k1}\, and\, x_2\, is\, A_{k2}\, and...and\, x_m\, is\, A_{km}\, THEN$$
$$u_{k1}\, is\, B_{k1}\, and\, u_{k2}\, is\, B_{k2}\, and...and\, u_{kl}\, is\, B_{kl}, k = \overline{1,K} \tag{1}$$

where $x_i, i = 1, m$ and $u_j, j = 1, l$ are total input and local output variables , A_{ki}, B_{kj} are fuzzy sets, and k is the number of rules. Note, that inputs $x_1, x_2, ..., x_m$ may be crisp or fuzzy variables. If input data are crisp, then fuzzifier will map these data into fuzzy sets. Decision of each agent is made by the composition rule, which is the basis of inference mechanism, as follows:

$$\tilde{U}_j = R_j \circ \tilde{X}, j = \overline{1,N} \tag{2}$$

where $\tilde{U}_j$ is fuzzy value of decision of j-th agent, Rj is the fuzzy relation corresponding to the fuzzy model (1), and $\tilde{X}$ is total input information after fuzzification.

Efficiency of inference engine considerably depends on the knowledge base internal organization and logic used for reasoning. Inference mechanism acts as follows. First, some objects take some values (initial data). Then, all production rules, containing each of these objects in antecedent, are chosen from the knowledge base.

For these rules the truth degree is computed (in other words, the system estimates the truth degree of the fact that current values of objects correspond to values fixed in antecedents). If the truth degree exceeds some threshold then imperatives from consequent are executed. At that time the same objects as well as a new one take new values and the process continues till work area contains "active" objects ("active" object means untested one).

By using the defuzzifier fuzzy decisions $\tilde{U}_j$ are mapped into the crisp value of solutions.

1.4 Optimization of Agents Behavior

Optimality of the objective function of full MADIS is mainly related with solution produced by each agent. Effectiveness of these solutions is determined mainly by knowledge base and inference mechanism of each agent. Optimization of the agents knowledge base means finding of scaling factors, membership functions, and rule set. Scaling factors and membership functions taken together represent the semantics of the symbols used by agent and the rule set represents the syntactic mapping among the symbols (Pratihar *et al.* 1999).

As effectiveness of the solutions of an agent significantly depend on type of inference engine, it is important to use switching engines for approximate reasoning by agents.

It is important to note that not all rules are necessary for the optimal solution generation by agents. So it is necessary to determine which rules and how many should be in the agents' rule base, the centers and shapes of the membership functions of the rules, the value of the scaling factors, and the kind of inference engine for agent use.

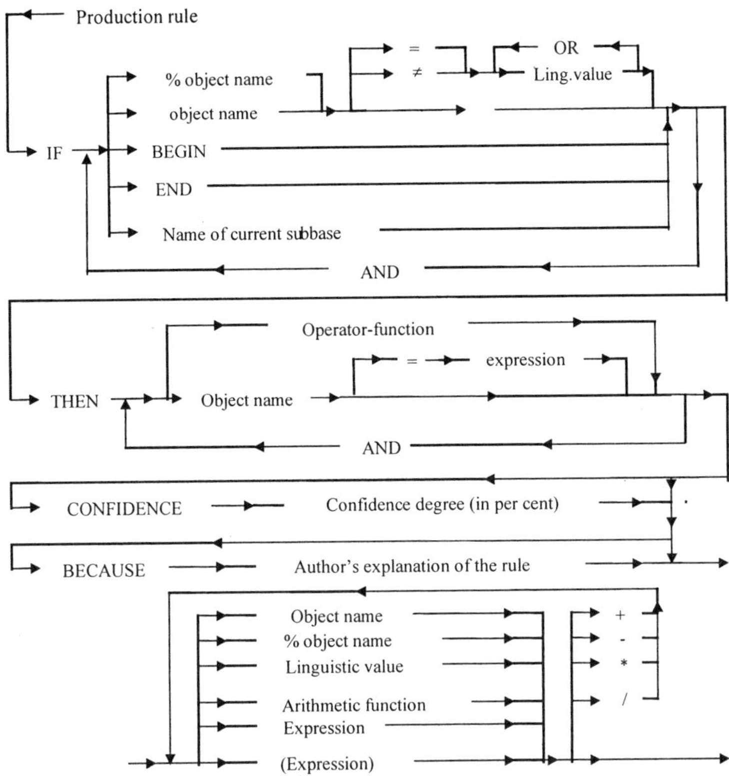

Figure 5. Production rules

To solve this problem we will use genetic algorithm, namely fuzzy-genetic approach. Assume that an agent has Q author pre-specified possible rules, each of which has M parameters (for example characteristic points of triangular membership functions).

At first step, the agents must be numbered. The inclusion of agent into multi-agent system should be represented by a 1 and rejection by a 0. Also, the rules in knowledge base of the agent must be numbered. The presence of rule should be represented by a 1 and the absence by a 0. Assume that number of switching logics for approximate reasoning is q and number of scaling factors is l. Suppose that each parameter needs a r coded array. Then a string of length $N+K+(M+q+l)r$ is formed. First N genes correspond to the size of decomposition (granulation) of total system intelligence (number of agents), K-fuzzy relational matrix. $(M+q+l)$ genes correspond to M parameters, q switching logics and l scaling factors.

After formation of an initial population of T strings each solution in the population is then evaluated to assign a fitness value. In this case, we have assigned a fitness value as

$$\tilde{J} = [1 + I]^{-1} \tag{3}$$

where I is fuzzy distance between desirable and actual outcomes of the system.

Since the objective of the considered multi-agent system is to minimize the fuzzy distance I, we use a GA to find a string that corresponds to the maximum fitness value (3). GA for learning rule bases is well described in (Aliev *et al.* 2000, Aliev and Aliev 2001).

After each solution in the population is evaluated and fitness is assigned, the population is modified by using three operators: selection, crossover and mutation (Aliev and Aliev 2001). After a new population of solutions is created, each of them is evaluated again to find a fitness value and all three operators are applied again. These generations proceed until pre-specified number of generations have elapsed.

Further we will continue discussion on optimization of an agent's behavior by selecting appropriate fuzzy implications.

Let the fuzzy system be appropriately described by a relational fuzzy equation (similar to (2)):

$$B = A \circ R,$$
(4)

where $A = \{z, \mu(z)\}$ is the input fuzzy set on Z and $B = \{v, \mu(v)\}$ - is the output fuzzy set on V; z and v are elements of fuzzy sets A and B respectively; $\mu(z)$ and $\mu(v)$ are corresponding membership functions; R is a fuzzy relation on $Z \times V$ in the form of rule with the structure IF...THEN...ELSE. The fuzzy relation R in $Z \times V$ has membership function

$$\mu(z,v) = \int_{Z \times V} [\mu_A(z) \to \mu_B(v)] \wedge [(1 - \mu_A(z)) \to (1 - \mu_B(v))] / (z,v)$$
(5)

where $\to$ is implication; $\wedge$ is logical minimum.

Solution of the equation (4) in known R and A can be shown as (Aliev and Aliev 2001);

$$\mu_B(v) = \max_z \min \{\mu_A(z), \mu_R(z,v)\}$$
(6)

Let's represent the measuring system as equations (Potiupkin 1996):

$$X(t) = z(t) + w_x, \quad U(t) = v(t) + w_u,$$
(7)

where $z(t) \in Z$ and $v(t) \in V$ is the input and output system parameters (see equation (2)), w_x and w_u are the corresponding measurement errors.

Let's define operators for the formation of fuzzy sets A, B $Q_x : X \to A$, $Q_u : U \to B$, where the parameters $X \subset [X_{min}, X_{max}]$ and $U \subset [U_{min}, U_{max}]$ are considered as source data for the formation of linguistic variables and for calculating appropriate values of membership functions $\mu(z)$ and $\mu(v)$. The index of efficiency is considered as:

$$J(R) = \sum_{i=1}^{n} \left[\mu_{B_i}(v) - \mu_{B_i^\wedge}(v) \right]^2,$$
(8)

where $\mu_{B^\wedge}$ is the estimate of membership function of $B^\wedge$, calculated on the basis of the solution to the equation (6) with the estimation of the matrix $R^\wedge$. R is determined from (8) as:

$$R = \arg \min_{R \subset \{R\}} (J),$$
(9)

where $\{R\}$ is the finite space of fuzzy relational matrixes.

Thus a class of models of the system in form of fuzzy relational equations (4), (6), a measurement model (7), operators for creating fuzzy sets of system's input and output and membership functions, an index (8) and criterion (9) are given. It is required to determine a

fuzzy relation R in form of a fuzzy relational matrix satisfying the given criterion.
In (Potiupkin 1996) it is shown in order for the system described by a fuzzy relational equation to be correctly-identifiable it is necessary for the associated relational matrix to be non-singular. Hence the domain of permissible fuzzy relations is determined as {RD}={R|det R≠0}.
For experimental test and determination of model, which would provide the existence of a correct solution in (Potiupkin 1996) an imitating model was developed. It used a simple model like U=100-X or IF X is X_{min} THEN U is U_{max} . To construct the matrix R the rule in form IF X is X_{min} THEN U is U_{max} ELSE U is U_{min} is used.
The following are the changing parameters of the model. Dimension of the system, i.e. the cardinality of fuzzy sets of input and output N=3, 5, 7, 9, 11. The type of membership function (MF) – three types:
a) stepped MF

$$\mu(z_i) = 1 - [1/(card\, Z_x - 1)] \times |\, z_i - ent[(card\, Z_x - 1)][(X - X_{min})/(X_{max} - X_{min})]\,|$$

where $z_i = ent\{(card\, Z_x - 1)[(X - X_{min})/(X_{max} - X_{min})]\}$, card Z_x is cardinality of the set of fuzzy variables ; X is the measured value of the parameter ;
b) exponential MF

$$\mu(z_i) = \exp\{-\gamma |K_i - X|\},$$

where $\gamma = 2\ln 0.5/\sigma$, $\sigma = a - b$, $\mu(a) = \mu(b) = 0.5$ is crossover points; K_i is support value of the parameter;
c) triangle MF

$$\mu(z_i) = 1 - \gamma \left| K_i - X \right|, \; \gamma = 1/\sigma.$$

The following 10 types of fuzzy implications frequently used in fuzzy computing are considered (Aliev and Aliev 2001):

1) min-logic

$$a \underset{min}{\to} b = \begin{cases} a, & if\ a \le b \\ b, & otherwise. \end{cases}$$

2) S# - logic

$$a \underset{S^\#}{\to} b = \begin{cases} 1, & if\ a \ne 1\ or\ b = 1, \\ 0, & otherwise. \end{cases}$$

3) S - logic ("Standard sequence")

$$a \underset{S}{\to} b = \begin{cases} 1, & if\ a \le b, \\ 0, & otherwise. \end{cases}$$

4) G - logic ("Gödelian sequence")

$$a \underset{G}{\to} b = \begin{cases} 1, & if\ a \le b, \\ b, & otherwise. \end{cases}$$

5) G43 - logic

$$a \underset{G43}{\to} b = \begin{cases} 1, & if\ a = 0, \\ min(1, b/a), & otherwise. \end{cases}$$

6) L - logic(Lukasiewicz's logic)

$$a \underset{L}{\to} b = \min(1, 1 - a + b).$$

7) KD - logic

$$a \underset{KD}{\to} b = ((1-a) \vee b) = \max(1-a, b).$$

8) ALI1 - logic

$$a \underset{ALI1}{\to} b = \begin{cases} 1-a, & \text{if } a < b, \\ 1, & \text{if } a = b, \\ b, & \text{if } a > b \end{cases}$$

9) ALI2 - logic

$$a \underset{ALI2}{\to} b = \begin{cases} 1, & \text{if } a \leq b, \\ (1-a) \wedge b, & \text{if } a > b \end{cases}$$

10) ALI3 - logic

$$a \underset{ALI3}{\to} b = \begin{cases} 1, & \text{if } a \leq b, \\ b / [a + (1-b)], & \text{otherwise.} \end{cases}$$

The comparative analysis of the first seven logics has been given in (Bandler and Kohout 1980). The analysis of these seven logics has shown that only S- and G-logics satisfy the classical principle of Modus Ponens and allow development of an improved rule of fuzzy conditional inference. At the same time the truthness of the implication operation in S-logic is equal either to 0 or 1, and only the truth value of logical conclusion is used in the definition of the implication operation in G-logic. Thus the degree of "fuzziness" of implication is decreased, which is a considerable disadvantage and restricts the use of these logics in approximate reasoning. The properties of fuzzy logics ALI1-ALI3 and their comparative semantic analysis are given in (Aliev and Aliev 2001).

Now we will discuss experimental investigation of these logics.

The following parameters have been watched: the count of events D during a series of tests, for which the identified fuzzy relation matrix R appears to be non-specific; and the count of correct solutions P.

A solution is considered to be correct if it allows the same solution to fuzzy equation (5) with the same input set A either for real or identified matrix $R^{\wedge}$; number of coincidences of events: identified matrix is non-singular, solution is correct Nc; number of coincidences of events: identified matrix is singular, solution is correct Nnonc. Relations of the above mentioned parameters with different combinations of changing parameters in series of 50 measurements with 39 test measurement have been researched under supposal of absence of errors in measurements (i.e. identification done with step 2, test done with step 2,564). Note that in all experiments the condition of necessity has been confirmed, Nc=P, Nnonc=0.

The analysis of the results has allowed the following conclusions. The necessary conditions are satisfied for all versions of structures. In case when the fuzzy sets of input and output are described by stepped MF (type a) the necessary conditions is also sufficient condition as the Zadeh composition minmax operator for this structure satisfies the condition of linearity. The versions of the structures are not equivalent, therefore, one can choose the best based on specific conditions. To make a choice of a type of implication one can use additional criteria, including human intuition criteria (Aliev and Aliev 2001).

Mentioned experiments have proved advantages of logics ALI1, ALI2, and ALI3 in comparison with other described logics. Further investigations of author (Potiupkin 1996) are based only on these three logics. A number of results of author (Potiupkin 1999) are shown in Table 1. In Table 1 exp is an exponential MF and ent is a stepped MF. Symbols "-, *, **, ***" are degrees of performance of necessary condition of correct identification: "***" marks practically global identification on the whole definitional domain of parameters and, consequently, absence of limitations on measurement procedure, "**" shows that in the center of definitional domain of parameters an area of incorrect solution exists, "*" - an increasing of its size and for "-" area of incorrect solution practically covers a definitional domain of parameters of input and output a system. Assigning known parameters (system dimensionality and type of membership functions of term sets) we can choose types of implication, ensuring existence of correct decision. For instance, the logic ALI2 is acceptable for N = 5 and exponential membership functions of exp type. In addition, the final choice should be generated upon conditions of solution problem, physical nature of prototyping object, as well as additional criterions, for instance, criterions of human intuitions (Aliev and Aliev 2001).

Table 1. Results of analyses of some fuzzy logics

Dimension N of the system	Membership function of input and output	Types of implication		
		ALI1	ALI2	ALI3
3	exp	*	*	*
	ent	***	**	* ***
5	exp	-	***	-
	ent	***	*	***
7	exp	-	*	-
	ent	***	***	***
9	exp	-	-	-
	ent	***	*	***
11	exp	-	*	-
	ent	***		***

1.5 Decision Generation through Cooperation and Competition among Intelligent Agents

The objective of the proposed MADIS is to generate such solution which produces the outcome nearest to the desirable value of the system outcome. Therefore, we will consider the following objective function (with one outcome index):

$$I = \sum_{j=1}^{N} \alpha_j \left| \widetilde{O}^d - \widetilde{O}_j^c \right| \tag{10}$$

$$\sum_{j=1}^{N} \alpha_j = 1, \alpha_j = \{0,1\}, \tag{11}$$

where $\widetilde{O}^d$ is fuzzy desirable value of the outcome index, $\widetilde{O}_j^c$ is the current fuzzy value of the j-th agent's outcome index, $\alpha_j, j = \overline{1, N}$ is the relative weight values for the contending agents. In the case of very complex unstructured systems, a designer may not have information about the desirable value of the system outcome. To maximize the actual outcome index we may take a large fuzzy number (larger than expected value of $\widetilde{O}_j^c$) as the value of $\tilde{O}^d$. Minimization of objective function (10) under conditions (11) is achieved through competition of agents with each other for the right to produce the total solution such that provides $\tilde{O}_j^c$ close to $\tilde{O}^d$.

For generation of solutions minimizing the objective function (10) each contending agent produces its own total solution as follows (Aliev *et al.*1991, Park *et al.*1997, Zadeh 1973:):

1. Each rule in (1) is formalized in the form of fuzzy relation $R_{kj}, k = \overline{1,K}$, defined as

$$R_{kj} = \int \mu_{A_K}(x) * \mu_{B_K}(u_{kj}),\tag{12}$$

where * is fuzzy implication operator

2. The set of fuzzy rules (1) is formalized using (12) in the form of composed fuzzy relation

$$R_j(X,U_j) = ALSO(R_{1j}, R_{2j}, ..., R_{Kj})\tag{13}$$

with the membership function

$$\mu_{R_j}(u_{1j}, u_{2j}, ..., u_{lj}, x_1, x_2, ..., x_m) = \max\left[\mu_1(\cdot), \mu_2(\cdot), ..., \mu_K(\cdot)\right]\tag{14}$$

3. The generation of agent's solution is performed on the basis of resulting fuzzy relation R_j by applying the compositional rule of inference

$$\tilde{U}_{jr} = \bigcap_{i=1}^{m} \tilde{X}_i^c \text{ o } R_j(X,U_{jr})j = \overline{1,N}, i = \overline{1,m}, r = \overline{1,l}\tag{15}$$

where o is a compositional operator and r is the index of output variable (solution).

To evaluate the agents' solutions $\tilde{U}_{jr}$, it is necessary to estimate the outcomes of the system in terms of their ability to minimize objective function (10) of the full system. Fuzzy neural networks with fuzzy and crisp inputs and fuzzy weights (Figure 2) is used to estimate solutions. Fuzzy inputs and weights may be described by different shapes, such as triangular, trapezoidal and Gaussian membership functions traditionally used in fuzzy logic. We use triangular membership functions to describe fuzzy inputs and weights. For learning of fuzzy neural network, i.e. tuning of weights, we use fuzzy arithmetic and genetic algorithms. Also, we use fuzzy arithmetic in testing mode of neuro-fuzzy estimator to calculate system outcomes.

1.5.1 Learning of Fuzzy-Neural Network

The fuzzy distance between actual output values $\tilde{O}_j$ and desired output values $\tilde{O}^d$ is calculated by the formula:

$$\tilde{E}_j = \sum_{s=1}^{S}\sum_{r=1}^{q}\left|\tilde{O}_{jrs}^d - \tilde{O}_{jrs}\right|,\tag{16}$$

where q is the number of outcomes related with agents, S is the number of learning pairs. Note, that learning of FNN is performed independently of agents' solutions.
The fitness function that we use is given by (17):

$$\widetilde{J} = \left[1 + \widetilde{E}\right]^{-1} \tag{17}$$

Each fuzzy weight is described by triangular membership function characterized with three parameters. Hence, if the number of adjusting weights is Q, then we must encode 3Q parameters. Each parameter takes value from a domain Di = [ai, bi].

The GA generates the optimal fuzzy membership function (in accordance with (16)) of weights as follows:

1. The GA starts its work, t = 1.
2. The initial population of candidate solutions is created.
3. The population of generation at time t, G(t), is evaluated.
4. If some termination conditions are met, go to step 8.
5. Generate new generation G(t+1) from G(t). Then crossover and mutation are applied.
6. Evaluate G(t+1).
7. Return to Step 4.
8. The termination of GA's work.
9. Among all the minimum errors stored in memory the smallest one is found. Membership functions by which the smallest error is obtained, are selected.
10. End.

1.5.2 Calculation of Fuzzy Value of System Outcome Indices

The trained fuzzy neural network based estimator receives fuzzy and/or crisp input data and solution values and using fuzzy arithmetic (Kaufmann and Gupta 1985) produces corresponding fuzzy outputs $\widetilde{O}_{j1}, \widetilde{O}_{j2}, ..., \widetilde{O}_{jq}$, $j = \overline{1, N}$.

1.5.3 Evaluation of Agents' Solutions and Selection of Total Problem Solution

The evaluator (see Figure 1) receives all the system outcome fuzzy values, corresponding to the solutions of each contending agent $\widetilde{O}_1, \widetilde{O}_2, ..., \widetilde{O}_N$, and evaluates them according to the objective function (10). For this purpose we use fuzzy ranking procedure for N fuzzy numbers to give a total ordering based on compatibility measure of fuzzy sets (Aliev *et al.*1993, Bortolan and Degani 1985, Chen and Hwang 1991, Setnes and Cross 1997). Each fuzzy outcome value, corresponding to agents solution, is presented by fuzzy number described with triangular membership function. The determining of the best $\widetilde{O}_j$ in terms of the objective function is performed by the following procedure.

1. Preparing of initial data by creating Table 2.
2. Calculation of the compatibility measure. As the compatibility measure we use the Jaccard index. The Jaccard compatibility measure can be presented by $N \times N$ relation $E_\ge$.
3. Calculation of the crisp ranking relation $R_>$ using operator ">".
4. Configuration of the order vector $O = [O_j]$ by summing the elements in each row of $R_>$. First component of vector O will be selected as nearest to the desirable value of system outcome in terms of (10). The solution that produced this outcome is accepted as system solution. For example, if j-th agent produced the nearest to the desirable solution, then this j-th agent receives the weight j=1, and rest $\alpha_i, i \ne j, i = \overline{1, N}$ receive weights $\alpha_i = 0$.

Table 2. Outcome fuzzy values

N	Set Name	Parameters
1	$\widetilde{O}_1$	[a1, b1, c1]
2	$\widetilde{O}_2$	[a2, b2, c2]
.	...	.
N	$\widetilde{O}_N$	[aN, bN, cN]

1.6 Multi-Agent Distributed Intelligent Marketing DSS

As an example, here we consider a simplified marketing system in an oligopolistic industry. We suppose that the firm's price and advertising strategies dominate the marketing strategy (Schott and Whalen 1994). The existing DSS are oriented to econometric models of the industrial history. In particular, as it is shown in (Schott and Whalen 1994) existing econometric models deal inadequately with the information about competitors future behavior assuming competitor actions are known. (Schott and Whalen 1994) presents procedure to model competitors behavior uncertainties as fuzzy information. The proposed multi-agent distributed intelligent marketing DSS consist of 5 agents (GA included 5 agents from author pre-specified 7). Input information are fuzzy variables of average price $\widetilde{x}_1$ (AvgPrice) and average advertising $\widetilde{x}_2$ (AvgAdv) of competitors, and are the same for all 5 agents. Using fuzzy inference rule each agent produces its output solutions: firm's own price ($\widetilde{u}_{i1}$) $i = \overline{1,5}$, and firm's own advertising $\widetilde{u}_{i2}, i = \overline{1,5}$. Fuzzy rules in knowledge base of each agent is of the following type (for example for the first agent):

IF Avg Price is HIGH and AvgAdv is MEDIUM, THEN
Price is HIGH and Advertising is MEDIUM

$$\vdots$$

    For the second agent:
IF AvgPrice is HIGH and Avg Adv is MEDIUM, THEN
Price is HIGH and advertising is LOW

$$\vdots$$

    Using switching procedure of 6 types of fuzzy inference rule, each agent produces its output solution: firm's own price, and firm's own advertising.

    Solutions of each agent for situation where AvgPrice is about three hundred dollars $325 and AvgAdv is about sixty thousand ($60,000) are shown in Table 3.

Table 3. Solutions proposed by 5 agents

Agent #	Price	Advertising
Agent 1	$331.59	$80,000
Agent 2	$331.67	$53,000
Agent 3	$313.61	$60,000
Agent 4	$331.59	$53,000
Agent 5	$331.59	$70,000

Coordinating agent receives values of solutions (price and advertising) of each agent and total input fuzzy information on AvgPrice and AvgAdv and calculates fuzzy profit. The output of the estimator is 5 fuzzy profits associated with the solutions of each agent. The fuzzy profits for the above situation are shown in Table 4.

Table 4. Fuzzy expected profits

Agent #	Fuzzy profit (in $)
Agent 1	(505,858; 84,195; 52,467)
Agent 2	(401,376; 56,963; 98,182)
Agent 3	(434,827; 29,321; 76,352)
Agent 4	(410,508; 56,823; 98, 130)
Agent 5	(501,342; 84,115; 50,786)

The evaluator component of coordinating agent performs fuzzy ranking of fuzzy profits and provides total ordering of 5 fuzzy profits as follows:

$$\widetilde{Pr}_1 > \widetilde{Pr}_5 > \widetilde{Pr}_3 > \widetilde{Pr}_4 > \widetilde{Pr}_2$$

First agents is the "winner" agent and its solution is accepted as solution for the given situation:

        Price =$331.59

        Advertising =$80,000

After optimization of relational matrixes, triangle membership functions, scaling factors and finding appropriate fuzzy inference mechanism the global solution of DSS (Price and Advertising for quarters 1, 2, 3, and 4) consists of the sequence of solutions of agent 1 for quarter 1, agent 5 for quarter 2, agent 5 for quarter 3, and agent 3 for quarter 4. All five agents competed for the total solution of the problem. In each quarter the most suitable agent for the situation was the "winner", while the other four agents were losers. For example, for situation in quarter 2 agent 5 was more suitable than the rest of the agents. Weights in objective function (2) are:

Quarter 1: $\alpha_1 = 1,\quad \alpha_2 = 0,\quad \alpha_3 = 0,\quad \alpha_4 = 0,\quad \alpha_5 = 0;$

Quarter 2: $\alpha_1 = 0,\quad \alpha_2 = 0,\quad \alpha_3 = 0,\quad \alpha_4 = 0,\quad \alpha_5 = 1;$

Quarter 3: $\alpha_1 = 0,\quad \alpha_2 = 0,\quad \alpha_3 = 0,\quad \alpha_4 = 0,\quad \alpha_5 = 1;$

Quarter 4: $\alpha_1 = 0,\quad \alpha_2 = 0,\quad \alpha_3 = 1,\quad \alpha_4 = 0,\quad \alpha_5 = 0$

respectively.

References

Aliev R.A., Fazlollahi B., Vahidov R.M. (2000) "Soft computing based multi-agent marketing decision support system". Journal of Intellegence and Fuzzy Systems 9, pp. 1-9.

Aliev R.A and Aliev R.R. (2001) Soft Computing and its Application. World Scientific, New Jersey, London, Singapore, Hong Kong.

Aliev R A , Mamedova G A, Aliev R R (1993) *Fuzzy Sets Theory and its Application*, Tabriz University, Tabriz.

Aliev R A, Aliev R R (1997) "Fuzzy Distributed Intelligence System for Continuous production. Application of Fuzzy Logic" In Jamshidi M, Titli M, Zadeh L, Bevrie S (eds.): Towards High machine Intelligence Quotient Systems. Prentice Hall PTR, Upper Sadle River, New Jersey, USA.

Aliev R A, Bonfig H, Aliev F T, Aliev R R (1993) "The Distributed Intelligent Manufacturing Systems" First European Congress on Fuzzy and Intelligent technologies, EUFIT, Aachen, Part II, Germany, pp. 229-235.

Aliev R A, Rashad R A, Aliev F T (1997): "Fuzzy Distributed Multi-Agent Manufacturing System" In Procedings of NAFIPS 97, Syracuse, New-York, pp. 311-316.

Aliev R, Aliev F, Babaev M (1991) Fuzzy Process Control And Knowledge Engineering In Petrochemical And Robotic Manufacturing, Koln: Verl. TUV Rheinland.

Aliev R.A. and Tsercovny A.E. (1988) ""Smart" manufacturing systems". *News of Academy of Sciences of USSR, Tech.* Cybernetics 6: 99-108, (in English and Russian).

Arlabosse, F. (1994) "ARCHON and its Environment". In J.W. Perram & J.P. Muller (Eds.) *Distributed Software Agents and Applications: MAAMA W'94* (pp.11-18). Berlin, Germany: Springer-Verlag.

Balabanowic, M. (1997) "An Adaptive Web Page Recommendation Service". *Proceedings of the First International Conference on Autonomous Agents.* New York: ACM, 378-385.

Bandler W. and Kohout L. (1980) "Fuzzy power sets and fuzzy implications operators". *Fuzzy Sets and Systems* 1:13-30.

Bonarini, A., (1993) "ELF: Learning Incomplete Fuzzy Rule Sets for an Autonomous Robot". *Proceedings of European Conference on Fuzzy and Intelligent Technologies* (EUFIT'93). Aachen, Germany: ELITE Foundation, 69- 75.

Bonarini, A., (1994) "Learning to Coordinate Fuzzy Behaviors for Autonomous Agents". *Proceedings of European Conference on Fuzzy and Intelligent Technologies* (EUFIT'94) Aachen, Germany: ELITE Foundation, 475-479

Bonarini, A. and Basso, F. (1997) "Learning to Compose Fuzzy Behaviors for Autonomous Agents". *International Journal of Approximate Reasoning*, 17, 409-432.

Bond, A.H. and Gasser L. (1988). Readings in Distributed Artificial Intelligence, Morgan Kaufmann, San Mateo, Ca.

Bond, A.H. and Gasser L. (1992) "A subject -indexed bibliography of distributed artificial intelligence (DAI)." *IEEE Transactions on Systems, Man and Cybernetics* 22(6), 1260-1281.

Bortolan G and Degani R (1985): "A review of some methods for ranking fuzzy subsets." *Fuzzy Sets and Systems*, 15 (1-19).

Brustoloni, J.C. (1991) *Autonomous Agents: Characterization and Requirements* (Carnegie Mellon Technical Report CMU-CS-91-204). Carnegie Mellon University.

Chavez, A., Dreilinger, D., Guttman, R., Maes P. (1997) "A Real-life Experiment in Creating an Agent Marketplace". In H.S. Nwana & N. Azarmi (Eds.) *Software Agents and Soft Computing* (pp.160-179). Berlin, Germany: Springer- Verlag.

Chavez, A., Moukas, A., Maes, P. (1997) "Challenger: A Multi-Agent System for Distributed Resource Allocation". *Proceedings of the First International Conference on Autonomous Agents*. New York: ACM, 323-321.

Chen S J and Hwang C L (1991) *Fuzzy Multiple Attribute Decision making: Methods and Applications*. Springer-Verlag, Heidelberg.

Clack, Ch., Farringdon, J., Lidwell, P., Yu, T. (1997) "Autonomous Document Classification for Business". *Proceedings of the First International Conference on Autonomous Agents*. New York: ACM, 201-208.

Corkill, D.D., Gallagher, K.Q., Murray, K.E. (1986) "A Generic Blackboard Development System". In *Proceedings of Conference of the American Association for Artificial Intelligence*, 1008-1014.

Corkill, D.D., Gallagher, K.Q., Johnson, Ph.M. (1987) "Achieving Flexibility, Efficiency, and Generality in Blackboard Architectures". In *Proceedings of 1987 Conference of the American Association for Artificial Intelligence*, 18-23.

Das, S.K., Fox, J., Elsdon, D., Hammond, P. (1997) "Decision Making and Plan - Management by Autonomous Agents: Theory, Implementation and Applications". *Proceedings of the First International Conference on Autonomous Agents*. New York: ACM,276-283.

Davies, N.J., Weeks, R., Revett, M.C. (1997) "Information Agents for the World Wide Web". In H.S. Nwana & N. Azarmi (Eds.) *Software Agents and Soft Computing* (81-99). Berlin, Germany: Springer- Verlag.

Davis, R. and Smith, R.G. (1983) "Negotiation as a Metaphor for Distributed Problem Solving". *Artificial Intelligence*, 20(1), 63-109.

Decker, K.S., and Lesser, V .R. (1995) "Designing a Family of Coordination Algorithms". *Proceedings of the First International Conference on Multi-Agent Systems*. San-Francisco, CA: AAAI Press/MIT Press, 173-180.

Denzinger, J. (1995) Knowledge-Based Distributed Search Using Teamwork. In *Proceedings of the First International Conference on Multi-Agent Systems*. San-Francisco, CA: AAAI Press/MIT Press, 81-88.

Doorenbos, R.B., Etzioni, O., Weld, D.S. (1997) "A Scalable Comparison-Shopping Agent for the World-Wide Web". *Proceedings of the First International Conference on Autonomous Agents*. Marina del Rey. New York: ACM, 39-48.

Durfee, E.H., and Lesser, V.R. (1987) "Using Partial Global Plans to Coordinate Distributed Problem Solvers". In *Proceedings of 1987 International Joint Conference on Artificial Intelligence*. 875-873.

Fazlollahi B., Aliev R.A., and Vahidov R.M. (2000) "Multi-agent distributed intelligent systems based on fuzzy decision-making". *International Journal of Intelligent Systems*, vol.15, 849-858.

Fischer, K., Muller, J.P., Pischel, M., Scier, D. (1995) "A Model for cooperative Transportation Scheduling". *Proceedings of the First International Conference on Multi-Agent Systems*. San-Francisco, CA: AAAI Press/MIT Press, 109-116.

Franklin, S. and Graesser, A. (1997) "Is it an Agent, or Just a Program?: A Taxonomy for Autonomous Agents". In J.P. Muller, M.J. Wooldridge & N.R. Jennings (Eds.) *Intelligent Agents III: Agent Theories, Architectures. and Languages* (pp.21-36). Berlin, Germany: Springer Verlag.

Gasser L and Huhns M (eds.) (1989) *Distributed Artificial Intelligence*, Vol. II, Morgan Kaufmann, San Mateo, California, pp. 259-290.

Georgeff, M.P. and Ingrand, F .F .(1989) "Decision-making in an Embedded Reasoning System". *Proceedings of 11th International Joint Conference on Artificial Intelligence* 972-978.

Georgeff, M.P. and Lansky, A.L. (1987) "Reactive Reasoning and Planning". *Proceedings of 6th National Conference on Artificial Intelligence*, 677-682.

Grand, S., Cliff, D., Malhotra, A. (1997) "Creatures: Artificial Life Autonomous --2]Software Agents for Home Entertainment". *Proceedings of the First International Conference on Autonomous Agents*. New York, N.Y.: ACM, 22-29.

Hayes-Roth, B. (1985) "A Blackboard Architecture for Control". *Artificial Intelligence*, 26, 251-321.

Hayes-Roth, B. (1995) "An Architecture for Adaptive Intelligent Systems". *Artificial Intelligence*, 72, 329-365.

Hayes-Roth, B. and Van Gent, R. (1997) "Story Making with Improvisational Agents". *Proceedings of the First International Conference on Autonomous Agents*. New York, N.Y.: ACM, 1-7.

Haynes, Th., Sen, S., Arora, N., Nadella R. (1997) "An Automated Meeting Scheduling System". *Proceedings of the First International Conference on Autonomous Agents*. New York, N.Y.: ACM, 308-315.

Jamshidi M (1997): *Large-Scale Systems: Modeling, Control, and Fuzzy Logic*. Prentice Hall, NJ.

Jennings, N.R. (1992) "On being Responsible". In Y.Demazeau & E.Werner (Eds.) *Decentralized AI*, 3, (pp. 93-102). Amsterdam, Holland: Elsevier.

Jong Y, Liang W, Reza L (1997) "Multiple Fuzzy Systems for Function Approximation." *Proceedings of NAFIPS 97*, Syracuse, New-York, pp. 154-159.

Kamel M and Chenniwa H (1994): "Coordination of distributed intelligent systems" In *Soft Computing: Fuzzy Logic, Neural Networks, and Disributed Artificial Intelligence*. Prentice Hall, pp. 261-297.

Kaufmann A and Gupta M M (1985): *Introduction to Fuzzy Arithmetic*, New York: Van Nostrand.

Khan, N.A. and Jain, R. (1985) "Uncertainty Management in a Distributed Knowledge Base system". In *Proceedings of International Joint Conference on Artificial Intelligence*. 318-320.

Kinny, D. and Georgeff, M. (1996) "Modelling and Design of Multi-Agent Systems". In J.P.Muller, M.J.Wooldridge, & N.R.Jennings (Eds.) *Intelligent Agents III: Agent Theories, Architectures, and Languages* (pp.1-20). Berlin, Germany: Springer Verlag.

Kusiak A (Ed.) (1988) *Artificial Intelligence: Implication for CIM*. Springer-Verlag, Berlin-Heidelberg, New-York-London-Paris-Tokyo.

Luck, M. and D'lnverno, M. (1995/a) "A Formal Framework for Agency and Autonomy". *Proceedings of the First International Conference on Multi-Agent Systems*. San-Francisco, CA: AAAI Press/MIT Press, 254-260.

Luck, M and D'Inverno, M. (1995/b) "Engagement and Cooperation in Motivated Agent Modeling". In *Distibuted Artificial Intelligence.Architecture and Modeling*. First Australian Workshop on DAI, Canberra, ACT, Australia, 70

Maes, P. (1994) "Agents that Reduce Work and Information Overload". *Communications of the ACM*, 37(7), 31-40, 146.

Maes, P. (1995/a) "Artificial Life Meets Entertainment: Life like Autonomous Agents". *Communications of the ACM*. 38(11), 108-114.

Maes, P. (1995/b) "Modeling Adaptive Autonomous Agents". In Langton, C.G. (Ed.) *Artificial Life: An Overview* (p.p. 135-162). Cambridge, MA: The MIT Press.

Malone, T.W., Fikes, R.E., Grant, K.R., Howard, M.T. (1988) "Enterprise: A Market-like Task Scheduler for Distributed Computing Environments". In B.Huberman, (Ed.) *The Ecology of Computation*, Amsterdam, Holland: North-Holland.

McCahon C S and Lee E S (1990) "Comparing fuzzy numbers: the proportion of the optium method" *International Journal of Approximate Reasoning*, 4: 159-181.

Miller, P. (1986) *Expert Critiquing Systems: Practice-Based Medical Consultation By Computer*. Berlin, Germany: Springer-Verlag.

Moukas, A. and Giorgos, Z. (1997) "Evolving a Multi-Agent Information Filtering Solution in Amalthaea." *Proceedings of the First International Conference on Autonomous Agents*. New York, N.Y.: ACM, 394-403.

Moulin B and Cloutier L (1994) "Collaborative work based on multiagent architectures: a methodological perspective" In Aminzadeh F, Jamshidi M (eds.): *Soft Computing: Fuzzy Logic, Neural Networks, and Disributed Artificial Intelligence*. Prentice Hall, pp. 261-297.

Munday, C., Dangedej, J., Cross, T., Lukose, D. (1995) "Motivation and Perception Mechanisms in Mobile Agents for Electronic Commerce". In *Distributed Artificial Intelligence. Architecture and Modeling*. First Australian Workshop on DAI, Canberra, ACT, Australia, 144-158.

Neves, M.C. and Oliveira E. (1997) "A Control Architecture for an Autonomous Mobile Robot". *Proceedings of the First International Conference on Autonomous Agents: New York, N.Y.: ACM*, 193-200.

Nwana, H.S. and Ndumu, D.T. (1997) "An Introduction to Agent Technology". In H.S. Nwana & N. Azarmi (Eds.) *Software Agents and Soft Computing* (pp. 3-26). Berlin, Germany: Springer- Verlag.

Nakamati G, Freitas R, Predo J, Gomide F (1994) "Fuzzy Distributed Artificial Intelligent Systems", IEEE, pp. 462-467.

O'Brien, P.D. and Wiegand, M.E. (1997) "Agents of Change in Business Process Management". In Nwana, H.S., Azarmi, N. (Eds.) *Software Agents and Soft Computing* (pp.132-145). Berlin, Germany: Springer- Verlag.

Park D, Kandel A, Langholz G (1997) "Genetic-based new fuzzy reasoning models with application to fuzzy control" *IEEE Transactions on Systems, Man, and Cybernetics - Part B: Cybernetics*, 24(1), 39-47

Potiupkin A.Yu. (1996) "Solving of the problem of fuzzy systems identification". *News of Academy of sciences of Russia* 4: 40-46.

Potiupkin A.Yu. (1999) "Estimation technical state of an objects described by fuzzy relational equations". *News of Academy of sciences of Russia* 4: 111-119.

Pratihar D.K., Deb K., Grosh A. (1999) "A genetic-fuzzy approach mobile robot navigation among moving obstacles". *International Journal of Approximate Reasoning* 20 145-172.

Rao, A.S. R and Georgeff, M.P. (1995) "BDI Agents: From Theory to Practice". In *Proceedings of the First International Conference on Multi-Agent Systems.* San-Francisco, CA: AAAI Press/MIT Press, 312-319

Rosenschein, J.S. and Genesereth, M.R. (1985) "Deals Among Rational Agents". In *Proceedings of 1985 International Joint Conference on Artificial Intelligenc*e 91-99

Russel, S.J. and Norvig, P. (1995) *Artificial Intelligence: A modern Approach.* Upper Saddle River, N.J.: Prentice Hall.

Schott B, Whalen T (1994) "Fuzzy uncertainty in imperfect competition." *Information Science* 76, 339-354.

Selker, T. (1994) "A Teaching Agent that Learns". *Communications of the ACM*, 37(7), 92-99.

Setnes M and Cross V (1997) "Compatibility-based ranking of fuzzy numbers" In *Proceedings of NAFIPS 97*, Syracuse, New-York.

Shoham, Y. (1993) "Agent Oriented Programming". *Artificial Intelligence*, .60, 51-92

Sikora, R. and Shaw, M.J. (1998) "A Multi-Agent Framework for the Coordination and Integration of Information Systems". *Management Science.* 44(11), S65-S78.

Singh, M.P. (1994) "Multi-Agent Systems: A Theoretical Framework for Intentions". *Know How and Communication*. Berlin, Germany: Springer Verlag.

Smith, D.C., Cypher, A., Spohrer, J. (1994) "Programming Agents without a Programming Language". *Communications of the ACM*. 37(7), 55-67.

Stephen T and Wong E (1989) "COSMO: A communication scheme for cooperative knowledge based systems." *IEEE Transaction on System, Man and Cybernetics* 23(3): pp. 809-822.

Tokoro, M. (1996) "Agents: Towards a Society in which Humans and Computers Cohabitate. Distributed Software Agents and Applications". *Proceedings of 6th European Workshop on Modeling Autonomous Agents in Multi-Agent World*. Berlin, Germany: Springer-Verlag, 1-10.

Tsuji T, Jazidie A, Kaneko M (1997/a) "Distributed trajectory generation for cooperative multi-arm robots via virtual force interactions." *IEEE Transactions on Systems, Man, and Cybernetics* - Part B: Cybernetics, 27(5) , 862-867.

Tsuji T, Nakayama S, Ito K (1997/b) "Parallel and distributed trajectory generation of redundant manipulators through cooperation and competition among subsystems." *IEEE Transactions on Systems, Man, and Cybernetics* - Part B: Cybernetics, 27(3), 498-509.

Vojdani N (1997) "A Fuzzy Contract Net Approach to Manufacturing Control. Application of Fuzzy Logic" In Jamshidi M, Titli A, Zadeh L, and Bevrie S, (eds.) *Towards High Machine Intelligence Quotient Systems*, Prentice Hall PTR, Upper Sadle River, New Jersey, pp. 289-299.

Werner E (1989): "Cooperative agents: A unified theory of communication and social structure." In Gasser L and Huhns M N (eds.): *Distributed Artificial Intelligence*. Vol. 2, Pitman morgan Kaufman, pp. 3-36.

Whinston, A. (1997) "Intelligent Agents as a Basis for Decision Support Systems". Decision Support Systems, 20(1), 1.

Wooldridge, M. and Jennings, N. (1995/a) "Agent Theories, Architectures, and Languages: a Survey." In M. Wooldridge. & N.R. Jennings (Eds.) *Intelligent Agents* (pp.1-22). Berlin, J Germany: Springer-Verlag.

Wooldridge, M. & Jennings, N. (1995/b) "Intelligent Agents: Theory and Practice. Knowledge Engineering Review", 10 (2),115-152.

Yager, R. (1997) "Intelligent Agents for World Wide Web Advertising Decisions". *International Journal of Intelligent Systems*.12, 379-390.

Zadeh L A (1973) "Outline of a new approach to the analysis of complex systems and decision processes." *IEEE Transactions on Systems, Man, and Cybernetics*, SMC3, 28-44.

Zadeh L A (1988) "Fuzy Logic" *IEEE Computer*, April 1988, pp. 83-93.

Zhang, Ch. (1992) "Cooperation Under Uncertainty in Distributed Expert Systems". *Artificial Intelligence*, 56, 21-69.

Zhang, M., and Zhang, Ch. (1995) "Neural Network Strategies for Solving Synthesis Problems in Non-Conflict Cases in Distributed Expert Systems". In *Distributed Artificial Intelligence. Architecture and Modeling*. First Australian Workshop on DAI, Canberra, ACT, Australia, 174-188.

Soft Computing Agents
V. Loia (Ed.)
IOS Press, 2002

Chapter 2

Incremental Synchronous Learning for Embedded Agents Operating in Ubiquitous Computing Environments

Hani Hagras
Victor Callaghan
Graham Clarke
Martin Colley
Anthony Pounds-Cornish
Arran Holmes
Hakan Duman

2.1 Introduction

In this chapter we introduce a novel learning and adaptation mechanism for embedded-agents that are embodied in devices making up ubiquitous computing environments. We illustrate the concept using eGadgets, which are types of ubiquitous computing devices developed by ourselves and our European partners, CTI (Patras, Greece) and NMRC (Cork, Ireland), as part of the EU Disappearing Computer programme. The concept of eGadgets is to create a conceptual and technological framework that will allow ordinary people to assemble and use, with ease, a collection of network-aware computer based products to provide collective functionality that will empower their lives beyond that provided by today's stand-alone products. Integrating useful amounts of intelligence into embedded devices is an essential enabling technology to achieve the vision of ubiquitous computing. In support of this vision we describe a fuzzy logic based Incremental Synchronous Learning (ISL) technique that provides online life-long learning that can be operated in a non-intrusive mode. A unique feature of our learning mechanism is that it seeks to *particularise* the agent's learnt behaviour to the individual user rather than work on behalf of the machine or adjust itself to the average behaviour of users. In order to assess such technology we have constructed the iDorm (intelligent dormitory) to act as a test-bed for intelligent inhabited environments. We report on an initial experiment in this new facility in which our intelligent embedded agents, powered by our ISL learning mechanism, learn a user's behaviour and control the iDorm for two days.

2.2 Project Framework

"Startrek" and similar science fiction films and series paint an intriguing picture of the future, one in which masses of unseen and tireless electronic devices and intelligent-agents attend to occupants every need; regulating the air they breath, the temperature of their cabins, their entertainment and communications. In fact their very existence in such alien environments is wholly dependent on technology. For many, space exploration and planetary habitats are not just the "final frontier" for mankind but the ultimate vision for ubiquitous computing and ambient intelligence. Fuelled by advances in microelectronics and Internet technology the variety of current computer-based networked artefacts, is growing at a huge rate. Some recent estimates showing of the order of 8 billion microprocessors were produced in 2001, of which only 2% went into PCs, the rest going into embedded computer devices most people wouldn't recognize as computers (Callaghan *et al.* 2000b). Such devices vary from, mobile telephones through home entertainment systems to cars. Thanks to pervasive networking (e.g. the Internet) such machines and artefacts can be configured by users into personalised and novel arrangements so that devices are able to coordinate their actions to support peoples lives. An obvious barrier to achieving this vision is the inherent complexity of the technology. People must be able to use such devices without needing to understand or deal with the underlying technology. One approach to achieving this is to embed intelligent agents into the devices that make up ubiquitous environments thereby transferring some of the cognitive load from people to machines; the extent to which this is done being sometimes referred to as the "cognitive disappearance metric".

It is anticipated that all forms of goods will be influenced by this development from items that are clearly electronic in nature today (e.g. mobile phones, home entertainment systems, kitchen appliances, etc.) to those that are currently not (e.g. clothing, desks, etc.) (Callaghan *et al.* 2000a). Such goods will find themselves in a variety of Intelligent Inhabited Environments (IIE); spaces such as cars, shopping malls, homes, clothes and even within our own bodies. However, in order to realise this vision, technologies must be developed that will support ad-hoc and highly dynamic (re)structuring of such networked arrangements of embedded computing devices whilst, wherever possible, shielding non-technical users from the need to understand or work directly with the underlying technology. The authors are engaged along with our European partners CTI and NMRC in the eGadgets project [http://www.extrovert-gadgets.net/] funded by the EU "Disappearing Computer" programme. A programme which, in part, aims at the development of compact intelligent embedded-agents (intelligence integrated into computational artefacts) and computational architectures to assist with the above.

The work proposed by this chapter focuses on the investigation and development of learning and adaptation techniques that seek to provide an online, life-long, personalised learning of anticipatory adaptive control in devices making up ubiquitous computing environments exemplified by our EU eGadgets project. To these ends we introduce our Fuzzy Incremental Synchronous Learning techniques and describe our intelligent dormitory (iDorm) as a testbed for our work in learning and adaptation, together with supporting experiments and results.

2.3 eGadgets

An eGadget is a tangible object (which can be an everyday object), it has a communication module (wired, radio or infrared), it has at least one plug (the abstraction of the ability to co-operate with other eGadgets). An eGadget also has a digital self (software running on the eGadget, on a host computer or both) and may or may not have processing power and memory and may or may not have sensors and actuators and may or may not be able to learn to adapt its operation to meet the users needs.

The concept of eGadgets is to create a conceptual and technological framework that will allow ordinary people to assemble and use, with ease, a collection of network aware computer based products (e.g. cellphones, music-players, washing machines, heating systems etc) to provide collective functionality which will empower their lives beyond that possible by today's stand-alone products. Embedding useful amounts of intelligence into eGadgets environments is an essential enabling technology to achieve the vision of the eGadgets (Callaghan *et al.* 2000b). In the terminology adopted by this project, individual devices are called eGadgets; collections of connected eGadgets are called GadgetWorlds;

the conceptual and technological framework is referred to as Gadgetware Architectural Style (GAS).

An example of a GadgetWorld might be a room in an intelligent-building in which environment and entertainment based eGadgets work together to form an integrated interactive environment. In this chapter we will describe our novel methods that supply compact reasoning and learning mechanisms that are able to deal with the numerous inputs and highly dynamic environments (both in the physical and network sense) that will characterise GadgetWorlds and provide useful amounts of intelligent functionality. We will use the iDorm as an example of GadgetWorlds and will show how can our Incremental Synchronous Learning (ISL) techniques provide an online, life-long, user-particularised, anticipatory, adaptive, control agent for a intelligent inhabited environments.

2.4 Intelligent Embedded Agents operating in Intelligent Inhabited Environments (IIE)

Ideally, for the vision described in the introduction to be realised, people must be able to use computer-based artefacts (or eGadgets) and systems without being cognitively aware of the existence of the computer within the machine. Clearly in many computer based products the computer remains very evident, for example, with a video recorder, the user is forced to refer to complicated manuals and to use his own reasoning and learning processes to use the machine successfully. This situation is likely to get much worse as the number, varieties and uses of computer based artefacts increase. We argue that if some part of the reasoning, planning and learning normally provided by artefact user, were embedded into the artefact itself, then, by that degree, the cognitive loading on the user would reduce and, in the extreme, disappear (i.e. a substantial part of the computer's presence would disappear). Put another way, the proportion of reasoning, planning and learning transferred to the artefact or eGadget (collectively referred to as "embedded-intelligence") is a measure of cognitive disappearance. Hence we view embedded intelligence as an essential property of artefacts for the cognitive disappearance of the computer and necessary to the successful deployment of new technology in Intelligent Inhabited Environments (IIE).

Embedded-computers that contain such embedded intelligence are normally referred to as *"embedded-agents"* (Callaghan *et al.* 2001). It is now common for such embedded-agents to have an Internet connection thereby facilitating multi embedded-agent systems. In a fully distributed multi embedded-agent systems each agent is an autonomous entity co-operating by means of either structured or ad-hoc associations with its neighbours.

2.4.1 Other work related to development of Intelligent Embedded Agents for IIE

There are a growing number of research projects concerned with applying Artificial Intelligence (AI) and intelligent agents to IIE. In Sweden, Davidsson (Davidsson 1998) utilises multi-agent principles to control building services. These agents are based on the AI thread that decomposes systems by function rather than behaviour as in our research. Their work does not address issues such as occupant based learning. In Colorado Mozer (Mozer 1998) uses a soft computing approach - neural networks - focusing solely on the intelligent control of lighting within a building. Their system, implemented in a building with a real occupant, achieved a significant energy reduction, although this was sometimes at the expense of the occupant's comfort. Work at MIT on the HAL project (Brooks 1997) concentrates on making the room responsive to the occupant by adding intelligent sensors to the user interface. In the University of Loughborough Angelov (Angelov *et al.* 2000) looked at the application of fuzzy rule-based models in HVAC system simulation and he was concerned with producing optimal models for buildings, which could be used later in control. The HIVE project at MIT (Minar *et al.* 1999) is an example of a particularly forward-looking distributed agent model. This model differs from our work principally in that their agents are soft (rather than our hard embedded-agents) with access to hard devices being via coded objects referred to as shadows. The soft agents reside on servers (e.g. PCs) and, as a consequence, do not have to consider the compactness of agent design, which is one central focus of our work. The University of Reading is active in the field of intelligent buildings and their view of intelligence is rooted in structural design and building utilisation concepts. Currently their research is mostly focusing on monitoring people over the network with the "talking sign" chips. There are also other high profile Intelligent Building projects such as the Microsoft Smart House, BT's Telecare and Cisco Internet Home. However most of these industrial projects are geared toward using networks and remote access with some smart control (mostly simple automation) with sparse use of AI and little emphasis on learning and adaptation to the user's behaviour. To the author's knowledge no other work has addressed the online learning and adaptation of intelligent embedded agents to specific users habitual behaviour operating within IIE.

2.4.2 Some Challenges facing Research in Intelligent Embedded Agents

Traditional AI techniques are well known for being computationally demanding and therefore unsuitable for 'lean' computer architectures. Historically most traditional AI system were developed to run on powerful computers such as workstations, whose specifications are at least two orders of magnitude removed from most embedded-computers. In addition traditional AI techniques have proved too fragile to operate real time intelligent machines. As a result, even implementing simplified traditional AI systems on embedded-computers has proved a considerable challenge to computer science.

Another problem is that most automation systems (which involve a minimum of intelligence) utilise mechanisms that generalise actions (e.g. set temperature or volume that is the average of many people's needs). However, we contend that AI applied to intelligent environments needs to particularise itself to the individual. A key underlying concept in the eGadgets model being that the technology should empower people to freely design novel configurations (often, not envisaged by the original gadget designers) thus providing a form of emergence. A fundamental axiom of our approach is that "the user is king", the users intentions (in the form of their usage actions) should, wherever possible (safety being one exception), be faithfully reflected in the eGadget or GadgetWorlds operation. In other words, programming or learning should support the notion of particularisation over generalisation, which is more common in other application domains. Thus, the value of an intelligent embedded agent lies in the agent's ability to learn and predict the human and the system needs and automatically adjust the agent controller to meet them and the agent's ability to do such learning and prediction based on a wide set of parameters. There is thus a need to modify effectors for environmental variables like heat and light etc on the basis of a *complex multi dimensional input vector*, which cannot be specified in advance. For example, something happening to one system (e.g. reducing light level) may cause a person to change behaviour (e.g. sit down) which in turn may result in them effecting other systems (e.g. needing more heat). An agent that only looks at heat levels is unable to take these wider issues into account. An added control difficulty is that people are essentiality non-deterministic and highly individual, therefore as explained above there is a need for a system that particularises for individual users rather than generalising for a group of users. When viewed in such integrated control terms it is possible to see why simple PID or fuzzy controllers are unable to deal satisfactorily with the problem of online learning for embedded agents.

The quality of agent decisions is limited by its knowledge of the world. It gets its knowledge from sensors directly attached to it and other agents (i.e. indirectly from their sensors). Naturally the question arises, which set of sensor information is sufficient for an agent to make a particular class of decision? Consider a simple heating controller and ask the question, "Why does the room's occupant alter the heat value?" Is it to do with the current temperature, the current level of activity of the user, what the user is wearing, where the user is in a room, where the user has just been or what? We may decide that it is based upon current temperature and therefore could operate with only one sensor, but later discover that an agent that used only one sensor was not working very effectively. At the other extreme we could decide we should sense 'everything' and then let the agent learn which of these sensed values was important. Clearly in this latter situation the agent would be able to make better-informed decisions and adapt to changing criteria. In addition this problem exposes a central dilemma, what is the best mechanism for selecting relevant sensory sets for agents? Is it the designer or the agents themselves? The problem with a designer is the assumption that people know best what the intelligent agent needs; but is this true (a dilemma sometimes referred to as the perception gap (Callaghan *et al.* 2000a)? We would argue that it is better to provide a large set of sensory inputs to agents and let them resolve which of the stimuli is important for any given decision wherever possible. Whilst this latter argument may have some appeal it carries with it a penalty, the need to compute using large sensory input vectors. Thus, large sensory sets are an issue for ubiquitous computing environments. One solution would be the development of mechanisms to allow embedded-agents to "focus" on sub-sets of data relating to specific decisions or circumstances.

2.5 The iDorm — A Testbed for Ubiquitous Computing and Ambient Intelligence

We have chosen the Essex Intelligent Dormitory Pictured in Figure 1 to be a demonstrator and test-bed for our intelligent learning and adaptation techniques applied to eGadgets and GadgetWorlds. Being an intelligent dormitory it is a multi-use space (i.e. contains areas with differing activities such as sleeping, working, entertaining etc) and can be compared in function to a room for elderly or disabled people or an intelligent student or hotel room. The room looks like any other with normal furniture that will allow the user to live comfortably as it has a bed, a working desk, bed side cabinet, wardrobe, a multi media PC which the user can use for working or entertainment as it has the capability of audio entertainment via playing music CD, radios using an up to date Dolby sound systems and it can also display normal TV programs and DVDs. The layout of the iDorm is shown in Figure 2.

In order to make the iDorm as sensitive as we can to the needs of the occupant we need to be able to comprehensively monitor activity in the room. For these reasons the iDorm is equipped with an array of embedded sensors such as temperature, occupancy, humidity and light level sensors, as well as a camera to be able to monitor what goes inside. It is possible to follow the activities inside the iDorm, via a live video link over the Internet (Pounds-Cornish and Holmes 2002) though this is not directly involved in our attempt to develop embedded intelligent mechanisms.

The iDorm makes provision for control of numerous systems such as entertainment, office-work and environmental control. In building the iDorm, the commercial reality is that the devices we have installed reside on several different types of network so that access needs to be managed and gateways *can therefore be regarded as critical components in such systems*, combining appropriate granularity with security. Currently the iDorm is based around three networks to be described later which are Lonworks, 1-wire (TINI) and IP although it would be possible to include others, providing a diverse infrastructure and for the development of network independent solutions (Homes *et al.* 2002). In what follows we summarise the sensors and actuators used.

Figure 1. Photo of iDorm

The room has eleven environmental parameters to be measured, which are;
- Time of the day (I1) measured by a clock connected to the 1- wire network
- Inside room light level (I2) measured by indoor light sensor connected to the Lonworks network
- Outside outdoor lighting level (I3) measured by an external weather station connected to the 1-wire network
- Inside room temperature (I4) measured by redundant sensors connected to the Lonworks and the 1-Wire networks
- Outside outdoor room temperature (I5) measured by external weather station connected the 1- wire network
- Whether the user is using his audio entertainment (I6) on the computer – either the radio or the CD player are sensed by Visual C++ code when running the Winamp program
- Whether the user is lying or sitting on the bed or not (I7) measured by a pressure pad connected to the 1-wire network
- Whether the user is sitting on the desk chair or not (I8) measured by a pressure pad connected to the 1- wire network
- Whether the window is opened or closed (I9) measured by a reed switch connected to the Tini-1 Wire network
- Whether the user is working or not (I10) sensed by a Visual C++ code that senses if the user is working on a Word document
- Whether the user is using video entertainment (I11) on the computer - either a TV program (via WinTV) or a DVD using the Winamp program sensed using Visual C++ code.

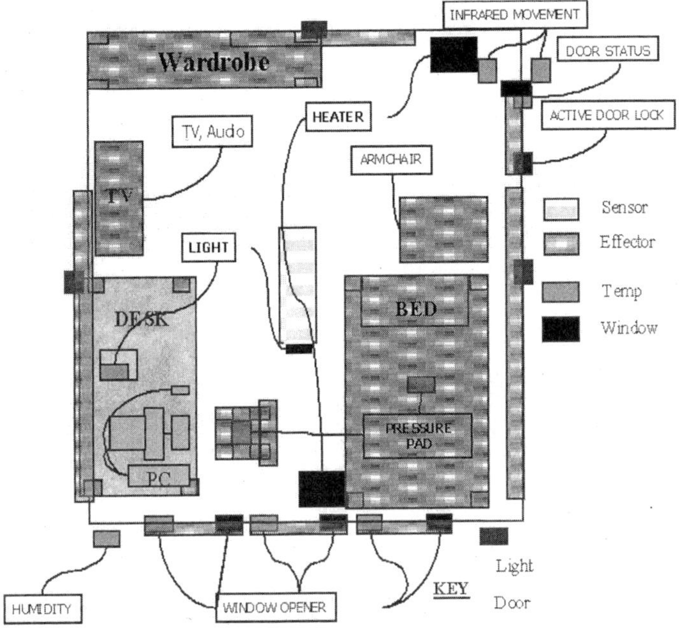

Figure 2. Layout of iDorm.

There are ten outputs to control;
- Fan Heater (O1)
- Fan Cooler (O2)
- A dimmable spot light above the Door (O3)
- A dimmable spot light above the Wardrobe (O4)
- A dimmable spot light above the Computer (O5)
- A dimmable spot light above the Bed (O6)
- A Desk Lamp (O7)
- A Bedside Lamp (O8)
- Whether the automatic blinds are opened or closed (O9)
- If the automatic blinds are closed their opening can be controlled (O10)

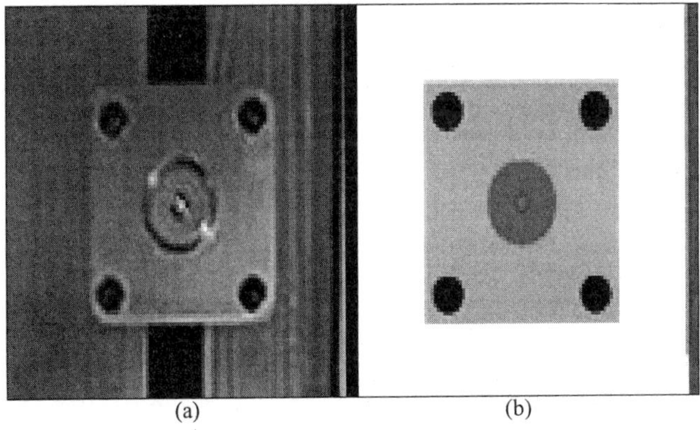

Figure 3. The iDorm Lock a) Real World b) VRML Model.

The room is also supplied by other sensors like smoke detector, humidity sensor, activity sensors, telephone sensor to sense whether the phone is on hook or off hook. However the above set of sensors and actuators are the ones used by our learning system

The Agent is designed to learn behaviour related to different individuals. In order to achieve this, it needs to be able to distinguish between users of the environment. This is achieved by using an active lock, designed and built by our research team based on Dallas Semiconductors 1-Wire protocol.

Each user of the environment is given an electronic key, about the size of a penny. It is mounted onto a key fob and contains a unique identification number inside its 2-kilobyte memory. The door to the iDorm contains an electronic keyhole that reads the address of any electronic key held against it; the lock is depicted both in the real world and in the VRML GUI in Figure 3.

The address is dynamically compared to a small user database where the address of a key is the index to the list of information shown in Table 1.

Table 1. Information held about each Key Holder

Last name
First name
Time last entered iDorm
Time last exited iDorm
Status (Student, Staff or Guest)
Unique ID Number
Electronic Key Unique ID Number

The Unique ID Number of the user is passed to the embedded agent so that it may retrieve and update rules learnt about that user previously. The lock is also able to support multiple connections to interrogate its state.

By gathering information from its sensors over a period of time, the embedded agent can notice how a particular person tends to react to particular circumstances, and can then *learn* to replicate that behaviour itself. Using our active lock system we can distinguish between different users, the system is able to learn different behaviours for different people. So for example, the agent might learn that Person A, who is only partially sighted, prefers a higher level of light than Person B, whose sight is normal. It could then adjust the lighting level appropriately, according to who was using the room at that time.

2.5.1 The iDorm Networking

Technology for networking building services is already widely deployed (e.g. Lonworks, BACnet, EIBUs, etc), as is technology for connecting domestic and mobile appliances (e.g. Cebus, Bluetooth). These are opening up the opportunities and technical difficulties afforded by highly connected and dynamic embedded-computing and networked gadgets.

One way intelligent embedded-agents are often deployed in the creation of intelligent environments (Sharples *et al.* 1999) is to assign an agent to control a localised space (e.g. a room, a body). These spaces can map quite naturally onto to the domain managed by network gateways. We believe that a marriage of network topologies and agent architectures would hold many synergetic advantages such as (Holmes *et al.* 2002):

1. The gateway domain could be readily made to match that of an intelligent building agent (i.e. both human activity and agent control equate to spaces such buildings, floors, rooms and bodies).
2. The gateway can bridge diverse sets of data and control networks (e.g. IP and LonTalk)
3. The gateway can provide a means of managing secure access.

4. The gateway can act as an area wide server providing managed access to the resources within its jurisdiction (e.g. remote home control via a web interface).
5. The gateway can "mine" information on activity under its control (for example, information on occupant's behaviour and use of equipment within the environment might be gathered and made available for the benefit of the occupant. In this case there would have to be agreement between individuals and manufacturers say on equipment usage.
6. The gateway could provide a low cost way of providing computational resource for agent deployment (i.e. gateways will be there anyway).
7. The gateway concept is both scalable and extensible in a downward (micro-world), upward (macro-world) and horizontal (more of same) direction.

For instance, in an intelligent building (which is an example of intelligent inhabited environments) there could be a gateway at the house level, further gateways to each room and gateways to complex devices within rooms (e.g. hi-fi systems) or body-wearable devices (e.g. with the mobile phone being the gateway). The use of gateways is therefore a scaleable solution to the problem of giving a degree of autonomy and security to different levels of any complex and hierarchical system (Holmes *et al.* 2002). In our example - the iDorm - there are in fact a number of sub-networks that the common interface disguises and protects at the same time.

The iDorm uses three main communication protocols to allow its devices to communicate with each other. Such a variety of networks and protocols were chosen because any successful intelligent agent produced for the iDorm can be shown to be network independent. In the following subsection we discuss the three main networks and their communication protocols.

2.5.1.1 Lonworks Network

Lonworks is Echelon's proprietary network and encompasses a protocol for buildings automation. It is a twisted pair network, similar to IP that comes in two flavours – one that provides power to the devices through the network and another that requires devices to have an external power supply. There are many commercially available sensors and actuators for this system. Each device has typed inputs and outputs. The Lonworks system allows association to be set up between inputs and outputs using a standard PC that is connected to the Lonworks network. The PC can then be disconnected and the associations will continue to function. The system has no central coordination system, just a set of devices. The physical network installed in the iDorm is Lonworks TP/FP10 network. The gateway to the IP network is provided by Echelon's iLon 1000 web server. This allows the states and values of sensors and actuators to be read or altered via a standard web browser using HTML forms. The majority of the sensors and effectors inside the iDorm are connected via a Lonworks network as shown in Figure 4.

2.5.1.2 Wire Network

Dallas semiconductor developed the 1-wire network protocol. It was designed for simple devices to be connected over short distances. 1-wire offers a large range of commercial devices including small temperature sensors, weather stations, ID buttons and switches. Unlike Lonworks the 1-wire system has a central coordination system. The 1-wire network is connected to a Tiny Internet Interface board (TINI board) which runs an embedded Java Virtual Machine (JVM). In the iDorm the Tini connected to the 1-wire network runs an embedded web server that serves out the status of the networked devices using a Java servlet. The servlet collects data from the devices on the network and responds to HTTP requests. The network layout and attached sensors are shown in Figure 5.

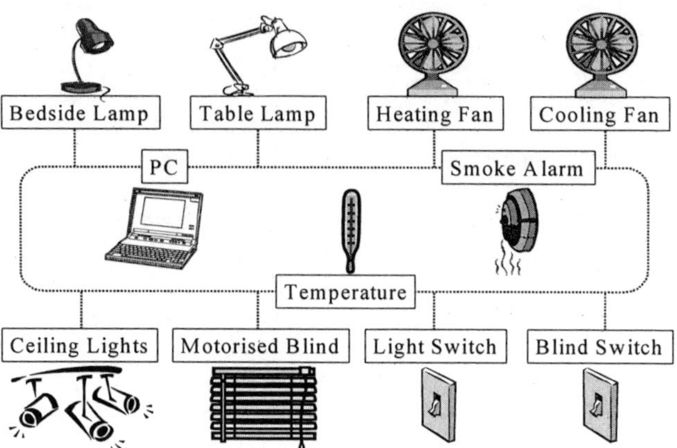

Figure 4. LonTalk network layout.

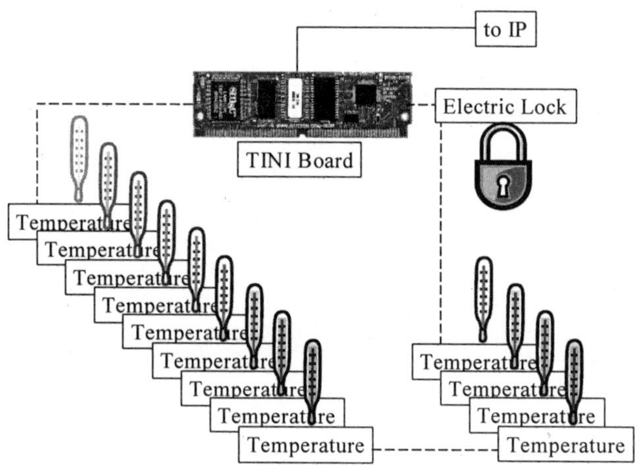

Figure 5. 1-Wire network layout

2.5.1.3 IP Network

The IP network forms a backbone to interconnect all networks and other devices like the Multi-media PC (MMPC). The MMPC will be the main focus for office-work and entertainment in the iDorm. Again the MMPC uses the HTTP protocol to display its information as a web page.

2.5.2 iDorm Gateway Server

The iDorm uses a single network (IPv4) as shown in Figure 6 to link the different networks together (Homes *et al.* 2002). This allows a common protocol to be produced so that all interfaces could use to communicate with the iDorm. There are several distinct advantages to this approach:

- The first is that a common interface immediately creates a scalable environment. More sensors can be added to existing networks or entirely new network protocols can be added to the iDorm without having to re-configure every other network that communicates in the room.
- The second is robustness. More than one network can provide similar information, if one fails the other can seamlessly provide that information. For example, the iDorm has temperature information available on both the Lonworks network and the 1-Wire network.
- The third advantage is that a common interface doesn't limit an interface to a certain way of expressing data. If all the iDorm's environmental information is available as simple states and values then it is entirely up to the interface designer as to how and in what format that data is used.
- The fourth advantage is that of security. If the iDorm's information is available through a single communication protocol, it is far easier to decide whether the client is entitled to receive this information. This entitlement can be decided on anything from identification or time. We use the latter concept to timeshare access to the iDorm when more than one experiment needs to run at one time.
- The fifth advantage is that a common protocol allows a dynamic interface to be created. An example of this is the voice recognition interface explained later in this chapter.
- The sixth advantage is that the processing power required to gather information from the room is greatly reduced by placing the onus on the common protocol to provide the information. This system reduces the amount of processing required from the interface.

The protocol that has been produced is an XML definition for the iDorm. All information requested from the iDorm must go through a central server. This server communicates with the iDorm's LonTalk and 1-Wire network across IP using HTTP requests to get environmental information and request changes to the states of the effectors

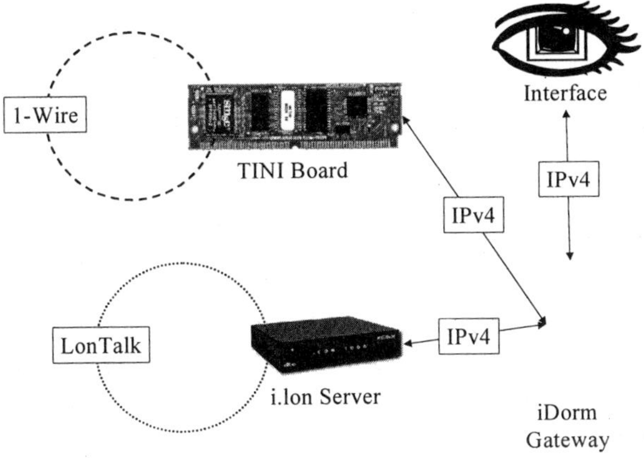

Figure 6. The high-level network

To create a standard interface to the iDorm we have an "iDorm gateway server". This receives XML formatted queries from an agent, then connects to all the network interface servers in turn and sends an HTTP GET request to make any changes to the network devices requested by the XML request. It then receives an HTML formatted page describing the states of all the devices on each network. This document is then parsed to remove the correct information and formatted in XML to retain its context, before being returned to the requesting agent as shown in Figure 7. XML is very portable and easy to parse which makes it ideal as cross platform communications syntax. Its other main advantage is that it is human readable and can be displayed easily in a number of ways depending on the applied style sheet.

The iDorm's gateway server is a practical implementation of an HTTP server acting as a gateway to each of the room's sub networks. This illustrates the concept that using a hierarchy of gateways it would be possible to create a scaleable architecture across such heterogeneous networks in IIE (Homes *et al.* 2002). The iDorm gateway server allows a standard interface to all of the room's sub networks. There could then be levels above this like a building server, or the granularity could be increased below this. This gateway system will allow the system to operate over any standard network such as EIBus, Bluetooth, Lonworks and could readily be developed to allow a 'Plug N Play' allowing devices to be automatically discovered and configured using intelligent mechanisms (surprisingly, Lonworks does not have such a facility) (Homes *et al.* 2002).

In addition, it is clear such a gateway is an ideal point to implement security and data mining associated with the sub network. Figure 8 shows a logical network infrastructure in the iDorm.

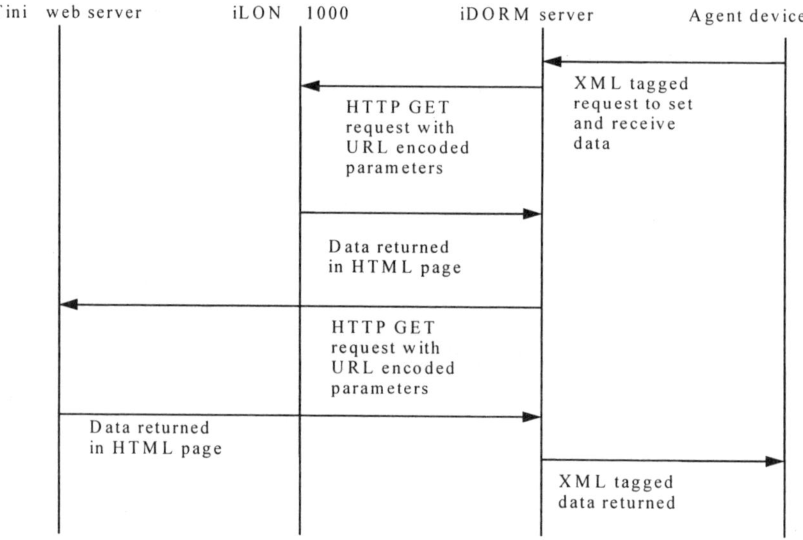

Figure 7. Diagram shows the XML based communication between the devices.

2.5.3 iDorm Interfaces

Our group has designed several interfaces to deal with the problem of being able to control the room with as few constraints as possible:

2.5.3.1 The Standard Interface

As mentioned previously, there are normal switches mounted on the walls in the iDorm that control all the effectors (lights, blind, heaters). However, these switches are not directly connected to the device they control. Each switch and button is a device on the Lonworks network. As such, it transmits a data packet across the network when it has been pressed.

2.5.3.2 The Web Interface

A small web page has been created which is accessible from any machine running a web browser. It shows the current status of the iDorm that automatically refreshes. The user can select the changes they wish to make to the environment; click on the "Update" button and the room will change. Because the web page is very simple and very small, it is possible to view it on smaller web enabled devices such as a palmtop.

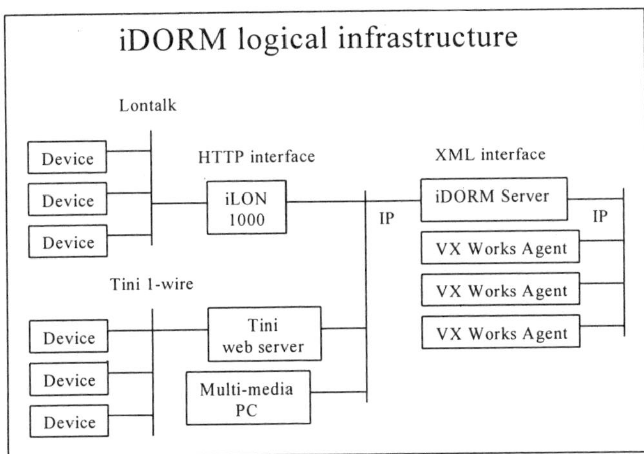

Figure 8. Diagram to show the logical network infrastructure in the iDorm.

2.5.3.3 The VRML Interface

This is a hybrid system that marries the Virtual Reality Modelling Language with a Java interface controlling the iDorm. Written in VRML 2.0, the model (depicted in Figure 9) provides a navigable virtual model of the environment that enables the user to see any part of the room and its current state. Any web browser with a VRML plug-in can view the model.

Using Java EAI, the model is linked to an applet running in the same browser window. It enables the user to choose a state for a variety of devices through a click and drag interface. Together, the model and the applet provide an information rich graphic user interface (GUI) where the user can see the current state of the iDorm both from the applet and the VRML itself (Pounds-Cornish and Holmes 2002).

The VRML runs two parallel processes, the first monitors the current state of the real world and reflects it in the model and in the interface. The second monitors the applet and notifies the agent when the user has requested a change.

The monitoring process requests a URL from the central server, which executes a TCL script to return an XML parsed document detailing the current state of the iDorm. It then parses this document and places all the pertinent values into a local vector. The process then walks down the vector changing the VRML model to reflect its recent scan of the real world. This process is looped so the model always reflects the latest state of the real world.

The notification process waits for the user to interact with the GUI, and then picks out what object was requested to change. The process then makes a GET request to the central server, which writes to a file containing the requested change(s).

When the agent is monitoring the human, it monitors the state of this file and when it spots the user's request it takes a snapshot of the current environment state and associates the request with it. The agent then allows the request through to the appropriate device. Because of the speed of communication, the delay in the user's request is negligible but the agent is still able to learn the circumstances that cause the user to change the environment.

The advantage of the iDorm GUI is that it functions alongside standard interfaces such as switches and buttons on the wall. It also allows the user to monitor and/or control the environment from a remote location (Pounds-Cornish and Holmes 2002). The iDorm GUI is also designed such that more than one instance of it can be run at the same time meaning that several people can monitor the environment whilst changes are being made.

One of the future development plans for the VRML model is to reduce the complexity of the GUI to enable it to run on a wireless palmtop device.

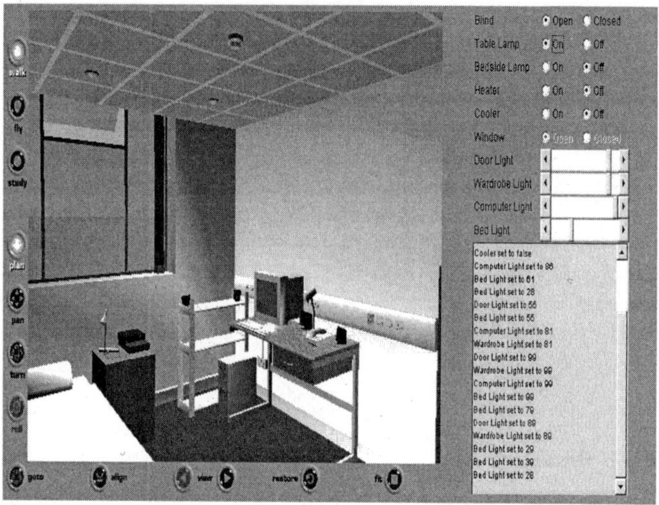

Figure 9. iDorm Graphical User Interface

2.5.3.4 WAP Interface

This interface is a simple extension of the web interface. Because the iDorm central server can also support the WML language it is possible to interact with the iDorm on mobile phones as depicted in Figure 10.

2.5.3.5 Voice Recognition Interface

Prof. Nikola Kasabov and Waleed Abdulla (Kasabov *et al.* 1999) from the University of Otago in New Zealand originated a speaker independent voice recognition system. Our research group is applying it using a room-based command set appropriate to the iDorm.

Based on Hidden Markov Models, the system contains commands created by the user. Several of the command's behaviours are dynamic, depending on the current state of the room. For instance, the command "brighter" takes an average of the ceiling light levels, adds 10% to the value and sets the spotlights accordingly. This command means the ambient light level of the room can be controlled without having to give individual commands to each spotlight.

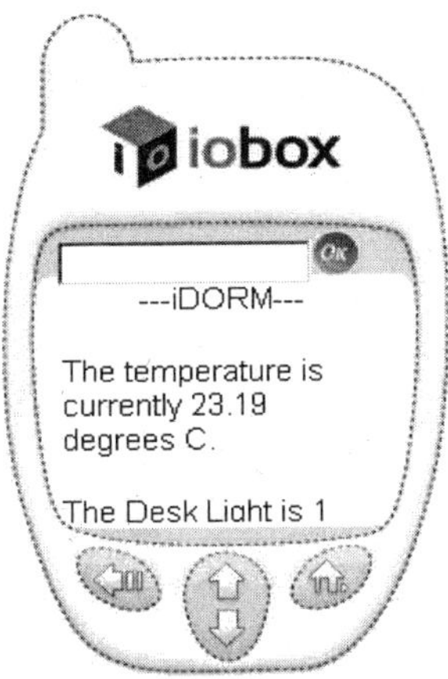

Figure 10. WAP Interface View.

2.6 Fuzzy Incremental Synchronous Learning (ISL) Technique

According to Kasabov (Kasabov 1998) an Intelligent Agent System (IAS) should be able to learn quickly from large amounts of data. He also sates that an intelligent system should also adapt in a real time and in an on-line mode as new data is encountered. Also the system should be able to accommodate in an incremental way any new problem solving rules, as they become known. It should be memory-based, plus possess data and exemplar storage and retrieval capacities. In addition, he says that an IAS should be able to learn and improve through active interaction with the user and the environment. It should have parameters to represent short and long term memory, age, forgetting, etc. Finally he states it should be able to analyse itself in terms of behaviour, error and success. To our knowledge, no system in the field of embedded agents operating in IIE had satisfied these criteria (Kasabov 1998).

Broadly speaking this work situates itself in the recent line of research that concentrates on the realisation of artificial agents strongly coupled with the physical world. A first fundamental requirement is that agents must be grounded in that they must be able to carry on their activities in the real world, in real time (Dorigo and Colombetti 1995). Another important point is that adaptive behaviour cannot be considered as a product of an agent considered in isolation from the world, but can only emerge from strong coupling of the agent and its environment (Dorigo and Colombetti 1995). Despite this, many embedded agents researchers regularly use simulations to test their models. However, the validity of such computer simulations to build autonomous embedded agents is often criticised and is the subject of much debate. Even so computer simulations may still be very helpful in the training and testing of agents models. However as Brooks (Brooks 1992) pointed out "it is very hard to simulate the actual dynamics of the real world". This may imply that effort will go into solving problems that simply do not come up in real world with a physical agent and that programs which work well on simulated agents will completely fail on real agents.

In this work we will refer to any learning carried out with user intervention and in isolation from the environment using simulation as *offline* learning. In our case learning will be done through interaction with the actual environment in a short time interval and we will call this *online* learning. Learning the agent controllers *online* enables the learnt controller to adjust to the real noise and imprecision associated with the sensors and actuators. By doing this we can develop rules that takes such defects into account, producing a realistic controller for embedded agents, grounded in the physical world that emerge from strong coupling of the agent and its environment not in simulation. These embedded agents are grounded in the real world (situated, embodied and operating in real time), as adaptive behaviours cannot be considered as a product of an agent in isolation from the world, but can only emerge from strong coupling of the agent and its environment.

2.6.1 The Hierarchical Fuzzy Control Architecture

The methodology of Fuzzy Logic Control (FLC) appears very useful when the processes are too complex for analysis by conventional quantitative techniques or when the available sources of information are interpreted qualitatively, imprecisely or uncertainly (Pedrycz and Gomide 1998), which is the case of embedded agents operating in IIE.

As most commercial Fuzzy Logic Control (FLC) implementations feature a single layer of inferencing between two or three inputs and one or two outputs. For embedded agents, however the number of inputs and outputs are usually large and the desired control behaviours are more complex. However, by using a *hierarchical* assembly of fuzzy controllers (HFLC), the number of rules required can be significantly reduced (Saffiotti 1997). We use a variant of the method suggested by Saffiotti (Saffiotti 1997) and Tunstel (Tunstel *et al.* 1997). In this we apply fuzzy logic to both implement the individual behaviour elements and the related arbitration (allowing both fixed and dynamic arbitration policies to be implemented) (Saffiotti 1997). To achieve this we implement each behaviour as an independent FLC aimed at a simple task. The use of this hierarchical fuzzy assembly has the following advantages.

- It uses the benefits of fuzzy logic to deal with imprecision and uncertainty.
- Using fuzzy logic for the co-ordination between the different behaviours which allows more than one behaviour to be active to differing degrees thereby avoiding the drawbacks of on-off switching schema (i.e. dealing with situations where several criteria need to be taken into account). In addition, using fuzzy co-ordination provides a smooth transition between behaviours with a consequent smooth output response.
- It offers a flexible structure where new behaviours can be added or modified easily. The system is capable of performing different tasks using identical behaviours by changing only the co-ordination parameters to satisfy a different high level objective without the need for re-planning.

In general we divide the behaviours available to the embedded agent operating in IIE and specifically in the iDorm into fixed or dynamic sets, where the dynamic behaviours are learnt to achieve the person's comfort and the fixed behaviours are pre-programmed. These latter behaviours need to be predefined because they cannot easily be learnt such as the temperature at which pipes freeze or what to do in the case of fire and so on. The fixed behaviours include a safety behaviour, an emergency behaviour and an economy behaviour. The *Safety behaviour* ensures that the environmental conditions in the room are always at a safe level. The *Emergency behaviour,* which in the case of a fire alarm or another emergency, might for instance open the emergency doors and switch off the main heating and illumination systems. In the case of an emergency this will be the only active behaviour. The *Economy behaviour* ensures that energy is not wasted so that if a room is unoccupied the heating and illumination will be switched to a sensible minimum value. All of the previous behaviours are fixed but settable. For dynamic behaviours we are going to use a monitoring system, which we call an ISL to record the user actions and learn to generate rules from this information to learn his *Comfort behaviour*. These will then be fine-tuned in an incremental and life long mode. The hierarchical fuzzy assembly is shown in Figure 11.

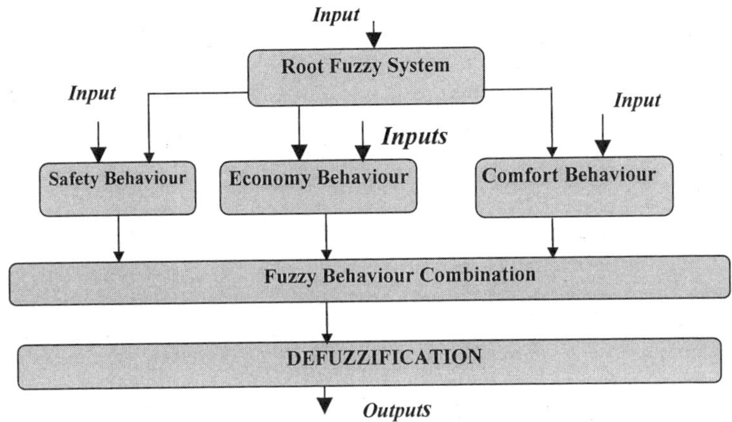

Figure 11. The Hierarchical Fuzzy Control System.

In our design each behaviour uses a FLC using singleton fuzzifier, triangular membership functions, product inference, max-product composition and height defuzzification. The selected techniques were chosen due to their computational simplicity and real-time considerations.

$$Y_t = \frac{\sum_{p=1}^{M} y_p \prod_{i=1}^{G} \alpha_{Aip}}{\sum_{p=1}^{M} \prod_{i=1}^{G} \alpha_{Aip}} \tag{1}$$

Where M is the total number of rules, y_p is the crisp output for each rule, $\Pi\alpha_{Aip}$ is the product of the membership functions for each rule's inputs and G is the number of inputs.
In case of using fuzzy numbers for preferences, product-sum combination and height defuzzification, the final output equation, provided by Saffiotti (Saffiotti 1997), is given below:

$$Y_{ht} = \frac{\sum_{i} (mm_y * y_i)}{\sum_{i} mm_y} \tag{2}$$

Where i represents the behaviours activated by context rules, which can be comfort, safety, emergency and economy. Y_t is the behaviour command output. mm_y is the behaviour weight which is calculated according to context rules which are suggested by the high level system and determine which behaviour is fired, and to what degree, for more information about the context rules please see (Hagras *et al.* 2000b)
The room has Eleven environmental parameters to be measured as follows:
- Time of the day (I1) measured by a clock connected to the 1-wire network represented by 4 triangular fuzzy sets (Night, Morning, Afternoon, and Evening). Note that we did not represent the time as binary sets as it very difficult to say for example that 4 am

belongs to the Night binary set and not to Morning binary sets, we think that 4 am belongs to both fuzzy sets but to different degrees. Also as the seasons change the differentiation between the sets changes, this is why we think it is more natural to set the time sets to be fuzzy sets to deal smoothly with season and timing changes and not having the abrupt changes that appears in the binary sets. Also note that the Afternoon fuzzy sets doesn't represent the time after 12 midday only but represents the midday period. The input Membership Function for the time input is shown in Figure 12

- Inside room light level (I2) measured by indoor light sensor connected to the Lonworks network represented by 3 triangular fuzzy sets (Dark Dim Bright)
- Outside outdoor light level (I3) measured by an external weather station connected to the 1-wire network represented by 3 triangular fuzzy sets (Dark Dim Bright). The input MF for both the inside and outside light levels is shown in Figure 13.
- Inside room temperature (I4) measured by redundant sensors connected to the Lonworks and the 1-Wire networks represented by 3 triangular fuzzy sets (Cold Temperate Warm)
- Outside outdoor room temperature (I5) measured by external weather station connected the 1- wire network represented by 3 triangular fuzzy sets (Cold Temperate Warm). The input MF for the inside and outside temperature is shown in Figure 14.
- Wither the user is using his audio entertainment (I6) on his computer by either he is listening to the radio or the CD player sensed by Visual C++ code when running the Winamp program represented by two binary states (Listening, Not Listening)
- Whether the user is lying or sitting on the bed or not (I7) measured by a pressure pad connected to the 1-wire network represented two binary states (On bed, Not on bed)
- Whether the user is sitting on the desk chair or not (I8) measured by a pressure pad connected to the 1- wire network represented by two binary states (On desk, not on desk)
- Whether the window is opened or closed (I9) measured by a reed switch connected to the Tini-1 Wire network represented two binary states (Open, Close)
- Whether the user is working or not (I10) sensed by a Visual C++ code that senses if the user is working on a Winword document represented two binary states (Working, Not Working)
- Whether the user is using his video entertainment (I11) on his computer by either he is watching a TV program via Wintv program or he is watching a DVD using the Winamp program, this is sensed using Visual C++ code represented two binary states (Watching, Not watching)

There are ten outputs to control;
- Fan Heater (O1) represented by ON-OFF Binary states
- Fan Cooler (O2) represented by ON-OFF Binary states.
- A dimmable spotlight above the Door (O3) represented by five triangular fuzzy sets (VLow, Low, Medium , High, VHigh).
- A dimmable spot light above the Wardrobe (O4) represented by five triangular fuzzy sets (VLow, Low, Medium, High, VHigh).
- A dimmable spot light above the Computer (O5) represented by five triangular fuzzy sets (VLow, Low, Medium, High, VHigh).
- A dimmable spot light above the Bed (O6) represented by five triangular fuzzy sets (VLow, Low, Medium, High, VHigh).
- a Desk Lamp (O7) represented by ON-OFF Binary states
- a Bedside Lamp (O8) represented by ON-OFF Binary states;
- Wither the automatic blinds are opened or closed (O9) represented by two Binary states (Open, Closed)

- If the automatic blinds are closed their opening can be controlled (O10) represented by 5 triangular fuzzy sets, where the fuzzy sets VLow, Low, deal with blind opening to the left and VHigh, High deal with blind opening to the right and Medium is 50 % opening. The output MF for the dimmable lights and the blind opening is shown in Figure 15.

This forms a rule base of 4*3*3*3*3*2*2*2*2*2*2 = 20736 possible rules. Which is a massive number of rules requiring large storage space and delaying the fuzzy system as each operation the system is required to perform the calculation over all these rules. We will show how the ISL will optimise this rule-base, reducing them to only those the user needs whilst allowing the ISL to add, delete and modify rules.

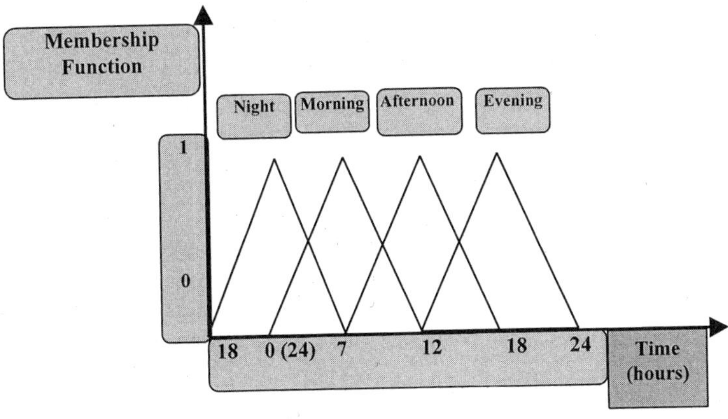

Figure 12. The input membership function of the time input

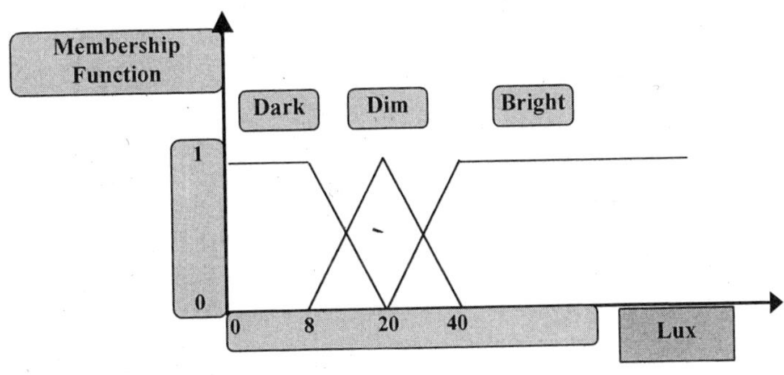

Figure 13. The input membership function of the inside and the outside light levels.

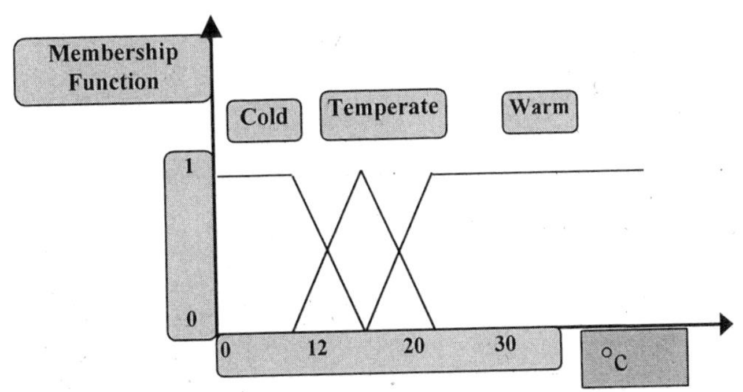

Figure 14. The input membership function of the inside and the outside temperatures.

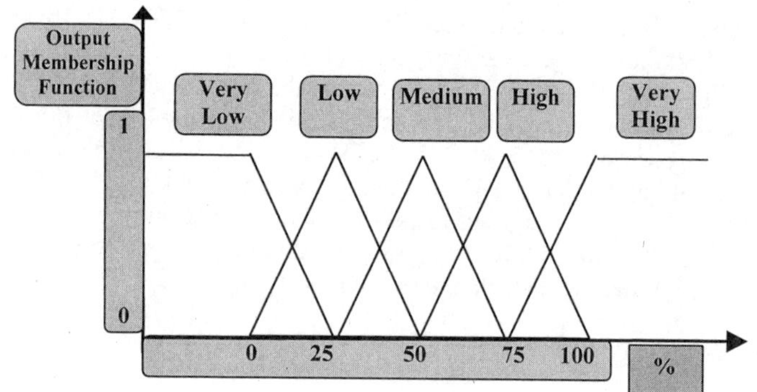

Figure 15. The output membership function of the dimmable spot lights and the blind opening.

2.6.2 The Incremental Synchronous Learning Description

The Incremental Synchronous Learning (ISL) architecture is shown in Figure 16. The embedded-agent needs to cater for somewhat different learning needs, on the one hand, short "initialisation" and on the other long "life-long" learning. In general a learning mechanism within an IIE would be life-long and non-intrusive. The ISL forms the learning engine within the control architecture and is the subject of British patent 99-10539.7. The agent is an augmented behaviour based architecture, which uses a set of parallel Fuzzy Logic Controllers (FLC), each forming a behaviour. The behaviours can be fixed or dynamic as explained above.

Each dynamic FLC (the comfort behaviour in the iDorm case) has one parameter that can be modified which is the *Rule Base* (RB) for each behaviour. Also, at the high level the co-ordination parameters can be learnt (Hagras *et al.* 2000a). The ISL system aims to provide life-long learning and adapts by adding modifying or deleting rules. It is also memory based in that it has a memory enabling the system to use its previous experiences (held as rules) to narrow down the search space and speed up learning.

The ISL works as follows:- when a new user enters the room he is identified by the active key button shown in Figure 3 and the ISL enters a Monitoring initialisation mode where it learns the users preferences during a non intrusive cycle. In the Experimental set-up we used a period of 30 minutes but in reality this is linked to how quickly and how complete we want the initial rule base. For example in a care house we want this rule base to be as complete as possible with some fine tuning, in a hotel we want this initialisation period to be small to allow fast learning. The rules and preferences learnt during the Monitoring mode form the basis of the user rules which are retrieved whenever the user renters the room. During this time the system monitors the inputs and users action and tries to infer rules from the user monitored actions. The user will usually act when given an input vector the output vector is unsatisfactory to him. Learning is based on negative reinforcement, as the user will usually request a change to the environment when he is dissatisfied with it.

After the Monitoring initialisation period the ISL enters a Control mode in which it uses the rules learnt during the Monitoring mode to guide its control of the rooms effectors. Whenever a user behaviour changes, so he needs to modify, add or delete any of the rules in the rule base the ISL goes back to the non intrusive cycle and tries to infer the rule base change to determine the users preferences in relations to the specific components of the rule that has failed. This is a very short cycle that the user is essentially unaware of and is distributed through the life-time of the use of environment, thus forming a life-long learning phase.

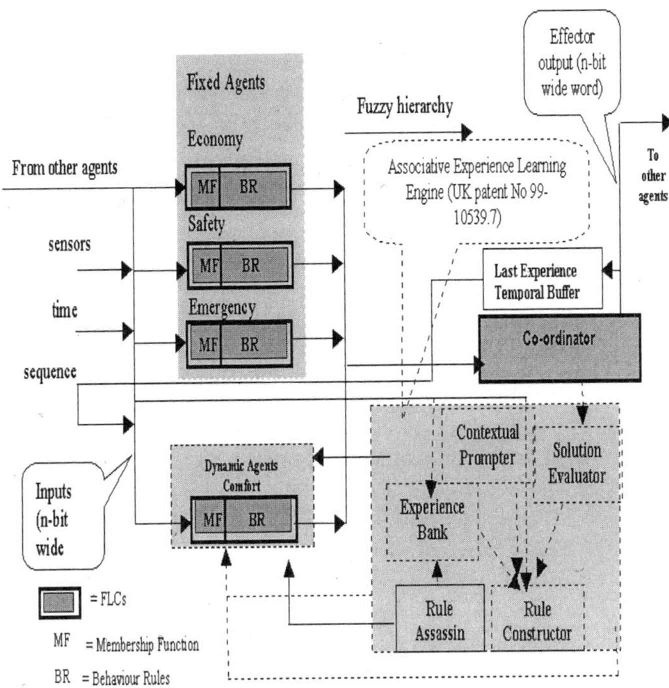

Figure 16. The ISL Embedded-Agent Architecture

As in the case of classifier systems, in order to preserve the system performance the learning mechanism is allowed to replace a subset of the classifiers (the rules in this case). The worst m classifiers are replaced by the m new classifiers (Bonarini 1999). In our case we will change all the consequences of the rules whose consequences were unsatisfactory to the user. We find these rules by finding all the rules firing at this situation where $\Pi\alpha Ai > 0$. We replace these rules consequents by the fuzzy set that has the highest membership of the output membership function. We have done this replacement to achieve the non-intrusive learning and to avoid direct interaction with the user. The learnt consequent fuzzy rule set is guided by the *Contextual prompter* which uses the sensory input to guide the learning.

The crisp output Y_t can be written as in (1). If the agent has N output variables, then we have Y_{tN}. The normalised contribution of each rule p output (Y_{pN}) to the total output Y_{tN} can be denoted by S_{rN} and is given by:

$$S_{rN} = \frac{\dfrac{Y_{pN} \prod\limits_{i=1}^{G} \alpha_{Aip}}{\sum\limits_{p=1}^{M} \prod\limits_{i=1}^{G} \alpha_{Aip}}}{Y_{t1}} \tag{3}$$

During the non-intrusive monitoring and life-long learning phases the agent is introduced to different situations, such as having different temperature and lighting levels inside and outside the room with the agent guided by the occupants desires as it attempts to discover the rules needed in each situation. The learning system consists of learning different episodes; in each situation only small number of rules will be fired. The model to be learnt is small and so is the search space. The accent on local models implies the possibility of learning by focusing at each step on a small part of the search space only, thus reducing interaction among partial solutions. The interaction among local models, due to the intersection of neighbouring fuzzy sets means local learning reflects on global performance (Bonarini 1999). So we can have global results coming from the combination of local models, and smooth transition between close models. By doing this we don't need to learn the whole 20736 rules at once but we learn only the rules needed by the user during the different episodes. It is necessary to point to a significant difference in our method of classifying or managing rules, rather than seeking to extract generalised rules we are trying to define particularised rules.

After the initial initialisation monitoring phase the system then tries to match the user derived rules to similar rules stored in the *Experience Bank* that were learnt from other occupiers. The system will choose the rule base that is most similar to the user-monitored actions. The system by doing this is trying to predict the rules that were not fired in the initialisation session thus minimising the learning time as the search is starting from the closest rule base rather than starting from random. Also this action will be satisfactory for the user as the system starts from a similar rule-base then fine-tuning the rules.

After this the agent will be operating with the rules learnt during the monitoring session plus rules that are dealing with uncovered situations during the monitoring process which are ported from the rule base of the most similar user, all these rules are constructed by the *Rule Constructor*. The system then operates with this rule-base until the occupant's behaviour indicates that his needs have altered which is flagged by the *Solution Evaluator* (i.e. the agent is event-driven). The system can then add, modify or delete rules to satisfy the occupant by re-entering briefly to the Monitoring mode. In this case again the system finds the firing rules and changes their consequence to the desired actions by the users. We also employ a mechanism - *learning inertia* - that only admits rules to the rule base when their use has exceeded some minimal frequency (we have used 3). One of our axioms is that "the user is king" by which we mean that an agent always executes the users instruction. In the case where commands are inconsistent with learned experience learning inertia acts as a filter that only allows the rule-base to be altered when the new command is demonstrated by its frequent use to be a consistent intention. It is in this way that the system implements a life long learning strategy. It is worth noting that the system can be monitoring for lengthy periods to learn the rules necessary for a care house. Also the system can start an accelerated (intrusive) monitoring period to learn the user behaviour fast (e.g. in a hotel room) and then switch to life long learning (non-intrusive) mode.

It is worth noting that as we are dealing with embedded agents with limited computational and memory capabilities it is very difficult to deal with a large number of possible rules in the rule base (e.g. in case of the iDorm, 20736) as this will lead to large memory and processor requirements which are not realistic in embedded agents. Therefore we set a limit on the number of stored rules to 450 (in our case, the maximum number the agent can store on the onboard memory without exceeding the memory limit or degrading the real-time performance). Each rule will have a measure of importance according to how frequently this rule is used. In calculating this *degree of importance* we also include a measure of most-recent-use. The overall *degree of importance* is the product of frequency-of-use- and period-since-last use. When the memory limit is reached the *Rule Assassin* retains rules according to the priority highest-frequency, followed by most-recently-used. If two rules share the same degree of relative rule frequency recall tie breaking is resolved by a least-recently-used rule. Although not included in the current implementation, we plan not to loose the rules that are chosen for replacement but rather store them in an external hard disk representing the *Experience Bank* so they can be recalled when needed. This action causes the onboard memory to only store the most efficient and the frequently used rules and not delaying or degrading the real time performance of the embedded agent.

Multi-Agent coordination is supported by making compressed information available to the wider network. The compressed data takes the form of a status word describing which behaviours are active (and to what degree). As with any data, the processing agent decides for itself which information is relevant to any particular decision. Thus, multi-agent processing is implicit to this paradigm. In addition, a collection of agents can be regarded as a higher-level agent, and in turn equivalent to a single sophisticated sensor. It can readily be seen that there is both a stigmatic and recursive view involved in this mechanism giving this system a simple, elegant but scaleable independent mechanism of coordination. The leads to its name RSC (Recursive Stigmatic Coordination) Paradigm (Callaghan *et al.* 2001). We have found that receiving high level processed information from remote agents, such as "the room is occupied" is more useful than being given the low level sensor information from the remote agent that gave rise to the high-level characterisation. This is because the compressed form both relieves agent-processing overheads and reduces network loading (Colley 2001).

2.7 Performance of Embedded Agents

From what was said earlier, embedded agents have comparably little computing resources. For example, the embedded agent we use in Essex shown in Figure 17 is based on 68000 Motorola processor with 4 Mbyte of RAM and an Ethernet network connection. It runs the VxWorks Real Time Operating System (RTOS). Clearly such agents have performance limitations in that they have limited I/O (24 lines in our case) and can only support a certain number of concurrent processes within real-time computational limits (16 medium size processes, each of less than 100 lines of code, with process pre-emption times of less a maximum of 2ms, in our case). That being said typical behaviours need only a handful of lines, 20 lines of core control code being large). As our processor is relatively modest in complexity, and quite capable of being fabricated using readily available microelectronics. The specification quoted above can readily be seen to be more than adequate for most ubiquitous devices such as security systems or, lighting controllers and so forth thus it is possible to state that useable agents can be realised from available technology. In addition, as larger systems (GadgetWorlds etc) are comprised of multiple eGadget systems (most with integrated agents) then the system scales without incurring computational constraints. As explained in the processing section, the RSC inter-agent coordination system being utilised simply treats other agents as sophisticated sensors, with coordination being achieved by observation of other agent's status rather than any sophisticated interacting involving computationally intensive messaging. The stigmatic status messages transmitted by agents are infrequent (e.g. 1 per minute) and small (e.g. a few bytes). As a large GadgetWorld would be no more than 100 eGadgets it can readily be seen that inter-agent coordination scale upwards to this level with negligible overheads leaving the basic limitation as being the relationship between the basic single agent and the control system it is embodied in.

2.8 Experimental Results

We have conducted a number of experiments with various different users staying in the iDorm for different lengths of time. We have performed some experiments with a limited number of inputs (the inside light level (I1) and outside light level (I2) and the inside temperature (I3) and the outside temperature (I4) and wither the user in on the bed or the desk (I5). The control outputs are as follows, O1 which is a row of dimmable spotlights above the desk and O2 is a row of dimmable spotlights above the bed, O3 is the Bedside Lamp, O4 is the desk Lamp, O5 is the blind opening and O6 is the fan heater and O7 is the Fan cooler

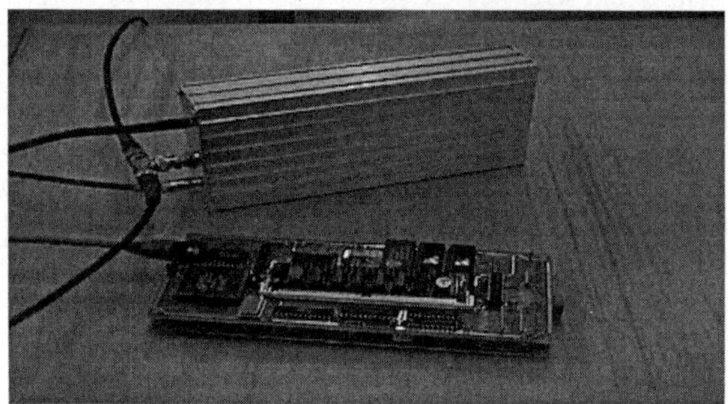

Figure 17. The Essex embedded agent.

Table 2 shows the learnt rule-base for "User-1" pictured in Figure 18 who occupied the room for more than two hours. In these experiments the user undertook many behaviours such as studying during the day (in which the lighting was bright) and studying in the evening (i.e. when external light was fading). This specific user preferred to use all the ceiling lights ON and the blind open to Norm. Another behaviour was lying in bed reading with the blind adjusted to his convenience and the bedside light sometimes being used. He would also close the blinds in the evening using combinations of the ceiling lamps and desk lamp. The experimental data also contains "going to sleep behaviours" including reading before sleeping and getting up spontaneously at night to work (they are students!).

Table 2. The learnt Rule Base for "User-1"

I1	I2	I3	I4	O1	O2	O3	O4	O5	O6	O7
XX	Med	Bright	Desk	Vhigh	Vhigh	OFF	OFF	Med	OFF	OFF
XX	High	Bright	Desk	Vhigh	Vhigh	OFF	OFF	Med	OFF	OFF
High	Low	Dim	Desk	Vhigh	Vhigh	OFF	OFF	Med	OFF	OFF
Med	Med	Bright	Bed	Vhigh	Vlow	ON	OFF	Vlow	OFF	OFF
Med	High	Bright	Bed	Vhigh	Vlow	ON	OFF	Vlow	OFF	OFF
High	Med	Bright	Bed	Vhigh	Vlow	ON	OFF	Vlow	OFF	OFF
High	High	Bright	Bed	Vhigh	Vlow	ON	OFF	Vlow	OFF	OFF
Med	Med	Dark	Desk	Med	Med	ON	ON	Med	OFF	OFF
Med	High	Dark	Desk	Med	Med	ON	ON	Med	OFF	OFF
High	Med	Dark	Desk	Vhigh	Vhigh	ON	OFF	Vhigh	ON	OFF
High	High	Dark	Desk	Vhigh	Vhigh	ON	OFF	Vhigh	ON	OFF
Low	Med	Dark	Bed	Vlow	Vlow	OFF	OFF	VLow	OFF	OFF
Low	High	Dark	Bed	Vlow	Vlow	OFF	OFF	VLow	OFF	OFF
Low	High	Dark	Desk	Med	Med	ON	ON	Med	OFF	OFF
Low	High	Dark	Desk	Med	Med	ON	ON	Med	OFF	OFF

The ISL learnt 15 rules of which the first 7 rules were learnt during the Initialisation phase. The next 4 rules were ported from similar users and were satisfactory to the user. The last 4 rules resulted from fine-tuning the ported rules, these rules dealt with darkness where the first two rules dealt with the user wanting to sleep and he wanted all lights off while the similar user slept with the desk lamp ON because he doesn't like darkness. The last two rules dealt with user returning to the desk to read as he couldn't sleep he switches all lights to Medium and switch ON the desk and the bedside lamp and the blind to Medium to allow more light, the similar user had the same behaviour but he was closing the blind. It is obvious that the room user and the similar user actions are very similar and we needed only a fine-tuning to satisfy the current user needs, this is an advantage of using the *Experience Bank* which reduces the life long learning time and satisfies the user. The XX in Table 2 indicate a No-Care situation, which resulted as the inside room lighting level was not important as when it was bright the user took always the same actions. This shows also that ISL besides optimising the rule base can help to identify and focus the input parameters required by the user and hence giving more optimisation to the system.

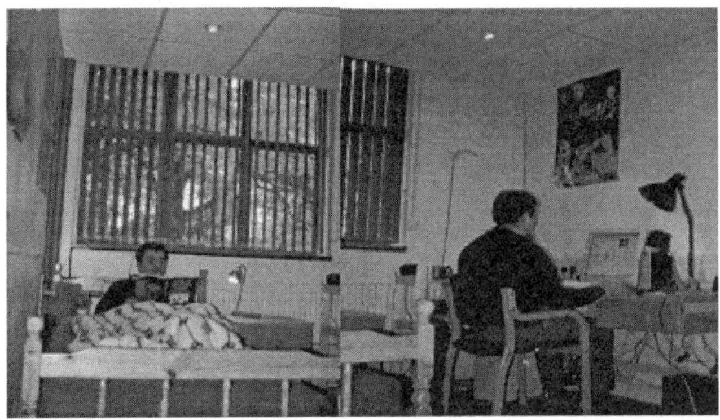

Figure 18. "User 1 in the iDorm".

We also conducted a set of interesting experiments with the whole set of sensors and actuators discussed in Section 2.6.1 in which another room user (user 2) had occupied the room continuously for a period of 51 hours over two nights while the room was controlled by our embedded agent implementing the ISL techniques. Since the room was originally designed as a multi-purpose space, it was possible to use it both as a dormitory and a workplace. The room was treated as a standard living space in which there were no artificial constraints such as periods of occupancy or behaviour. The Agent was connected to the iDorm server and the user was given access to the VRML GUI to adjust the environment as they saw fit.

The user was identified by his intelligent key, which activates the active lock explained in Section 2.5. Figure 19 shows the user using his intelligent key to access the room.

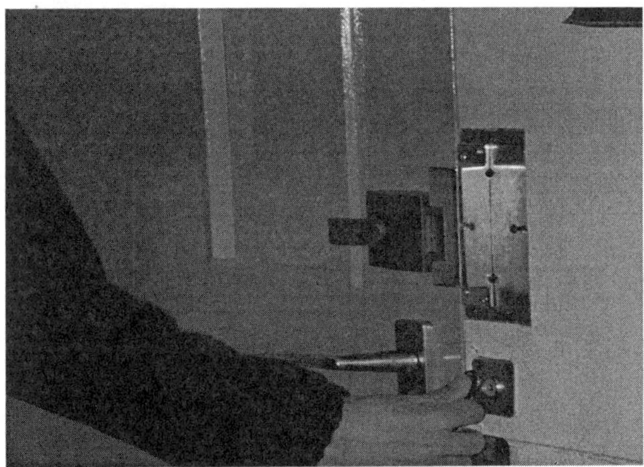

Figure 19. User (2) accesses the room via his intelligent key.

Throughout the experimentation period, the user adjusted the environment using the VRML GUI whenever they were not happy with the current state of the environment and made a note of the decisions they were making in a journal. Whenever this action occurred, the Agent received the request, generated a new rule or adjusted a previously learnt rule and allowed the action through (see Figure 20). The agent would react to similar environmental states by taking the learnt user action.

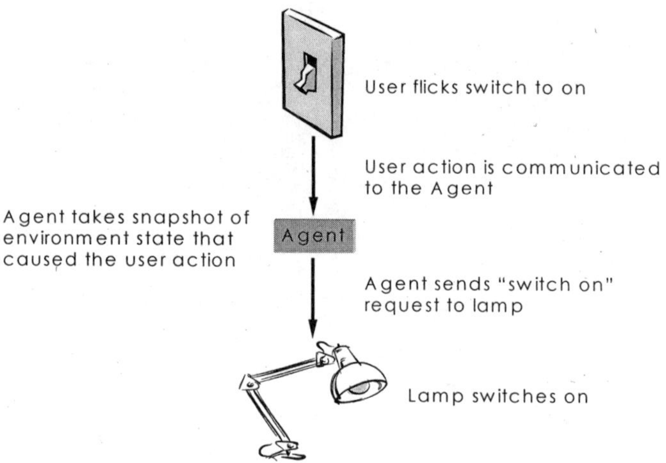

Figure 20. The Agent Communication Path

At the end of the experiment, the results returned by the agent would be a set of fuzzy rules about the user's behaviour over the previous 51 hours and a list of journal entries provided by the user.

A small parsing tool was written to convert the text file containing the fuzzy rule set into a human readable format. At the end of the experiment, the rules were converted into this form and examined in two different ways. The first involved comparing the human readable rules to the journal entries from the user to ensure that the Agent had successfully learnt the behaviours the user was exhibiting. The second was to compare the number of rules learnt over time. The Agent's success can be measured by monitoring how well it matches the environment to the user's demands. If it does well, the user will have to generate fewer rules over time. If it does badly, the user will have to generate more rules over time.

At the end of the 51-hour period, the Agent had learnt 324 rules. Table 3 gives the first ten rules learnt by the Agent and Table 4 gives the first and the eighth rules translated by the parsing software tool. In Table 3 for I1 "0" represents the Night fuzzy set while "1" represents the Morning fuzzy set and "2" represents the Afternoon fuzzy set and "3" represents the evening fuzzy set. For the inside and the outside light levels (I2, I3) "0" represents Dark fuzzy set, "1" represents the Dim fuzzy set and "2" represents the Bright fuzzy sets. For the inside and outside temperatures (I4, I5) "0" represents the Cold fuzzy set and "1" represents the temperate fuzzy sets and "2" represent the Warm fuzzy set. For O3, O4, O5, O6, O10, "0" represents the Very Low fuzzy set, "1" represents the Low fuzzy set, "2" represents the Medium fuzzy set, "3" represents the High fuzzy set and "4" represents the Very High fuzzy set. All the other inputs and outputs are represented by binary sets in which "0" is False and "1" is ON. For the blind "0" is open and "1" is closed.

Figure 21 shows the ISL activating rule 1 in Table 3 in which it is afternoon time and the user is sitting on his chair to read. Figure 22 shows the ISL output during night time when the user is sleeping in which he prefers the bed side lamp to be ON and the blinds to be closed.

Table 3. First 10 Rules Learnt by Agent

I1	I2	I3	I4	I5	I6	I7	I8	I9	I10	I11	O1	O2	O3	O4	O5	O6	O7	O8	O9	O10
2	2	2	1	1	0	0	1	1	0	0	0	0	0	0	4	0	0	0	0	0
2	2	2	1	2	0	0	1	1	0	0	0	1	0	0	4	0	0	0	0	0
2	2	2	2	1	0	0	1	1	0	0	0	0	0	0	4	0	0	0	0	0
2	2	2	2	2	0	0	1	1	0	0	0	1	0	0	4	0	0	0	0	0
3	2	2	1	1	0	0	1	1	0	0	0	1	0	0	4	0	0	0	0	0
3	2	2	1	2	0	0	1	1	0	0	0	1	0	0	4	0	0	0	0	0
3	2	2	2	1	0	0	1	1	0	0	0	1	0	0	4	0	0	0	0	0
3	2	2	2	2	0	0	1	1	0	0	0	1	0	0	4	0	0	0	0	0
2	2	2	1	1	0	0	0	1	0	0	0	0	0	0	0	0	0	0	0	0
2	2	2	1	2	0	0	0	1	0	0	0	0	0	0	0	0	0	0	1	0

Table 4. The Parsed First and Eighth Rules Learnt by Agent

In the afternoon when it is bright inside and bright outside, temperate inside and temperate outside, sitting on the chair, with the window open I switch the heater off, switch the cooler off, switch the door spotlight Very Low, switch the wardrobe spotlight Very Low, switch the computer spotlight Very High, switch the bed spotlight Very High, turn off the bed lamp turn off the table lamp and open the blind.
In the evening when it is bright inside and bright outside, warm inside and warm outside, sitting on the chair, with the window open I switch the heater off, switch the cooler on, switch the door spotlight Very low, switch the wardrobe spotlight Very Low, switch the computer spotlight Very High, switch the bed spotlight Very Low, turn off the bed lamp turn off the table lamp and open the blind.

Figure 21. User (2) is sitting at the desk in the afternoon in the iDorm, which is controlled by the ISL.

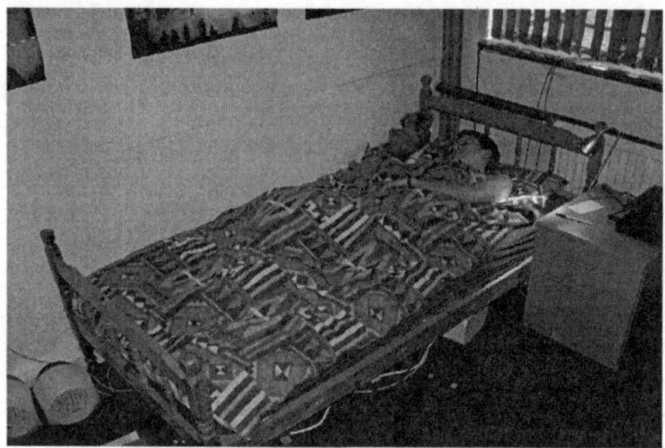

Figure 22. User (2) is sleeping in the bed in the iDorm, which is controlled by the ISL.

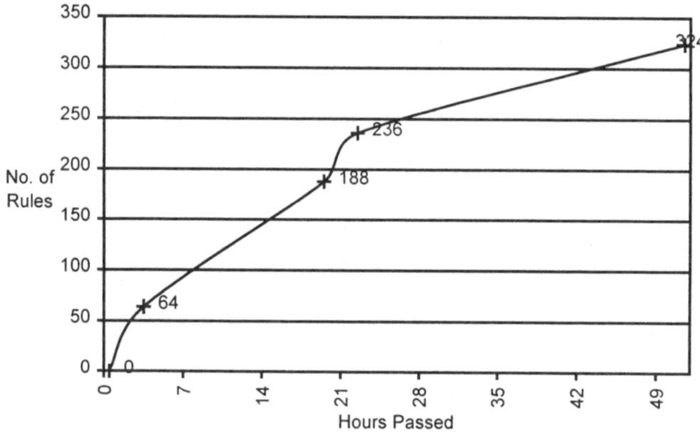

Figure 23. Rules Learnt by Agent Over Time

The agent had learnt the 324 rules needed to capture the behaviour of this user over the 51-hour experiment, which demonstrated that our system can learn effectively using the ISL and it doesn't need to learn the whole 20736 to act optimally. Figure 23 shows the number of rules learnt over the duration of the experiment. Figure 23 suggests that the Agent had to learn less new rules about the user as the experiment progressed; the latter was one of our criteria for measuring the Agent's success. Using the evidence of the continual reduction in the learning rate, we can conclude that the Agent managed to pick out the pertinent behaviour of the user over time. We can also conclude from matching the journal entries to the learning rate that the agent adapts the size of its rule set to the frequency of user behaviour. That is to say, 21 hours into the experiment there is a significant rise in the learning rate. This can be matched to mid-morning where the user leaves the iDorm for a coffee break and changes the state of a number of devices before leaving the room. If the agent didn't remember this behaviour then at the same time the following day (45 hours into the experiment), there would be a similar sharp rise where the user repeated the same behaviour. However, it can be seen from the graph that the Agent's learning rate is unaffected at this time suggesting that the user was content with the Agent's behaviour.

These experiments had offered surprising results in terms of the little information the agent had to gather in order to autonomously create a comfortable environment with diminishing need for user correction. Based on these results, it is feasible for the research team to give the Agent access to more of the input vector – increasing the complexity of the behaviour it can monitor. These learning techniques are very important for embedded agents operation in IIE populated by a large number of eGadgets.

2.9 Conclusions

In this chapter we have presented our Incremental Synchronous Learning (ISL) mechanism for online learning and adaptation of embedded-agents embodied in intelligent inhabited environments populated with eGadgets (which we have developed as an exemplary ubiquitous computing model). This work is part of the EU Disappearing Computer programmes eGadgets project. The main goal of this project is to support user-driven design of ad-hoc assemblies of a computer based artefacts that will make up many envisaged ubiquitous computing environments. Embedding useful amounts of intelligence into eGadgets environments was seen as an essential enabling technology to achieve the vision of the eGadgets project. In particular, it solves the problem of how would an eGadget (or other ubiquitous computing device) adapt its control to whatever ad-hoc set of connections a user decided to provide a particular device with.

We have also discussed how transferring some cognitive capabilities from people into artefacts is a natural way to facilitate the disappearance of computers as computers are increasingly embedded into our daily environment. We have also argued that embedded-intelligence can bring significant cost and effort savings over the evolving lifetime of product by avoiding expensive programming (and re-programming). In particular, if people are to use collections of computer based artefacts to build systems to suit their own personal tastes (which may be unique in some sense) then self programming embedded-agents offer one way of allowing this without incurring an undue skill or time overhead.

Our techniques were evaluated in the Essex iDorm which is an intelligent dormitory that makes an excellent evaluation platform for ubiquitous computing and ambient intelligence work as it provides a compact multi-use space with occupant that are sympathetic to exploring new technology. We had carried unique experiments in which the iDorm has been occupied by various people and up to two day of continuous occupancy. Our fuzzy logic based ISL had demonstrated the capability of the method to provide online learning in both set-up and life long learning cycles. We have demonstrated a novel feature of this agent in that it particularises itself to the users behaviour (including idiosyncratic actions) rather than to the machine or by generalising for a group of users.

For our current and future work we have plans to conduct more and longer experiments with the iDorm (up to a year to get a full climatic cycle), significantly expand the sensor-effector set and explore more fine-grained and course grained distributed embedded-agents (e.g. with agents in eGadgets, communities of eGadgets forming GadgetWorlds and even inter-communicating rooms). We are also investigating the integration of mobile agents such as robots (Colley *et al.* 2001) and wearable agents (e.g. cellphones, watches etc).

Acknowledgements

We are pleased to acknowledge the funding support from the EU IST Disappearing Computer program (eGadgets) and the Korean-UK Scientific Fund programme (cAgents). We are also pleased to acknowledge our eGadget partners Kieran Delaney (NMRC), Achilles Kameas, Irene Mavrommati and Manolis Koutlis (CTI) and our cAgents partners from KAIST Professor Zenn Bien and Mr. Kim and Mr. Lee and Mr. Myung whose numerous and challenging scientific discussions have contributed to our thinking in this area.

References

Angelov, P., Buswell, R., Hanby,V. (2000), " Automatic Generation of Fuzzy Rule-based Models from Data by Genetic Algorithms, *Proceedings of International Conference on Recent Advances on Soft Computing, Leicester, UK.*

Bonarini, A. (1999), "Comparing Reinforcement Learning Algorithms Applied to Crisp and Fuzzy Learning Classifier systems", *Proceedings of the Genetic and Evolutionary Computation Conference*, pp. 52-60.

Brooks, R. (1992), "Artificial Life and Real Robots", MIT press.

Brooks, R. (1997), "Intelligent Room Project", *Proceedings of the 2nd International Cognitive Technology Conference (CT'97)*, Japan.

Callaghan, V., Clarke, G., Pounds-Cornish, A. (2000a) "Buildings As Intelligent Autonomous Systems: A Model for Integrating Personal and Building Agents", *The 6th International Conference on Intelligent Autonomous Systems (IAS-6), Venice, Italy.*

Callaghan, V., Clarke, G., Colley, M., Hagras, H. (2000b), " Embedding Intelligence: Research Issues for Ubiquitous Computing", *Proceedings of the Ubiquitous Computing in Domestic Environments Conference, Nottingham-UK.*

Callaghan, V., Clarke, G., Colley, M., Hagras, H. (2001), "A Soft-Computing based DAI Architecture for Intelligent Buildings" *Studies in Fuzziness and Soft Computing on Soft Computing Agents, Physica-Verlag-Springer.*

Colley, M., Clarke, G., Hagras, H., Callaghan V. (2001), "Intelligent Inhabited Environments: Co-operative Robotics & Buildings", *32nd International Symposium on Robotics (ISR 2001), Seoul, Korea.*

Davisson, P. (1998), "Energy Saving and Value Added Services; Controlling Intelligent-Buildings Using a Multi-Agent System Approach" *in DA/DSM Europe DistribuTECH, PennWell.*

Dorigo M., Colombetti, M. (1995), "Robot Shaping: Developing Autonomous agents through learning", *Artificial Intelligence Journal*, Vol (71), pp. 321-370.

Hagras, H., Callaghan, V., Colley, M. (2000a),"Learning Fuzzy Behaviour Co-ordination for Autonomous Multi-Agents Online using Genetic Algorithms & Real-Time Interaction with the Environment " *Proceedings of the 2000 IEEE International Conference on Fuzzy Systems, San Antonio-USA*, pp. 853-859.

Hagras, H., Callaghan, V., Colley, M., Clarke, G. (2000b) "A Hierarchical Fuzzy Genetic Agent Architecture for Intelligent Buildings Sensing and Control", *Proceedings of the International Conference on Recent Advances in Soft Computing, Leicester, UK.*

Holmes, H. Duman, A. Pounds-Cornish, A. (2002), "The iDorm: Gateway to Heterogeneous Networking Environments", *International ITEA Workshop on Virtual Home Environment, Paderborn, Germany.*

Kasabov, N. (1998), "Introduction: Hybrid intelligent adaptive systems", *International Journal of Intelligent Systems,* Vol.6, pp.453-454.

Kasabov, N., Kozma, R., Kilgour, R., Laws, M., Taylor, J., Watts, M. (1999), "A. Hybrid connectionist-based methods and systems for speech data analysis and phoneme-based speech recognition". In: *Neuro-Fuzzy Techniques for Intelligent Information Processing*, N. Kasabov and R.Kozma, Eds. Heidelberg, Physica Verlag.

Minar, N., Gray, M., Roup, O., Krikorian, R., Maes, P. (1999), "HIVE: Distributed Agents for Networking Things". MIT Media Lab, *Appeared in ASA/MA*.

Mozer, M. (1998), "The Neural Network House: An Environment That Adapts To Its Inhabitants", *Proceedings of American Association for Artificial Intelligence Spring Symposium on Intelligent Environments, AAAI Press,* pp. 110-114.

Pedrycz, W., Gomide, F. (1998), " An Introduction to Fuzzy Sets: Analysis and Design", MIT press, Cambridge.

Pounds-Cornish, A., Holmes, A. (2002), "The iDorm - a Practical Deployment of Grid Technology" *Proceedings of 2nd IEEE International Symposium on Cluster Computing and the Grid* (CCGrid2002), Berlin, Germany.

Saffiotti, A. (1997), " Fuzzy Logic in Autonomous Robotics: Behaviour Co-ordination" Proceedings of the 6th IEEE International Conference on Fuzzy Systems, Spain , pp. 573-578.

Sharples, S., Callaghan, V., Clarke, G. (1999), "A Multi-Agent Architecture For Intelligent Building Sensing and Control", International Sensor Review Journal, Vol. 19. No. 2.

Tunstel, E., Lippincott, T., Jamshidi, M. (1997), "Behaviour Hierarchy for Autonomous Mobile Robots: Fuzzy Behaviour Modulation and Evolution", *International Journal of Intelligent Automation and soft computing, Vol .3, pp. 37-49.*

Chapter 3

Component Based Distributed Multi-Agent Architecture for Soft Computing

Rajiv Khosla[1]

3.1 Introduction

Intelligent agents today are being applied in distributed environments on the Internet, process control, engineering and others. Further, a new area, namely, soft computing agents has emerged recently. It represents merger of techniques from soft computing area with those in distributed artificial intelligence. In this paper we outline a multi-layered multi-agent soft computing architecture for designing agents at clerical, tool and task levels respectively. The clerical support is provided in terms of fetching and depositing data across different machines in a distributed environment.

Tool support is provided in terms of applying various soft and hard computing technologies like fuzzy logic, neural networks, genetic algorithms, knowledge based systems and their hybrid configurations for designing and developing optimum models of various real world problems. Finally, task level support is provided in terms of modelling user's tasks and problem solving models. The multi-layered architecture is motivated by the human-centred approach and consistent problem solving structures/strategies employed by practitioners while designing solutions to complex problems or situations The multi-layered multi-agent architecture has been applied to problems in image processing, data mining, process control, electronic commerce, diagnosis, forecasting, and sales recruitment.

The chapter is organized as follows. Section 3.2 outlines the characteristics of various software models which form the basis of the component based design of multi-agent soft computing architecture. Section 3.3 constructs the multi-layered multi-agent architecture. The layers represent various components of the soft computing architecture. Agent definition of agents in different layers is outlined. The layers also represent the clerical, tool and task levels of modeling soft computing systems. In this section the emerging characteristics as well as the semantic and pragmatic quality of the architecture are also outlined. Section 3.4 describes a novel application of the architecture of the tool level for fault diagnosis in electrical power systems. Section 3.5 concludes the chapter.

3.2 Software Models

An architecture is an information processing mechanism that can operate on the information represented in a form that is specific to the architecture (Chandrasekaran, 1990). In order to construct the computational level architecture we outline the characteristics of the object-oriented, agent and intelligent technology models in this section. These models help to define the information and its form, which will be used by

---

[1] This work has been supported by VPAC grant no. EPPNLA002/2001

the architecture to design and develop the computer-based artifacts. We also outline the complementary properties of these models from the perspective of integrating them in the next section.

3.2.1 Object-Oriented Model

The research and practice in artificial intelligence and software engineering has shown that the natural modeling strength of object-oriented models is structural abstraction of data and determining structural relationships (Brow, 1991; Coad et al., 1992; Dillon et al., 1993; Iivari, Rumbaugh et al. 1990).

Knowledge is generally organized into hierarchies with a twofold goal: to devise a conceptually clean model of the represented world, and to provide a compact storage organization which may also enable easier navigation through and search of knowledge. Various knowledge representation formalisms such as frames, semantic networks, and objects have been developed over decades of symbolic AI research. These three formalisms are based on hierarchical configurations of symbolic knowledge representation.

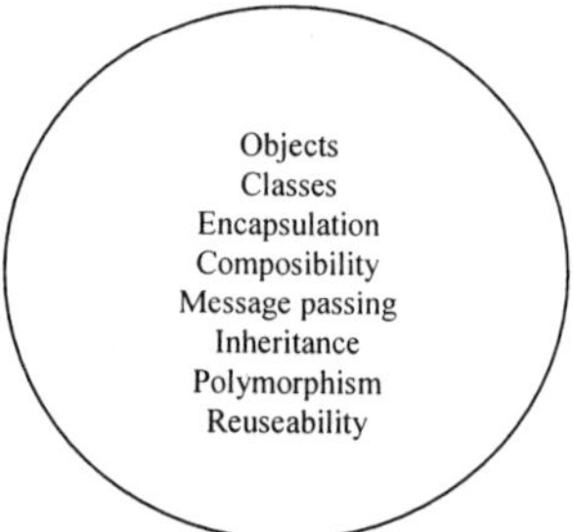

Figure 1. The Object-Oriented Model

An object-oriented model as seen in Figure 1 derives itself cognitively from human cognition related studies in symbolic knowledge representation and computationally from the research in object-oriented programming, object-oriented software engineering and databases. The characteristics of objects include inheritance, composability and other non-hierarchical relationships between concepts from a modeling viewpoint. From a software implementation viewpoint, an object-oriented method provides attractive features like strong encapsulation, polymorphism and reusability. A common set of characteristics which define the general object-oriented model are shown in Figure 1. These characteristics, are unique object identifier, data and operations, encapsulation, inheritance, composition, message passing, polymorphism and reusability.

3.2.2 Agent Model

As described by (Farhoodi et al., 1997a and b), agents have some remarkable features as distinct from objects. An agent has both temporary (active in workspace) and permanent knowledge (permanent means intrinsic in this context; it stays stable from one execution cycle to the next). It has a controller (representing its head), which can be given alternative behavioral characteristics (e.g. stimulus-response-like, actor-like, or blackboard-like). An agent performs tasks which have both declarative and procedural components. An agent's repertoire of tasks represents its capabilities. Each task can have its procedural "how to do" component represented as rules, knowledge sources (rule sets), or methods.

Figure 2. The Agent Model

Figure 2 shows some of the features of an agent model as distinct from an object-oriented model. An agent model promotes a societal view of computation. An agent possesses knowledge and methods and the ability to engage in complex communication with other agents, including human agents, in order to obtain information or request their help in accomplishing its goals and tasks.

3.2.3 Object-Oriented vs. Agent Models

The object-oriented model and the agent model share some common as well as some complementary characteristics. The aim of this section is to bring out these common and complementary characteristics to facilitate the integration of the two models and provide object-oriented support in a multi-process, distributed environment. Although each model interprets some characteristics differently, their similarities allow them to be merged together.

Both models provide a mechanism for communication using some form of message passing. However, each message employed by an agent is also defined in terms of mental activities. An agent may engage another (or itself) with messaging activities from a predefined class of messages protocol (Parks, 1998). The class of message protocol is mainly borrowed from the speech-act theory (Searle, 1969; Winograd et al. 1986) such as informing, requesting, offering, accepting, rejecting, competing, and assisting.

An important point to note here is that the agent model is primarily driven by task abstraction and task-oriented behavior. On the other hand, the object-oriented model is primarily driven by structuring objects in the real world and identifying relationships between them. In addition, an agent is dynamic by nature as against objects which are passive by nature. Further, an agent facilitates task-based communication and defines the nature of communication between different agents that can be intricate and complex (e.g. negotiation) depending upon the application domain. An agent may change its behavior dynamically during its lifetime whereas the behavior of an object is fixed during specification time.

Objects and agents can be organized in a class hierarchy and their properties can also be inherited by their subclasses. Objects in the object-oriented models are typically passive, becoming active only when requested to do so, whereas, agents are active in nature and can negotiate with others and work in a cooperative manner in order that goals can be fulfilled.

3.2.4 Operating System Process Model

Distributed control and parallelism are two activities that can be effectively simulated in a multi-process operating system environment. The term *process* in the operating system process model shown in Figure 3 denotes a program or component of a program which can be independently scheduled by an operating system in order to accomplish some tasks (Bourne, 1983). In a single process design, all of the processing capabilities of a program are encapsulated into a single package. A multi-process application distributes processing services across several processes and may use operating system communication facilities to pass results and data among the processes. Communication facilities allow processes to execute and communicate across process or machine boundaries.

In multi-process environments, the interaction among processes must be coordinated in order to prevent unsynchronized access and updates of data. One of the effective ways of coordinating interaction among processes in a multi-process environment is through inter-process communication. Pipes are an effective means of communication in a multi-process environment (Christian, 1988). A pipe is a communication channel which couples one process to another. A process can send data "down" the pipe by using the *Write* system call, and another process can receive the data by using the *Read* system call at the other end.

Figure 3. The Operating System Process Model

Thus, firstly, a multi-process architecture makes provision for concurrent and distributed processing of information. Secondly, the ability to simulate concurrent execution is conducive to the idea of competition for enhancing the computation reliability in a real time domain. Thirdly, inter-process communication provides an effective means for synchronous and asynchronous communication, cyclic and continuous operation in a real time and dynamic environment. Fourthly, distributed and parallel processing, synchronous and asynchronous communication facilitate hierarchical and autonomous control over inferencing done by various processes. The inter-process communication channels make provision for hierarchical control in terms of what type of data will be processed by the lower level process. The parallel and distributed processing feature contributes to the autonomous control each process has over its inferencing. These features also provide more flexibility for dealing with any temporal reasoning constraints associated with real time systems.

3.2.5 Operating System Process vs. Object-Oriented Models

An operating system process model like the object-oriented model encapsulates data and operations in the process paradigm. Objects in an object-oriented system generally reside in a class hierarchy, while processes are not organized in this manner. Rather, a process is an independent entity, which can initiate its own activity. Objects in the object-oriented model are typically passive, becoming active only when requested to do so (some classes may remain passive as they exist only for facilitating inheritance). Processes are inherently active and become passive only when necessary.

Communication ports provide the vehicle for message passing in the process model. Ports may be typed in order to affect the manner in which messages may be sent and delivered. In contrast, typing exists throughout the object-oriented model, both internally with respect to the vehicles manipulated by the operations, and externally with respect to the messages and class structures supported by the model.

The operating system process and object-oriented models differ in their overall architecture within a multi-processing environment. In the object-oriented model, all data and operations normally reside in a global object structure. The process model encapsulates only the operations and data used by a single process as no global structure which organizes a process exists.

3.2.6 Intelligent Technology Model

Intelligent technologies include expert systems, neural networks, fuzzy systems, and genetic algorithms. The intelligent technology model as shown in Figure 4 captures various characteristics of those intelligent technologies as well as their hybrid configurations.

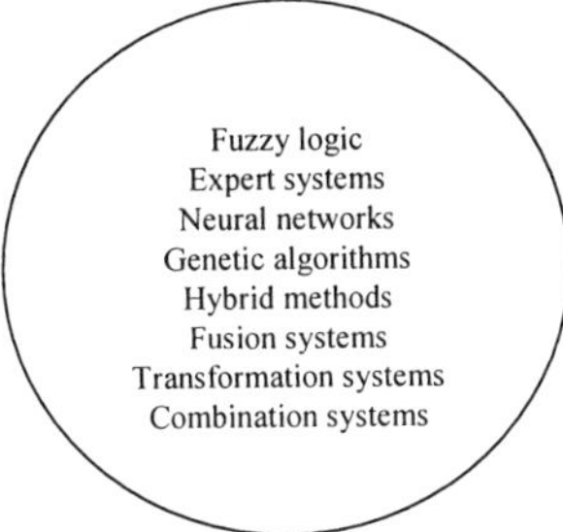

Figure 4. The Intelligent Technology Model

The representing formalisms employed by expert systems are grounded on four architectures (i.e. rule based, rule and frame (object) based, model based, and blackboard architectures). They include predicate calculus, production rules, semantic networks, frames and objects. Although these properties are very useful to help model real world problems and are widely used in various industrial applications, nevertheless they suffer from a number of limitations including combinatorial explosion of rules, inability to handle problems of a non-deterministic or fuzzy nature, and others. The inability to handle non-deterministic problems can be overcome by exploiting the features provided by neural networks. That is, neural networks are best for problems with random and non-deterministic characters. Although there are number of supervised and unsupervised neural network based learning algorithms, the most commonly used ones are backpropagation and self-organizing Kohonen maps. Radial basis function networks which incorporate both supervised and unsupervised characteristics are also used.

Fuzzy logic which, like neural networks involving approximate reasoning, is very capable of handling fuzzy problems. This is done through a fuzzy system construction that involves determination of fuzzy sets and fuzzy membership functions, fuzzification of inputs, fuzzy inferencing and rule evaluation, and defuzzification of outputs.

Genetic algorithms refer to a class of adaptive search procedures based on principles derived from the dynamics of natural population genetics. The general characteristics of genetic algorithms include working with a coding of the parameter set, searching from a population of points, rather than a single point, using a pay-off or fitness function, and using probabilistic transition rules.

Under the banner of real world application, expert systems, fuzzy systems, neural networks, and genetic algorithms have been used in various industrial applications. These applications, however, have also highlighted limitations of these technologies (Khosla et al., 1997b). In order to develop more powerful problem solving strategies, the hybridization of these technologies is encouraged. On the human information processing side, studies in cognitive psychology, cognitive science and artificial intelligence indicate that information processing takes place at a macrostructure level and a microstructure level. At macrostructure level, information processing takes place in the order of few seconds to minutes, whereas at the microstructure level, it takes place in the order of few milliseconds to a few hundred milliseconds. In recent times, the macrostructure and microstructure levels have also been known as the artificial intelligence and computational intelligence levels respectively. The hybrid approaches adopted to model these two levels can be grouped into intelligent fusion systems, transformation systems, combination systems and associative systems. More details of intelligent hybrid systems can be found in (Khosla et al., 1997a).

Table 1. Summary of Problem Solving Ontology Model

PHASE	(SOME) TASKS	INTELLIGENT METHODS (optional)	HYBRID CONFIGURATION
Global preprocessing phase	Eliminates global noise which is peculiar to problem under study, input conditioning	Symbolic Methods, Fuzzy Methods	Transformation
Decomposition phase	Analyzes and decomposes the problem domain into set of abstract concepts/classes	Symbolic Methods Neural Network Methods	Combination
Control phase	Operates within each abstract class and performs tasks like local noise filtering, input validation and problem formulation, determination of decision level classes, and resolving conflicting outcomes of decision level classes	Symbolic/Fuzzy Methods, Neural Network Methods, Fuzzy-Neural Network Methods, Genetic Algorithm Methods	Fusion, Transformation
Decision phase	Determines/predicts specific classifications with each decision-level class and provides outcomes to problem solver	Neural Network Methods, Numerical Methods Mathematical Algorithms, Fuzzy-Neural Network Methods, Genetic Algorithm Methods	Fusion, Transformation
Postprocessing phase	Validates decision, explains and presents decisions made in the decision phase	Symbolic/Fuzzy Methods, Neural Network Methods, GA methods	Fusion, Transformation

3.2.7 Problem-Solving Ontology Model

The problem solving ontology model developed by Khosla and Dillon (1997) has been derived from a number of human-centered perspectives such as neurobiological control, cognitive science, man made physical systems, user acceptability, learning, knowledge representation, task complexity, conscious and automated behavior, and others.

The problem solving ontology model is described in terms of the five information phases, tasks to be accomplished in each phase, intelligent methods used to accomplish the tasks in different phases, and hybrid configuration of intelligent methods. The intelligent methods are selected based on top down or bottom up knowledge engineering strategy (Khosla et al. 1997a)[2]. Some characteristics of problem solving ontology model are shown in Table 1.

The intelligent methods reflect integration of artificial and computational intelligent levels of problem solving involving symbolic, fuzzy, neural network, and genetic algorithm methods. The problem solving ontology model incorporates fusion, transformation, and combination methods as a mean to maximize both quality of solution and range of tasks to be handled. More details on the problem solving ontology model can be found in (Khosla et al. 1997a).

3.3 Multi-Layered Multi-Agent Architecture for Soft Computing

The multi-layered multi-agent architecture is shown in Figure 6. It is derived from integration of characteristics of technological artefacts like intelligent technologies (e.g., fuzzy logic, neural network, genetic algorithms), agents, objects and distributed process model with the problem solving ontology model shown in Figure 5. It consists of five layers, namely, the object layer, which defines the data architecture or structural content in the context of the work activity. The software agent layer helps to define the distributed processing constructs. The intelligent agent layer defines the constructs for intelligent technologies. The hybrid layer defines constructs for intelligent fusion, combination and transformation technologies. Finally, the problem solving ontology agent layer defines the constructs related to modeling of tasks in a domain.

This layer employs the services of the other layers for accomplishing various tasks. The five layers facilitate a component based approach for agent based software design. The generic agent definition used for defining the agents in the problem solving agent layer, intelligent hybrid agent layer, intelligent agent layer and software agent layer is shown in Figure 6.

The *parent agent* construct in the generic agent definition identifies the generic agents in the four agent layers, whose constructs and services have been inherited by a particular application or domain based agent. *Goal* is a desire or desired outcome or state. *Task* is a goal directed process, in which people consciously or unconsciously engage. *Task Constraints* are pragmatic constraints imposed by the stakeholders and the environment for successful accomplishment of a task. The task constraints primarily determine the selection knowledge required for selecting a technological artefact for accomplishing a task.

The generic agent definition includes communication constructs employed by an agent. These communication constructs are based on human communicative acts like request, command, inform, broadcast, explain, warn and others. The *communicates with* construct in Figure 7 identifies all the agents and objects that an agent communicates with in the five layers. The linguistic and non-linguistic features represent the sensed data from the external

---

[2] Top down knowledge engineering strategy is used where knowledge required for accomplishing tasks is available while bottom up fashion is used where the knowledge is not available.

environment as well as computed data by the agent. The sensed and computed data are used by the agents in the four layers to gather data from the environment (in this case human is the data source) and also assist the direct stakeholders in interpreting the computing data. *Represented Features* are the conceptual and perceptual features of artefacts in a domain. Conceptual features are perceptual categories (e.g. high temperature, low temperature) which can have binary, structured, fuzzy or continuous values. Perceptual categories are derived from perceptual features while a perceptual feature is a stable signature in a raw sensory signal.

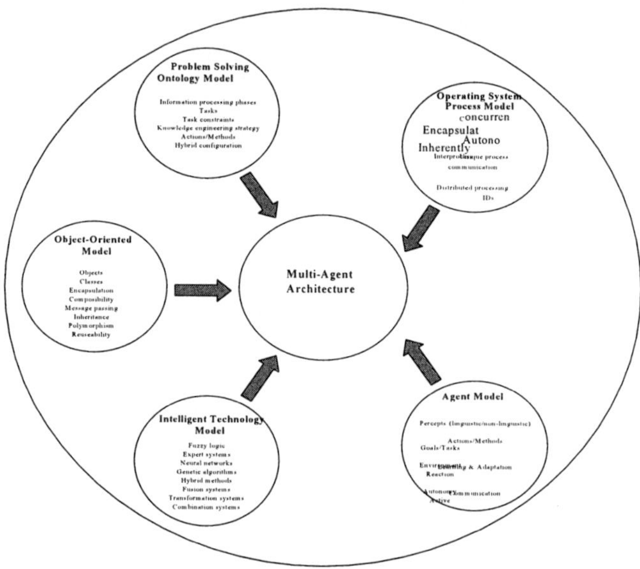

Figure 5. Integration of Object, Agent, Operating System Process, Intelligent Technology, Multimedia Interpretation, and Problem Solving Ontology

Representing Dimension is the physical or abstract dimension used to represent conceptual or perceptual features. For example, a conceptual feature like temperature can be represented using a physical dimension such as density high/mild or low temperature. These physical dimensions can help to identify the perceptual features and perceptual categories of a given artefact. *Psychological Scale* is the abstract measurement property of the physical or abstract dimension of a represented feature or types of scale including nominal, ordinal, interval and ratio. The purpose of using the representing dimension and scale information is twofold. Firstly, from a human-centred perspective, the representing dimension and scale information provide insight into the distributed

The *external tools* construct in Figure 7 refers to those computer-based or other tools that are external to the definition of an agent. On the other hand, *internal tools* are those tools that are defined internally by an agent. The *external tools* include simulated training data files used by an agent. On the other hand, the sensitivity algorithms and the back propagation rule are *internal tools* defined and used by the neural network agent. Since the neural network agent is a generic agent it does not have any parent agent or communication constructs.

The *internal state* construct refers to the beliefs of an agent at a particular instant in time. Finally, the actions construct is used to define the sequence of actions for accomplishing various tasks.

All the agents in Figure 6 are defined based on the generic agent definition shown in Figure 7. Some characteristics of the agents in the four agent layers are defined in the next section.

3.3.1 Clerical Agent Layer

The role of the clerical agent layer is to enable mobile agents in a distributed computing environment to fetch and drop useful data on behalf of its users. The useful data may involve documents from remote sites, processed results from soft computing agents located on different machines in a distributed computing environment, etc.

The clerical agent layer employs distributed communication and processing agent and belief agent to accomplish this role. These agents are briefly described next.

- **Distributed Communication and Processing Agent:** The goal of the communication agent is to facilitate distributed communication between problem solving agents in a hierarchical as well as a lateral fashion. The functionality of this agent is based operating system level like Process ID, Pipes; data and functions like *Fork*, *Write* and *Read*. The operating system process also defines the distributed nature of the multi-agent architecture.

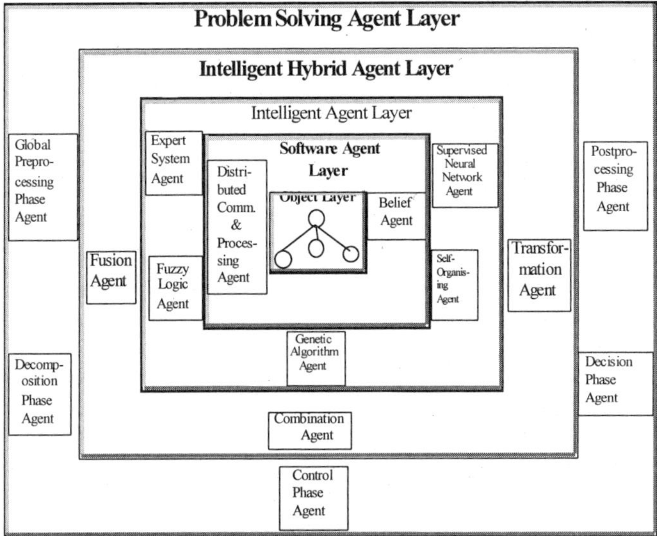

Figure 6. Multi-Layered Multi-Agent Architecture

- **Media Agent:** The media agent is associated with the agents in the other four layers for generation, display, layout and coordination of various media artefacts. The external tools used by a media agent can involve use of graphic objects, audio objects and text objects. The actions can involve learning and reasoning for generation, display, layout and coordination of various media artefacts. An example of a media agent will be shown in the next chapter.

3.3.2 Intelligent Agent Layer

The intelligent agent layer consists of artificial intelligent agents like expert system agent as well as soft computing agents like neural network agents, fuzzy logic agent, and genetic algorithm agent.

Name:
Parent Agent:
Goals:
Tasks:
Task Constraints:
Precondition:
Postcondition:
Communicates With:
Communication Constructs:
Linguistic/non-linguistic Features:
Psychological Scale:
Representing Dimensions:
External Tools:
Internal Tools
Internal State:
Actions:

Figure 7. Generic Agent Definition

- **Expert System Agent:** The primary goal of an expert system agent is to enable the problem solving agent to do high level reasoning, such as problem formulation and context validation. The action like Rules is used for inferencing on a given set of percepts. Initialise Rule Variables is used to initialise the rule variables based on the internal state of a problem solving agent. The Actions like *Loadkb* and *UnlLoadkb*, as their name signifies, are used for loading (into working memory) and unloading (removing from working memory) the knowledge base of an expert system agent. The percept *KBName* uniquely identifies the knowledge base name of a particular instance of the expert system agent. Thus the expert system agent provides an environment for a problem solving agent to build application dependent expert or knowledge based system agents.

- **Neural Network Agent:** There are two types of neural network agent: supervised and unsupervised neural network agents. The percepts of the supervised neural network agent involve both input and output symbols or patterns, whereas the percepts of the unsupervised neural network agent involve only the input patterns. The supervised neural network agent may engage in classification, whereas the unsupervised neural network agent may engage in clustering. The actions associated with the supervised neural network are applicable to multilayer perceptron using a backpropagation algorithm and other supervised learning algorithms. Similarly, the actions associated with the unsupervised neural network are applicable in neural network architectures like (Kohonen 1990) nets and ART (Carpenter et al. 1988). Figure 8 shows the agent definition of a neural network agent.

- **Fuzzy Logic Agent:** The actions in the fuzzy logic agent to a large extent represent the problem independent part of fuzzy logic. The problem dependent part is represented by the percepts like fuzzy membership functions, linguistic symbols, and the structure of the fuzzy antecedent and consequent. The action *Fuzzy Inferencing* can represent min-max operation, compositional inference, and other forms of fuzzy inference. The *Defuzzify Data* can employ most commonly used centre of gravity method or methods for defuzzifying data.

- **Genetic Algorithm Agent:** The genetic algorithm agent is used for optimisation of fuzzy rules, learning data sets, neural network structure, etc. The action *Create Gene Type* is used for representing the percepts as a bit, integer, floating point, or as a case chromosome. The actions Initialise *Population, Select Parents, Reproduce, Evaluate Offspring,* and *Replace Parents* represent the genetic algorithm agent optimisation life cycle. The *Select Parents* action selects parents who can possibly produce a filter offspring. The *Reproduce* action involves crossover and mutation operators to produce the new offspring. The *Evaluate Offspring* action evaluates an offspring based on a given fitness function percept. Finally, *Replace Parents* replaces certain parents with the new or filter offspring.

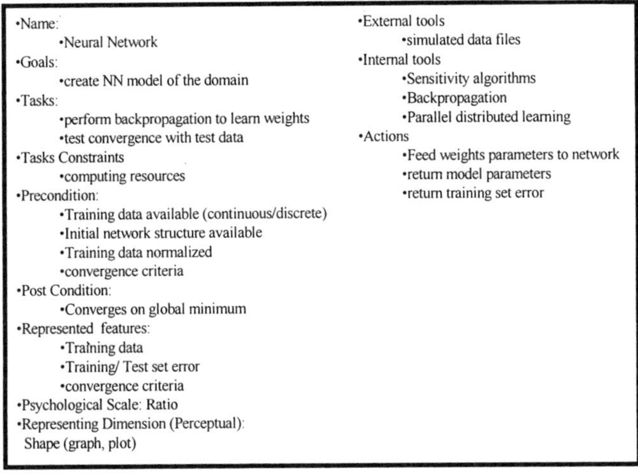

Figure 8. Neural Network Agent Definition

3.3.3 Intelligent Hybrid Agent Layer

The intelligent hybrid agent layer makes use of intelligent features and methods provided by the intelligent agent layer (e.g. those of expert system agent, fuzzy logic agent, and genetic algorithm agent). The intelligent features and methods can be utilized based on fusion, transformation and combination configuration.

The concepts of fusion, transformation, and combination have been used in different situations or tasks, and by applying top-down and/or bottom up knowledge engineering strategy. All these hybrid configurations have a number of advantages in that a hybrid arrangement is able to successfully accomplish tasks in various situations.

The fact of the matter is that the fusion, transformation, and combination configurations have been motivated by and developed for different problem solving tasks/situations. Thus, it is the role of the intelligent hybrid agent layer to select each of these hybrid configurations that suits problem/situations faced by the agents in the problem solving agent layer.

The three classes of hybrid agents consisting of fusion, combination, and transformation are represented in Figure 6. An agent definition of a fuzzy-neural fusion is shown in Figure 9.

3.3.4 Problem Solving Agent Layer

Whereas, the intelligent agent and intelligent agent layers provide tool support to the users, the problem solving agent layer enables the user/problem solver to structure and model tasks in a domain. It provides a task vocabulary to the user for complex domains. The task vocabulary is defined through five problem solving agents namely, preprocessing, decomposition, control, decision, and postprocessing agents respectively. The problem solving agents employ the services of the agents in the other three agent layers to accomplish various problem driven tasks. The definition of the decision agents is shown in Figure 10. It can be seen that the main task engaged by the decision phase adapter involves determination decision instance. Decision instance, or instances, represent partly or wholly user defined outcomes from a computer-based artifact. These outcomes are realized within each decision concept invoked by the control phase adapter. These outcomes are, for example, specific faulty components in an electronic circuit board, actual faces in a face recognition problem, or a product with desired features in an electronic commerce application, etc.

In some real time systems it may be necessary to compute the computational resources and the time required by different decision level classes to determine solutions. Thus, certain decision level classes may not be considered viable under these constraints and thus may not be activated. For accomplishing this task, symbolic or fuzzy methods are employed. The task constraints imposed on this decision phase adapter involve scalability, reliability, maintainability learning, adaptability, generalisation, and domain dependence.

<table>
<tr><td valign="top">

- Name:
  - Fuzzy Neural Network Agent
-
  -
- Goals:
  - create optimized control action 2
- Tasks:
  - create Fuzzy NN Model of control system
  - perform fuzzy decent to learn Fuzzy Rules
  - test convergence with test data
  - extract rules
- Tasks Constraints:
  - Normalized Training data available
  - optimized Fuzzy Model not known
- Precondition:
  - control data/parameters available
  - Training data normalized
  - convergence criteria is known
- Post Condition:
  - Converges on global minimum
  - optimized fuzzy rule base
- Communicates with:
  - Problemsolving Agent
  - Clerical Agent
  - Communication constructs:
- Receive data from problem solving agent
  - inform of network parameters to user
  - receive feedback data from environment
- Preceptual features:
  - Training / test set error shapes
  - Convergence graphs

</td><td valign="top">

- Linguistic/nonlinguistic percepts:
  - Control input parameters (location, velocity)
  - Control Output
- External tools:
  - simulated data files
  - Intelligent NN Agent
- Internal tools:
  - sensitivity algorithms
  - Fuzzy Decent Algorithm
  - Fuzzy Logic
- Actions:
  - Feed control input to network
  - return control parameters
  - return training set error

</td></tr>
</table>

Figure 9. Fuzzy-Neural Fusion Agent Definition

The qualitative or linguistic features employed by the decision phase adapter can be fine grain fuzzy or even binary. For example, in a alarm processing problem (illustrated later in this chapter) two properties of the alarm data are used. First, existence or absence (i.e. binary property) of a circuit breaker alarm in a decision class (candidate faulty section) is determined. Second, the fine grain fuzzy contribution value of a circuit breaker alarm and associated relay towards a fault in a particular network component is modeled in terms of their protection proximity to a possible faulty component. This contribution value is determined in terms of the fuzzy feature activity level of a path consisting of alarm and relay.

The non-linguistic represented features employed can be continuous decision data. For example, in the face recognition problem, color pixel data related to a face candidate and spatial coordinates of facial features like eyes, mouth and nose are used to identify actual faces and track eye movements in the decision phase.

The nominal scale can be used to measure binary features like existence or non-existence of an alarm, whereas fine grain fuzzy features can be measured on the ordinal, interval or ratio scales, depending on the scale properties, by the fuzzy features. For example, in an animal classification (more specifically, tiger classification) domain, some of the scale properties of fuzzy features *heavy cheek hair* are category (cheek hair), magnitude (heavy > light) and absolute zero (no cheek hair). These properties represent the ratio scale.

As mentioned earlier, representing dimension is useful for determining the perceptual aspects (e.g. shape, size, length, distance, density, location, position) of data and reasoning in problem domain. For example, in the alarm processing domain, the representing dimension of the fuzzy feature activity level is distance.

DECISION AGENT	
Name:	Decision
Goal:	Provide user/stakeholder defined outcomes from the system
Precondition:	Decision concept case data, Decision level concepts (optional)
Tasks:	Determine decision instance (e.g. faulty components, control action in control problems
Task Constraints:	Domain Independent: Scalability, Maintainability, Reliability, Learning, Generalisation and Adaptability plus Domain dependent
Communicates With:	Intelligent hybrid Agents, Intelligent agents, Clerical Agents, and Domain Objects
Communication Constructs:	Request, Command
Domain Model (optional):	Structured, Functional, Causal, Geometric, Heuristic, Spatial, Shape, Colour, etc.
Represented Features:	Quantitative/Linguistic – binary, fine grain fuzzy decision concept data Non-Linguistic – continuous decision concept data
Psychological Scales:	Nominal, Ordinal, Interval, Ratio or None
Representing Dimensions (Perceptual):	Shape, Size, Length, Distance, Density, Location, Position, Orientation, Colour, Texture
Actions:	Hard (e.g. symbolic rule based), Soft (e.g. neural networks, fuzzy logic, genetic algorithms)
Postcondition:	Specific instance of the concept determined

Figure 10. Definition of Decision agent Definition

The actions of the decision agents can involve soft computing mechanisms like neural network, fuzzy logic, genetic algorithm) or other statistical/mathematical algorithms. The soft computing mechanisms can satisfy task constraints like pattern recognition, learning, generalization and adaptability. Optimization may be another constraint which may need to be satisfied. Genetic algorithms are ideal for satisfying the optimizing, learning and generalization characteristics of soft computing mechanisms like neural networks.

Figure 11 shows a typical instance of execution precedence of the five problem solving agents in a complex data intensive application. It also integration of agents from other layers.

3.3.5 Emerging Characteristics

In order to get an overall picture of the multi-agent architecture, it is useful to look at its emergent behavior. The emergent behavior of the framework is defined by outlining its architectural characteristics.

The architectural characteristics define the significance of the multi-agent architecture in terms of its emergent design characteristics. Some of the emergent design characteristics are outlined in this section.

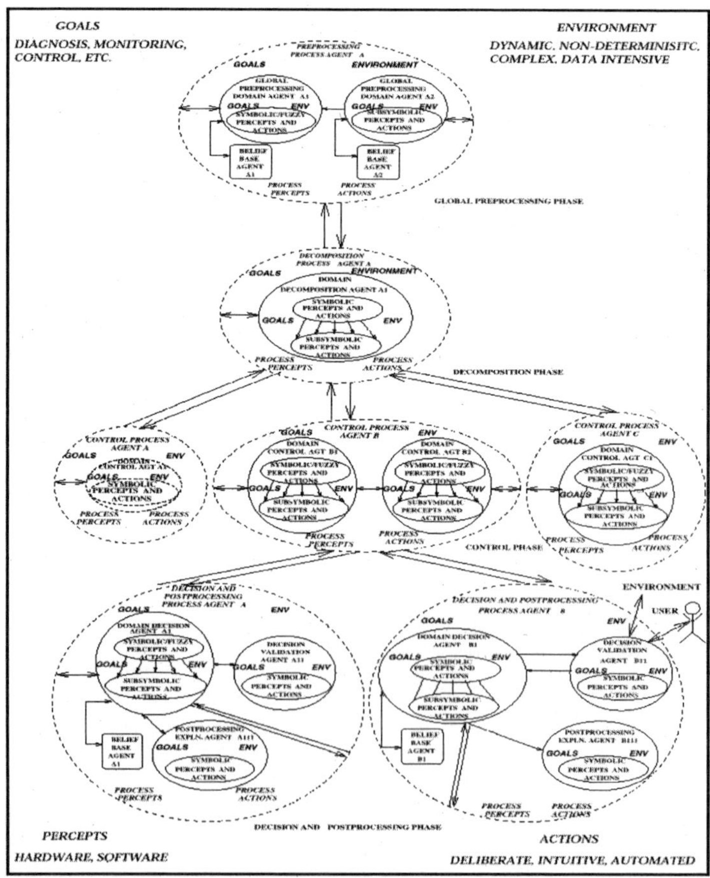

Figure 11. An Example of Execution Precedence of Problem Solving Agents in a Complex Data Intensive Application

3.3.5.1 Task Orientation

The solutions to real world problems are determined by engineers, designers, accountants, sales managers, etc. in a task context (Chandrasekaran et al., 1992, Preece, 1997) rather than a technological context. Various intelligent technologies like knowledge based systems, fuzzy logic, neural networks and their hybrid configuration (e.g. fusion, transformation and combination), propose a technology-based solution to real world problems. The problem solving ontology component of the framework is a task-oriented system in which technological artifacts are considered as primitives for accomplishing various tasks.

The use of one or more technological primitives is contingent upon satisfaction of task constraints.

The task orientation enables the framework to match a given task to one or more technologies among a suite of technologies rather than match a given technology to tasks in a work activity.

3.3.5.2 Flexibility

Most complex real world problems require satisfaction of a number of task constraints ranging from incomplete and noisy information, learning, fast response time to explanation and validation as one technology is not enough to provide a satisfactory solution. A technology-based solution constrains a problem solver to force-fit a particular software design onto a task or problem. The five problem solving adapters and their agent definitions allow the problem solver to use multiple domain models in terms of multiple hybrid agent layers and the intelligent agent layer provides flexibility of intelligent techniques and their hybrid configurations that can be employed to satisfy various task constraints. That is, the user can follow the five problem solving adapters in different sequences or even use five or fewer phases in a decision making sequence. This characteristic will be illustrated in the next chapter.

3.3.5.3 Versatility

Technologies like expert systems and fuzzy logic rely heavily on the availability of domain knowledge. In a number of real world problems (e.g. data mining) explicit domain knowledge is not available or may involve a long and cumbersome knowledge acquisition process. The framework is versatile in that it can model solutions in the presence or absence of domain knowledge.

3.3.5.4 Forms of Knowledge

Real word problems involve use of multiple forms of knowledge (e.g. continuous, discrete, symbolic and fuzzy). Unlike a number of intelligent technologies, associative systems are not limited to one or two forms of knowledge but can model any real world problem with continuous, discrete, or fuzzy knowledge because of the multiplicity of techniques used by them.

3.3.5.5 Learning and Adaptation

The ability to learn new tasks and adapt to novel solutions are essential properties of the framework. The multi-agent architecture involves task-based learning in which a problem solver employs multiplicity of learning techniques (e.g. supervised, self-organized, evolutionary, their variations and hybrid configuration) to match the needs of various learning tasks.

3.3.5.6 Distributed Problem Solving and Communication – Collaboration and Competition

In order to deal with the complexity of real world problems in general and World Wide Web (WWW) based problems (e.g. Web searching, Web mining, etc.) in particular, distributed problem solving has become a necessity. The task-oriented approach of the framework not only enables distribution of tasks among different system components, which may be executed on remote machines, but also facilitates collaborative and competitive problem solving. That is, agents can collaborate with each other by performing different tasks. They can be mobile and perform multiple techniques or agents can compete with each other on the same task (by performing it using different techniques like neural networks, knowledge-based systems, etc.) and thus enhance overall system reliability.

3.3.6 Syntactic, and Semantic Quality

In this section of the chapter we wish to establish the validity of the distributed multi-agent architecture along the syntactic, semantic and pragmatic quality dimensions respectively.
The syntactic quality determines the intuitiveness of the constructs used to model a domain. That is, how close are the software artifacts used by a particular technology to those used by humans (i.e. users/stakeholders and not system designers). The software artifacts like objects and agents have been used based on their intuitive strengths to model structural and task aspects of a problem domain respectively. The provision of hard and soft methods for accomplishing various tasks has been based on the assumption of satisfying a range of pragmatic constraints governed by epistemological limitations of humans and computers.
The semantic quality, unlike the syntactic quality, determines how people use various artifacts to solve problems. That is, how close is the software design to the human solution of that problem. In our case the problem solving agent layer has been derived from generalizations and persistent structures used by people in solving complex problems. The problem solving agents assist in modeling human tasks and are technology independent.

3.4 Fuzzy Application in Electrical Power System

For the purpose of illustration, a model of power system protection (consisting of CBs and Relays), as shown in Figure 12, is used (Sekine et al. 1989). In this example, fuzzy logic is applied for fault diagnosis in Bus 1 (B1) in Figure 12. The previous work on fault diagnosis has employed either expert systems (Inoue et al. 1989; Jongpier et al. 1991; Liu 1993).
There are eight possible paths in B1 (Bus 1 in Figure 12) in this example. The paths have been configured based on the operation or maloperation of the following circuit breakers.

B1m CB2 CB3 CB4 CB5 CB6 CB7 CB9 CB10 T1s L1Cs T2s L2Cs

The eight paths are as follows:
Path-1: B1m L2Cs CB10
Path-2: B1m CB6 L2Cs CB10
Path-3: B1m CB6 T2s CB3 CB5
Path-4: B1m T2s CB3 CB5

Path-5: B1m CB7 L1Cs CB9
Path-6: B1m L1Cs CB9
Path-7: B1m CB4 T1s CB4 CB2
Path-8: B1m T1s CB4 CB2

Fault diagnosis at B1 is determined by the activity level of each path. The activity level is based on the number of active(1) / non-active(0) relays and circuit breakers in a path and their protection proximity to B1. The proximity of the components to B1 enables us to determine their contribution values to the fault in B1 For example, the contribution ratio in Path-5 (B1m:CB7:L1Cs:CB9) is 2:2:1:1. B1m and CB7 have higher contribution values as compared to L1Cs and CB9 because they are topologically closer to B1. If B1m and CB7 are the two components, which have operated in Path-5, then the contribution value of this path to a fault at B1 is 2/3. The contribution value of a path is mapped to the active membership function in shown in Figure 6 to determine its activity level. Thus, the activity level of Path-5 with its operational components as above is 1/12.

The input patterns to a fuzzy-neural agent can be of two forms. They can consist of the operational status of the circuit breakers and relays mentioned above, or the activity level of each path (which is a fuzzy feature) based on the contribution value of each path to a fault in B1. The fuzzified/preprocessed input patterns in the second case amounts to providing a priori knowledge to the fuzzy-neural agent for training. Our results show that the output of the fuzzy-neural agent using preprocessed input patterns (inputs with prior knowledge) is closer to the truth value of their corresponding validation fuzzy rules. The fuzzy rules used for validating the output of the fuzzy-neural agent are of the form:

IF Path-1 is active THEN Bus 1 is faulty

where active is a fuzzy set. The membership function for active at each path is shown in Figure 13. The degree of certainty that B1 is at fault based on the activity level in each path leading to B1 has to be determined. The inferencing method chosen is the additive method. In this method, the truth value of a consequence is determined by adding up the truth value of all fuzzy rules having the same consequence. For the power system diagnostic problem, there are many paths leading to a fault area. The additive inferencing method is used because the activity level at each path contributes to the possibility of fault in the diagnosed area. Therefore, the truth values of the rules leading to a diagnosed area are added up to determine the truth value of the area at fault.

The final truth value is, however, bounded by 1. The decision made by the fuzzy-neural agent, that an input pattern is faulty, is validated if its truth value assessed by fuzzy rules is above an alpha-cut threshold value. In this example, the alpha-cut threshold value for fuzzy rules is set at 0.5.

Test patterns 1 & 2 show the results with some unseen input patterns with the ANN outputs using both binary (a) and fuzzified inputs (b).

Test pattern 1:
a) Input:1 1 0 0 0 0 0 1 1 0 1 1 1
b) Fuzzified Inp:1.00 0.67 0.43 0.50 0.67 1.00 0.43 0.50
    output for B1 (a):0.900
    output for B1 (b):0.694
Truth value of the fuzzy validation rule:0.649

Test pattern 2:
a) Input:0 1 0 0 1 0 1 0 1 1 1 1 1
b) Fuzzified Inp:0.67 0.33 0.29 0.50 0.500 0.33 0.29 0.50
　　output for B1 (a):0.200
　　output for B1 (b):0.502
Truth value of the fuzzy validation rule:0.426

It can be seen from the test pattern results that the fuzzy-neural agent outputs using fuzzified inputs (inputs with prior knowledge) are closer to the truth value of the fuzzy validation rule than the ones with binary inputs. Although the decision made by the fuzzy-neural agent may be validated or invalidated by fuzzy rules, the assessment of the certainty that B1 is at fault varies between the fuzzy-neural agent and fuzzy rules. In the case of test pattern 2 where a fault at B1 is invalidated by the fuzzy rule because 0.426 is lower than the alpha-cut threshold value, the decision can be left to the user. Rules are both close to their alpha-cut thresholds.

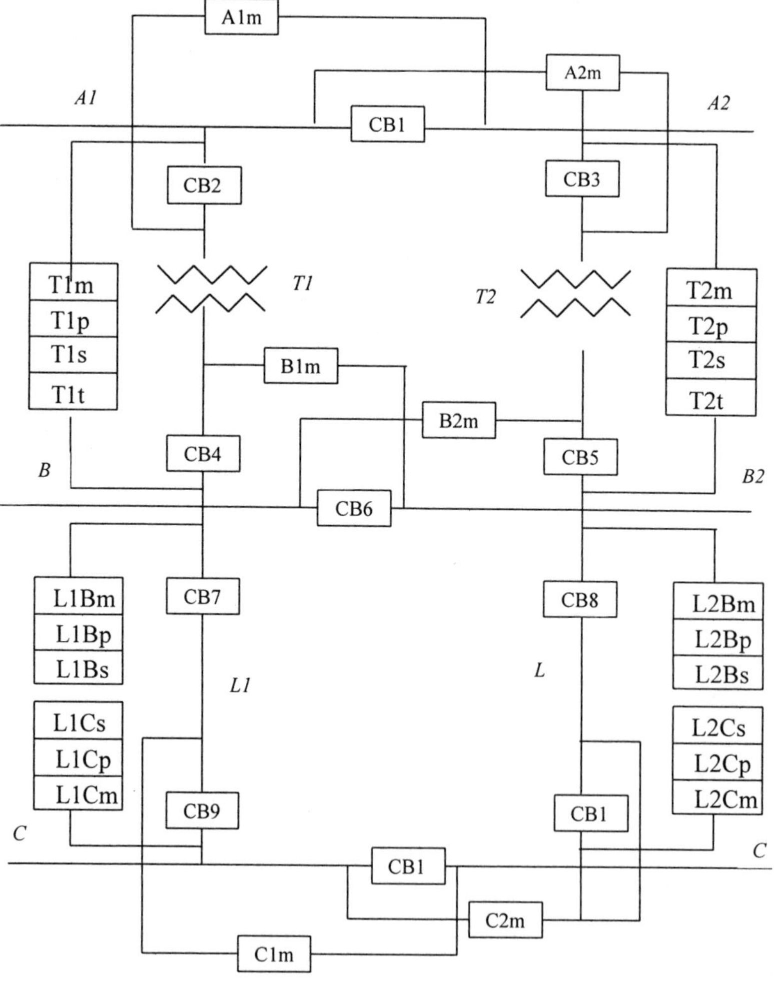

Figure 12. Model of a Power System and a Protection System Subscripts m, main protection; p, remote backup protection (distance 1); s, remote backup protection (distance 2); t, remote backup protection (distance 2, opposite direction to subscript s)

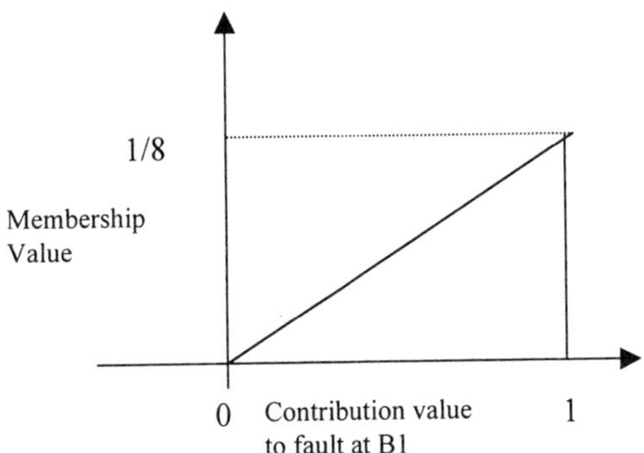

Figure 13. Membership function for active fuzzy set

3.5 Conclusion

In this chapter we have described a component based multi-agent architecture for complex soft computing applications. The architecture can assist practitioners and problem solvers in modelling clerical, tool and task level of soft computing applications. The architecture is derived through integration of several software models including object-oriented model, agent model, operating system process model, intelligent technology model and problem solving ontology model. The five layers of the multi-agent distributed architecture facilitate component based agent design of soft computing systems. We have described the constructs used by the agents along with agent definition of agents in different layers. The emerging characteristics and the syntactic and semantic quality of the architecture are also described. The application of the tool level of the architecture in electrical power system demonstrates that how power system operator's a prior knowledge and human-like reasoning is incorporated in the modelling process by using the fuzzy-neural soft computing agent.

References

Booch, G. (1986), Object-Oriented Development," IEEE Transactions Software Engineering, vol. SE-12, no. 2, February, pp. 212-220.

Bourne, S.R. (1983), The Unix System, Addison-Wesley, Massachusetts, USA.

Brow, A.W. (1991), Object-Oriented Databases: Application in Software Engineering, McGraw-Hill, New York, USA.

Carpenter, G.A. and Grossberg, S. (1988), The ART of Adaptive Pattern Recognition by Self-Organizing Neural Network, *IEEE Computer*, 21, 3, 77-88.

Chandrasekaran, B. (1990), What Kind of Information Processing is Intelligence, in "The Foundations of AI: A Sourcebook, Cambridge, UK: CambridgeUniversity Press, pp. 14-46.

Chandrasekaran, B., Johnson, T.R. and Smith, J.W. (1992) Task-Structure Analysis for Knowledge Modeling, Communications of the ACM, 35, 9, 124-136.

Christian, K., (1988), The Unix Operating System, Wiley-Interscience Publication, New York.

Coad, P. and Yourdon, E. (1990), Object-Oriented Analysis, Prentice Hall, Englewood, NJ, USA.

Coad, P. and Yourdon, E. (1992), Object-Oriented Design, Prentice Hall, Englewood, NJ, USA.

Cox, B.J. (1986), Object-Oriented Programming, Addison-Wesley.

Dillon, T. and Tan, P.L. (1993), Object-Oriented Conceptual Modeling, Prentice Hall, Sydney, Australia.

Farhoodi, F. and Fingar, P. (1997a) Competing for the Future with Intelligent Agents, URL: http://home1.gte.net/pfingar/agents_doc_rev

Farhoodi, F. and Fingar, P. (1997b) Developing Enterprise Systems with Intelligent Agent Technology, URL: http://home1.gte.net/pfingar/docmag_part

Iivari, J. (1995) Object-orientation as structural, functional and behavioural modelling: a comparison of six methods for object-oriented analysis, *Information and Software Technology*, **37**, 3, 155-163.

Inoue, N., Fuji, T., Shinohara, T., Mochizuki, J., and Kajiwara, J., (1989) An Expert System for Intelligent Alarm Processing in EMS and SCADA Systems, Proceedings of 2nd Symp. Expert System Applications to Power Systems, 89-95.

Jacobson, I., Ericsson, M. and Jacobson, A. (1995) *The Object Advantage: Business Process Reengineering with Object Technology*, ACM Press. A division of the Association for Computing Machine Inc. (ACM).

Jongepier A.G., Dijk H.E., Sluis, L.V.D. (1991) Neural Networks Applied to Alarm Processing, *Proc. 3rd Symp Expert System Applications in Power Systems*, 615-620.

Khosla, R. and Dillon, T. (1995), Integration of Task Structure Level Architecture with O-O Technology," in Seventh International Conference on Software Engineering and Knowledge Engineering (SEKE'95), Maryland, USA. Published under the section Advances in O-O Technology.

Khosla, R. and Dillon, T. (1997a) *Engineering Intelligent Hybrid Multi Agent Systems,* Kluwer Academic Publishers, Norwell, MA 02061, USA.

Khosla, R. and Dillon, T. (1997b) Fusion of Knowledge-Based Systems and Neural Networks and Applications, in *1st Conference on Conventional and Knowledge-Based Intelligent Electronic Systems*, Adelaide, Australia, 27-44.

Khosla, R. and Dillon, T. (1997c) Learning Knowledge and Strategy of a Generic Neuro Expert System Architecture in Alarm Processing, *IEEE Transaction on Power Systems,* 12, 12, 1610-1618.

Kim, Ballou, Chou, Garza and Woelk (1988), Integrating an Object-Oriented Programming system with a Database System, in ACM OOPSLA Proceedings, October.

Kohonen, T. (1990) Self Organisation and Associative Memory, Springer-Verlag.

Liu CC (1993) Practical Use of Expert Systems in Power Systems, Invited paper in Proc. 4th Symp. on Expert System Applications in Power Systems.

Murphy, G.L., and Wright, J.C. (1985), Changes in conceptual Structure with Expertise: Differences Between Real-World Experts and Novices, in Journal of Experimental Psychology: Learning, Memory and cognition, vol.10, pp. 144-155.

Myer, B. (1988), Object-Oriented Software Construction, Prentice Hall.

Parks, D. (1998) Agent-Oriented Programming: A Practical Evaluation,URL, http://http.cs.berkeley.edu/~davidp/cs263/oop.html

Preece, J. (1997) *Human-Computer Interaction,* Addision-Wesley, Massachusetts, USA.

Rosch, E., Mervis, C.B., Gray, W.D., Johnson, D.M. and Boyes-Braem, P. (1976), Basic Objects in Natural Categories, Cognitive Psychology, vol. 8, pp. 382-439.

Russell, S., and Norvig, P. (1995), Artificial Intelligence - A Modern Approach, Prentice Hall, New Jersey, USA.

Rumbaugh, J. et al. (1990), Object-Oriented Modeling and Design, Prentice Hall, Englewood Cli_s, NJ.

Searle, J. (1969) *Speech Acts,* Cambridge University Press, Cambridge, UK.

Sekine Y., Okamota H., and Shibamoto T., (1989) "Fault Section Estimation using cause-effect network," Second Symp. on Expert Systems Application to Power Systems, Seattle, USA, 17-20 July.

Sigfried, S. (1996) *Understanding Object-Oriented Software Engineering,* The Institute of Electrical and Electronics Engineering, Inc., New York.

Slatter, P.E. (1987), Building Expert Systems: Cognitive Emulation, Ellis Horwood Limited, Chichester.

Unland, R. and Schlageter, G. (1989), An Object-Oriented Programming Environment for Advanced Database Applications, in Journal of Object-Oriented Programming, May/June.

Wang X., Dillon, T. (1992) A Second Generation Expert System for Fault Diagnosis, International Journal of Electrical Power and Energy Systems, vol. 14, no. 2-3, 212-216.

Winograd, T. and Flores, F. (1986) Understanding Computers and Cognition: A New Foundation for Design, Addison-Wesley, Readings.

Whitfield, T.W.A. and Slatter, P.E. (1979), The Effects of Categorization and Prototypicality on Aesthetic Choice in a Furniture Selection Task, in British Journal of Psychology, vol. 70, pp. 65-75.

Soft Computing Agents
V. Loia (Ed.)
IOS Press, 2002

Chapter 4

Similarity-based Knowledge Discovery for Web Information Retrieval

Vincenzo Loia
Sabrina Senatore
Maria I. Sessa

4.1 Introduction

With the great amount of information available through Internet, and with the increasing demand for more powerful information-oriented services, the development of advanced Web search engines becomes one of the most critical issues in Web-based information society. The remarkable progress made by Web searching engines to strengthen the techniques of indexing and clustering can difficulty keep up with the continuum Internet expansion, even today in progress. The combination of two features, huge size and document heterogeneity, leads to several difficulties in all the basic operations, such as visualization, storage, indexing, classification and retrieval. Many lessons have been learnt by pre-existing information-based systems, especially in the fields of hypermedia, very large database and information retrieval systems, but it is clear that the nature of the Web demands new resolution approaches, in term of theories and systems. As pointed out by Yao (Yao *et al.* 2001), the creation of new disciplines focused on Web related research and applications could have an important impact in the future. Among these new research trends, we stress the area where deduction takes a central role in the processing of unstructured and imprecise information. Current Web search engines have remarkable capabilities when there is a matchable success between the query parameters and the available data. In many cases the retrieved documents fit to the users request in a vague manner. This situation is compared by Lawrence and Giles (Lawrence and Giles 1999) to "a search in a phone book which is updated irregularly, is biased toward listing more popular information, and has most of the pages ripped out". This problem is (also) due to the users difficulty in formulating a rich search query. Restricting the query to a sequence of keywords may cause two common drawbacks: an enormous returned list of results (so large to be irrelevant) or, as opposite, a very limited answer that does not reflects the wider users view.
Herein, we propose a Web information retrieval approach, based on mobile agent computation and flexible deductive reasoning: the agents cover the spidering task, looking for Web pages related to a user-given argument. They extract information from the reached Web pages in form of Prolog rules. Then a deductive activity is performed: the agents are equipped with deductive behaviour so to be autonomous in applying inference-based reasoning. A similarity model is embedded in the reasoning engine in order to correctly process the approximation level established at user level side.
This methodology has been realized by extending the classical SLD Resolution procedure (Sessa 2002), in order to handle the unification between different terms linked by similarity relationships. The basic idea is to overcome failures of the inference process by weakening the equality constraint in the unification procedure.
The paper is so structured: first we briefly point out on some issues around Information Retrieval and its role in Web searching activity. Then, we start the discussion of our

approach by describing MASIR (Sections 4.3 and 4.4), the architecture that realizes our model of Web searching. In particular, the theoretical framework is faced in Section 4.5, where we detail the similarity relation and how it is possible to handle subjective definition of the Similarity Relation. Section 4.6 focuses on the deductive definition capability, achieved thanks to an extension of SLD resolution mechanism. To discuss about experimental results, in Section 4.7 we illustrate Info-Miner, an application that runs on the MASIR architecture, designed for document searching. Lastly, in Section 4.8 we present recent results obtained by reinforcing the deductive reasoning model through goal-oriented spidering and context-based processing. Within this aim, we introduce a new operator, named MIS (Matching In Similarity) which allows us to provide a relation, based on similarity, between parts of text. This operation is employed as a simple and powerful mechanism to directly represent the user's intentions.

4.2   Besides Standard Information Retrieval

The Information Retrieval (IR) concerns with the study of systems for indexing, searching, and recalling data, particularly text or other unstructured forms. As stated by (Lancaster 1968), an IR-based system does not inform the user on the subject of his inquiry. It merely informs on the existence (or non-existence) and whereabouts of documents relating to his request. The goodness of an IR system is evaluated according to different criterions (Dunlop 1997), but, roughly speaking two factors are essential: the relevant information extracted from the available one, and the time spent by the system in satisfying the user's request. Until some years ago, the limited quantity of information, available on the Internet, guaranteed an accurate response to common user's needs: the classification systems were defined to operate with limited databases, indexes and restricted criterions could be sufficient to get satisfactory responses.

Now the uncontrolled growth and the dissemination of information on the Internet is very hard to manage: information is difficult to reach, due to the lack of direct link; documents are logically related to others but the relationship has gone unnoticed, or some documents have unlinked parts of information, the examination of which would produce new knowledge (Baeza-Yates R. *et al.* 1999).

Traditional IR systems look for the subject according to the exact keywords or a combination of some words of the whole expression. In general, the searching tools are unable to capture the complete objective of the user's request. Independently from the efficiency of the search tools, standard Web search engines prefer handling queries quickly and simply. Sometimes, the retrieved documents fit to the user's request in a vague manner. In many cases this is due to the user difficulty in formulating the search query: restricting the natural human language expression in a poor sequence of keywords may cause two common drawbacks: an enormous returned list of results (so large to be irrelevant) or, as opposite, a very limited answer that does not reflects the wider user's view.

To build up a flexible IR system we need, contemporaneously, to better characterize the searchable information, and to enlarge the user description model of the searchable terms.

As in (Loia *et al.* 2001a), we introduce our model of distributed IR, by presenting our architecture proposal, namely MASIR, standing for Mobile Agents for Similarity-based Retrieval. MASIR provides a wide range of information retrieval services by exploiting mobile computation of similarity-based agents. These agents are skilled to access remote Web information resources. They search relevant information according with a reasoning scheme in order to extract knowledge during their information analysis. This knowledge is then used to deduce new relevant information by applying a similarity-based matching mechanism.

4.3 Distributed Information Retrieval in MASIR: basic concepts

MASIR is an architecture (mostly implemented in Java and running on top of TCP/IP derived protocols) that provides information retrieval services by exploiting mobile computation of similarity-based agents. MASIR includes different User Applications, which can work independently, or may co-operate via transparent interoperability. MASIR is characterized by three basic technologies:

- Mobile Agents
  Software robots, or crawlers, spiders, etc., are all terms of an undefined computation entity usually identified by the term "agent"; it is not novelty the use of agents to retrieve Web documents. It is worth stressing that often agents are interpreted, erroneously, as mobile entities, even if in many cases the agents used for information discovery are stationary. Mobile agents, differently from "normal" agents, are able to be dispatched to a target Web site and, over it, to perform an activity. MASIR is based on this technology: to design network-aware agents useful for distributed application not restricted to a given execution environment.

- Knowledge-based Web View
  Hypertext Markup Language (HTML) documents are largely spread all over the Internet. Usually the Web search tools, such as *Lycos, NetFind, Infoseek* just to cite few of them, perform resource discovery comparing the keywords specified by the user with some HTML-oriented information (titles, reference hypertext, meta-tags, etc.). Independently from the efficiency of the search methods, these tools deal with some common features:
  - *Query*. Standard Search engines prefer handling queries quickly and provide simple input schemes based either on entering keyword of the wished document or on selecting a search mode. As discussed in (Gallaire and Nicolas 1978) and (Reiter 1984), queries in *model-theoretic view* are formulas that are evaluated on the interpretation using the semantic definition of truth, whereas queries in *proof-theoretic view* are considered as theorems that are to be proven. MASIR treats queries in a proof-theoretic view.
  - *Search*. Since the queries are considered through the perspective of a logic-based proof, this means that all search domains must be interpreted as collection of logic formulas. A Web document D gives rise to a set S of Horn clauses C_i, ..., C_j, where a single rule C_i reflects a specific property P_i. Then, this set of the clauses is a knowledge-based representation of the complete document D. Thanks to an inference-based mechanism performed by MASIR, it is possible to create interconnection, dependencies, among Web documents, or inside a document itself. This represents a useful answer to the need of knowledge restructuring, considering that in the Web, we find partial, unstructured information sources.
  - *Results*. Usually, traditional information retrieval strategies return myriad of independent, disaggregated solutions. The final result is difficult for the final user because of a lack of conciliation-based mechanisms. This task becomes affordable if the single spots of information may be submitted to a further deductive process that returns the final result, free from redundancy and inconsistence.

- Similarity-based Matching

  It may be interesting to extend the concept of precision or equality towards a more flexible interpretation, considering the "similarity" as a weaker relation of indiscernibility. Rather than viewing the similarity as a technique to treat situations of vagueness, uncertainty or imprecision, for which fuzzy theory, evidence theory, probably theory may be employed with success, we consider the similarity as a tool to maintain equivalence relations among objects whose diversity is relaxed with a certain degree of tolerability. In IR, an important operation necessary to evaluate the goodness of search discovery, is to compare the available information U_a (the discovered information) with that wanted U_w (user request). MASIR bridges U_a and U_w through a set of equivalence classes provided by the exploited similarity relation.

4.4 MASIR: the Architecture

The MASIR architecture takes benefit from a stable integration of software synergies background, which provides an environment that guarantees a straightforward interaction between different application layers and the bulk of the agent technology used to implement the discovery process, hiding to the user some low-level details related to security and reliability of the architecture.

MASIR is a hierarchic infrastructure, based on two fundamental layers, each one coupled with the underneath level: TCP/IP, the bottom layer supporting the communication-based application, and Grasshopper platform that provides an environment to support the agent's creation, execution, localization, migration, communication and security control.

In the following, operating details about the different layers are given.

4.4.1 TCP/IP protocol

TCP/IP (Transmission Control Protocol/Internet Protocol) is the basic communication language or protocol of the Internet. It uses the client/server model of transmission and guarantees the correct performance of Grasshopper. Grasshopper's environment uses several high level protocols on top of TCP/IP in order to provide the agent's communication, migration and security.

4.4.2 Grasshopper platform

The Grasshopper platform (Grasshopper Development System) provides an environment to support the agent's creation, execution, localization, migration, communication and security control.

It is a run-time development environment, compliant with the international Mobile Agent System Interoperability Facility (MASIF) standard of the Object Management Group (OMG) that aims to achieve interoperability between several agent-based applications. Grasshopper provides sophisticated security mechanisms against every kind of threats and assures a set of basic features by means of access control, certificates and encryption. The Grasshopper environment is completely written in Java and is based on CORBA technology.

Figure 1 shows the main components of Grasshopper system environment. It consists, essentially, of agent systems (agencies), grouped within a domain (region), as better explained below.

Agency. It is a Java process that manages the execution, transport, communication and security control of Grasshopper agents. Every agency manages the following services:

- security: it protects the hosts from unauthorized agent access (internal security mechanism); Grasshopper provides external security mechanism which allows to encrypt the code and the agent's state during their migration, by means of the Secure Socket Layer (SSL) protocol.
- registration: each agency stores information about every agent, runs locally and enables agents to find each other for data exchange.
- persistence: this service periodically allows to save the agent's data; in the case of system crash, it can recuperate the internal agent state and continues the execution from stopped point.

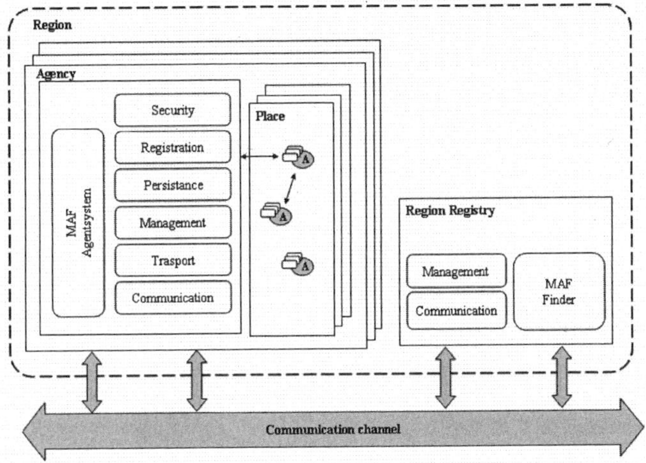

Figure 1 Grasshopper's platform

- management: the agency can manage the creation, removing, suspension/resume and coping of agents.
- transport: the service enables the serialization of agent's state, the transfer of agent to the destination location.
- communication: it permits the transferring of agent between different agencies and it supervises interactions between remote agents and non-agent-based entities.
- MAF AgentSystem: current component defines an OMG MASIF standard interface to increase the interoperability between Grasshopper and other mobile agent platforms.

Region Registry. An agency can register itself as a region registry. It maintains the information about the agencies and agents running inside. The region registry is automatically updated, every time an agent migrates to another agency. It provides the following basic services.

- management system: it allows to locate agents inside region.

- communication service: it enables interactions between region registry and remote entities.
- MAF Finder: the component provides an OMG MASIF standard interface to increase interoperability between this platform and others.

4.4.3 MASIR: a Logical View

Figure 2 shows the logical components of MASIR environment. It consists, essentially, of different types of task-oriented agents, which cooperate to reach a specific goal.

- Similarity Definition. It appears as a user-side interface tool: it allows the user to acquire the defined Similarity relationships upon a suitable fixed set of terms (the universe or *dictionary*) in order to assure the correct similarity-based settings.
- Similarity Agent. It collects the similarity relations, defined upon the input dictionaries and, when the user does not specify the current similarity relation, proactively loads the dictionary and relative similarity that better match the input clause (user's query).
- User Applications. Different IR-oriented services are available in MASIR. MASIR started initially as a smart Mailbot system (Loia *et al.* 2001b) able to send electronic messages to unknown, legitimate readers. Additional tasks have been added, such as the searching of scientific papers, conferences, scientists, and so on. Each User Application exhibits a user interface designed to transform the user's request into a logic goal to be proven with a related knowledge-base.
- Discovery Agent. The agent owns an appropriate knowledge extractor (depending on the application domain) and a logic-based reasoning model. The agent moves on the net: reaching a site, its goal is to proof the logic query corresponding to the user's request, thus it interprets the web resources and extracts new knowledge in terms of clause forms. Through the similarity-based reasoning, and on the base of the acquired knowledge, the agent triggers a resolution procedure returning, as result, answers to the query. This deduction process exploits the similarity notion to overcome failures in the exact matching of the unification between the required information and the available ones. Thus the obtained answers have an associated degree of approximation that expresses a measure of the weakening of the equality constraint.
- Collector Agent. This agent gathers all returned information from the Discovery Agents. Its ability is in filtering the messages by assuring the data consistency. Finally it returns the refined information to the corresponding User Application.

The MASIR platform works in background (transparent mode) on the user's machine managing the interaction among the different User Applications. Usually, each User Application can be executed in a separate mode, even though the major potentiality is achieved when some of its services work together, transparently, through co-operating activities.

The Similarity Definition gives the current similarity in logic-compliant structure to the Similarity Agent which updates the stored Similarity Relations among the terms in different dictionaries. The proof-based query and the current Similarity are hence injected into the Discovery Agents, becoming part of its knowledge. The Discovery Agent, with this baggage, moves on the net to reach the destination site, parses the web documents and extracts the inherent knowledge. While it examines the local page, it clones itself, every time that an external link is founded (that allows the agent to reach another machine).

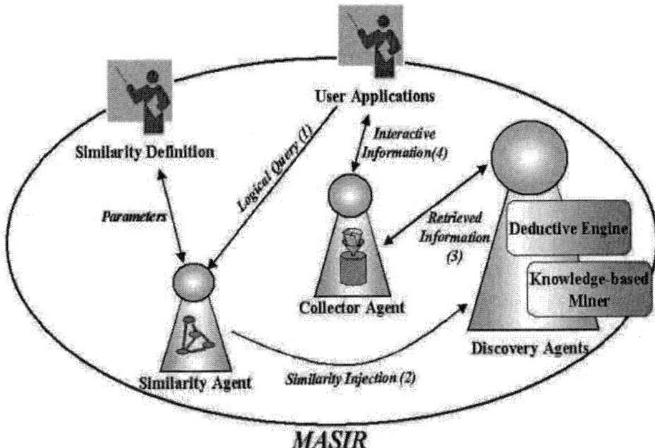

Figure 2: MASIR - Logical Architecture

Adopting this scheme, a Discovery Agent copes with a portion of the input domain; the collection of the several Discovery Agents' results is gathered by the Collector Agent, active on the user's machine. Its ability in filtering enables to obtain a synthetic and error-pruned answer. This information is then sent to the User Application (or to all the User Applications, if the interoperability mode is active), in order to customize the final exploitation.

4.5   Similarity-based Features of the Discovery Agent

Agent technology characterizes the current state of software design in the area of distributed systems and applications (Genesereth and Ketchpel 1994). Even though there is no universal definition accepted for the term "agent", the scientific community sees an agent as a software component running in specific environment. This component is equipped by a set of characteristics such as: autonomy, persistence, social ability, reactivity, pro-activeness. These features are important especially to handle real-world problems that are characterized by a wide space of solutions. In this case, the difficulty (or often, the impossibility) to provide a complete, precise model of the problem is faced thanks to the agent's ability to tolerate and process approximate or vague information.

The mathematical notion of *Similarity Relation* is a many valued extension of the equality, and it is widely exploited in any context where a weakening of the equality constraint is useful (Zadeh 1971).

The following paragraph better explains the notion of similarity, combining formal definitions with simple examples and gives, through a graphical interface, some functional aspects to assist the user during the building of Similarity Relation.

4.5.1 Similarity Relation

More formally, the Similarity relation is a mathematical notion that provides a way to manage alternative instances of an entity that can be considered "equal" with a given degree (Klawonn and Castro 1994). The formal definition exploits the notion of T-norm which is a binary operation $\wedge : [0,1] \times [0,1]$ associative, commutative, non-decreasing in both the variables, and such that $x \wedge 1 = 1 \wedge x = x$ for any $x \in [0,1]$. In the sequel, we assume that $x \wedge y$ is the minimum between the two elements $x, y \in [0,1]$.

Definition 1: A Similarity on a domain $\mathcal{U}$ is a fuzzy subset $\mathcal{R}: \mathcal{U} \times \mathcal{U} \to [0, 1]$ of $\mathcal{U} \times \mathcal{U}$ such that the following properties hold

i) $\mathcal{R}(x, x) = 1$ for any $x \in \mathcal{U}$ (reflexivity)
ii) $\mathcal{R}(x, y) = \mathcal{R}(y, x)$ for any $x, y \in \mathcal{U}$ (symmetry)
iii) $\mathcal{R}(x, z) \geq \mathcal{R}(x, y) \wedge \mathcal{R}(y, z)$ for any $x, y, z \in \mathcal{U}$ (transitivity).
we say that $\mathcal{R}$ is strict if the following implication is also verified
iv) $\mathcal{R}(x, y) = 1 \Rightarrow x = y$.

The following notion of λ-cut is crucial in fuzzy set theory (Zadeh 1965), and it allows us to define a similarity by means of a suitable family of equivalence relations:

Definition 2: Let $\mathcal{U}$ be a domain and $\mathcal{R}: \mathcal{U} \times \mathcal{U} \to [0, 1]$ a fuzzy relation in $\mathcal{U}$. Then, for any $\lambda \in [0, 1]$, the relation $\approx_{\mathcal{R},\lambda}$ in $\mathcal{U}$ defined as

$$x \approx_{\mathcal{R},\lambda} y \Leftrightarrow \mathcal{R}(x, y) \geq \lambda$$

is named cut of level λ (in short λ-cut) of $\mathcal{R}$

The notion of λ allows us to define a similarity by means of a suitable family of equivalence relations according to the following result that can be easily proven.

Proposition 3: Let $\mathcal{R}$ be a similarity in a domain $\mathcal{U}$ and, for any $\lambda \in [0, 1]$ let $\approx_{\mathcal{R},\lambda}$ be the λ-cut of $\mathcal{R}$ Then, $\{\approx_{\mathcal{R}\lambda}\}_{\lambda \in [0,1]}$ is a family of equivalence relations such that,

i) for any μ and λ in $[0, 1]$ $\quad \mu \leq \lambda \Rightarrow \approx_{\mathcal{R}\lambda} \supseteq \approx_{\mathcal{R}\mu}$

ii) for any μ in $[0, 1]$, $\displaystyle\bigcap_{\lambda \leq \mu} \approx_{\mathcal{R}\lambda} = \approx_{\mathcal{R}\mu}$.

Conversely, let $\{\approx_{\mathcal{R}\lambda}\}_{\lambda \in [0, 1]}$ be a family of equivalence relations satisfying conditions i) and ii). Then the relation $\mathcal{R}$ defined by setting

$$\mathcal{R}(x, y) = Sup\{\lambda \in [0,1] \mid x \approx_{\mathcal{R}\lambda} y\}$$

is a similarity whose family of λ-cuts is equal to the family $\{\approx_{\mathcal{R}\lambda}\}_{\lambda \in [0, 1]}$

We concern with similarity defined in a finite domain $\mathcal{U}$. It implies that we have a discrete and ordered set of possible similarity values $\lambda_i \in [0,1]$, with i belonging to a finite set I of indexes. Then, the family $\{\approx_{\mathcal{R}\lambda}\}_{\lambda \in [0, 1]}$ in Proposition 3 is given by $\{\approx_{\mathcal{R}\lambda i}\}_{i \in I}$. The following example given in (Sessa 2001) shows the idea that a similarity can be described level-by-level by means of the family $\{\approx_{\mathcal{R}\lambda i}\}_{1 \leq i \leq n}$ of λ-cuts relations.

Example 4

Let U be the set

U={M, B, G, E, P, H, S, T, C, W, D }

where these letters stand for

M=*man,* B=*bear,* G=*gorilla,* E=*eagle,* P=*pigeon,* H=*hawk,*

S=*shark,* T=*tiger,* C=*cat,* W=*wolf,* D=*dog.*

We can define a similarity R between elements in U by setting for any x, y $\in$ U

R(x, y) = R(y, x)
R(x, y) = 1 if x=y
R(D, W) = R(E, H) =.8
R(M, G) = R(C, T)=.5
R(M, B) = R(B, G) = R(E, P) = R(H, P) = R(D, C) = R(D, T) = R(W, T) = R(W, C) = .2
R(x, y) = 0 otherwise. ·

As an example, by considering the cut relation $\approx_{R.2}$ of level λ =.2, the equivalence class of the element W is {W, D, C, T}, whereas by considering the cut relation $\approx_{R.7}$ of level λ =.7, the equivalence class of the element W is {W, D}.

An equivalent representation of R can be given by considering the quotient sets of the λ_i - cuts in the family $\{\approx_{R\lambda i}\}_{0 \leq i \leq 4}$, corresponding to the different similarity levels $\{\lambda_0, \lambda_1, \lambda_2, \lambda_3, \lambda_4\} = \{ 0, .2, .5, .8, 1\}$

$U/\approx_{R_1}$ = {{M}, {B}, {G}, {E}, {P}, {H}, {S}, {T}, {C}, {W}, { D}},

$U/\approx_{R.8}$ = {{M}, {B}, {G}, {E, H}, {P}, {S}, {T},{C}, {W, D}},

$U/\approx_{R.5}$ = {{M, G}, {B}, {E, H}, {P}, {S}, {T, C}, {W, D}},

$U/\approx_{R.2}$ = {{M, B, G}, {E, P, H}, {S}, {T, C, W, D}},

$U/\approx_{R.0}$ = {{M, B, G, E, P, H, S, T, C, W, D}}= {U}

For any x, y in U, the similarity value R (x, y) can be obtained by considering the maximum level $\lambda_i,$ with i $\in$ { 0, 1, 2, 3, 4}, such that the elements x and y belong to the same equivalence class in $\approx_{R\lambda i}$.

It is not easy to define a similarity in a set of elements by providing the similarity values R (x, y) for any x, y $\in$ U. Indeed, the transitivity constraint in Definition 1 can produce side effects which can contradict the assigned similarity values. According to Proposition 3, a level-by-level construction of the family $\{\approx_{R \lambda i}\}$ of λ_i-*cuts* allows to overcome this problem. The following algorithm, given in (Sessa 2001) is an interactive step-by-step procedure which in output provides the quotient sets of the family of λ_i-*cuts*. These partitions are defined according to guided choices interactively provided by the user.

Algorithm 5 BOTTOM-UP ALGORITHM.

INPUT: a domain $U = \{a_1, ..., a_m\}$ and the ordered set $\Delta = \{\lambda_0, ..., \lambda_n\}$, of similarity levels, with $0 = \lambda_0, \leq ... \leq \lambda_n = 1$

OUTPUT: the quotient sets $Q_i = \{ C_1^i, ..., C_{k_i}^i \}$, associated with the $\lambda_i\text{-}cuts$ in the family $\{\approx_{\lambda_i}\}_{0 \leq i \leq n}$.

set $k_0 = 1$, $C_{k_0}^0 = U$ and $Q_0 = \{C_{k_0}^0\}$;
for $i = 1, ..., n$
    set $Q_i = Q_{i-1}$;
    for $j = 1, ..., k_{i-1}$
        if C_j^{i-1} is a singleton;
            then continue;
      else
            get in input from the user $C_{j_1}^i, ..., C_{j_h}^i$ such that:
$$C_j^{i-1} = \bigcup_{1 \leq r \leq h} C_{j_r}^i \ \text{and}$$
$$C_p^i \cap C_q^i = \varnothing, \text{for any } p, q \in \{j_1, ..., j_h\};$$
            set $Q_i = (Q_i - C_j^{i-1}) \cup \{C_{j_1}^i, ..., C_{j_h}^i\}$;
        end for
end for
end

The previous algorithm starts from the trivial partition $Q_0 = U/\approx_0 = \{U\}$ corresponding in the intended similarity to the cut of level 0, where all the elements are in the same equivalence class. At any step a refinement of the previous partition is constructed.
More precisely, at any iterative step, the user provides the splitting of an equivalence class C_j^{i-1} in the quotient set Q_{i-1} of $\approx_{\lambda-1}$, on the basis of a subjective evaluation of a more significant similarity-level $\lambda_i > \lambda_{i-1}$ between elements in this class.
A top-down procedure can be also defined starting from the partition $Q_n = U/\approx_{\lambda n}$ corresponding to the cut of level 1. At any step, the user provides the new classes in Q_{i-1} as union of classes in the previous partition Q_i by relaxing the similarity constraint.
The following example shows an application of the Algorithm 5 (Sessa 2001).

Example 6

Let $\Delta = \{0, .4, .6, .8, 1\}$ be an ordered set of similarity values and U a set of geometric figures denoted with $U = \{F_3, F_4, F_5, F_6, F_8, C\}$ where these letters stand for

F_3 = triangle F_4 = square F_5 = pentagon

F_6=hexagon F_8 =octagon C =circle

The following steps can be obtained by exploiting the Algorithm 5

- $Q_0 = U/\approx_0 = \{\{ F_3, F_4, F_5, F_6, F_8, C\}\}$

- $Q_1 = U/\approx_{0.4} = \{\{ F_3\}, \{F_4, F_5, F_6, F_8, C\}\}$

- $Q_2 = U/\cong_{0.6} = \{\{ F_3\}, \{F_4, F_5, F_6 \}, \{F_8 , C\}\}$

- $Q_3 = U/\cong_{0.8} = \{\{ F_3\}, \{F_4, F_5\}, \{F_6\}, \{F_8 , C\}\}$

- $Q_1 = U/\cong_1 = \{\{ F_3\}, \{F_4\}, \{F_5\}, \{F_6\}, \{F_8\}, \{C\}\}$

This family of λ_i-cuts provides the similarity in U such that

$$\mathcal{R}(F_4, F_8) = \mathcal{R}(F_4,C) = \mathcal{R}(F_5, F_8) = \mathcal{R}(F_5, C) = \mathcal{R}(F_6, F_8) = \mathcal{R}(F_6, C) = .4$$

$$\mathcal{R}(F_4, F_5) = \mathcal{R}(F_4, F_6) = \mathcal{R}(F_8, C) = .6$$

$$\mathcal{R}(F_5, F_6) = .8$$

$$\mathcal{R}(x, y) = 0 \text{ otherwise.}$$

Let us stress that in the bottom-up Algorithm 5 the user provides the definition of the new classes $C^i_{j1}, ..., C^i_{jh}$ on the basis of subjective choices.

If, for the current level of similarity λ_i, the user thinks that there is not significant difference with respect to the previous level λ_{i-1}, the resulting quotient set Q_i will be equal to Q_{i-1}.

4.5.2 Implementation issues of Similarity Relation Building

The system provides a user-friendly way to characterize a subjective definition of the Similarity Relation (see subsection 4.5.1 and relative examples), on a given dictionary (compound of related terms which depict a shared topic).

The Figure 3 shows the user interface panel, aimed to assist the user during the building of the similarity relationship among the given terms.

According to the bottom-up Algorithm 5 in Subsection 4.5.1, the Similarity Builder panel in Figure 3 allows the user to define a new similarity relation, through the creation of the family of quotient sets which represent the λ_i-cut, $1 \leq i \leq n$. The system provides a default set of similarity values λ_i given by:

$$\lambda_0 = 0, \qquad \lambda_{i+1} = \lambda_i + 0.1 \qquad 1 \leq i < 10.$$

An interactive procedure helps to define the similarity among the terms of the chosen dictionary by showing these default similarity levels in a growing order. For any level λ_i, the user can define a new partition (corresponding to the λ_i-cut) by constructing the related equivalence classes as a refinement of the previous λ_{i-1}-cut. With this aim, the user subjectively selects some terms belonging to a class of the λ_{i-1}-cut (shown in the left-side list in the figure) and put them into the same class of the new λ_i-cut (shown in the right-side list). We recall that elements in the same class of a partition are related by similarity values greater than the considered λ_i level.

The construction starts from the trivial λ_0-cut, with $\lambda_0 = 0$, where all the elements belong to the same class. The text area at the bottom of the panel in Figure 3 shows the classes of the last specified partition (*previous partition*) and stands out the *splitting class* of this partition (the elements of the splitting class are listed in the left-side list).

In the example, the user is defining a new class of terms in the quotient set of the λ_i-cut, with $\lambda_i = .5$ by splitting the class C3 of the previous λ_{i-1}-cut, with $\lambda_{i-1} = .4$. In order to build the new class, the user puts in this class the terms that (with respect to a subjective evaluation) are linked by a similarity value greater than .5. In the text area on the bottom of the panel, the classes C1, C2, C3, C4, C5 of the previous λ_{i-1}-cut, with λ_{i-1} =.4, are listed and the current *splitting class* C3 is evidenced. When the splitting of this class is completed, the user clicks on the *Apply* button and the new established class is memorized. When the construction of the current λ_i -cut, with λ_i $_{-1}$ =.5 is completed through this refinement process of the previous λ_i $_{-1}$ -cut, with λ_i $_{-1}$ =.4, the user clicks on the *Save Partition* and the new λ_i-cut is saved. When the trivial λ -cut with only singleton classes is reached, a message "No refinement is possible" alerts that the splitting activity can be considered concluded. In any case this trivial partition automatically appears when the value of similarity λ =1 is reached. Once the construction of the family of λ-cuts has been completed, the user clicks on *Save Similarity* button and the overall similarity relation is saved on the disk: an appropriate window appears on the top of the screen, to assign a name to the new similarity relation.

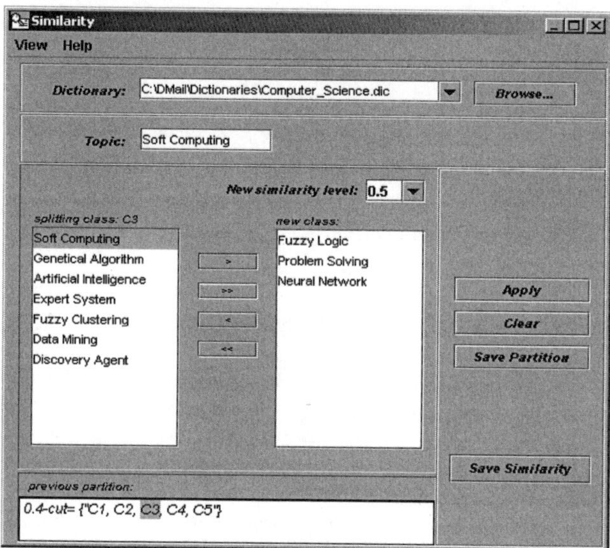

Figure 3: Graphical User Interface

4.6 Reasoning Model of Discovery Agents

The Discovery Agent performs its deduction using the similarity-based reasoning. This inference model is based on an extension of SLD Resolution, through a modified unification algorithm which becomes more tolerant when two not identical terms are compared: where, in the traditional approach, the classical algorithm fails, now the unification of them is successful, if there is a non zero similarity value between them.

The flexible inference system is performed through the encapsulation of Similarity relation in the deductive process, introduced in (Genesereth and Ketchpel 1994). Roughly speaking, we inject into an agent a similarity-based logic that is used as decision mechanism to capture local knowledge, during the spidering activity. This leads to the definition of *Similarity-based Agent*, i.e. an agent that inspects a site, recuperates some information to increase its knowledge baggage and, finally, according with the user request, deducts a useful evaluation of the interest of user in receiving the discovered information.

By exploiting mobile computation, the agent migrates on a web site, parses HTML-based pages and extracts information that are represented as ground predicates, i.e., *facts* of a classical Prolog program. These facts are, then, processed by the agent itself by means of an extension of an SLD Resolution towards similarity-based reasoning.

The following paragraph depicts the similarity-based extension of the Logic Programming paradigm, providing a more flexible SLD Resolution during the unification process.

4.6.1 Approximate deduction

In general, approximate reasoning capabilities are introduced in the Logic Programming framework by considering the inference system based on fuzzy logic rather than on conventional two-valued logic. Several approaches extend the resolution rule to some fuzzy logic systems as K-standard sequence logic (Lee 1972) and possibilistic logic (Dubois and Prade 1990). In (Kifer and Li 1988) a general formal semantics for rule-based systems with uncertainty is presented. Function free rules of the form $p(x, ...) : f(\alpha,..., \gamma)$ $\longleftarrow a(y,...) : \alpha, ..., c(u, ...) : \gamma$ are considered, where $p(x,...),\ a(y, ...),\ ...,\ c(u,...)$ are usual literals, $\alpha\ ...\gamma$ are variable or constant values in [0,1] representing certainty information about the associated literal, and f belongs to a finite set of functions. A generalization of the semi-naive bottom-up query evaluation procedure is also provided.

Several PROLOG interpreters based on fuzzy logic have been also presented in literature. The first implementation of the fuzzy resolution rule proposed in (Lee 1972) is given in (Ishizuka and Kanai 1985) with the PROLOG-Elf. In this system the inference takes care only of formulas with associated truth value greater than .5. Weighted rules are also exploited in the Fuzzy-PROLOG proposed in (Mukaidono *et al.*1989). However, the heuristic technique which enables to compute these weights, i.e. the truth values of the rules, hardly works and does not share the logical feature of the system. The language FPROLOG given in (Martin *et al.* 1987) tries to implement the capability of managing uncertain data represented by fuzzy sets. The basic idea is that some facts have associated truth value in [0,1] representing their degree of membership in the set of true assertions. The truth value of a rule is computed by the truth values of its conditions, according to a given combination operator. A PROLOG interpreter based on Lukasiewicz logic, named LULOG and written in Common Lisp, is presented in (Klawonn and Kruse 1994). Finally, for completeness sake, we also recall the fuzzy relational inference language FRIL presented in (Baldwin and Zhou 1984), which is a query language exploiting fuzzy relations, i.e., to any tuple t is associated a truth value $\chi(t) \in [0,1]$ denoting the degree to which t satisfies the relation. A fuzzy relational algebra is introduced. An operation in this algebra (as union, join, projection, etc.) takes one or more fuzzy relations as its operand(s) and produces a new fuzzy relation.

A new methodology that enhances the Logic Programming paradigm with approximate reasoning capability has been introduced in (Gerla and Sessa 1999). With respect to the previous literature, this approach is very different since the approximation is represented and managed at a syntactic-level, instead of at rule-level. Indeed, the fuzziness feature is provided by an abstraction process which exploits Similarity relations defined between elements in the alphabet of the language (constants, functions, predicate symbols). On the contrary, in the underground logic theory, the inference rule as well as the usual crisp representation of the considered universe is not modified. This avoids both the introduction of weights on the clauses, and the use of fuzzy sets as elements of the language. In order to introduce approximate reasoning capabilities in a logic program P on a function free language $\mathcal{L}$, in (Gerla and Sessa 1999) a Similarity Relation $\mathcal{R}$ is considered in the alphabet of $\mathcal{L}$. This relation provides non-zero Similarity value for constant or predicate symbols with the same arity, whereas it is the identity relation for variables. Then, the Similarity is extended to formulae in $\mathcal{L}$ and the inference process is enhanced by adding to the given program P all the clauses which have a non zero Similarity degree with a clause in P. A declarative fixpoint semantics has been also provided.

The operational counterpart of this approach is given in (Sessa 2002), where the *Similarity-based SLD Resolution* is introduced. A computed answer substitution provided by this procedure has an associate approximation degree λ in [0, 1] which gives a measure of the needed "tolerance" level to obtain such a solution. This procedure exploits a simple variation of the standard unification algorithm that provides the m.g.u. of two atoms. We recall that a mismatch between two function symbols or relation names causes a failure of the unification process. Then, it is rather natural to admit a more flexible unification in which the syntactical identity between function and predicate names is substituted by a Similarity $\mathcal{R}$.

In other words, if corresponding function or predicate symbols which are different have a non-zero Similarity degree in $\mathcal{R}$, the unification process does not fail. A consequence of this assumption is that atoms can be unified with different "tolerance" level of approximation.

As an example, let us consider the atoms p(a) and q(x), a Similarity $\mathcal{R}$ such that $\mathcal{R}(p, q) = .7$ and $\mathcal{R}(a, b) = .5$, and the substitutions

$$\vartheta_1 = \{x / a\} \qquad \vartheta_2 = \{x / b\}$$

which provide the instances

$$p(a)\,\vartheta_1 = p(a) \neq q(x)\,\vartheta_1 = q(a)$$
$$p(a)\,\vartheta_2 = p(a) \neq q(x)\,\vartheta_2 = q(b).$$

By assuming that the Similarity $\mathcal{R}$ replaces the equality relation, we have that the instances obtained by applying ϑ_1 and ϑ_2 can be considered "equal", but some "tolerance" must be exploited to overcome the mismatch between the predicate symbols p and q and the constant symbols a and b. In a straight way, a measure of this "tolerance" level can be expressed for ϑ_1 by the similarity value $\mathcal{R}(p, q) = .7$, and for ϑ_2 by $\mathcal{R}(p, q) \wedge \mathcal{R}(a, b) = .7 \wedge .5 = .5$ (i.e., the minimum between the similarity values which relate the mismatching symbols). It is intuitive that for higher values of Similarity exploited to overcome failures of matching, corresponds to a better value of "tolerance" which is needed to consider "equals" different symbols. Thus, it is natural to assume that an acceptable unifier must provide the maximum value of Similarity between the obtained instances.

The formalization of this extended notion of unification has been given in (Formato *et al.* (2000), where a generalized definition of *most general unifier* has been also provided as follows.

Definition 7: Given a Similarity $\mathcal{R}$, a substitution θ and two atoms with the same arity $A=p(t_1, ..., t_n)$ and $B=q(t'_1, ..., t'_n)$ in a first order language. We define the unification-degree $\upsilon_\mathcal{R}(A\theta, B\theta)$, of A and B, with respect to θ and $\mathcal{R}$, as follows.

$$\upsilon_\mathcal{R}(A\theta, B\theta) = \mathcal{R}(A\theta, B\theta) = \mathcal{R}(p, q) \wedge \left(\bigwedge_{i=0}^{n} \mathcal{R}(t_i\theta, t'_i\theta) \right).$$

If the predicate symbols of A and B have different arities, $\upsilon_\mathcal{R}(A\theta, B\theta) = 0$.

We say that a substitution θ is a weak unifier of A and B with unification-degree λ up to $\mathcal{R}$ (in short a λ-unifier) if

$$\lambda = \upsilon_\mathcal{R}(A\theta, B\theta) = \max_{\varphi \in \Psi} \upsilon_\mathcal{R}(A\varphi, B\varphi)$$

where Ψ denotes the set of all the substitutions.

Two atoms A and B are λ-unifiable up to R if there exists a λ-unifier for A and B with $\lambda >$ 0, otherwise we say that they are not unifiable.

It is easy to verify that θ is a classical unifier of A and B if and only if $\upsilon_R(A\theta, B\theta) = 1$.

In order to extend the classical pre-order between substitution, the equality is replaced by the λ-cut of R:

Definition8: Let θ and σ be two substitutions and R a similarity relation. We say that θ is more general than σ at the level λ up to R, denoted with $\theta \leq_{R,\lambda} \sigma$, if then exists a substitution ξ such that, for any variable x

$$x\sigma \approx_{R,\lambda} x\theta\,\xi$$

or equivalently $R(x\sigma, x\theta\,\xi) \geq \lambda$.

Then, the notion of most general unifier is extended as follows.

Definition 9: Given a substitution θ and two atoms A and B in a first order language with a Similarity R We say that θ is a weak most general unifier of A and B with unification-degree λ up to R (in short a λ-m.g.u.) if the following conditions hold:

i) θ is a λ-unifier of A and B

ii) $\theta \leq_{R,\lambda} \sigma$, for any σ which is a λ-unifier of A and B.

The Similarity-based SLD Resolution procedure introduced in (Sessa 2002) exploits the following modification of the classical unification algorithm in (Apt R.K. 1990), which provides a λ-m.g.u. for two atoms, if they are λ-unifiable, and a negative answer otherwise. The computed unification degree λ is considered as a constraint that must be satisfied in the derivation process. Then, the approximation degree associated to a computed answer substitution by a successful Similarity-based SLD derivation is the minimum of these constraints obtained in the derivation process. Obviously, an exact solution has approximation degree equal to 1.

WEAK-UNIFICATION ALGORITHM

Given two atoms $A=p(s_1, ..., s_n)$ and $B=q(t_1, ..., t_n)$ of the same arity to be unified, construct the associated set of equation:

$W = \{p = q, s_1 = t_1, ..., s_n = t_n\}$.

If $R(p, q) = 0$, the algorithm ends with failure, otherwise, set $U = R(p, q)$ and $W = W-\{p = q\}$. Non deterministically choose from the current set of equation W an equation of a form below and perform the associated action.

1. $f(s_1, ..., s_n) = g(t_1, ..., t_n)$ where $R(f, g) > 0$: replace by the equations $s_1 = t_1, ...,$ $s_n = t_n$, and set $U = U \wedge R(f, g)$
2. $f(s_1, ..., s_n) = g(t_1, ..., t_n)$ where $R(f, g) = 0$: halts with failure;

3. $x = x$: delete the equation;

4. $t = x$ where t is not a variable; replace by the equation $x = t$;

5. $x = t$ where $x \neq t$ and x has another occurrence in the set of equations: if x appears in t then halt with failure, otherwise perform the substitution $\{x/t\}$ in every other equations.

The following example highlights the main features of the previous weak-unification algorithm (Sessa 2002). Let us recall that constant symbols can be considered as functions with zero arity.

Example 10

Let us consider a Similarity $\mathcal{R}$ such that $\mathcal{R}(p, r) = .5$, $\mathcal{R}(f, g)=.7$, $\mathcal{R}(a, c)=.3$ and the two atoms $p(f(x), a, y)$, $r(g(b), c, f(x))$ to be unified. The weak-unification algorithm performs the following steps:

– Since $\mathcal{R}(p, r) = .5 \neq 0$ we consider the set $W_1 = \{f(x) = g(b), a = c, y = f(x)\}$ and $U=.5$.

– Choosing the equation $f(x) = g(b)$ in W_1, since $\mathcal{R}(f, g) = .7 \neq 0$ we have the new set $W_2 = \{x = b, a = c, y = f(x)\}$ and $U=.5 \wedge .7=.5$.

– Choosing the equation $x = b$ in W_2, since x has another occurrence in W_2, we have the new set $W_3 = \{x = b, a = c, y = f(b) \}$.

– Choosing the equation $a = c$ in W_3, since $\mathcal{R}(a, c) = .3 \neq 0$ we have the new set $W_4 = \{ x = b, y = f(b) \}$ and $U = .5 \wedge .3=.3$.

– Since W_4 is a solved set, the computed weak m.g.u. is $\xi = \{x/b, y/f(b)\}$ with $U=.3$.

Let us verify that ξ has unification degree .3.
$\upsilon_{\mathcal{R}}(\, p(f(x), a, y)\xi, r(g(b), c, f(x))\xi\,) =$
$$= \mathcal{R}(p, r) \wedge \mathcal{R}(f(b), g(b)) \wedge \mathcal{R}(a, c) \wedge \mathcal{R}(f(b), f(b)) = .5 \wedge .7 \wedge .3 \wedge 1 = .3.$$

Practically, the classical unification module is modified exploiting the Similarity Relation to guarantee a more flexible approach: where the traditional unification algorithm provides a m.g.u. between two atoms if and only if they match, the "weak" unification algorithm succeeds if two terms are not identical, but a similarity relation is defined between them.
Our bridge between approximate reasoning capabilities and fuzzy logic consists in the *Similarity-based SLD Resolution* (Sessa 2002).
This approach allows the approximation to be represented and managed at a syntactic-level, instead of at a rule-level. A computed answer substitution provided by this procedure has an associate approximation degree $\lambda \in [0, 1]$ which gives a measure of the needed "tolerance" level to obtain such a solution. We recall that a mismatch between two function symbols or relation names causes a failure of the unification process. The Similarity-based SLD Resolution exploits a more flexible unification in which the syntactical identity between function and predicate names is substituted by a Similarity $\mathcal{R}$. In other words, if corresponding function or predicate symbols which are different have a non-zero Similarity

degree in $\mathcal{R}$, the unification process does not fail. A consequence of this assumption is that atoms can be unified with a "tolerance" level λ of approximation. The unification algorithm introduced in (Sessa 2002) provides a λ-m.g.u. for two atoms, if they are λ-unifiable, and a negative answer otherwise. In MASIR platform, this algorithm is exploited to process information extracted from the HTML page, in order to compute the *relevance degree* of the returned information for a given request. The similarity-based inference engine is implemented by an extension of an existent Prolog, integrated with the Similarity Relation.

4.6.2 Similarity-based Prolog

This section details the extension of an existing Prolog interpreter towards similarity-based resolution (Loia *et al.* 2001/c). The extension has been realized considering Java as implementation tool. Figure 4 shows the main classes involved in this extension according to the UML description.

- *Engine* implements the parsing of the Prolog program and of the input goal. It handles the choice points and the variables to be un-bound upon backtracking.

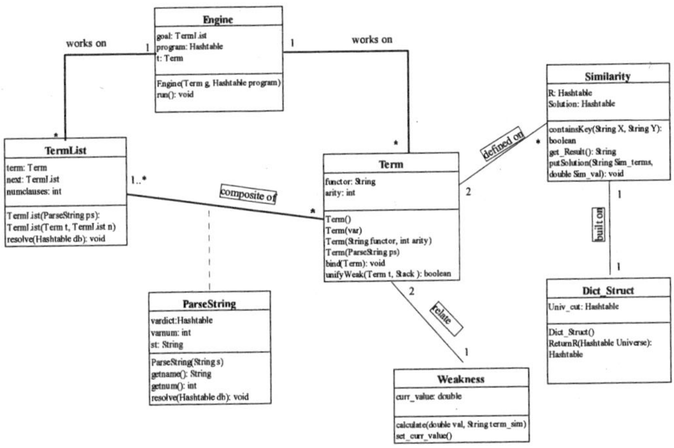

Figure 4: UML Classes Diagram

- *TermList* focuses on the execution on clauses with head by checking their syntactic correctness.
- *Term* represents the basic data structure in Prolog; it has several constructors, in particular it provides the extended similarity-compliant unification algorithm as explained in the following.
- *Weakness* checks, during the resolution process, if the value of similarity between the terms under unification, is smaller than the current one.
- *Dict_Struct* maintains, through an efficient structure, the λ-cut relations, in order to apply the similarity effects between the dictionary terms.
- *Similarity* keeps trace of the values deriving from similarity relations among elements of a dictionary. This class provides, moreover, some methods to check and update the similarity structure.

4.6.3 Weak Unification

Definitively, the weak unification realizes the extension of the inference engine. In fact, where the traditional unification algorithm provides a m.g.u. between two atoms if and only if they match, the "weak" unification algorithm succeeds if two terms are not identical, but a similarity relation is defined between them   (Sessa 2002). Here, the correspondent algorithm follows.

```
// INPUT: t₁, t₂ terms to unify
// OUTPUT: boolean value TRUE or FALSE


1  BOOLEAN UnifyWeak(t₁, t₂) {
2    if t₁ is a reference to another term then
3          return unifyWeak(ref(t₁), t₂);
4    if t₂ is a reference to another term then
5          return unifyWeak(t₁, ref(t₂));
6    if t₁ and t₂ are values (bound and not referenced) then
7          if (t₁.arity == t₂.arity) AND Check_Similar(t₁.functor, t₂.functor) {
8              // recursive call on arguments functor
9              for i=0 to t₁.arity
10                      return unifyWeak(t₁.arg(i), t₂.arg(i))
11            return TRUE
12        } else
13            return FALSE
14        } // at least one arg not bound ...
15   if (t₁ is bound) {
16      //verify occur check
17      if (t₁ not occurs in t₂) {
18          bind t₁ to t₂
19          return TRUE
20      } else return FALSE
21   } else
22   if (t₂  not occurs in t₁) {
23      bind t₁ to t₂
24      return TRUE
25   } else return FALSE
26 }
```

```
// INPUT: f₁, f₂ term functors to check if they are equal
// OUTPUT: boolean value TRUE or FALSE


1  BOOLEAN Check_Similar( f₁, f₂)
// R is a structure (an hashtable) to store the similarity relations among the terms.
2      if f₁ == f₂ then return TRUE     // f₁ and f₂ are equal
3    else
4        if ∃ couple (f₁, f₂) in Similarity.R :  sim_degree: = R.getValue(f₁, f₂)  ≠ 0 then
5            if sim_degree < current_minimal_degree then
6                current_min_degree = sim_degree
7            return TRUE
8      else
9            return FALSE
```

The *UnifyWeak* algorithm realizes a traditional unification between two terms: the lines above show the case when the terms are some references to other terms, are bound or are free variables. The extension of inference process towards a more "tolerant" unification is performed in line 7, where a call to another function is shown. *Check_Similar* realizes a test to verify if the functors of terms are identical or not. If the functors are equal (line 2), the algorithm works in the classical way and returns TRUE to the UnifyWeak algorithm. Otherwise, if the previous test fails (the functors are not identical), the lines 4-9 of *Check_Similar* are executed: the system verifies if there is a similarity value R between the two functors f_1 and f_2. The Similarity class, in Figure 4, maintains the complete similarity relation among dictionary terms: the relation R can be structured as a hashtable, associating each couple of terms to a similarity degree.

The value of similarity, *sim_degree*, is compared with the stored current one (line 5), *current_min_degree* in order to maintain the minimal similarity value between term couples (line 76). If the test in line 4 succeeds (a relation between f_1 and f_2 exists), the system updates the values and returns TRUE to *UnifyWeak* algorithm.

Then the execution proceeds via recursive calls on function arguments (lines 8-10).

Let us suppose there is the following similarity degree between two terms *Fuzzy Logic* and *Neural Network*:

$$R(\text{'}Fuzzy\ Logic\text{'},\ \text{'}Neural\ Network\text{'}) = 0.6.$$

During the inference process, the system has to prove some goals such as *topic(Paper, `Fuzzy Logic')* on the specified Prolog program.

So, it tries to unify the goal with all the clauses which have the predicate *topic* in the head.

For example, let us assume that the following fact of the program is reached:

topic(paper_102, 'Neural Network').

where both the arguments are ground terms.

In accordance with the *UnifyWeak* algorithm, the test in the line 7 succeeds; indeed the two functors *topic* have the same arity and the function *Check_Similar* returns TRUE, because the functor names are equal. Then applying the recursive procedure on arguments (lines 9-10 of *UnifyWeak*), the variable *Paper* is bound to the ground term *paper_102*, and the test of line 7 succeeds (the lines 4-7 of *Check_Similar* function are verified).

Since an entry in the R structure exists for the couple *Fuzzy Logic* and *Neural Network* with associated similarity degree 0.6 is extracted, the unification process successfully ends.

4.7 Info-Miner: Example of User Application

This section is devoted to give an example of an application that runs on the MASIR environment. Figure 5 shows the Info-Miner query interface. It can be splitted in two different areas: the upper one is dedicated to specify the Grasshopper's parameters setting, the other one is the interface to be filled by the user during the query formulation.

The parameters related to configure the agent-based environment are applied to use the Grasshopper platform, in order to guarantee reliable agent's communication, migration and interaction. The MASIR environment localizes the available running mobile agent domain: through the physical addresses where the Grasshopper regions and places are active, the agent are launched to execute their tasks.

The query specification area is build through a tabbed panel. The user can insert the appropriate information, both defining the search criterion and selecting the expected information to be returned, when the Web searching is completed.

The information required by the user concerns scientific documents, and is defined in terms of correlated fields (authors, proceedings or journal contribution, publication date, topic(s), ...).

At query mode, the user specifies the search mode, by setting the web domain to be analyzed and the depth level searching (a parameter that limits the visiting of possible Web sites).

Finally, by activating options at the bottom of the query interface, the user may choose what kind of information the search returns as result of the spidering search.

In our example of Figure 5, the user looks for papers appeared in a *Conference* after the year *1999*, dealing with the topic *Soft Computing*.

The query is transformed in the following Prolog-like goal:

*? - doc(IdPage, IdDoc, Author, Title), topic(IdDoc, ['Soft Computing']),
    doc_reference(IdDoc, 'Conference'), after(IdDoc, Date, 1999),...photo(IdPage, Author, File).*

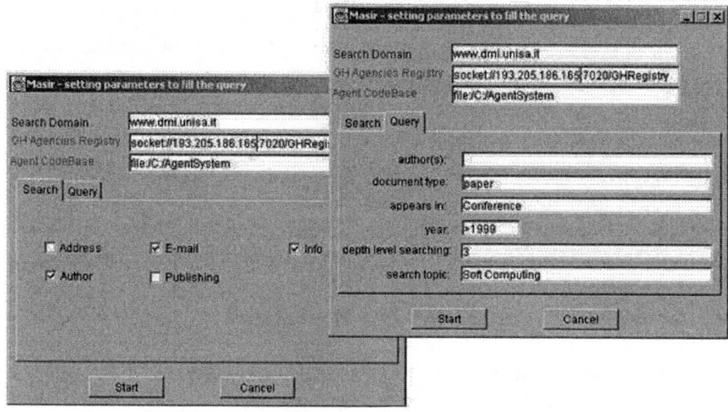

Figure 5: Web Search Interface

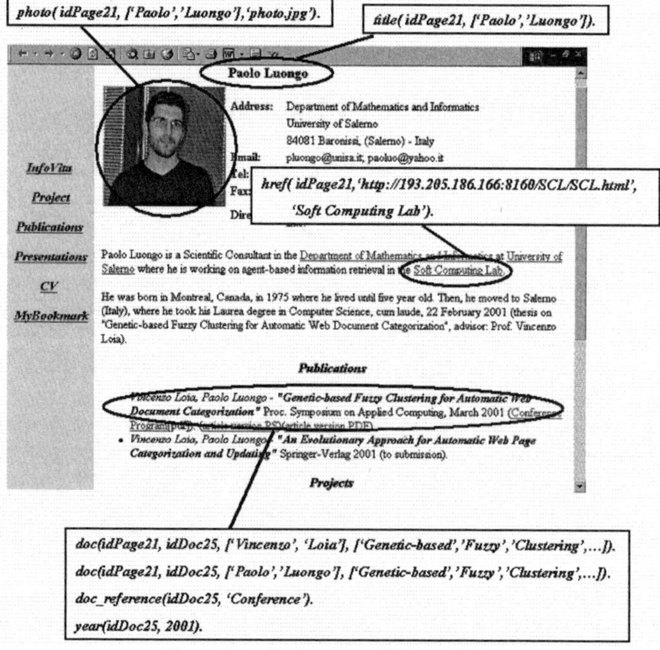

Figure 6: A Web page and its knowledge

The Discovery Agent dispatched on the specified Web area (in the example our department site), tries to prove the previous goal, using the facts extracted from the "contacted" Web page and its knowledge-base of Prolog rules.

In particular, Figure 6 shows a Web page where the Discovery Agent extracts useful knowledge in terms of Prolog facts.

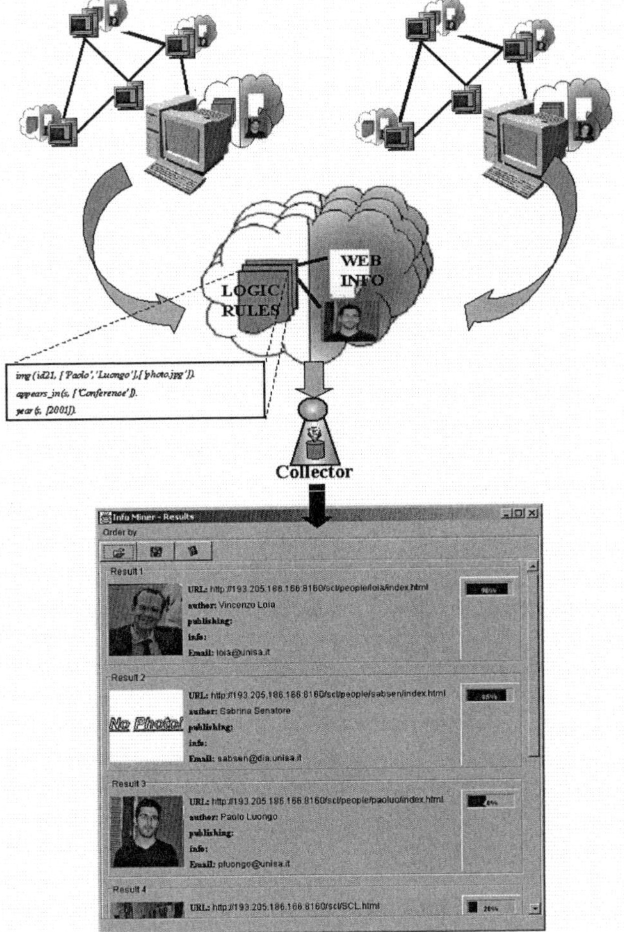

Figure 7: From Single spots of information to unified view

These facts are processed by the Similarity-based Resolution, taking into account the similarity relations established by the user.

To better clarify the extended resolution procedure, let us suppose the user has defined a similarity degree $\lambda = 0.7$ between the term *Soft Computing* and the term *Fuzzy* and that, in the proof of the main goal, the variable IdDoc has as value 'idDoc25'. During the SLD resolution process, the subgoal *topic(IdDoc, ['Soft Computing'])* has to be proved.

The knowledge-base used in the proof consists of a number of logic predicates, among them the ones used to treat the subgoal *topic*.

Let us consider one of these predicates:

topic(IdDoc, Arg) :- doc(IdPage, IdDoc, Author, Title), is_in(Arg, Title).

This rule succeeds when in the title of the document (logic variable *Title*) appears the term *Arg*. The unification of the two values *['Genetic-based', 'Fuzzy', 'Clustering', ...] (Title)* and *'Soft Computing' (Arg)*, does not fail, as in the case of "standard" SLD Resolution, thanks to an existing similarity relationship.

Thus the subgoal *topic(IdDoc, 'Soft Computing')* succeeds with approximation degree 0.7.

The results are finally returned to the Collector Agent, charged to fuse the different replies in an efficient visualization, as shown in Figure 7. The system displays the authors' photos (if available) and other information related to the found Web page, according to the user's requirements. The relevance of the results is expressed through the Similarity value computed for the specific Web page.

4.8   Related pages through the Similarity Relation

The described architecture is designed to extract useful information, according to a user's request. The user must fill the fields of the interface by following a specific format: this behavior could be viewed as a rigid formalism. It is useful to relax these constraints to guarantee a more user-friendly, flexible approach, without functional restrictions.

In the following we discuss a different approach to Web searching where the input to the retrieval process is not a user query, but a well-specified Web page: frequently users want to look for Web pages that present aspects (structural and contextual) that are similar to a given page. The system responds to this kind of query returning a set of Web pages that have similar context and deals with related arguments.

In this section we propose an enhancement of the Similarity notion, by introducing into the system a query model exploiting a similarity-based context analysis. Within this aim, we introduce a new operator, named *MIS* (Matching In Similarity) which allows us to provide a relation, based on similarity, between parts of text. This operation is employed as a simple and powerful mechanism to directly represent the user's intentions.

4.8.1   Matching in Similarity between Parts of Text

Let V be the vocabulary of the given natural language, without the articles. With V^+ here we denote the set of all the *sequences* of elements in V. Let $\mathcal{R}$ be a similarity defined in V , which states degrees of approximation between different elements in V and let $I = \{ \lambda_1, \lambda_2, ..., \lambda_n \}$ with $0 = \lambda_1 < \lambda_2 < ... < \lambda_n = 1$ the set of the considered similarity values.

Definition 11: The Matching in Similarity, denoted with MIS is an operator MIS : $V^+ \times V^+ \rightarrow I^+$, such that for any A, B $\in V^+$ with A = (a_1, a_2, ..., a_n), B = (b_1, b_2, ..., b_m) and m $\leq$ n, it is:

$$MIS(A, B) = (\mathcal{R}(a_{h1}, b_1), \mathcal{R}(a_{h2}, b_2), ..., \mathcal{R}(a_{hm}, b_m))$$

where $\mathcal{R}(a_{hk}, b_k) = \max_{1 \leq i \leq n} \{\mathcal{R}(a_i, b_k)\}$ for any k = 1,..., m.

The previous definition can be given in a similar way in the case that n $\leq$ m.
Roughly speaking, the MIS operator manages parts of text as lists of words. Assuming without loss of generality that the length of the first list is less or equal than the second, for any word in the first list the best similarity value with respect to the element of the second list is computed.

4.8.2 Some MIS functions

The application of MIS operator returns a sequence of similarity degrees which represents the combination of words whose matchings (similarity relation) are closer. In order to obtain an adequate filtering tool, several kinds of evaluation can be made on the output of the MIS operator. In the following some function of the MIS operator are shown.
More formally, we introduce the following notion:

Definition 12: Let $\theta : \Gamma^+ \rightarrow [0, 1]$ be a function. The function θ, named valuer, is applied on the output of the MIS operator. Some simple examples of valuers are shown in the following, where $A, B \in V^+$ and MIS $(A, B) = (\gamma_1, \gamma_2, ..., \gamma_m)$ with $\gamma_i \in \{ \lambda_1, \lambda_2, ..., \lambda_n \}$:

$$average(MIS\ (A,\ B)) = \frac{1}{m} \sum\nolimits_{i=1}^{m} \gamma_i$$

$$max(MIS\ (A,\ B)) = \max_{1 \leq i \leq m} \gamma_i$$

$$percent(MIS\ (A,\ B)) = \frac{k_\lambda}{m}$$

where k_λ is the number of values in $\{\gamma_1, \gamma_2, ..., \gamma_m\}$, that are greater or equal to a fixed $\lambda \in (0, 1]$.

4.8.3 Related Pages

In order to provide a suitable measure to compare parts of text (extracted from different Web pages), we use the similarity valuer applied on a sequence of MIS values. Every MIS value is obtained by comparing "homogeneous" features extracted from the Web page. In particular we use as set of features some HTML tags, by distinguishing content-based from context-based information. More formally, given two Web pages P_1 and P_2 we define the function:

*Definition 13: $Sim(P_1, P_2) = \Delta\ (\theta_1(MIS(X_1, Y_1)), \theta_2(MIS(X_2, Y_2)), ..., \theta_i(MIS(X_i, Y_i)))$
where $X_i \in \{ title(P_1), h1(P_1), href(P_1), ... \}$, $Y_i \in \{ title(P_2), h1(P_2), href(P_2), ... \}$ and $\Delta, \theta_1, ..., \theta_i$ are valuers.*

The operators in the set {title, h1, href, ...} correspond to agent-based entities that are designed to recognize specific sections in the Web page and to convert the section data into a knowledge-based representation.

4.8.4 Content/Contextual View

Currently there is no standard in the realization of a Web page. In our approach, to gain flexibility in the Web page analysis, the interpretation of the overall page is handled by a set of distinct, independent extractor agents. An extractor is an agent entity specialized to:

1. identify the corresponding view;
2. extract the information related to the tag;
3. transform this information into a deductive-oriented representation.

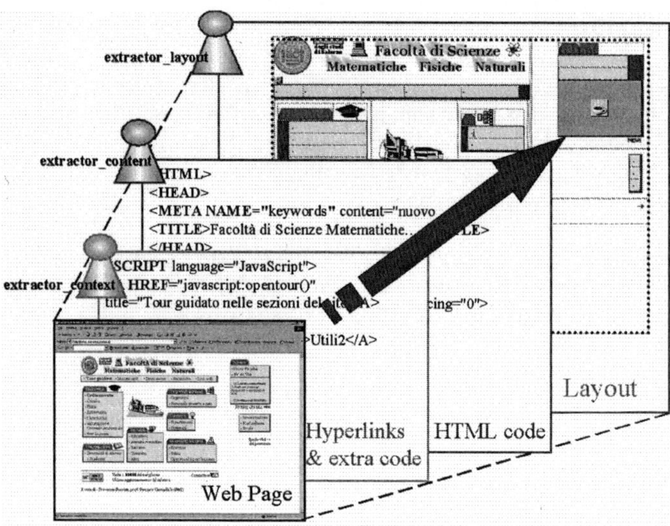

Fig. 8. Different views of a Web page: every view characterizes a meaningful portion, handled by a designed agent.

The logical union of the extractors, comprehensive of their cooperation activities, gives a uniform, complete model of the Web page. The model is essentially composed of two kinds of information. The first is originated from the tags identifying content-based data (title, body, meta, h1, l1, etc.). The second kind of information concerns the contextual nature of the Web page, expressed in terms of other tags, among them the href tag, used to link the page to another Web resource. The href tag contains, in some cases, useful textual information that is appropriately filtered from other data inherent to href, and exploited to acquire important knowledge about the page itself.

4.8.5 Agents Classification

The architecture is based on the interaction of different typologies of agents, according to the assigned task to solve. Some task-oriented agents concern the knowledge-based extraction, in order to acquire information from the Web portions of the given pages (see Figure 8); other agents operate to realize the spidering activity and to collect relevant information, in order to return a ranked sequence of similar pages.

Considering the knowledge-based extraction activity, we outline the following agents:

- *meta extractor*: it is a coordinator agent that realizes a light analysis of the Web page, organizing it in some specific, distinct areas. For each area, the agent, successively, triggers a more skilled extractors designed to handle a restricted section of a Web page.
- *extractor layout*: this agent examines the framework of a Web page, considering some structural part, relative to the layout of the page (frameset, table, etc.). They realize a comparison (skeleton level) between the two Web documents.
- *extractor content*: its ability is to process specific sections of a Web page (HTML tags as <title>, <p>, <h1>, <meta>, etc.), to extract textual patterns, and finally to translate them into formal knowledge (Prolog facts, ground terms). This knowledge is then injected into the discovery agent.

- *extractor context*: this agent processes the tags of hyperlinks (<href>) and some extra code enclosed in <script> tags.

The other group of agents, useful for Web searching is organized as discovery and collector agents:

- the *discovery agent* moves on the net to reach the destination site (Figure 9). The parsing activity is realized in collaboration with the extractor agents which are created during the parsing. Initially a single discovery agent starts and moves towards the destination: once reached the Web page, it starts its activities, cloning himself when an external hyperlink (to a domain external to the current one) is found;
- the *collector agent* is able to manage the visualization by performing some predefined ranking.

4.8.6 Interactions among agents

Given a Web page as input, the goal is to look for pages whose structure, layout and arguments are similar to the input page. The agents realize the cooperation and interaction activities to converge towards this target.

When the user provides the model page, the meta extractor scans it and triggers an appropriate extractor agent according with the considered section. Each extractor agent contributes to extract additional information to increase the knowledge of the discovery agent. This means to generate Prolog facts, such as:

```
metatag(IdPage, TypeTag, TextTag).
title(IdPage, TextTitle).
h1(IdPage, TextHeading).
href(IdPage, Url, TextUrl).
```

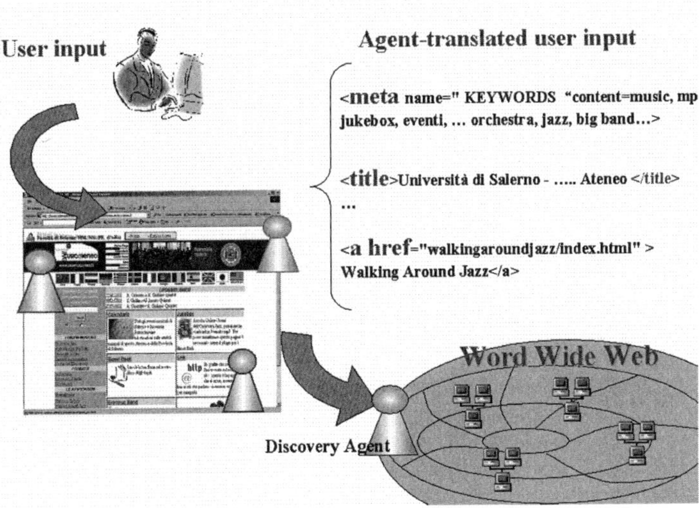

Fig. 9. Input Web page for the spider activity

The collected knowledge is injected into the discovery agent, which is designed to explore the net. When this agent reaches the destination site, it creates and triggers the meta extractor; this last starts a light parser activity and then runs the appropriate extractor agents when relevant Web tags are encountered. The new information becomes part of the discovery agent knowledge.

The process is repeated each time a new page is analyzed.

4.8.7 Attitudes of the Discovery Agent

The deductive model of a discovery agent is extended through the MIS operator, introduced in subsection 4.8.1. During the examination of the current page, the discovery agent interacts with the extractor agents, each one dedicated to analyze specific HTML sections. Knowledge (in forms of Prolog rules) is extracted from the Web page given as input by the user. The Web documents, analyzed during the spidering activity, become part of this knowledge. More precisely, for each contacted Web document, the discovery agent compares the knowledge representation of the input page with the acquired knowledge of the just analyzed page. The discovery agent, through the SIM operator, is able to evaluate how the Web pages are similar (Figure 10).

Operatively, this task is accomplished by the following glance of code.

```
sim(InputPage, ReachedPage) :-
            compare(title(InputPage, TextTitle1), title(ReachedPage, TextTitle2)),
            compare(h1(InputPage, TextHeading1), h1(ReachedPage, TextHeading2)),
            compare(metatag(InputPage, TypeTag, TextKeywords1),
            metatag(ReachedPage, TypeTag, TextKeywords2)),
            compare(href(InputPage, Url1, TextUrl1), href(ReachedPage, Url2,
            TextUrl2)), ...
```

where the variables *InputPage, TextTitle1, TextHeading1, TextKeywords1, Url1, TextUrl1* are relative to the user-given Web page; the other variables *ReachedPage, TextTitle2, TextHeading2, TextKeywords2, Url2, TextUrl2* are inherent to spidering-returned pages.

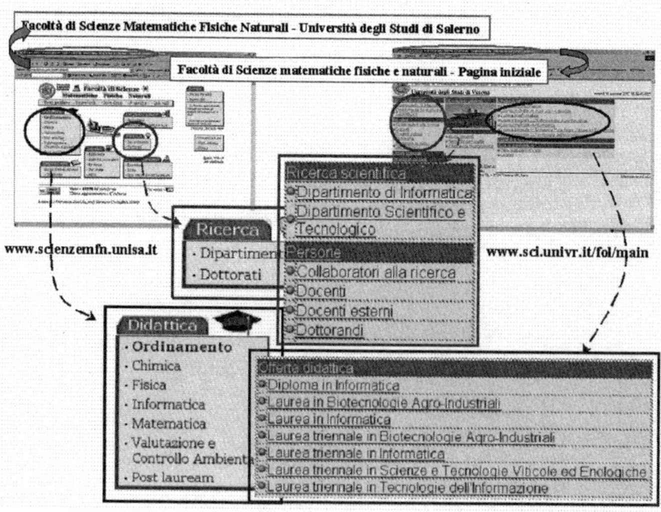

Fig. 10. Two similar pages: a Web page from Univ. of Salerno and a Web page from Univ. of Verona

The variable TypeTag enables to characterize the type of meta-tag, when more than one tag of this kind is encountered. The predicate *compare* allows us to define some rules to characterize the MIS operator (see subsection 4.8.1). As an example of a rule defined for this predicate, the following form is given:

```
compare(title(InputPage, TextTitle1), title(ReachedPage, TextTitle2)) :- mis(TextTitle1, TextTitle2).
```

To emphasize the agent's behavior, some details about the Prolog-like code (in the previous glance of code mis predicate are not described) are missed, delineating a basic idea of the deductive reasoning model of the discovery agent. Exploiting the MIS operator, the agent infers additional information to decide the relevance of a page in the provided Web context.

Conclusion and Future Works

The Web is a cheap and powerful utilitarian medium. Its explosion is due to the simple fact that common users are able to communicate, to find answers, to locate services, to download. Nowadays users find difficulties in achieving these goals, in particular in locating resources. This important goal is compromised by the unexpected, irregular evolution of the Internet. To reduce this problem, it is necessary to explore alternative strategies able to introduce deductive capabilities inside the core of Web search engines (Nikravesh *et al.* 2002).
Within this frame, we are studying the role of similarity-based approximate reasoning, to make more flexible the model of query management and, concurrently, to better bridge the gap between the available information and the wanted one.
The similarity-based reasoning model takes a central role in the design of intelligent system (Itan and Mukaidono 2001). This approach is pursued in the design of our agent-based architecture suitable for advanced Web-based Information Retrieval: previous experiments done in different area, such as email address mining (Loia *et al.* 2001b, 2001d) or scientific document retrieval (Loia *et al.* 2002) proved the utility in combining similarity with agent-based deductive systems.
In this paper the role played by deductive mobile agents has been presented as key issue of Distributed Information Retrieval framework, supported by the MASIR platform. Agents become tolerant to approximate information thanks to a similarity-based reasoning embedded into a logic programming deductive system. MASIR offers different information-retrieval features. Its structure allows future developments without significant changes in the bulk architecture. In the study of new techniques for Web searching (Tajima and Takagi 2001), the last part of this paper introduces an extension of Web searching technique for discovering "similar" Web documents, by using fuzzy-context reasoning. Instead of putting one or more keywords in the query, the user introduces (the URL) of a Web Page describing the user expectations. The system is then responsible to return a list of URLs, characterizing similar Web pages.

References

Apt R.K. (1990) "Logic Programming", *in: J. van Leeuwen (Ed.)*, volume B, pages 492-574. Elsevier, Amsterdam.

Baeza-Yates R., Ribeiro-Neto B. (1999) *Modern Information Retrieval*. Addison Wesley Longman Publishing Co. Inc.

Baldwin J.F. and Zhou S.Q. (1984) *A fuzzy relational inference language*, pages 155-174, 14.

Dubois D. and Prade H. (1990) "A fuzzy evolutionary approach to the classification problem". *Resolution principles in possibilistic logic, Int. Journal of Approximate Reasoning*, 3:1-21.

Dunlop M. (1997) "Time relevance and interaction modeling for information retrieval". In *Proceedings of the 20th Annual International ACM-SIGIR Conference on Research and Development in Information Retrieval*. Belkin N. J., Narasimhalu A. D. and Willett P. eds.

Formato F., Gerla G., Sessa M.I. (2000) "Similarity-based unification". *Fundamenta Matematicae*, 40:1-22.

Gallaire H. and Nicolas J. M. (1978) "Database:Theory vs. interpretation". In H. Gallaire and J. Minker Eds., editors, *Logic and Database*, pages 33-54. Plenum Press.
Genesereth, M.R. and Ketchpel S.P. (1994) Software agents. *Communications of the ACM*, 38(8):48-53.

Gerla G. and Sessa M.I. (1999) "Similarity in Logic Programming". In *G. Chen, M. Ying, K.-Y. Cai (Ed.s). Fuzzy Logic and Soft Computing,* pages 19-31. Kluwer Acc. Pub., Norwell.

Grasshopper Development System, Light Edition, Release 1.2.2 URL: http://www.ikv.de/products/grasshop- per/ index.html

Ishizuka M. and Kanai N. (1985) "Prolog-Elf incorporating Fuzzy Logic". *In Proceedings of 9th Int. Joint. Conf. on Artificial Intelligence*, pages 801.803. Springer, Berlin.

Itan R. and Mukaidono M. (2001) "Redundant Object and Dependency of Domain Attributes in α-Coverings of the Universe". *In The 10th IEEE International Conference on Fuzzy Systems*, Melbourne, Australia, December 2-5.

Kifer M. and Li A. (1988) "On the semantic of rule-based expert systems with uncertainty". In *Proceedings of Inter. Conf. on Databases Theory 1988, Lecture Notes in Computer Science*, volume 326, pages 186-202. Springer, Berlin,

Klawonn F. and Castro J.L. (1994) "Similarity in Fuzzy Reasoning". *Mathware and Soft Computing*, pages 197-228, 1995.

Klawonn F. and Kruse R. (1994) "A Lukasiewicz Logic based Prolog". *Mathware and Soft Computing*, 1:5-29.

Lancaster, F.W. (1968) *Information Retrieval Systems: Characteristics, Testing and Evaluation*. Wiley, New York,.

Lawrence S. and Giles L. (1999) "Accessibility and Distribution of Information on the Web". *In Proceedings of The International Symposium on Language for Intensional Programming*, volume 400, pages 107-109. Nature.

Lee, R.C.T. (1972) "Fuzzy logic and the resolution principle". *Journal of the ACM*, pages 109-119.

Loia V., Luongo P., Senatore S. and Sessa M.I., (2001a) "A Similarity-based View to Distributed Information Retrieval with Mobile Agents", in *The 10th IEEE International Conference on Fuzzy Systems*, Melbourne, Australia, IEEE Press.

Loia V., Luongo P., Senatore S. and Sessa M.I., (2002) "Info-Miner: bridging agent technology with approximate information retrieval", in *2002 AFSS International Conference on Fuzzy Systems*, Science City, Calcutta, India, 3-6 February, Lectures Notes in Computer Science, Springer.

Loia V., Senatore S. and Sessa M.I. (2001b) "Similarity-based Agents for Email Mining." *In Proc. of the joint Conference IFSA/NAFIPS 2001*, Vancouver, Canada, July 25-28.

Loia V., Senatore S. and Sessa M.I., (2001c) "Similarity-based SLD Resolution and its implementation in an Extended Prolog System", in *The 10th IEEE International Conference on Fuzzy Systems*, Topic Area: T5, Melbourne, Australia, IEEE Press.

Loia V., Senatore S. and Sessa M.I. (2001d) "Given a message, find legitimate readers: a flexible MailBot-based Approach". *2001 IEEE International Conference on Systems, Man and Cybernetics (IEEE SMC 2001)*, October 7-10.

Martin T.P., Baldwin J.F., Pilsworth B.W. (1987) "The implementation of FProlog a Fuzzy Prolog interpreter". *Fuzzy Sets and Systems*, 23:119-129.

Mukaidono M., Shen Z.L., Ding L., (1989) "Fundamentals of Fuzzy PROLOG", *Int. Journal of Approximate Reasoning* volume 3, pages 179-193.

Nikravesh M., Loia V., Azvine B. (2002) "Fuzzy Logic and the Internet" *Soft Computing*, 6:287-299.

Reiter R. (1984) "Towards a logical reconstruction of relational database theory". In M.L. Brodie, J. Mylopoulous, J. W. Scmidt Eds., *On Conceptual Modelling*, pages 191-238. Springer.

Sessa M.I. (2002) "Approximate Reasoning by Similarity-based SLD Resolution", *Theoretical Computer Science*, 275:389-426.

Sessa M.I. (2001) "Translations and Similarity-based logic programming". *Soft Computing Journal*, 5 issue 2:160-170.

Tajima M. and Takagi T. (2001) "Query Expansion Using Conceptual Fuzzy Sets For Search Engine". *In The 10th IEEE International Conference on Fuzzy Systems*, Melbourne, Australia, December 2-5.

Yao Y. Y., Zhong N., Liu J., Ohsuga S. (2001) "Web Intelligence: Research Challenges and Trends in the New Information Age, in Web Intelligence: Research and Development." In Lectures *Notes in Artificial Intelligence*, volume 2198, pages 1-17. Springer-Verlag.

Zadeh L.A., (1965) "Fuzzy sets", *Information and Control*, issue 8:338-353.

Zadeh L.A., (1971) "Similarity Relations and Fuzzy Orderings", *Information Sciences*, volume 3, pages 177-200.

Chapter 5

Collaborative Agents in Data Exploration

Witold Pedrycz
George Vukovich

5.1 Introduction

In the ocean of data over the Internet, we are interested in the development of agents that help make sense of data. The agents collaborate between themselves by exchanging information or knowledge they have acquired on an individual local basis. By their nature, agents do not explore the complete WWW space but concentrate on some domain while gaining a global picture through collaboration, refer to Figure 1.

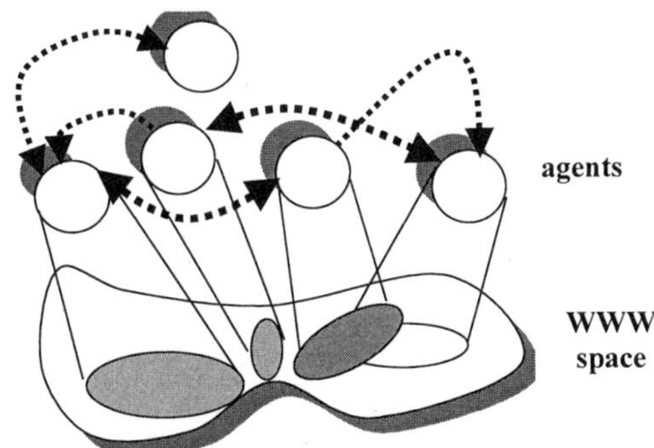

Figure 1. Agents exploring the WWW space and their collaborative links (higher level); note that the collaboration occurs in a reciprocal manner (two-directional links shown as dotted lines) and functional manner (in which one of the agents assumes a leading role - the corresponding link is one-directional).

We distinguish between two evident levels: the first one concerns an interaction with the WWW while the second dwells on the collaboration between the agents. As the first one is completed at the level of numeric entities, the second is about the interaction and collaboration being inherently realized at the level of information granules. At the implementation end, this concept is realized in the framework of fuzzy clustering.

The collaboration-driven task outlined above calls for an orchestrated effort and implies a highly collaborative nature of search for dependencies in data so that such findings are common and relevant to all databases (as such discoveries of global character are of genuine interest). To shed light on the spectrum of the processing problems, we identify possible scenarios along with existing drawbacks and envision potential mechanisms of collaboration:

Search for a common structure in databases. Within a given organizational structure (company, network of sales offices, etc.), there are several local databases of customers (e.g., each supermarket generates its own database or a sales office maintains a local database of its customers). Generally, we can assume that all databases have the same attributes (features) while each database consists of different objects (patterns). To derive some global relationships that are common to all these databases, we should allow the databases to collaborate at the level of the patterns. Quite commonly, we may not be permitted to have access to all databases but eventually could be provided with some general aggregates (say, some synthetic indexes describing data; a mean value or median are a good example in this case). Refer to Figure 2 that illustrates the underlying concept. Bearing this in mind, we can talk about *vertical* (data based) collaboration in the process of knowledge elicitation (that is revealing a common structure in the data).

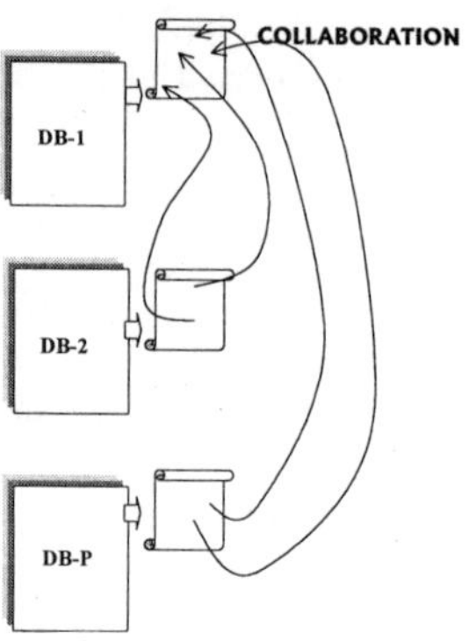

Figure 2. Vertical collaboration between databases at a local level; in each database objects are located in the same data space but deal with the different patterns.

Security issues and discovery of data structures across different datasets. Consider now that information about the same group of clients is collected in different databases where an individual company (bank, store, etc.) builds its own database. Because of confidentiality and security requirements, the companies cannot share information about clients in a direct manner. However all of them are vitally interested in deriving some associations that help them learn about clients (namely, identifying their profiles and needs). As they are concerned with the same population of clients, we may anticipate that the basic structure of the population of such patterns, in spite of possible minor differences, should hold across all databases. The approach taken in this case would be to build clusters in each database and exchange information at the level of the clusters treated here as information granules. Subsequently, we allow all collaboration processes to be realized at this particular level. In this manner, the security issues are not compromised while a sound mechanism of collaboration/ interaction between the databases becomes established. Graphically, we can envision the situation of such collaboration as the one portrayed in Figure 3. Evidently, in this case we are concerned with a *horizontal* (that is feature-based) collaboration in the search for the data structure.

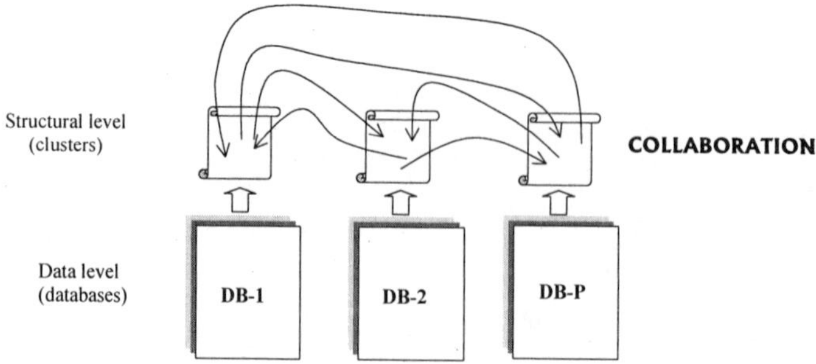

Figure 3. Collaboration between databases at the level of "local" structures (clusters) discovered there; note that no direct collaboration at the data level is allowed.

As the structure elicitation is profoundly a user-oriented and user-friendly process, we are interested in the collaborative clustering as its results are information granules. In the sequel, this gives rise to a certain type of collaboration as indicated before, namely a vertical collaborative clustering that involves databases involving various objects and horizontal clustering where we are faced with the same objects but being characterized by various attributes.

The general picture of collaboration showing a bi-directional and one directional facets of collaboration is outlined in Figure 4. This sets up an overall scheme of reasoning behind the proposed algorithms.

Moving on to the algorithmic issues are concerned, the underlying idea of collaboration dwells on a well-known Fuzzy C-Means (FCM) cf. (Bezdek 1981).

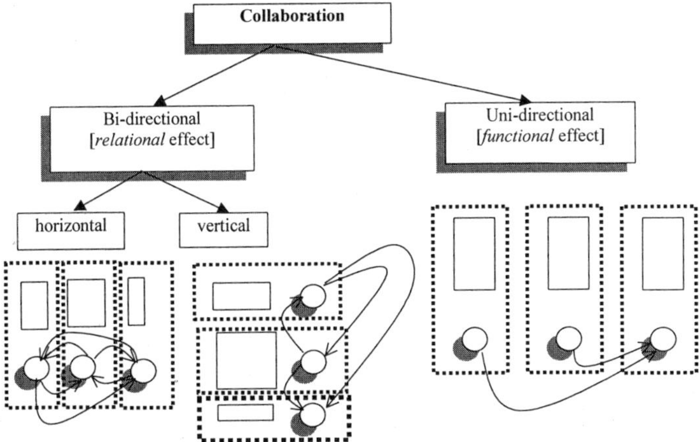

Figure 4. Various facets of collaboration and interaction between the algorithmic frameworks.

The reader may refer to pertinent details as to the generic method that is used as a canvass of the collaborative schemes developed in the study. In general, we can think of clustering (Bezdek 1981, Duda *et al.* 2001, Kandel 1986, Kersten 1999, Pedrycz 1998) as a vehicle of forming information granules. It is also worth stressing that fuzzy clustering arose as a fundamental and highly appealing technique in construction of fuzzy models; refer e.g., to (Delgado *et al.* 1997, Delgado *et al.* 1998, Pedrycz, W., 1995). Moreover the collaborative clustering can be cast in the realm of intelligent agents cf. (Loia and Sessa 2001) whose activities may center around discovering and sharing knowledge.

Owing to the nature of the problem in which we address its relational and directional facet we will be referring to it as a *collaborative* information granulation. The satisfaction of relational and directional requirements helps reflect the structure in the data as well as optimize the mapping itself (in the sense being outlined above). To link the problem more closely with fuzzy modeling, it is worthwhile to refer to relational models that are models developed in the framework of fuzzy relational equations. Commonly, we proceed with a collection of fuzzy relations (or fuzzy sets) defined in the input and output space and design (estimate) a fuzzy relation that attempts to form the best mapping between these information granules. Evidently, this formulation deals with the directional aspect of the problem. The relational aspect must have been dealt with earlier (when the fuzzy relations were formed, e.g., through some clustering) and is totally disjoint from the estimation of the mapping. Intuitively, it would be advantageous to have a unified approach where the relational and directional aspects are handled together.

In this study, we propose a new scheme of building information granules in the collaborative fashion to capture the relational and directional aspects of information granulation. We formulate the problem first and then cast it in an operational framework of fuzzy clustering, especially the commonly used FCM environment. It is discussed how the objective function has to be modified and what type of the constraint optimization problem arises there. The type of the granular mapping to be optimized is in the form of the logic–based expression using OR and AND logic connectives.

The chapter is so organized as follows. In Section 5.2, we start with a problem formulation by discussing an overall scheme of horizontal clustering. The derivation of the complete optimization algorithm is discussed in Section 5.3 that is followed by a discussion of the flow of the optimization pursuits in Section 5.4. Next we quantify the mechanisms of collaboration by looking at the impact the locally discovered structures have on each other. Vertical collaboration is studied in Section 5.6 and this is followed by unidirectional (functional) collaboration covered in Section 5.7. Discussion on an optimization phase is given in Section 5.8.

5.2 Horizontal Clustering: Fundamentals

In what follows, we consider "p" subsets of data located in different spaces (viz. the patterns there are described by different features). As each subset concerns the same patterns (that is each pattern results as a concatenation of the corresponding subpatterns), the number of elements in each subset is the same and equal to N. We are interested in partitioning the data into "c" fuzzy clusters. The result of clustering completed for each subset of data comes in the form of a partition matrix and a collection of prototypes. We use a bracket notation to identify the specific subset. Hence we use the notation $U[ii]$ and $v_i[ii]$ to denote the partition matrix and the i-th prototype produced by the clustering realized for the ii-th set of data. Similarly, the dimensionality of the patterns (number of their features) in each subset could be different; to underline this we use a pertinent index, say $n[ii]$, $ii=1, 2, \ldots,p$. The distance function between the i-th prototype and k-th pattern in the same set is denoted by $d_{ik}^2[ii]$, $i=1, 2, \ldots,c$, $k=1, 2, \ldots,N$. Again, the index used here underlines the fact that we are dealing with a certain data space pertinent to the ii-th data set (database). Furthermore we confine ourselves to the weighted Euclidean distance that takes the form

$$d_{ik}^2[ii] = \| x_k - v_i[ii] \|_{ii} = \sum_{j=1}^{n[ii]} \frac{(x_{kj} - v_{ij}[ii])^2}{\sigma_j^2[ii]}$$

where $\sigma_j[ii]$ is a standard deviation of the j-the feature. The objective function guiding the formation of the clusters that is completed for each subset assumes a well-known form as being encountered in the standard FCM method

$$\sum_{k=1}^{N} \sum_{i=1}^{c} u_{ik}^2[ii] d_{ik}^2[ii]$$

$ii=1,2, \ldots,p$. The collaboration between the subsets is established through a matrix of connections (interaction coefficients or interactions, for brief). Each entry of the collaborative matrix states describes an intensity of the interaction. In general, $\alpha[ii, kk]$ assumes nonnegative values. The higher the value of the interaction coefficient, the stronger the collaboration between the corresponding subsets. To accommodate the collaboration effect in the optimization process, the objective function is expanded into the form

$$Q[ii] = \sum_{k=1}^{N} \sum_{i=1}^{c} u_{ik}^2[ii]d_{ik}^2[ii] +$$

$$+ \sum_{\substack{jj=1 \\ jj \neq ii}}^{P} \alpha[ii, jj] \sum_{k=1}^{N} \sum_{i=1}^{c} \{u_{ik}[ii] - u_{ik}[jj]\}^2 d_{ik}^2[ii]$$

ii=1, 2, …, p. The role of the second term standing in the above expression is to make the clustering based on the ii-th subset "aware" of some other partitions. It becomes obvious that if the structures in all datasets are similar then the differences between the partition matrices tend to be lower. On the other hand, if we encounter higher differences, we anticipate that the collaboration will be able to address these needs.

As usual, we require that the partition matrix satisfies 'standard" requirements of membership grades summing to 1 for each patterns and the membership grades contained in the unit interval. All in all, the collaborative clustering converts into the following family of "p" optimization problems with membership constraints

$$\text{MinQ[ii] subject to } U[ii] \in \mathbf{U}[ii]$$

where $\mathbf{U}[ii]$ is a family of all fuzzy partition matrices (Delgado *et al.* 1998). The minimization is carried out with respect to the fuzzy partition and the prototypes. This problem and its solution are discussed in detail in the ensuing section.

5.3 The Optimization Scheme

The above optimization task splits into two problems, namely a determination of the partition matrix U[ii] and the prototypes $v_1[ii]$, $v_2[ii]$, …, $v_c[ii]$. These problems are solved separately for each of the collaborating subsets of patterns. To determine the partition matrix, we exploit a technique of Lagrange multipliers. The augmented objective function V[ii] that we consider separately for each "k" comes in the form

$$V[ii] = \sum_{i=1}^{c} u_{ik}^2[ii]d_{ik}^2[ii] + \sum_{\substack{jj=1 \\ jj \neq ii}}^{P} \alpha[ii, jj] \times$$

$$\times \sum_{i=1}^{c} \{u_{ik}[ii] - u_{ik}[jj]\}^2 d_{ik}^2[ii] -$$

$$- \lambda(\sum_{i=1}^{c} u_{ik}[ii] - 1)$$

where λ denotes a Lagrange multiplier. The necessary conditions leading to the local minimum of V[ii] read as follows

$$\frac{\partial V[ii]}{\partial u_{st}[ii]} = 0, \quad \frac{\partial V[ii]}{\partial \lambda} = 0$$

s = 1, 2, …,c, t = 1, 2, …,N. To come up with a concise expression, we introduce some auxiliary notation

$$\varphi_{st}[ii] = \sum_{\substack{jj=1 \\ jj \neq ii}}^{P} \alpha[ii, jj]u_{st}[jj]$$

and

$$\psi[ii] = \sum_{\substack{jj=1 \\ jj \neq ii}}^{P} \alpha[ii, jj]$$

The solution to the optimization problem is the partition matrix

$$u_{st}[ii] = \frac{\varphi_{st}[ii]}{1 + \psi[ii]} + \frac{1}{\sum_{j=1}^{c} \frac{d_{st}^2}{d_{jt}^2}}[1 - \sum_{j=1}^{c} \frac{\varphi_{jt}[ii]}{1 + \psi[ii]}]$$

In the calculations of the prototypes we use explicitly the weighted Euclidean distance between the patterns and the prototypes. The prototypes are computed in the form

$$v_{st}[ii] = \frac{A_{st}[ii] + C_{st}[ii]}{B_s[ii] + D_s[ii]}$$

$s=1,2, \ldots, c, t=1, 2, \ldots, n[ii], ii=1, 2, \ldots P$

The coefficients in the above expression are computed as follows

$$A_{st}[ii] = \sum_{k=1}^{N} u_{sk}^2[ii]x_{kt}[ii]$$

$$B_s[ii] = \sum_{k=1}^{N} u_{sk}^2[ii]$$

$$C_{st}[ii] = \sum_{\substack{jj=1 \\ jj \neq ii}}^{P} \alpha[ii, jj] \sum_{k=1}^{N} (u_{sk}[ii] - u_{sk}[jj])^2 x_{kt}[ii]$$

$$D_s[ii] = \sum_{\substack{jj=1 \\ jj \neq ii}}^{P} \alpha[ii, jj] \sum_{k=1}^{N} (u_{sk}[ii] - u_{sk}[jj])^2$$

(note that $x_k[ii]$ denotes a k-th pattern coming from the ii-th subset of patterns).

5.4 The General Scheme of Collaboration

The general clustering scheme consists of two phases:

(i) generation of clusters without collaboration. This phase involves the use of the FCM algorithm applied individually to each subset of data. Obviously, the number of clusters needs to be the same for all the datasets. During this phase we seek independently a structure in each subset of data

(ii) collaboration of the clusters. Here we start with the already computed partition matrices, set up the collaboration level (through the values of the interaction coefficients arranged in $\alpha[ii,jj]$) and proceed with a simultaneous optimization of the partition matrices

Moving on to the formal algorithm, the computational details are organized as a sequence of steps

<u>Given</u>: subsets of patterns $\mathbf{X}_1$, $\mathbf{X}_2$, ..., $\mathbf{X}_P$

<u>Select</u>: distance function, number of clusters (c), termination criterion, and collaboration matrix $\alpha[ii,jj]$.

Initiate randomly all partition matrices $U[1]$, $U[2]$, ..., $U[p]$

<u>Phase I</u>

For each data

    repeat

    compute prototypes $\{\mathbf{v}_i[ii]\}$, i=1, 2, ...,c and partition matrices $U[ii]$ for all subsets of patterns

    until a termination criterion has been satisfied

<u>Phase II</u>

    repeat

    For the given matrix of collaborative links $\alpha[ii,jj]$ compute prototypes and partition matrices $U[ii]$

    until a termination criterion has been satisfied

The termination criterion relies on the changes to the partition matrices obtained in successive iterations of the clustering method.

5.5 Quantification of Collaboration Mechanism

There are two levels of assessing a collaboration effect occurring between the clusters, namely the level of data and the level of information granules (that is fuzzy sets included in the partition matrix). In this latter quantification, we use the results of clustering without any collaboration as a point of reference.

The *level of data* involves a comparison carried out at the level of the numeric representatives of the clustering, that is the prototypes. The impact of the collaboration is then expressed in the changes of the prototypes occurring as a result of the collaboration.

At the *level of information granules* (partitions and fuzzy sets), the effect of collaboration is expressed in two ways as shown schematically in Figure 5 where the collaboration involves two datasets (viz. p=2) indicated by **1** and **2**. Similarly, by **1-ref** and **2-ref** we denote the results (partition matrices) resulting from the clustering carried out without any collaboration. First, we express how close the two partition matrices are as a result of the collaboration. The pertinent measure reads as an average distance between the partition matrices $U_1=[u_{ik}[\mathbf{1}]]$ and $U_2=[u_{ik}[\mathbf{2}]]$, that is

$$\delta = \frac{1}{N*c}\sum_{k=1}^{N}\sum_{i=1}^{c}u_{ik}[\mathbf{1}] - u_{ik}[\mathbf{2}]|$$

Evidently, the stronger the collaboration (higher values of the corresponding α), the lower the values of δ. In this sense, this index helps us translate the collaboration parameters (α) into the effective changes in the membership grades (that are the apparent final result of such interaction). The plot of δ regarded as a function of α can be useful in revealing how the collaboration phenomenon takes place. It tells how much the data subset is susceptible to the collaborative impact coming from the other subsets of patterns. For instance, no changes in the values of δ for increasing values of αs is an indicator of strong differences existing between the structures in the two datasets.

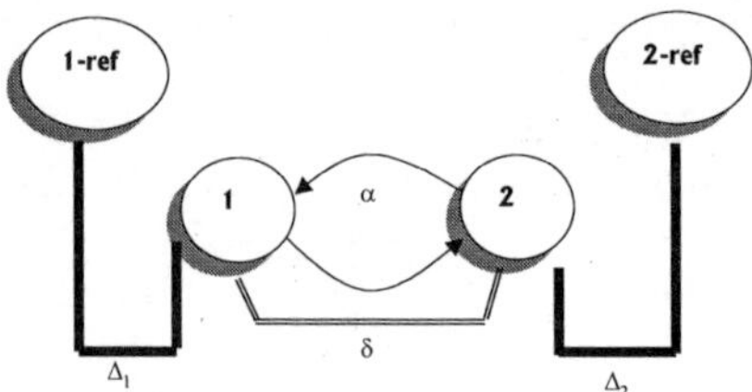

Figure 5. Quantification of collaboration at the level of information granules; see a detailed description in text.

The second criterion takes into consideration the results of clustering obtained without any collaboration and treats this as a reference point. Using such partition matrices, we quantify how far the collaboration affects the results of clustering. For instance, for the first data set we get

$$\Delta_1 = \frac{1}{N*c} \sum_{k=1}^{N} \sum_{i=1}^{c} u_{ik}[\mathbf{1}] - u_{ik}[\mathbf{1-ref}]|$$

For the second data subset the expression reads in the form

$$\Delta_2 = \frac{1}{N*c} \sum_{k=1}^{N} \sum_{i=1}^{c} u_{ik}[\mathbf{2}] - u_{ik}[\mathbf{2-ref}]|$$

While the above index exhibits a global character, one can investigate the changes at the level of the individual cluster and patterns. This local behavior of the collaboration is helpful in identifying elements whose membership grades are affected quite significantly as a result of collaboration and those whose structure is compatible across all datasets.

5.5.1 Experiments

In the series of numeric experiments, we use a Boston housing data available on the WWW, see ftp://ftp.ics.uci.edu/pub/machine-learning-databases/housing/. It consists of 506 patterns describing real estate in the Boston area. There are 14 features describing the patterns. These include crime rate, nitric acid concentration, median value of the house, just to name a few. We distinguish between two subsets of features where the first one can be treated as descriptors of social aspects of the data

> **A** ={per capita crime rate by town, nitric oxides concentration (parts per 10 million), proportion of owner-occupied units built prior to 1940, weighted distances to five Boston employment centers, pupil-teacher ratio by town, % lower status of the population, median value of owner-occupied homes in $1000's}

and

> **B** ={proportion of residential land zoned for lots over 25,000 sq.ft, proportion of non-retail business acres per town, Charles River dummy variable (equal to 1 if tract bounds river; 0 otherwise), average number of rooms per dwelling, index of

accessibility to radial highways, full-value property-tax rate per $10,000, 1000(Bk - 0.63)^2 where Bk is the proportion of blacks by town}

In the following experiments we set up the number of the clusters to be equal to 5, c=5. Several scenarios of collaboration are discussed; see Figure 6 for its schematic notation. As only two subsets of data are involved, we drop indexes in the collaboration matrix; the meaning of collaboration becomes obvious from the context.

In all experiments we start with clustering that takes place without any collaboration (it was found that the number of iterations equal to 60 was enough to assure no changes to the partition matrices that is the optimization process could be deemed complete). At the next phase the collaboration takes place.

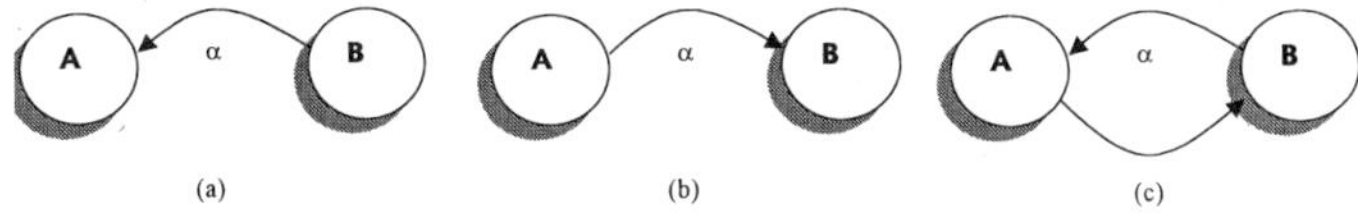

Figure 6. Scenarios of collaborative clustering used in the experiments.

a. There is a collaborative link originating from **B** and affecting **A**. The values of this link (α) are set successively to 0.05, 0.1, 0.5 and 1. The values of the objective function are shown in Figure 7; as expected the objective function assumes higher values for the increasing levels of collaboration (this is not surprising by noting that the collaboration component contributes additively as a part of this objective function). Noticeable are the drops in the values of the objective function occurring at the beginning of the entire optimization.

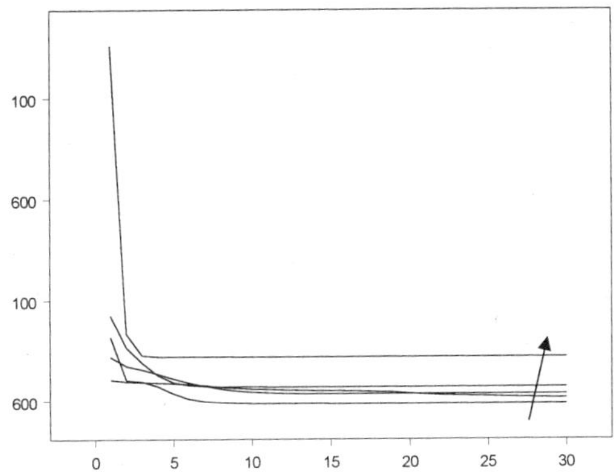

Figure 7. The values of the objective function in successive iteration steps of the algorithm and selected values of the collaborative link (namely 0.05, 0.1, 0.5, and 1).

The resulting prototypes change once the collaboration assumes different intensity as shown below

α=0.5
v_1= [12.840698　0.675343　92.033089　1.984616　19.896008　21.301111　13.195952]
v_2= [0.291484　0.437043　32.688419　6.474721　16.880703　6.680616　27.994970]
v_3= [0.880803　0.528872　68.019592　3.802059　18.728121　12.382829　21.436878]
v_4= [0.639216　0.500246　60.230255　4.270203　17.784111　8.671939　26.960485]
v_5= [8.554115　0.661536　89.209915　2.277547　19.955612　17.302109　17.229208]

$\alpha=1.0$
$v_1=$ [13.185606 0.673498 91.076195 2.016629 19.926291 20.879652 13.254309
$v_2=$ [0.264656 0.435453 33.055351 6.535963 16.788097 6.537128 28.447708
$v_3=$ [0.759657 0.527652 67.316498 3.848079 18.747555 12.533010 21.190838
$v_4=$ [0.561581 0.500323 59.888401 4.340404 17.798523 8.690695 26.753359
$v_5=$ [9.424790 0.663229 88.969498 2.242356 19.995226 17.504406 17.110945

For comparative reasons, the prototypes of the subset **A** without any collaboration are listed as follows

$v_1=$ [11.491062 0.688633 94.221016 1.930663 19.940283 21.444845 13.103884]
$v_2=$ [0.394793 0.439771 31.897591 6.384313 17.012272 6.963907 27.159363]
$v_3=$ [0.860573 0.489002 52.550468 4.605259 18.520782 9.673503 24.041653]
$v_4=$ [1.307117 0.536930 75.181625 3.334807 17.237040 9.618564 27.298693]
$v_5=$ [3.288866 0.601333 86.465401 2.696251 19.858582 15.527621 18.926182]

One can note that higher values of α lead to more evident translations of the prototypes in comparison to their original location when no collaboration took place. The prototypes in each data set start resembling each other. The collaboration effect can be quantified in the language of membership functions (partition matrices). Following the notation introduced in Section 5.3, the values of the indexes δ and Δ_1 are illustrated in Figure 8.

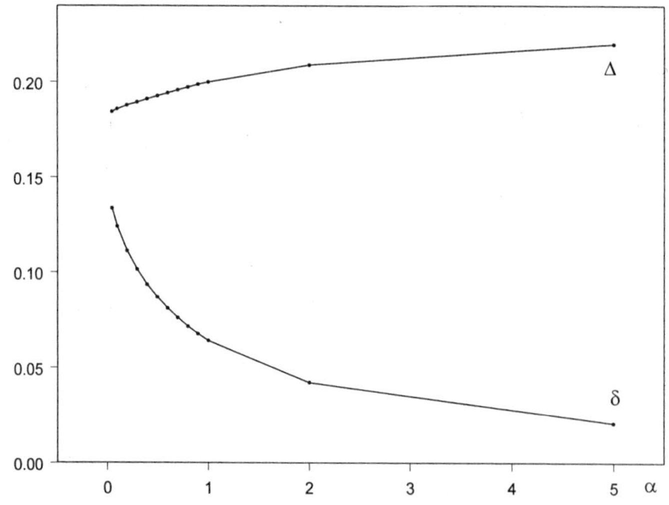

Figure 8. Values of δ and Δ for selected values of α.

As anticipated, the values of δ become lower as the collaboration level increases while Δ_2 gets higher as we depart from the "local" partition matrix (viz. the one computed without any collaboration) being under collaborative pressure to accept some other sources of information about the overall data structure.

b. This experiment deals with the collaboration originating from the second group. The collaboration effect is quantified in Figure 9. In comparison to the other collaborative scheme, there is a quite comparable level of changes in the membership grades. The only significant jump is reported when a collaboration effect comes into a play.

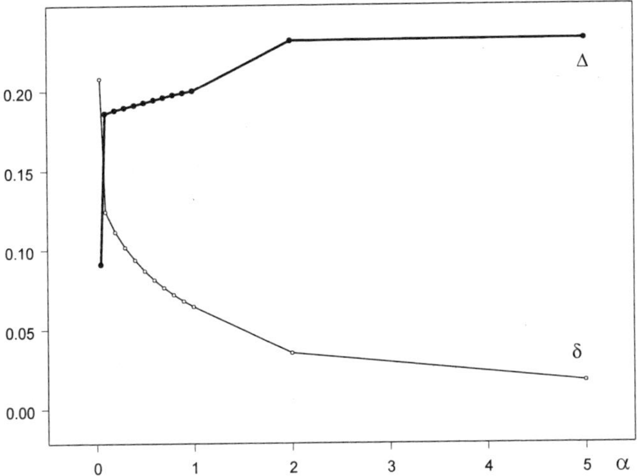

Figure 9. Values of δ and Δ for some selected values of α.

c. In this case, we allow for the collaborative links to be reciprocal that is **A** and **B** interact; see Figure 10. The results are shown in the form of δ as well as Δ_1 and Δ_2. The values of δ go down monotonically as values of α go higher. An interesting effect occurs in terms of the collaboration: **A** tends to be more stiff as to the collaborative interaction; the values of Δ_1 in spite of the increasing interaction (higher values of α). **B** is more flexible in terms of the collaboration more readily accepting collaborative signals that manifest in the increasing values of Δ_2.

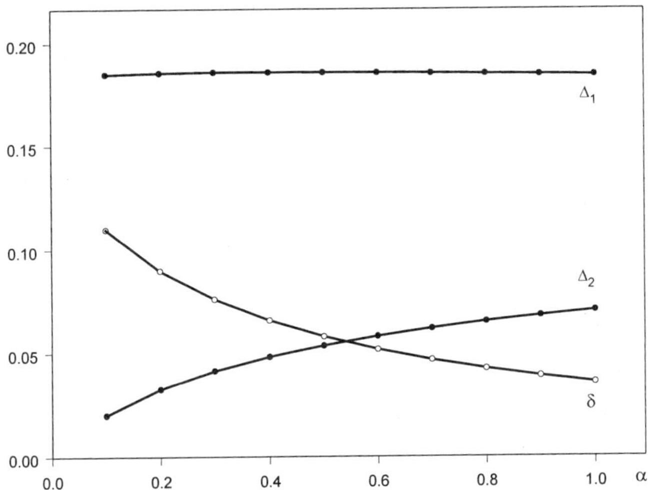

Figure 10. Values of δ and Δ for selected values of α.

In the following experiments, we split the features into two groups: the first one (**A**) includes all the features but the price of real estate that forms the second group (**B**). The collaborative link is activated by the first group (namely this group affects the clustering realized within **B**).

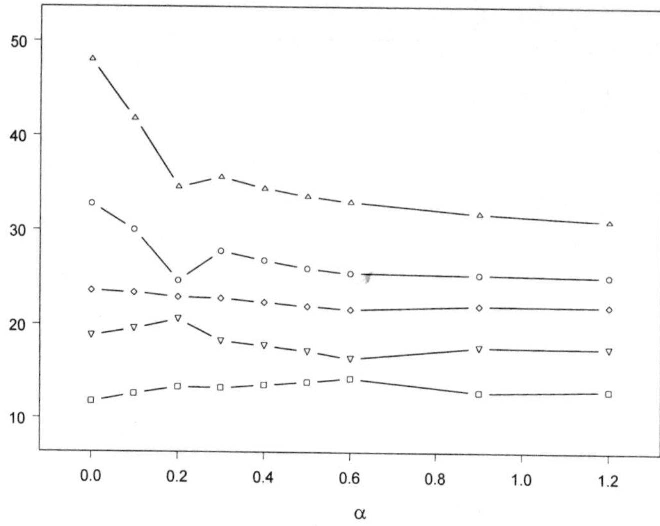

Figure 11. Prototypes in the median value of real state as a function of the collaboration linkage α.

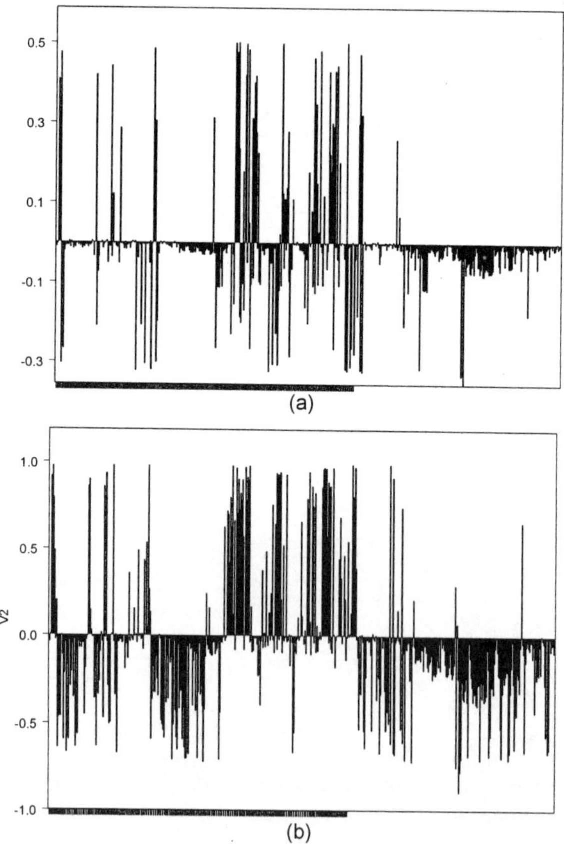

Figure 12. Changes in the membership grades for the first cluster for α =0.2 (a) and α=0.5 (b).

The prototypes in the median value of house change depending on the values of the collaborative feedback. Noticeably, with the increase of the collaboration (denoted by α) the prototypes tend to occupy more narrow range in comparison to the situation where no interaction was present, refer to Figure 11.

There is also another way of investigating the way of visualizing the effects of collaboration by looking at the changes in the membership grades caused by the collaboration. The changes in the membership grades occurring for the two selected levels of collaboration are shown in Figure 12.

Now we keep changing the number of clusters while retaining the same level of collaboration ($\alpha = 0.5$) to analyze how this affects the changes of δ and Δ.

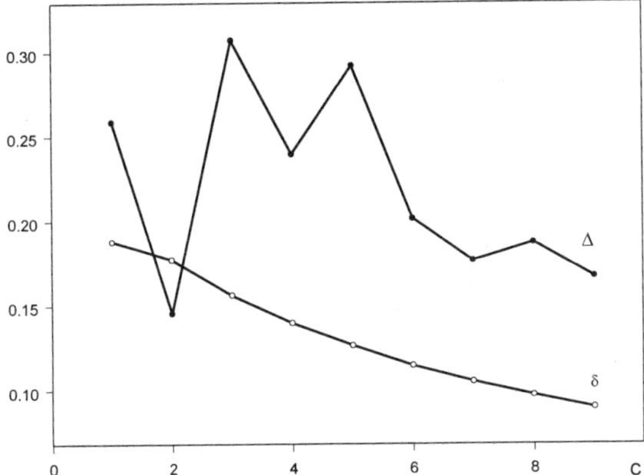

Figure 13. δ and Δ as functions of the number of the clusters (c).

As expected, the values of δ go down with the increasing number of the clusters, Figure 13. The reason for this trend is obvious: we get more clusters, the individual membership grades go down and the differences become lower. As to the second index, it less monotonic as with the changes of the number of clusters each dataset has its own "plausible" number of clusters and this could vary between them.

5.6 Vertical Collaboration

As already discussed, the vertical collaborative clustering is concerned with a collection of databases involving different patterns defined in the same feature space so that the patterns do not repeat across the databases. As the feature space is common throughout the databases we can use prototypes as a means of facilitating the collaboration between the databases. With the same notation as before, the objective function is given in the form

$$Q[ii] = \sum_{i=1}^{c} \sum_{i=1}^{N[ii]} u_{ik}^2[ii]d_{ik}^2 +$$

$$\sum_{\substack{jj=1 \\ jj \neq ii}}^{P} \beta[ii.jj] \sum_{k=1}^{N[ii]} \sum_{i=1}^{c} u_{ik}^2[ii] \parallel v_i[ii] - v_i[jj] \parallel^2$$

where $\beta[ii,jj]$ (> 0) describes a level of collaboration between the datasets and $\parallel \parallel$ denotes a distance function between the prototypes. The optimization of the objective function is carried out for the partition matrix U[ii] and the prototypes of the clusters v[ii]. The final expression governing computations of the partition matrix reads as

$$u_{st} = \cfrac{1}{\sum_{j=1}^{c} \cfrac{D_{st}^2}{D_{jt}^2}}$$

$t=1, 2,\ldots, N[ii]$, $s=1,2,\ldots,c$ where D_{st} is given in the form

$$D_{st}^2 = d_{st}^2 + \sum_{\substack{jj=1 \\ jj \neq ii}}^{P} \beta[ii, jj] \, \| \, v_s[ii] - v_s[jj] \, \|^2$$

Proceeding with the optimization of the prototypes, we obtain

$$v_{st}[ii] = \frac{F_{st}[ii] - A_{st}[ii]}{C_{st}[ii] - B_{st}[ii]}$$

$s=1, 2, \ldots, c$, $t=1,2,\ldots,n$ with the following expressions

$$A_{st}[ii] = \sum_{k=1}^{N[ii]} u_{sk}^2[ii] x_{kt}[ii]$$

$$B_{st}[ii] = \sum_{k=1}^{N[ii]} u_{sk}^2[ii]$$

$$C_{st}[ii] = \sum_{\substack{jj=1 \\ jj \neq ii}}^{P} \beta[ii, jj] \sum_{k=1}^{N[ii]} u_{sk}^2[ii]$$

$$F_{st}[ii] = \sum_{\substack{jj=1 \\ jj \neq ii}}^{P} \beta[ii, jj] \sum_{k=1}^{N[ii]} u_{sk}^2[ii] v_{st}[jj]$$

Table 1 Three datasets used in the experiment of vertical clustering.

No. of data	Data Set #1	Data Set #2	Data Set #3
1	1.1 1.6	1.1 1.6	1.1 1.6
2	1.3 2.1	1.3 2.1	1.3 2.1
3	2.2 2.5	2.2 2.5	2.2 2.5
4	2.3 2.7	2.3 2.7	2.3 2.7
5	3.5 **6.7**	3.8 8.7	3.8 8.7
6	3.9 6.1	3.9 6.1	3.9 6.1
7	**3.3** 5.8	5.3 5.8	5.3 5.8
8	2.9 6.2	2.9 6.2	2.9 6.2
9	7.1 9.2	7.1 9.2	**5.1** 3.2
10	8.3 9.1	8.3 9.1	8.3 **3.1**
11	7.8 8.5	7.8 **5.5**	7.8 **3.5**
12	7.4 7.9	7.4 7.9	2.4 **3.9**

To illustrate how the method of this collaborative clustering works, we consider three collections of two-dimensional synthetic data collected in Table 1 where we identify the indexes of data points in the set. The elements substantially different from one data set to another are indicated in boldface. We partition the data into 3 clusters. The number of iterations the clustering algorithm has been run is equal to 15 (practically, at this number, there are no further changes in the objective function).

For comparative reasons, we start with a scenario in which there is no collaboration. The resulting partition matrices and prototypes are listed below

- partition matrix; first data set

```
0.962885  0.029110  0.008005
0.987977  0.009657  0.002366
0.973869  0.021538  0.004593
0.948994  0.042514  0.008491
0.010942  0.977999  0.011059
0.013902  0.973516  0.012582
0.010637  0.983763  0.005600
0.015808  0.975499  0.008693
0.007394  0.024593  0.968013
0.006575  0.017805  0.975620
0.000675  0.002018  0.997307
0.009464  0.031015  0.959521
```

partition matrix; second data set

```
0.025856  0.964681  0.009462
0.008925  0.988080  0.002995
0.014625  0.981004  0.004371
0.029609  0.961978  0.008414
0.708906  0.075178  0.215916
0.982872  0.008537  0.008591
0.780051  0.067610  0.152339
0.875552  0.078263  0.046185
0.054116  0.012098  0.933786
0.044340  0.012775  0.942884
0.284482  0.093742  0.621776
0.011821  0.002588  0.985591
```

partition matrix; third data set

```
0.039863  0.032573  0.927565
0.017405  0.012870  0.969724
0.003631  0.002755  0.993615
0.009680  0.006951  0.983369
0.818173  0.091730  0.090097
0.975737  0.011179  0.013085
0.754797  0.161347  0.083856
0.913704  0.030640  0.055656
0.207793  0.492985  0.299222
0.013797  0.974664  0.011539
0.001866  0.996727  0.001407
0.183367  0.071699  0.744934
```

In all cases, we have several clearly visible clusters of data. The prototypes of the three datasets as tabulated below, are significantly different. In particular, the second and third prototype varies a lot across the datasets.

Dataset #1- prototypes	Dataset #2 - prototypes	Dataset #3- prototypes
[1.718665 2.222599]	[1.746825 2.253552]	[1.908616 2.492797]
[3.399974 6.196972]	[4.024643 6.495806]	[3.865419 6.565224]
[7.655201 8.676819]	[7.545924 8.293676]	[7.655816 3.344443]

Now, let us set up a collaboration level equal to 1; more specifically, $\beta[ii,jj]=1.0$ for all $ii \neq jj$. The collaboration established in this way results in similar prototypes as quantified in the following table

Dataset #1- prototypes	Dataset #2 - prototypes	Dataset #3- prototypes
[1.865954 2.338975]	[1.869684 2.344301]	[1.944257 2.400455]
[3.720608 6.258747]	[3.834615 6.340519]	[3.858967 6.242465]
[7.444662 7.334947]	[7.412808 7.155983]	[7.358653 6.138383]

Noticeably, the prototypes start exhibiting a strong resemblance across the data that is a visible indicator of the ongoing collaboration. The effect of collaboration driving the prototypes closer for each dataset translates into changes in membership grades of the individual data points. Computationally, the change is taken as the sum of the absolute differences taken over all clusters that is

$$\sum_{i=1}^{c} | u_{ik} - u_{ik}(no\_collaboration) |$$

with $u_{ik}(no\_collaboration)$ denoting the membership grade of the k-th pattern in the i-th cluster in case no collaboration is present. This effect of collaboration is shown in Figure xx. Immediately, we recognize that some patterns are quite strongly affected by the collaboration. Those are the patterns that are different between datasets. With the increasing values of βs, the collaboration becomes more vigorous. Subsequently, the values of the changes in the membership grades are shown in Table 2. It can be seen that some of the patterns are heavily affected by the collaboration meaning that at these points the structure are quite distinct and any reconciliation between them requires a substantial level of effort. These particular patterns are indicated in boldface. These results correlate very evidently with the data, see Table 1. The method reveals that data points 9, 10, 11, and 1 are different – an observation included in Table 1. Interestingly, these patterns are the same that resulted in a substantial level of changes in membership occurring during the process of collaboration.

Table 2. Changes in the membership grades of the individual data points in three datasets for $\beta=1.0$.

Pattern no.	Change in membership (first dataset)
1	0.032886
2	0.022677
3	0.027390
4	0.043216
5	0.011151
6	0.029918
7	0.064940
8	0.100724
9	**0.398732**
10	**0.323950**
11	**0.274974**
12	**0.144609**

Pattern no.	Change in membership (second dataset)
1	0.035287
2	0.022392
3	0.014654
4	0.020496
5	0.024933
6	0.012801
7	**0.186115**
8	0.056257
9	**0.366174**
10	**0.287519**
11	**0.302670**
12	**0.186651**

Pattern no.	Change in membership (third dataset)
1	0.032886
2	0.022677
3	0.027390
4	0.043216
5	0.011151
6	0.029918
7	0.064940
8	0.100724
9	**0.398732**
10	**0.323950**
11	**0.274974**
12	**0.144609**

In the sequel, a total change in the membership (Δ) determined as

$$\Delta = \sum_{k=1}^{N} \sum_{i=1}^{c} | u_{ik} - u_{ik}(no\_collaboration)|$$

and now regarded as a function of β is summarized in Figure 14. Again, there is a strong monotonic relationship between the level of this collaboration and the manifesting changes in the partition matrix; the detailed relationships vary between datasets (groups of data).

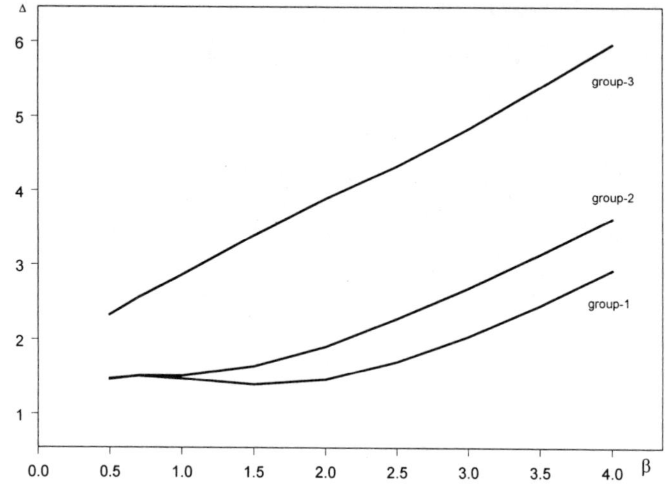

Figure 14. Δ as a function of β for datasets used in the experiment

Next we consider the same synthetic data now using the vertical clustering where the methods collaborate at the level of the membership functions (partition matrices). First the prototypes obtained at $\beta[ii][jj]=1$ are summarized in Table 3. Subsequently, we show the changes in the membership grades, Table 4. Finally, Figure 15 visualizes how the values of Δ are affected by the assumed level of the collaboration.

Table 3. Prototypes of the clusters for β [ii][jj]=1.

Dataset-1	Dataset-2	Dataset-3
1.822371 2.348398	1.820462 2.341236	2.105824 2.529360
4.116829 6.610057	4.585076 6.841259	4.256230 6.166471
7.632895 8.640197	7.563589 8.204105	7.440859 3.623372

Table 4. Changes in membership grades for the three datasets; the most significant changes (with the values over 0.3) indicated in boldface.

Dataset-1	Dataset-2	Dataset-3
1 0.041962	1 0.045628	1 0.030457
2 0.031656	2 0.032021	2 0.009927
3 0.037368	3 0.023017	3 0.002122
4 0.065780	4 0.039695	4 0.004779
5 0.105568	5 0.093528	5 0.233347
6 0.044639	6 0.063337	6 0.050150
7 0.296192	7 0.082744	7 0.148840
8 **0.340145**	8 0.142058	8 0.160036
9 **0.486945**	9 **0.417606**	9 **0.473936**
10 **0.424982**	10 **0.358432**	10 **0.871235**
11 **0.410413**	11 0.025409	11 **0.891050**
12 **0.371832**	12 **0.422575**	12 0.031298

In general, the patterns that are identified as those requiring a high level of collaboration by the previous method, are also highlighted as such by this approach. Comparing the plots of the changes in Δ, Figure 14 and 15, we see that they are both monotonic yet the type of monotonicity is not identical.

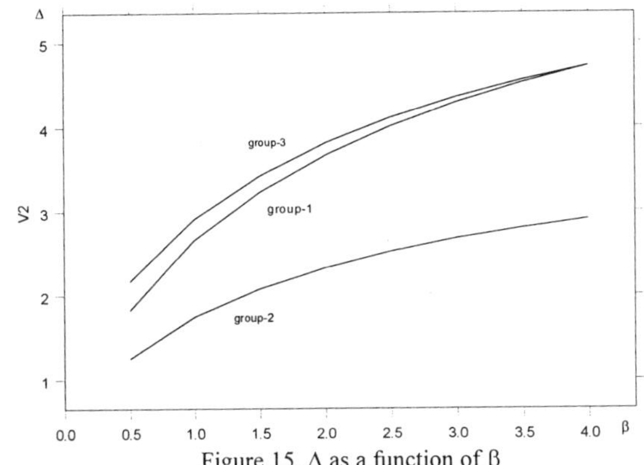

Figure 15. Δ as a function of β

5.7 Unidirectional (functional) collaboration

The unidirectional collaboration is concerned with the clustering in which the activities of data structuring is conveyed (impacts) the other activities occurring at the level of other subsets. To get into the details, we consider two datasets. Given are two data sets (patterns) $\mathbf{X}[1]$ and $\mathbf{X}[2]$ where $\mathbf{X}[1]= \{\mathbf{x}_1[1], \mathbf{x}_2[1], ...\mathbf{x}_N[1]\}$ and $\mathbf{X}[2]= \{\mathbf{x}_1[2], \mathbf{x}_2[2], ...\mathbf{x}_N[2]\}$ where $\mathbf{x}_k[1] \in \mathbf{R}^{n_1}$ and $\mathbf{x}_k[2] \in \mathbf{R}^{n_2}$. The clustering of $\mathbf{X}[1]$ involves $c[1]$ clusters. For the second data set, the clustering gives rise to $c[2]$ clusters. The clusters constructed in $\mathbf{X}[1]$ are denoted by $A_1, A_2, ...A_{c[1]}$. For $\mathbf{X}[2]$ the resulting clusters are $B_1, B_2,..., B_{c[2]}$. In what follows, the terms cluster and information granule are used interchangeably. Furthermore, as we are dealing with two data sets, all constructs pertaining to the data are indexed by square brackets, namely [1] and [2].

The mapping between the granules in $\mathbf{X}[1]$ and $\mathbf{X}[2]$ exhibits an evident logic flavor meaning that we assume a logic form of the relationship between the information granules, namely we express an information granule B_i as a logic aggregation (ϕ) involving the information granules developed in $\mathbf{X}[1]$, that is

$$B_i = \phi_i(A_1, A_2, ...A_{c[1]}, \mathbf{w}_i)$$

i=1. 2, ...,$c[2]$. Formally the above mapping (ϕ) transforms a $c[1]$ dimensional unit hypercube into a unit interval.

The above expression includes also a weight vector (parameters) $\mathbf{w}_i$ that is used to calibrate the links between A_j and B_i. We discuss the details of the logic expression in the next section. More descriptively, we are interested in the development of information granules $\{A_i\}$ and $\{B_j\}$ so that they satisfy the requirements of relational and directional nature. We have not specified the form of the logic mapping. A general category of these transformations emerges in the setting of fuzzy relational equations where the weight vectors are combined together in the form of a single fuzzy relation.

5.7.1 The objective function and its generalization

In what follows, we discuss a case of two subsets of data (it generalizes quite easily to any number of the subsets however the notation requires more attention). Let us consider that for $\mathbf{X}[2]$ the clusters built there are affected by the collaboration coming from $\mathbf{X}[1]$ as we are concerned about the mapping (logic transformation between $\mathbf{X}[1]$ and $\mathbf{X}[2]$). This is taken into consideration by expanding the objective function in the following additive form

$$Q[2] = \sum_{i=1}^{c[2]} \sum_{k=1}^{N} u_{ik}^{2}[2] d_{ik}^{2}[2] + \beta \sum_{i=1}^{c[2]} \sum_{k=1}^{N} (u_{ik}[2] - \phi_i(U[1]))^2 d_{ik}^{2}[2] \qquad (1)$$

The first term (of relational character) is just a standard component encountered in the FCM that looks after the structure in $\mathbf{X}[2]$. The second one (being of directional character) captures differences between U[2] and the mapping of the structure detected in $\mathbf{X}[1]$ (viz. the fuzzy partition U[1]) to $\mathbf{X}[2]$, that is ϕ_i (U[1]). It characterizes the performance of the mapping between the information granules. The weight coefficient (β) is used to quantify a balance between the structure in $\mathbf{X}[2]$ and the impact from the mapping requirement (the second term in the above objective function). Considering the two goals of this process of information granulation, we say that β strikes a compromise between the relational and directional aspects of such optimization.

The optimization of (1) requires detailed investigation as it departures from the standard FCM scheme. The minimization of the objective function Q[2] is completed with respect to the partition matrix U[2] (structure), prototypes and the parameters of the logic transformation (ϕ_i).

5.7.2 The logic transformation

The granular mapping from $\mathbf{X}[1]$ to $\mathbf{X}[2]$ is realized as a logic transformation between the information granules. It is worth stressing that there is a panoply of possible types of mappings and our choice is implied by the transparency of the logic mapping that comes hand in hand with the logic type of the spaces between which the mapping takes place. Two classes of mappings are discussed

- *OR-based* As the name stipulates, we consider the information granule B_i to be an OR aggregation of the granules in the input space, that is

$$B_i = A_1 \; or \; A_2 \; or \; ... \; or \; A_{c[1]} \qquad (2)$$

Not all fuzzy relations in the input space contribute to the formation of B_i nor each of them may exhibit an equal impact on the membership of B_i. To gain this flexibility, we allow for a weight vector (connections) $\mathbf{w}_i$ whose role is to articulate (quantify) the contribution coming from A_j's. The following modification is made to (2)

$$B_i = (A_1 \; and \; w_{i1}) \; or \; (A_2 \; and \; w_{i2}) \; or ... \; or \; (A_{c[1]} \; and \; w_{ic[1]}) \qquad (3)$$

where $\mathbf{w}_i = [w_{i1} \; w_{i2} \; ... \; w_{ic[1]}]$ are weights with the values confined to the unit interval. If all weights are set to 1, then (3) reduces to (2). The logic operations are realized by t- and s-norms and this leads to the equivalent expression of (3) (which is a s-t realization of the logic expression)

$$B_i = (A_1 \; t \; w_{i1}) \; s \; (A_2 \; t \; w_{i2}) \; s ... \; s \; (A_{c[1]} \; t \; w_{ic[1]})$$

and

$$B_i = \overset{c[1]}{\underset{j=1}{S}} (A_j \, t w_{ij}) \qquad (4)$$

In particular, (4) translates to a well-known max-min composition for the following realization: t-norm- minimum, s-norm – maximum. In this sense, (4) becomes a well known fuzzy relational equation. Note that the above logic mapping concerns a single fuzzy relation in $X[2]$. In the similar fashion we can realize the mapping for the remaining information granules. After a careful examination of the mappings being viewed together, we come up with the following concise notation. Arrange all weights into a matrix form

$$R = [r_{ij}] = \begin{bmatrix} w_{11} & \cdots & & w_{1c[2]} \\ \cdots & & & \\ & & w_{ij} & \\ & & & \\ w_{c[1]1} & \cdots & & w_{c[1]c[2]} \end{bmatrix} \tag{5}$$

Then the mapping from information granules in $X[1]$ to information granules in $X[2]$ is nothing but a fuzzy relational equation with a standard s-t composition (denoted here by a small dot)

$$\mathbf{B} = A \circ R \tag{6}$$

where $A = [A_1 \ A_2 \ A_{c[1]}]$ and $B = [B_1 \ B_2 \ B_{c[2]}]$
Similarly, we can introduce an AND type of aggregation of the information granules meaning that we consider B_i to be a combination of A_js aggregated AND-wise, that is

$$B_i = A_1 \ and \ A_2 \ and \ \ldots \ and \ A_{c[1]} \tag{7}$$

The straightforward generalization of the above aggregation includes a weight vector with the values in [0,1] and, subsequently, the combination of the t-s type

$$B_i = (A_1 \ or \ w_{i1}) \ and \ (A_2 \ or \ w_{i2}) \ and \ldots \ and \ (A_{c[1]} \ or \ w_{ic[1]}) \tag{8}$$

$$B_i = (A_1 \ s \ w_{i1}) \ t \ (A_2 \ s \ w_{i2}) \ t \ldots \ t \ (A_{c[1]} \ s \ w_{ic[1]}) = \mathop{T}_{j=1}^{c[1]} (A_j \ s \ w_{ij}) \tag{9}$$

Note that (9) is realized in terms of the t- and s-norms.
These two aggregation mechanisms (s-t and t-s combination) are dual in the sense of their functionality. Owing to the character of the AND and OR operations, intuitively we use them depending on the number of the information granules existing in the respective spaces. If $c[1] > c[2]$ we consider the OR type of aggregation (in anticipation that the element in the output space is constructed as a union of several information granules in the input space). Similarly, for $c[1] < c[2]$, the AND–type of aggregation is more appealing (as we project that B_i is made more specific in relation to the information granules existing in $X[1]$).

5.7.3 The algorithm

Now we are ready to proceed with the computational details that lead us to the complete algorithm. The objective function implies the following optimization task

$$\min_{U[2], v_1[1], v_2[2], \ldots, v_{c[2]}} Q[2]$$

subject to

$$U[2] \in \mathbf{U}$$

and

$$R \in \mathbf{R} \tag{10}$$

where the family of partition matrices $\mathbf{U}$ is defined in a usual manner (namely, we require that the elements in each column of $U[2]$ sum up to 1 and the sum of elements in each row of R is nonzero and lower than N). R is an element of the family of the fuzzy relations $\mathbf{R}$ (viz. matrices with elements confined to the unit interval). The above optimization problem concerns a way of forming a structure in $\mathbf{X}[2]$ with an inclusion of the mapping properties. The clustering mechanisms in $\mathbf{X}[1]$ follow the standard FCM and will not be discussed here. We start with the determination of the partition matrix and then move on to the optimization of the fuzzy relation R.

The optimization of the partition matrix $U[2]$ in the objective function uses a technique of Lagrange multipliers (because of the constraint that we need to satisfy in the development of the partition matrix). For a given data point (k), we form an augmented objective function

$$V = \sum_{i=1}^{c[2]} u_{ik}^2[2]d_{ik}^2[2] + \beta\sum_{i=1}^{c[2]} (u_{ik}[2] - \phi_i(U[1]))^2 d_{ik}^2[2] + \lambda(\sum_{i=1}^{c[2]} u_{ik}[2] - 1) \tag{11}$$

where λ is a Lagrange multiplier (the problem is handled separately for each pattern, k=1, 2, …,N). Proceeding with the necessary conditions for the minimum of V

$$\frac{\partial V}{\partial u_{st}[2]} = 0 \qquad \frac{\partial V}{\partial \lambda} = 0$$

where s=1, 2, …, c[2], t=1, 2, …N, we calculate

$$2u_{st}[2]d_{st}^2[2] + 2\beta(u_{st}[2] - y_{st})d_{st}^2[2] + \lambda = 0 \tag{12}$$

y_{st} stands for a logic-based mapping between the information granules that is ϕ_s taken over the t-column of U[1]

$$y_{st} = \mathop{S}_{j=1}^{c[1]} (u_{st}[1]tr_{sj})$$

Computing $u_{st}[2]$ from (12) we obtain

$$u_{st}[2] = \frac{2\beta y_{st}d_{st}^2[2] - \lambda}{2d_{st}^2[2](1 + \beta)} \tag{13}$$

As the membership grades sum up to 1, this leads us to the expression

$$\sum_{j=1}^{c[2]} \frac{\beta y_{jt}d_{jt}^2[2] - \lambda}{2d_{jt}^2[2](1 + \beta)} = 1 \tag{14}$$

In the sequel we obtain

$$\frac{\lambda}{2(1+\beta)} = \frac{-1 + \dfrac{\beta}{1+\beta}\displaystyle\sum_{j=1}^{c[2]} y_{jt}}{\displaystyle\sum_{j=1}^{c[2]} \dfrac{1}{d_{jt}^2[2]}} \tag{15}$$

Introduce the notation

$$\tilde{u}_{st}[2] = \frac{1}{\displaystyle\sum_{j=1}^{c[2]} \dfrac{d_{st}^2[2]}{d_{jt}^2[2]}}$$

and plug (15) into (13). This leads to the expression

$$u_{st}[2] = \frac{\beta}{1+\beta} y_{st} - \frac{1}{d_{st}^2}\frac{\lambda}{2(1+\beta)} = \frac{\beta}{1+\beta} y_{st} - \tilde{u}_{st}[2]\left(\frac{\beta}{1+\beta}\sum_{j=1}^{c[2]} y_{jt} - 1\right)$$

Finally arranging all terms we get

$$u_{st}[2] = \tilde{u}_{st}[2] + \frac{\beta}{1+\beta}\left(y_{st} - \tilde{u}_{st}[2]\sum_{j=1}^{c[2]} y_{jt}\right) \tag{16}$$

s=1, 2, …, c[2], t=1, 2,…,N.
The previous formula has an interesting interpretation: if β is equal to zero then it reduces to the well-known formula for the partition matrix encountered in the FCM. When β increases, then $u_{st}[2]$ is affected by the second term in (13).
The calculations of the prototypes do not come with any constraints so we follow the necessary condition for the minimum of Q[2], namely $\dfrac{\partial Q[2]}{\partial v_{st}[2]} = 0$, s=1, 2, …,c[2], t=1, 2, …n₂.
In light of the weighted Euclidean distance governed by the expression,

$$d_{ik}^2[2] = \sum_{j=1}^{n_2} \frac{(x_k[j] - v_{ij}[2])^2}{\sigma_j^2[2]} \tag{17}$$

(where $\sigma_j^2[2]$ denotes a variance of the j-th variable in $\mathbf{X}[2]$, j=1, 2, …,n₂), the above derivative is equal to

$$\frac{\partial Q[2]}{\partial v_{st}[2]} = -2\sum_{k=1}^{N} u_{sk}^2[2]\frac{(x_k[t] - v_{st}[2])}{\sigma_t^2[2]} - 2\beta\sum_{k=1}^{N} \psi_{sk}\frac{(x_k[t] - v_{st}[2])}{\sigma_t^2[2]} \tag{18}$$

with the following shorthand notation

$$\psi_{sk} = (u_{sk}[2] - y_{sk})^2$$

Bearing in mind the necessary condition for the minimum of Q[2] with respect to the prototypes, namely $\dfrac{\partial Q[2]}{\partial v_{st}[2]}$ we derive

$$v_{st}[2] = \frac{\sum_{k=1}^{N} x_k[t](u_{sk}^2 + \beta \psi_{sk})}{\sum_{k=1}^{N}(u_{sk}^2 + \beta \psi_{sk})} \tag{19}$$

Noticeably, when $\beta=0$, we arrive at the standard expression for the prototypes that is identical to the one encountered in the FCM method.

Finally, we optimize the fuzzy relation R describing the logic mapping between the spaces. In general, the solution is not expressed analytically and we have to proceed with some iterative optimization. The underlying expression governing this optimization reads as

$$R(iter+1) = R(iter) - \gamma \nabla_{R(iter)} Q[2] \tag{20}$$

where the fuzzy relation is transformed on a basis of the gradient of the performance index Q[2]. The learning rate shown above ($\gamma > 0$) controls a pace of changes of the updates of the fuzzy relation. The constraint on the entries of the fuzzy relation is maintained by containing the updates to the unit interval. There are no analytical methods for solving this problem (in essence what we have is a system of fuzzy relational equations with the s-t composition to be solved with respect to the unknown fuzzy relation R).

The gradient of Q[2] can be computed once we confine ourselves to some specific triangular norms and co-norms. In what follows (and all experiments shown in Section 5.5 will exploit this selection), we consider two common models of the logic connectives such as a product (t-norms) and probabilistic sum (s-norm). Then the detailed computations are as follows

$$\frac{\partial Q[2]}{\partial r_{st}} = -2\beta \sum_{k=1}^{N}(u_{sk}[2] - \Phi_{ik})d_{sk}^2[2]\frac{\partial \Phi_{ik}}{\partial r_{st}}$$

where

$$\Phi_{ik} = \overset{c[1]}{\underset{j=1}{S}}(r_{ij}tu_{jk}[1])$$

Bearing in mind the realizations of the t- and s-norm we obtain

$$\frac{\partial \Phi_{sk}}{\partial r_{st}} = (1 - A_{st})u_{tk}[1] \tag{21}$$

where A_{st} denotes an s-t composition that excludes the currently optimized element of the fuzzy relation

$$A_{st} = \overset{c[1]}{\underset{\substack{j=1 \\ j \neq t}}{S}}(u_{jk}[1]tr_{sj}) \tag{22}$$

5.7.4 The overall development framework: a flow of optimization activities

The way in which the information granules are built stipulates a certain flow of optimization activities. These can be grouped into two main phases, see Figure 5. The initial phase concentrates on the clustering completed independently for the two data sets $X[1]$ and $X[2]$. The intent here is to establish some preliminary structure in the data so that we could have a reasonable starting point to proceed with the collaboration and further refine the initial relationships. During the second phase, the clustering processes start to collaborate through the mapping. At the same time the fuzzy relation is subject to the gradient-based optimization (as illustrated in Figure 16, this as an integral portion of the collaboration process and negotiation of the granular structures). Because of the direction of the mapping, the clustering in $X[1]$ is not affected per se while the relational and directional facets of the clusters emerge at the side of $X[2]$.

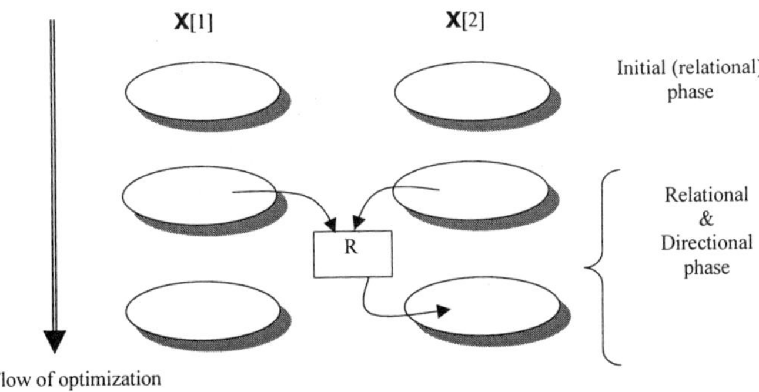

Figure 16. Relational and directional optimization of information granules
-an overall iterative development scheme.

The selection of the numeric value of β in the optimized objective function Q[2] requires a few words of comment. The higher the value of β, the more emphasis becomes placed on the directional aspects of the problem. It is easy to envision a situation when with the increasing values of β the two criteria may lead to competitive situations. A practical guideline would be to gradually increase the value of β and monitor the behavior of Q[2] over the process of optimization. One should not exceed the level of collaboration (value of b) over the point where we start noticing oscillations in the values of the performance index. This becomes a sign of moving from collaboration to competition; too "tightly" coupled features of relational and directional optimization start competing.

5.8 The design of relational collaboration through an optimization interface

The essence of the directional collaboration discussed in the previous section dwelled on a mechanism that conveyed an immediate impact the clustering technique realized in the space of independent variables exerted on the optimization of Q[2] (the second term of the objective function weighted by some scaling factor β). One can envision another optimization scenario that involves an intermediate optimization block as shown in Figure 17.

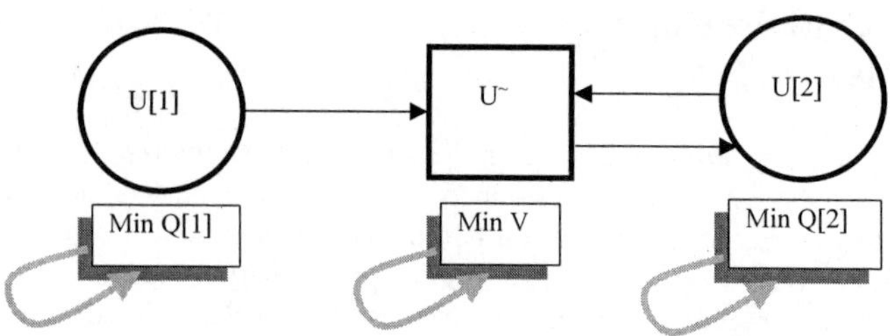

Figure 17. A general scheme of relational collaboration; see details in text

This block plays a role of a mediator between the two processes of local optimization. More specifically, we have three optimization processes going on when the two of them exchange information expressed in the language of some partition matrices. First, there is an independent optimization realized for U[1] and this is just a standard FCM. The second is the FCM guided by the following objective function

$$Q[2] = \sum_{i=1}^{c[2]} \sum_{k=1}^{N} u_{ik}^2[2]d_{ik}^2 + \beta \sum_{i=1}^{c[2]} \sum_{k=1}^{N} (u_{ik}[2] - u_{ik}^{\sim})^2 d_{ik}^2$$

where $U^{\sim} = [u_{ik}^{\sim}]$, $i=1, 2,.., c[2]$, $k=1, 2, …,N$ is an auxiliary matrix whose role is to assure communication and negotiation mechanisms between the data (and agents, respectively). As before β is a positive weight factor. The crux of the negotiation process is realized by the minimization of the performance index

$$V = \sum_{k=1}^{N} \sum_{i=1}^{c[1]} (u_{ik}[1] - F(u_{jk}^{\sim}[2]))^2$$

with $F(U^{\sim})$ transforming $U^{\sim}$ into the partition space with c[1] clusters. The minimization of V is carried out with respect to $U^{\sim}$. The origin of the starting values of $U^{\sim}$ will become clear through the description of the overall optimization activities. They are outlined as follows

optimize Q[1]; this results in U[1]

initiate optimize the standard FCM for the second data (no interaction with other ssources of data) and treat the resulting partition matrix as $U^{\sim}$
iterate //main iteration loop

> optimize V with respect to the elements of $U^{\sim}$ (they need to be maintained in the [0,1] range but they do not necessarily sum up to 1 for each data point. Quite commonly we may encounter an iterative scheme here meaning that it invokes some gradient-based optimization as follows

$$u_{ik}^{\sim}(iter + 1) = u_{ik}^{\sim}(iter) - \gamma \frac{\partial V}{\partial u_{ik}^{\sim}(iter)}$$

> with γ being a positive learning rate

> optimize Q[2] with respect to the partition matrix U[2] and the prototypes of the data set; again this is an iterative optimization process so one can envision this to be another loop of iterations

until a given termination criterion has been satisfied.

The form of the mapping (F) depends on the specificity of the problem. For instance, we may consider this to be a sum mapping matrix U~ onto the clusters in the first space. Then the minimized performance index reads as follows

$$V = \sum_{k=1}^{N} \sum_{i=1}^{c[1]} (u_{ik}[1] - \sum_{j \in K_i} u_{jk}^{\sim}[2])^2$$

where the internal sum is taken over all clusters (j) located in the second space that were associated with the i-th cluster in the first space (denoted here by K_i). The main computational activities contributing to the overall scheme are also indicated in Figure 17 by arrows pointing at the corresponding phases of the process.

5.9 Conclusions

The two modes of collaboration between computing agents give rise to an interesting taxonomy as far as the space of collaboration is concerned
(A) In the horizontal collaboration, the methods exchange information in the space of information granules while not being involved in any communication occurring in the data space. We can say that the collaboration happens at more abstract level as the partition matrices being provided to other collaborators are defined in the space of general data structures (partition matrices).
(B) In the vertical collaboration, we may encounter two models of collaboration. The first one is the same as outlined in the horizontal collaboration, namely the methods communicate at the level of their partition matrices. This collaboration at the level of information granules that is more abstract than the one going on in the data space itself. The difference lies in the fact that now such partition matrices used for communication purposes are induced).
In the entire discussion presented so far, we have assumed that while there is some collaboration and the optimization processes interact between themselves, there is no centralized optimization mechanism. As a consequence, the minimization was carried out having the individual objective functions (Q[1], Q[2], …Q[P]) in mind. The communication links imply that these processes collaborate by exchanging information (e.g., partition matrices). There is a possibility for an introduction of a centralized aspect of collaboration by forming a global performance index in the additive form Q = Q[1] + Q[2]+…+ Q[P]. The graphic illustration of this computing model is visualized as in Figure 18.

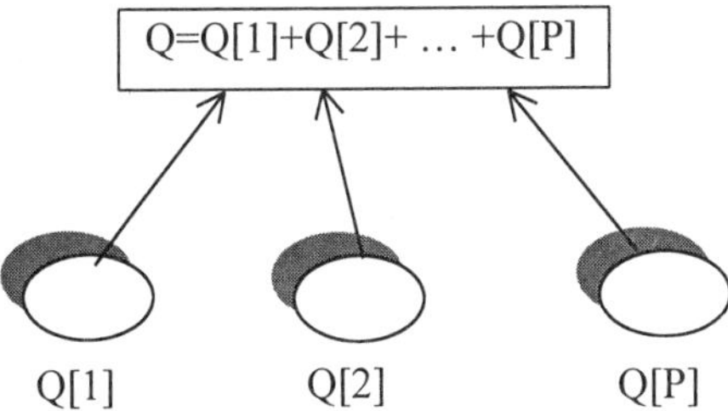

Figure 18. Centralized aspects of collaboration; in addition to the optimization at the level of the individual agents, developed is a higher level aimed at the minimization of Q.

References

Bezdek, J.C. (1981) *Pattern Recognition with Fuzzy Objective Function Algorithms*, Plenum Press, N. York.

Delgado, M., Gomez-Skarmeta, A.F., Martin F., (1997) "A fuzzy clustering-based prototyping for fuzzy rule-based modeling", *IEEE Transactions on Fuzzy Systems*, 5(2), 223-233.

Delgado, M., Gomez-Skarmets, A.F., Martin F., (1998) "A methodology to model fuzzy systems using fuzzy clustering in a rapid-prototyping approach", *Fuzzy Sets and Systems*, vol. 97, no.3, 1998, 287-302.

Duda, R.O., Hart, P.E., Stork, D.G. (2001) *Pattern Classification,* 2nd edition, J. Wiley, N. York, NY.

Kandel, A. (1986) *Fuzzy Mathematical Techniques with Applications*, Addison-Wesley, Reading, MA, 1986.

Kersten, P.R. (1999) "Fuzzy order statistics and their application to fuzzy clustering", *IEEE Trans. on Fuzzy Systems*, 7, no. 6, 708-712.

Loia V. and Sessa S., (2001) "A soft computing framework for adaptive agents." In: *Soft Computing Agents: New Trends for Designing Autonomous Systems-* Studies in Fuzziness and Soft Computing volume 75.Springer-Verlag, forthcoming in June.

Pedrycz, W., (1995) *Fuzzy Sets Engineering*, CRC Press, Boca Raton, FL.

Pedrycz, W., (1998), Conditional fuzzy clustering in the design of radial basis function neural networks, *IEEE Transactions on Neural Networks*, 9 no. 4, 601- 612.

Soft Computing Agents
V. Loia (Ed.)
IOS Press, 2002

Chapter 6

Semi-metric Behavior in Document Networks and its Application to Recommendation Systems

Luis M. Rocha

6.1 Introduction

Recommendation systems for different Document Networks (DN) such as the World Wide Web (WWW), Digital Libraries, or Scientific Databases, often make use of distance functions extracted from relationships among documents and between documents and semantic tags. For instance, documents in the WWW are related via a hyperlink network, while documents in bibliographic databases are related by citation and collaboration networks. Furthermore, documents can be related to semantic tags such as keywords used to describe their content. The distance functions computed from these relations establish associative networks among items of the DN, referred to as Distance Graphs, which allow recommendation systems to identify relevant associations for individual users. However, modern recommendation systems need to integrate associative data (defined by distance graphs) generated from multiple sources such as different databases, web sites, and even other users. Thus, we are presented with a problem of combining evidence (about associations between items) from different sources characterized by distance functions. In this paper we describe our work on (1) inferring relevant associations from, as well as characterizing, semi-metric distance graphs and (2) combining evidence from different distance graphs in a recommendation system. Regarding (1), we present the idea of semi-metric distance graphs, and introduce ratios to measure semi-metric behavior. We compute these ratios for several DN such as digital libraries and web sites and show that they are useful to identify implicit associations. We also propose a model based on semi-metric behavior that allow us to quantify the amount of important latent associations in a DN. Regarding (2), we describe an algorithm to combine evidence from distance graphs that uses Evidence Sets, a set structure based on Interval Valued Fuzzy Sets and Dempster-Shafer Theory of Evidence. This algorithm has been developed for a recommendation system named *TalkMine*.

6.2 Document Networks and Recommendation Systems

The prime example of a Document Network (DN) is the World Wide Web (WWW). But many other types of such networks exist: bibliographic databases containing scientific publications, preprints, internal reports, as well as databases of datasets used in scientific endeavors[1]. Each of these databases possesses several distinct relationships among documents and between documents and semantic tags or indices that classify documents appropriately.

DN typically function as information resources for communities of users who query them to obtain relevant information for their activities. We often refer to collections of document

---

[1] Such as MEDLINE (http://www.nlm.nih.gov), the e-Print Arxiv (http://xxx.lanl.gov/), and the GenBank (http://www.ncbi.nlm.nih.gov/Genbank/) for Nucleic Acid Sequences.

networks and communities of users as Distributed *Information Systems* (DIS) (Rocha 2001b). DIS such as the Internet, Digital Libraries, and the like have become ubiquitous in the past decade, demanding the development of new techniques to both cater to the information needs of communities of users as well as to understand several aspects of the structure and dynamics of DN. The first set of techniques, needed to respond to engineering needs, come from the field of Information Retrieval, and are typically known as Recommender Systems (Krulwich & Burkey 1996, Konstan et al. 1997, Herlocker et al. 1999, Rocha 2001b). The second set of techniques, needed to respond to scientific interest in DN, come from the desire to analyze networks of documents and/or communities and is more related to Graph theory, Algebra, Complex Systems, as well as Linguistics (Kleinberg 1999, Chakrabarti et al. 1999, Berry, Dumais, & Obrien 1995, Li, Burgess, & Lund 2000, Newman 2001). Clearly, the scientific and engineering techniques complement and influence each other. We expect to use scientific knowledge about DN to improve recommendation algorithms, namely by better understanding users and information resources, and by producing adaptive DN, or adaptive webs (Bollen & Heylighen 1998, Bollen & Rocha 2000, Rocha 2001a).

The information retrieval and recommendation systems we have developed in this area are based on Multi-Agent algorithms which integrate knowledge about the association amongst elements of DN, amongst users, and about the interests of individual users and their communities. In particular, a soft computing algorithm (*TalkMine*) has been created to integrate such evidence and in so doing adapt DN to the expectations of their users (Rocha 2001b). The process of integration of knowledge in *TalkMine* requires the construction of distance graphs from DN that characterize the associations amongst their components. We summarize in sections 6.9 and 6.10 how *TalkMine* uses evidence theory and fuzzy set constructs to integrate such distance graphs to obtain measurements of relevance and produce recommendations. Before that, we detail the main goal of the present work, which is to study distance graphs extracted from DN. We show that their metric behavior can be used (1) as an indicator of the relevance of collections of documents and the interests of users who have selected certain sets of documents, (2) to identify the trends in communities associated with sets of documents, and (3) to study the characteristics of such DN in general, particularly, the amount of important latent associations.

Our approach to the third of these goals, in particular, is based on empirical evidence accumulated from several real and artificial DN. It is also independent of the particularities of *TalkMine* or any other specific recommendation algorithm. Indeed, our approach aims at a general characterization of how associative knowledge is stored in DN. Goals 1 and 2 are detailed in sections 6.6 and 6.7. Goal 3 is detailed in section 6.8. Sections 6.3 to 6.5 outline the foundations of semi-metric behavior required for later sections.

6.3 Characterizing Document Networks with Distance Functions

6.3.1 Harvesting Relations from Document Networks

For each DN we can identify several distinct relations among documents and between documents and semantic tags used to classify documents appropriately. For instance, documents in the WWW are related via a hyperlink network, while documents in bibliographic databases are related by citation and collaboration networks (Newman 2001). Furthermore, documents are typically related to semantic tags such as keywords used to describe their content. Although all the technology here discussed would apply equally to any of these relations extracted from DN, let us exemplify the problem with the datasets we have used in the *Active Recommendation Project* (ARP) (http://arp.lanl.gov), part of the Library Without Walls Project, at the Research Library of the Los Alamos National Laboratory (Bollen & Rocha 2000).

Table 1. Most Common (stemmed Keywords and their frequency)

Frequency	Keyword
188498	cell
144294	system
140258	studi
138128	express
129679	protein
122587	model
116900	activ
112538	rat
107240	gene
106497	human

ARP is engaged in research and development of recommendation systems for digital libraries. The *information resources* available to ARP are large databases with academic articles. These databases contain bibliographic, citation, and sometimes abstract information about academic articles. One of the databases we work with is *SciSearch*, containing articles from scientific journals from several fields collected by ISI (Institute for Scientific Indexing).

We collected all SciSearch data from the years of 1996 to 1999. There are 2,915,258 records[2], from which we extracted 839,297 keywords (semantic tags) that occurred at least in two distinct documents. The sources of keywords are the terms authors and/or editors chose to categorize (index) documents, as well as title words. Note that these do not include any other words that may occur in the text of the articles – only words specified as keywords and title words were included in this study. We removed typical stop words and stemmed all remaining keywords. The 10 most common (stemmed) keywords in the ARP dataset are listed in Table 1.

The relation between documents and keywords allows us to infer the semantic value of documents and the inter-associations between keywords. Naturally, semantics is ultimately only expressed in the brains of users who utilize the documents, but keywords are symbolic tokens of this ultimate expression, which we can try to infer from the relation between documents and keywords. Such semantic relation is stored as a very sparse *Keyword-Document Matrix* **A**. Each entry $a_{i,j}$ in the matrix is boolean and indicates whether keyword k_i indexes ($a_{i,j} = 1$) document d_j or not ($a_{i,j} = 0$).

The structure of a DN is likewise defined by the relations between documents in the document collection. In academic databases these relations refer to citations, while in the WWW to hyperlinks. In subsequent sections we work mostly with the semantic relation of DN (as defined here), but in section 6.8 we also work with the hyperlink structure of web sites.

6.3.2 Computing Distance Functions: Associative Semantics

To discern closeness between keywords according to the documents they classify, we

---

[2]Records contain bibliographical information about published documents. Records can be thought of as unique pointers to documents, thus, for the purposes of this article, the two terms are interchangeable.

compute the *Keyword Semantic Proximity* (*KSP*), obtained from **A** by the following formula:

$$KSP\left(k_i, k_j\right) = \frac{\sum_{k=1}^{m}\left(a_{i,k} \wedge a_{j,k}\right)}{\sum_{k=1}^{m}\left(a_{i,k} \vee a_{j,k}\right)} = \frac{N_{\cap}\left(k_i, k_j\right)}{N\left(k_i\right) + N\left(k_j\right) - N_{\cap}\left(k_i, k_j\right)} \qquad (1)$$

The semantic proximity[3] between two keywords, k_i and k_j, is the probability that keywords k_i and k_j co-index the same document in a DN whose semantics is defined by matrix **A**. It depends on the sets of documents indexed by each keyword, and the intersection of these sets. $N(k_i)$ is the number of documents keyword k_i indexes, and $N_{\cap}(k_i, k_j)$ the number of documents both keywords index. This last quantity is the number of elements in the intersection of the sets of documents that each keyword indexes. Thus, two keywords are near if they tend to index many of the same documents.

From the inverse of *KSP* we obtain a distance function between keywords:

$$d(k_i, k_j) = \frac{1}{KSP(k_i, k_j)} - 1 \qquad (2)$$

d is a distance function because it is a nonnegative, symmetric, real-valued function such that $d(k, k) = 0$ (Shore & Sawyer 1993). It defines a weighted graph *D*, which we refer to as a *distance graph*, whose vertices are all of the keywords extracted from a given DN, and the edges are the values of $d(k_i, k_j)$ for pairs of keywords (k_i, k_j). A small distance between keywords implies a strong semantic association between keywords, in the case of the ARP dataset, inferred from the probability of co-indexing documents. This way, this distance function indicates how far, semantically, a keyword is from another given a specific set of documents. In this sense, the *associative semantics* captured by *d* is context-dependent, as discussed next.

6.3.3 Characterizing Information Resources and Users

Clearly, many other types of distance functions can be defined on the elements of a DN. Naturally, the conclusions drawn cannot be separated by how well, and how appropriately for a given application, a distance function is capable of discerning the elements of the set it is applied to. Thus, distance functions applied to citation structures or collaboration networks would require distinct semantic considerations than those used for keyword sets.

In any case, we characterize an information resource with sets of distance functions such as formula 2. We assume that the collection of all relevant associative distance graphs extracted from a DN, is an expression of the particular knowledge it conveys to its community of users as an information resource. Notice that different information resources may share a very large set of keywords and documents. However, these are organized differently in each resource, leading to different associative semantics. Indeed, each resource is tailored to a particular community of users, with a distinct history of utilization and deployment of information. For instance, the same keywords will be related to different sets of documents in distinct resources, thus resulting in different distances for the same

---

[3]This measure of closeness, formally, is a proximity relation (Klir & Yuan 1995, Miyamoto 1990) because it is a reflexive and symmetric fuzzy relation. Its transitive closure is known as a similarity relation (Ibid).

pairs of keywords. Therefore, we refer to the relational information, or associative semantics, of each information resource as a *Knowledge Context* (Rocha 2001b). We do not mean to imply that information resources possess cognitive abilities. Rather, we note that the way documents are organized in information resources is an expression of the knowledge traded by their communities of users. Documents and keywords are only tokens of the knowledge that is ultimately expressed in the brains of users. A knowledge context simply mirrors some of the collective knowledge relations and distinctions shared by a community of users. The distance graphs which relate elements of DN define an associative semantics. They convey how strongly associated pairs of elements in the specific network are.

More specifically, we characterize an information resource R by a structure named Knowledge Context:

$$KN_R = \{X, \mathcal{R}, d\} \tag{3}$$

Where X is a set of available sets of elements X_i, e.g. $X = \{K, M, U\}$, where K is a set of keywords, M a set of documents, and U a set of users. $\mathcal{R}$ is a set of available relations amongst the sets in X, e.g. $\mathcal{R} = \{\mathbf{C}(M, M), \mathbf{A}(K, M)\}$, where $\mathbf{C}$ denotes a citation relation between the elements of the set of documents, and $\mathbf{A}$ a semantic relation between documents and keywords, such as the keyword-document matrix defined in section 6.3.1. Finally, d is a set of distance functions applicable to some subset of relations in $\mathcal{R}$, e.g. $d = \{d_k\}$, where d_k is a distance between keywords such as the one defined by formula (2). The application of these distance functions results on distance graphs D whose vertices are elements from the sets in X.

In our architecture of recommendation (Rocha 2001b), users are themselves characterized as information resources, where X may contain, among other application-specific elements, the sets of documents previously retrieved by the user and their associated keywords. Ultimately, what feeds recommendation algorithms, are the distance functions d of knowledge contexts. In this article, we deal in particular with the metric behavior of such functions. We discuss below how an analysis of the metric behavior of distance graphs extracted from DN, allows us to produce appropriate recommendations, and also to better understand the quality of the knowledge stored in information resources. We note that the metric analysis detailed below is not tied to our particular view of recommendation systems, which we discuss in section 6.10.

6.4 Semi-Metric Behavior

The distance graph D obtained from applying distance function d (formula 2) to the KSP proximity relation obtained from formula (1), is not Euclidean because, for a pair of keywords k_1 and k_2, the triangle inequality may be violated: $d(k_1, k_2) \leq d(k_1, k_3) + d(k_3, k_2)$ for some keyword k_3. This means that the shortest distance between two keywords in D may not be the direct link but rather an indirect pathway[4]. Such distance functions are referred to as semi-metrics (Galvin & Shore 1991).

Naturally, the distance graphs obtained from applying a distance function such as d can be made Euclidean. If we compute the transitive closure of the proximity relation derived from

---

[4]Given that most social and knowledge-derived networks possess Small-World behavior (Watts 1999), we expect that vertices which tend to be clustered in a local neighborhood of related vertices, show large distances to vertices in other clusters. But because of the existence of "gateway" vertices relating vertices in different clusters (the small-world phenomenon), smaller indirect distances between vertices in distinct clusters, through these "gateway" vertices, are to be expected.

formula (1), we would obtain a similarity relation on the set of keywords. The application of distance d (formula 2) to a similarity graph would result in a metric distance graph. Indeed, it is very common in the analysis of social or document networks to impose a metric requirement on the distance graphs generated. The purpose of this article is to show that loosening the metric requirement, results in a methodology capable of identifying important characteristics of DN – which we loose with metric distance graphs.

Most ideas are born out of anecdotal, often personal, evidence. The one put forward here is no exception. It arose from questioning what could one infer from the semi-metric behavior of the distance graphs calculated from DN. Given a distance function, what can we say about a pair of highly semi-metric elements from a finite set? And what can we say about the resulting distance graph, from the pairs of highly semi-metric pairs it contains? To construct an intuition to answer these questions, one needs to deal with very familiar examples. In this case, the author could think of no DN more familiar than the set of books cited by his own dissertation (Rocha 1997a)! A database similar (but much smaller) to the one used by ARP contains the relevant information. This database contains about 150 books, each indexed by the respective Library of Congress Keywords, for example:

Kearfott, R. Baker and Vladik Kreinovich (Editors) (1996). *Applications of Interval Computations*. Kluwer. Keywords: Optimization algorithms, Fuzzy logic, Uncertainty, Mathematics, Reliable Computation, Interval Computation.

Table 2. Distance function for 5 keywords in the dissertation database

	Adaptive Systems	Evolution	Modeling systems	Complex Systems	Social Systems
Adaptive Systems	0.00	3.89	12.00	10.33	16.00
Evolution	3.89	0.00	21.50	4.22	35.00
Modeling Systems	12.00	21.50	0.00	5.75	10.00
Complex Systems	10.33	4.22	5.75	0.00	19.00
Social Systems	16.00	35.00	10.00	19.00	0.00

From this database, 86 keywords were extracted. A distance graph D was calculated using function d according to formula (2). Table 2 shows the values of the edges of this graph $d(k_1, k_2)$ for 5 of the keywords. One needs to note that this distance graph is obtained from the relations extracted from a very particular set of documents (in this case 150 books). Therefore, one should not expect the distance values to represent a universally accepted thesaurus or the associations one would anticipate from common sense semantics. Indeed, this kind of distance function is used to characterize particular information resources, as discussed in section 6.3. In this case, the distance graph on the set of keywords denotes only the derived associative semantics from the set of books cited in the dissertation.

To obtain the shortest distance between vertices (keywords) of D, we used a $(+, \min)$ matrix composition of D until closure is achieved – note that traditional algebraic matrix composition is $(*, +)$. Table 3 shows the shortest distances for the same 5 keywords. We see for instance that the shortest indirect distance between MODELING SYSTEMS and EVOLUTION is 9.97, whereas the direct distance is 21.5. This means that the distance between the keyword pair MODELING SYSTEMS-EVOLUTION is semi-metric. This is not the case of the metric pair ADAPTIVE SYSTEMS-EVOLUTION, for which the shortest distance is the direct one.

Table 3. Shortest distance for 5 keywords in the dissertation database (semi-metric pairs shown in italics).

	Adaptive Systems	Evolution	Modeling systems	Complex Systems	Social Systems
Adaptive Systems	0.00	3.89	12.00	*8.11*	16.00
Evolution	3.89	0.00	*9.97*	4.22	*19.89*
Modeling Systems	12.00	*9.97*	0.00	5.75	10.00
Complex Systems	*8.11*	4.22	5.75	0.00	*15.75*
Social Systems	16.00	*19.89*	10.00	*15.75*	0.00

6.5 Characterizing Semi-metric Behavior

Clearly, semi-metric behavior is a question of degree. For some pairs of vertices the indirect distance provides a much shorter short-cut, a larger reduction of distance, than for others. One way to capture this property of pairs of semi-metric vertices (keywords) is to compute a *semi-metric ratio*:

$$s(k_i, k_j) = \frac{d_{direct}(k_i, k_j)}{d_{shorthest}(k_i, k_j)}$$

(4)

where $d_{shortest}$ is the shortest distance between the keyword pair. s is positive and ≥ 1 for semi-metric pairs, where $d_{shortest}$ in an indirect distance between the two keywords. In our example, s(MODELING SYSTEMS, EVOLUTION) = 21.5/9.97 =2.157. This ratio is important to discover semi-metric behavior necessary for our analysis as discussed below, but given that larger graphs tend to show a much larger spread of distance, s tends to increase with the number of vertices of D. Therefore, to be able to compare semi-metric behavior between different DN and their respective different sets of keywords, a *relative semi-metric ratio* is used:

$$rs(k_i, k_j) = \frac{d_{direct}(k_i, k_j) - d_{shortest}(k_i, k_j)}{d_{max} - d_{min}}$$

(5)

rs compares the semi-metric distance reduction to the maximum possible distance reduction in graph D. d_{max} is the largest distance in the graph, and $d_{min} = 0$ is the shortest distance in the entire graph. This ratio varies between 0 and 1 for semi-metric pairs, and it is negative for metric pairs.

Often, the direct distance between two keywords is ∞ because they do not index any documents in common. As a result, s and rs are also ∞ for these cases. Thus, s and rs are not capable of discerning semi-metric behavior for pairs that do not have an initial finite direct distance. To detect relevant instances of this infinite semi-metric reduction, we define the *below average ratio*:

$$b(k_i, k_j) = \frac{\overline{d_{k_i}}}{d_{shorthest}(k_i, k_j)}$$

(6)

where $\overline{d_{k_i}}$ represents the average direct distance from k_i to all k_k such that $d_{direct}(k_i, k_k) \geq 0$. b is only applied to semi-metric pairs of keywords (k_i, k_j) where $d_{shortest}(k_i, k_j) < d_{direct}(k_i, k_j)$

and it measures how much the shortest indirect distance between k_i and k_j falls below the average distance of all keywords k_k directly associated with keyword k_i. Note that $b(k_i, k_i) \neq b(k_j, k_i)$. Of course, b can also be applied to pairs with finite semi-metric reduction. $b > 1$ denotes a below average distance reduction.

6.6 Analysis of a Collection of Documents: The Global Interests of the Collector

The three semi-metric ratios were applied to graph D of the dissertation database. Table 4 lists the top 5 pairs for semi-metric ratio s. If we rank pairs for the relative semi-metric ratio rs, there is a slight reordering of the top as the pair EVOLUTION-DNA drops to rank 11 and the pair LIFE-COGNITION to 6th, while the pair EVOLUTION-CONTROL rises to rank 3 (from 6th) and the pair EVOLUTION-INFORMATION THEORY rises to 5th (from 20th).

Table 4. Semi-metric pairs with highest s in dissertation database.

(k_i,k_j)	$s(\ k_i,k_j)$	$rs(\ k_i,k_j)$
ADAPTIVE SYSTEMS-COGNITION	6.39	0.84
EVOLUTION-CONSTRUCTIVISM	5.00	0.76
EVOLUTION-PSYCHOLOGY	5.00	0.73
EVOLUTION-DNA	4.69	0.64
LIFE-COGNITION	4.55	0.66

What is most interesting about these results is that these pairs denote the original contributions that were offered by the dissertation! Indeed, the dissertation was about using ideas and methodologies from Complex Adaptive Systems, Evolutionary Systems, and Artificial Life and apply them to Artificial Intelligence and Cognitive Science. In particular, the mathematical models (from Psychology) of cognitive categories were expanded using evolutionary ideas, by drawing an analogy with the symbolic characteristics of DNA. Furthermore, this framework was named Evolutionary Constructivism, a term that did not exist previously, but draws both from Evolutionary Theory and the Philosophy of Constructivism in Cognitive Science and Systems Theory.

To understand these results, we need to remember that the distance function d is derived from the finite set of books used in the dissertation. A high degree of semi-metricity for a keyword pair means that this pair of keywords co-indexes very few of the books in the database, but that there exists a strong indirect association between the two keywords via some indirect path, whose short distances require the existence of many books co-indexed by the keyword pairs in the edges of the indirect pathway. Thus, a keyword pair with high values of semi-metric ratios, implies a strong keyword association that is a global property of the specific collection of documents, but not one identifiable in many included documents, and rather constructed from an indirect series of strongly related documents. In other words, the highly semi-metric pairs represent associations that are *latent* in this specific collection of documents – novel associations "begging to be made". Indeed, the two pairs (EVOLUTION-CONTROL and EVOLUTION-INFORMATION THEORY) ranked in the top 5 for the relative semi-metric ratio, identify two associations that are certainly implied by the collection of books (given its large subsets of Cybernetics and Information Theory books), but which were not dealt with in this dissertation – offering some topics for other dissertations!

We can see how the semi-metric analysis of a set of documents associated with a person, say the set of documents retrieved by a user of some information resource, can reveal a set of implied interests of the user, which she has not been able to satiate with individual documents (she may not even be aware of the need). These refer to those interests which are implied by the global associative semantics, but not by previously retrieved (or collected) individual documents. In this sense, semi-metric pairs discover a demand for novel documents to fill a gap implied by the overall DN. If we had used a metric distance function, this specific need would go unnoticed. Finally, the ability to discover an implied demand for documents with this semi-metric analysis is clearly useful for recommendation systems. We detail the development of such systems in a separate article. Here, we want to strengthen our evidence of the utility of semi-metric analysis by applying it to several other larger DN, and proposing a classification of DN according to semi-metric behavior.

6.7 Analysis of Larger Datasets: Latent Trends

The anecdotal analysis of the author's dissertation database served the purpose of creating an intuition of what semi-metric behavior may mean for DN, but we also applied it to other more "subject-independent" datasets. The same semi-metric behavior ratios were used to study the ARP dataset describe above. A distance graph D was calculated using function d (formula 2) for the set of the 500 most common keywords. The semi-metric ratios (formulas 4 to 6) were then calculated for all edges of D (keyword pairs). Table 5 shows the 5 keyword pairs with highest values of s.

Table 5. Semi-metric pairs with highest s in ARP dataset.

(k_i,k_j)	$s(k_i,k_j)$	$rs(k_i,k_j)$
LEUKEMIA-MYOCARDI	272.20	0.4981
HORMON-THIN	214.08	0.9953
CARE-EXCIT	213.59	0.9953
GENE-EQUAT	205.76	0.9951
FILM-TRANSCRIPT	204.51	0.9951

To analyze these results, again, one must remember the original collection of documents, in this case, all the scientific articles published in journals indexed by *ISI* in *SciSearch* between the years of 1996 to 1999. An edge of D with high values of semi-metric ratios r and rs, implies that while very few articles are co-indexed by the respective keyword pair, a series of articles exists which creates an indirect path in D between these two keywords. To obtain a large semi-metric ratio, it is necessary that all edges in the shortest indirect path be defined by short direct distances, which in turn require the existence of many articles co-indexed by both keywords in every edge of this path. Thus, a highly semi-metric keyword association between two keywords implies that very few documents are co-indexed by the keyword pair, but that there are sets of documents indirectly supporting the pair.

The existence of indirect support for a pair of keywords (particularly in scientific databases) may identify a trend that can be expected to be picked up. While it is hard to understand all associations identified in a dataset such as ARP containing so many different topics, at least one association is observed in the data set which is meaningful to the author. The high semi-metricity of the GENE-EQUAT[5] pair may be a result of the trend observed in the late 1990's towards computational and mathematical biology, as molecular biology started to move into a post-genome bioinformatics mode (Kanehisa 2000).

---

[5]Notice that ARP keywords are stemmed to group different constructions of the same term: e.g. Equation and Equations.

Indeed, the analysis of the keyword pairs with infinite semi-metric reduction characterized by a high below average ratio b, seems to give further evidence for this claim, as the highest values of b are observed for the pairs EQUAT-MESSENGERRNA, EQUAT-TRANSCRIPT, and EQUAT-GENE-EXPRESS. These pairs associate the keyword *Equation* with keywords that describe the chief technology that enabled the greatest advances in bioinformatics in the late 1990's and today: the *Gene Expression* Arrays that allow the rapid measurement in parallel of *messenger RNA transcribed* from DNA in the cell (the process of gene expression). Ratio b seems to be useful for larger datasets not collected by a single author. As discussed in more detail in section 6.8, such large datasets are very incomplete in the sense that many potentially semantically associated keyword pairs do not co-index a single document, resulting in an infinite distance for those pairs. Ratio b picks associations between those pairs of keywords that do not co-index <u>a single</u> document but that are strongly implied by the overall collection.

In the case of the ARP database, which contains almost 3 million documents (see section 6.3.1) collected between 1996 and 1999, not a single document was co-indexed by the keywords in the pairs picked up with high values of b (e.g. *Equation* and *Gene Expression*). But the entire collection of documents strongly implied such keyword associations, identifying a *latent* relationship in the literature. We can interpret a latent association between two keywords as evidence that a direct association may be instantiated later by the appearance of documents co-indexed by both keywords, in other words, it identifies a plausible trend. Indeed, we note that in 2001, we observed that in the same collection of journals used by ISI and SciSearch, a very small set of papers started appearing which are co-indexed by both keywords *Equation* and *Gene Expression*, for instance:

Pasto M et al [2001]. "Metabolic activity of the external intercostal muscle of patients with COPD". *Archivos De Bronconeumologia*, v. 37(#3), pp. 108-114, Mar 2001

We expect to observe more articles using this pair of keywords, as the publication of papers in scientific journals typically lags 1 or 2 years from the submission date. In any case, the semi-metric ratios defined in section 6.5 are useful to identify latent associations implied by a collection of documents, and to give a measure of strength for this latent, semi-metric behavior. Below we use them also to characterize different DN, including known public datasets.

We would like to note that in information retrieval, the term latent is associated with a particular technique known as *Latent Semantic Analysis* (LSA) (Landauer, P.W.Foltz, & D.Laham 1998) or *Latent Semantic Indexing* (Berry, DUMAIS, & Obrien 1995). This technique uses Singular Value Decomposition (related to Principal Component Analysis) to group keywords which are semantically associated directly or indirectly in a collection of documents. In this sense, our usage of the term latent is similar to LSA. But our semi-metric analysis is proposed here both as a means to identify those <u>specific</u> pairs of keywords which are *most* latent (useful for recommendation), and as discussed in section 6.8, to characterize types of networks (useful to advance our knowledge of networks).

6.8 Characterizing Document Networks

The behavior of the three semi-metric ratios above (formulas 4 to 6) can also be used characterize the type of DN we encounter. We expect different DN to possess different semi-metric behavior. As discussed in section 6.3.3, we assume that the way keywords are semantically associated in information resources is an expression of the knowledge traded by their communities of users. Thus, we expect semi-metric behavior to allow us to better understand how knowledge is stored in DN, and furthermore determine types of DN.

6.8.1 Additional Document Networks

To investigate this hypothesis, in addition to the dissertation and ARP databases, we have applied this study to other DN such as[6]:

1. ***Distance graph built from web-site Hyperlink Structure*** (PCPStruct). We used a structural proximity measure computed by Bollen (Bollen 2001) for all pairs of the 423 web pages of the *Principia Cybernetica Project* (PCP) Web site (http://pespmc1.vub.ac.be/), which its editors deemed most important. This web site is a collection of dictionary-like definitions about Systems Research topics; each of these 423 web pages is associated with a specific concept (e.g. "Adaptive Systems"). These web pages/concepts were taken as vertices of a non-directed graph, whose edges are weighted with a value computed by a structural proximity measure very similar to formula (1): P_{struc} = max (P^{in}, P^{out}). P^{in} is an inwards proximity where two web pages are considered near if they tend to be linked from many of the same pages, formally it is the probability that two web pages are both linked from a page that links to one of them. P^{out} is an outwards proximity where two web pages are considered near if they tend to link to the same pages, formally it is the probability that two web pages tend to link to the same page that one of them links to(see (Rocha & Bollen 2001) for details). We then normalized all P_{struc} values linearly against the highest value. Finally, using formula (2), we obtained a distance graph D for the set of web pages.

2. ***Distance graph built and adapted from web-site collective usage*** (PCPAdap). Based on the methodology of (Bollen & Heylighen 1998), Bollen (Bollen, Vandesompel, & Rocha 1999) utilized user paths derived from the web server logs of the *Principia Cybernetica Project* (PCP)Web also used in 1. These web pages/concepts were taken as vertices of a directed graph, whose edges are weighted with a value computed from three reinforcement rules: *frequency* (reinforces the edge a $\rightarrow$ b every time it is traversed by a user), *symmetry* (reinforces the edge b $\rightarrow$ a every time a $\rightarrow$ b is traversed), *transitivity* (reinforces the edge a $\rightarrow$ c every time the path a $\rightarrow$ b $\rightarrow$ c is traversed)[7]. For the present work, we constructed a non-directed graph from this user-adapted network by taking the maximum of both directed links between two vertices. We then normalized the weights of this graph linearly against its highest value, which we took as a measure of proximity between vertices. Finally, using formula (2), we obtained a distance graph D.

3. ***Distance graph built and adapted from usage of Journal titles in LANL's research digital library*** (ISSN). Similarly, Bollen (Bollen & Vandesompel 2000) utilized user paths derived from the weblogs of the Los Alamos National Laboratory Research Digital Library (http://lib-www.lanl.gov/) to adapt a network of 472 Research Journal Titles (e.g. "Communications of the ACM" and "BioSystems"), identified by their ISSN. Using the same methodology used for PCPAdapt (point 2 above), we obtained a distance graph on the set of these journal titles.

4. ***Distance graph built from free word association norms*** (Word Norm) Nelson et al (Nelson, McEvoy, & Schreiber 1998) have computed tables of associations between pairs of words from free association experiments with more than 6000 subjects. These tables are in effect directed graphs between words, whose weights are taken to characterize the semantic proximity between words as understood by the population of subjects. These kinds of norms can be seen as a measurement of the associative

---

[6]The additional DN used here were produced by Johan Bollen for the Active Recommendation Project. The author wishes to thank him for making them available.
[7]For more details of this adaptive hypertext mechanism see (Bollen & Heylighen 1998, Bollen, Vandesompel, & Rocha 1999), or (Rocha & Bollen 2001).

semantics of a population. In the present work, we used a subset of 150 words from this dataset (of about 5000 words). Our 150 words were the same used by Bollen and Heylighen (Bollen & Heylighen 1998) in their hypertext experiments, described as the 150 most common English nouns, (words such as "art", "car", "face"). Similarly to the cases above, we constructed a non-directed graph by taking the maximum of both directed links between two words. We then normalized the weights of this graph linearly against its highest value, which we took as a measure of proximity between vertices. Finally, using formula (2), we obtained a distance graph D.

5. ***Random distance graphs.***
   a. *Uniform.* We computed 50 proximity graphs of 150 vertices, and 20 of 500 vertices, whose random weights are uniformly distributed in the unit interval. Using formula (2), we derived the respective distance graphs.
   b. *Exponential.* An analysis of the weights of the PCPAdapt, ISSN, and Dissertation proximity graphs reveals that they fit an exponential random distribution[8] ($\lambda = 15.3$; 18.8; and 10.15 respectively). We computed exponential proximity graphs with $\lambda = 5, 10, 15, 20, 30, 40$, and 100. For each λ, we produced 10 proximity graphs of 150 vertices, and 5 of 500 vertices. Using formula (2), we derived the respective distance graphs.
   c. *Hyper-exponential.* An analysis of the weights of the PCPStruct, ARP, and Word Norm proximity graphs reveals that they fit a hyper-exponential random distribution[9] ($\lambda_1 = 8.3, \lambda_2 = 39.2, p = 0.38; \lambda_1 = 8.8, \lambda_2 = 37.8, p = 0.11$; and $\lambda_1 = 7.6, \lambda_2 = 33.3, p = 0.5$ respectively). We computed random hyper-exponential proximity graphs with similar parameters: $\lambda_1 = 8, \lambda_2 = 39, p = 0.4; \lambda_1 = 9, \lambda_2 = 38, p = 0.1$; and $\lambda_1 = 8, \lambda_2 = 33, p = 0.5$. For each of these two cases, we produced 10 proximity graphs of 150 vertices, and 5 of 500 vertices. Using formula (2), we derived the respective distance graphs.

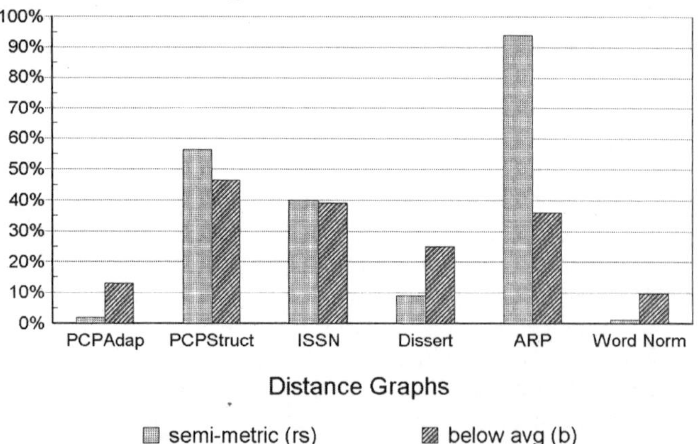

Figure 1. Semi-metric behavior of the several non-random distance graphs.

6.8.2 Semi-metric Behavior: Measuring Associative Semantics

Figure 1 depicts the percentages of pairs with semi-metric behavior described by ratios *rs*

---

[8]The exponential probability distribution function is $F(t) = \lambda e^{-\lambda t}$, $t \geq 0, \lambda > 0$.
[9]The hyper-exponential probability distribution function is $F(t) = \lambda_1 p e^{-\lambda_1 t} + \lambda_2 (1-p) e^{-\lambda_2 t}$, $t \geq 0, \lambda_1, \lambda_2 > 0$.

(formula 5) and b (formula 6) for all non-random distance graphs described above. Table 6 summarizes all the values. From this figure alone we can observe that the Word Norm distance graph shows very small semi-metric behavior: only 1% of all word pairs have $rs >$ 0.0, and only 10% have $b > 1.0$.

We would expect this behavior since, given the large pool of subjects in the Word Norm experiments, the appropriate distance between pairs of the most common English words has been directly established. We can say that the Word Norm distance graph captures most of the common sense word associations in a population; it is a fairly *complete* measurement of its semantics.

Table 6. Percentage of semi-metric pairs for ratios rs and b for all distance graphs. Values for random cases are averages, standard deviation also shown.

	N	%rs	stdv %rs	%b	stdv %b
ARP	500	94		36	
Dissert	86	9		25	
PCPAdap	423	2		13	
PCPStruct	423	56		47	
ISSN	472	40		39	
Word Norm	150	1		10	
Uniform	150	96.3223	0.2166	14.7703	0.5616
	500	98.6466	0.0307	12.3738	0.2558
Exp λ=5	150	97.939	0.2699	15.4505	0.4949
	500	99.2856	0.0093	13.2108	0.3351
Exp λ=10	150	87.9974	0.4723	15.208	0.6997
	500	93.6482	0.0444	14.3884	0.0757
Exp λ=15	150	85.029	0.4908	16.0492	0.5618
	500	90.5042	0.0596	14.784	0.0972
Exp λ=20	150	83.3281	0.3757	16.6791	0.7992
	500	89.0098	0.1100	15.4748	0.2250
Exp λ=30	150	82.2659	0.4815	17.3846	0.5559
	500	87.8064	0.0968	16.1488	0.1528
Exp λ=40	150	81.6992	0.5263	18.0295	0.4917
	500	87.1862	0.1472	16.8334	0.2021
Exp λ=100	150	80.1878	0.3540	20.3974	0.4448
	500	85.7592	0.1337	19.618	0.1233
HyperExp (8, 39, 0.4)	150	92.1146	0.21	16.655	1.0188
	00	96.1634	0.451	16.0852	0.2362
HyperExp (8, 33, 0.5)	150	97.939	0.3230	15.4505	0.5107
	500	95.9424	0.1351	15.342	0.1588
HyperExp (9, 38, 0.1)	150	91.5947	0.3893	17.6178	0.4240
	500	96.3464	0.0661	16.7052	0.0991

The ARP distance graph on the other hand, has been built from automatic analysis of keywords present in a large set of scientific documents from several fields of inquiry (e.g. Biology, Physics, Chemistry). In this dataset, we expect the same keyword to have distinct meanings for distinct communities of authors (polysemy) and the same concept to be described by several keywords (synonymy).

Furthermore, when keywords co-index a document, unlike the Word Norm experiments, authors and/or editors are not expected to list possibly associated keywords. Thus the ARP distance graph is very far from capturing all the possible, relevant, associations between pairs of keywords, it indeed provides only a very incomplete measurement of the semantics of the population of its authors. This is apparent from the percentage of semi-metric pairs observed: 94% of all keyword pairs have *rs* > 0.0 (meaning that there is a shorter indirect distance for most pairs), and 36% have *b* > 1.0. The other datasets also observe an expected semi-metric behavior. The PCPAdap distance graph (*rs*: 2% and *b*: 13%) behaves similarly to the Word Norm case, which shows that Bollen's adaptive hypertext algorithm succeeded in capturing the semantics of its user community in a fairly complete manner. Especially when we contrast it to the PCPStruct distance graph (*rs*: 56% and *b*: 47%), which contains many more pairs of web pages/concepts with shorter indirect distances. The distance graph of PCPStruct was built exclusively from the hyperlink structure of the web site as designed by its authors. Because we observe a large percentage of semi-metric pairs, we can conclude that many associations between web pages are not explicitly made by the web site authors, but implied by the overall hyperlink structure. Using Bollen's algorithm on this same web site, which integrates the traversal paths from the user population with a transitivity rule, brings about a substantial reduction of indirect associations. In other words, the population of users whose traversal behavior was integrated by Bollen's algorithm, identified most of the relevant associations between web pages.

However, the same adaptive hypertext algorithm, was not as successful in deriving a complete measurement of the semantic associations between journal titles in the ISSN distance graph (*rs*: 40% and *b*: 39%). Several reasons for this can be found. The user community used to adapt the PCP web site is more thematically coherent. PCP is a web site dedicated to the study of Systems Research, thus, its community of users functions in the same research universe. In contrast, the user community used to adapt the ISSN distance graph is the population of scientists and engineers at the Los Alamos National Laboratory, which contains a rather diverse pool of people from such fields as Physics, Biology, Material Science, Computer Science, etc. Indeed, the 472 journals in this network cover all areas of science and technology. Thus, such a heterogeneous community may not possess a complete associative semantics to begin with. By this we mean that distinct communities fail to see associations outside of their usual set of journals and terminology. As shown in section 6.7, in such heterogeneous DN such as ARP and ISSN, many relevant associations are not explicitly observed in individual documents or by users of the dabatases, but rather implied by the network.

Furthermore, Bollen's (Bollen 2001) methodology to recover user paths from user logs may not be as appropriate for the ISSN network as it was for the PCP case. Whereas PCP users were browsing a web site, ISSN users were retrieving documents from a digital library. The first were more prone to pursue links thus creating longer paths which can be used by the transitivity rule of Bollen's algorithm to discover indirect associations. The users of a research library tend to be looking for specific papers from references or retrieving documents from keyword searches. This fact could perhaps be alleviated by collecting web logs for a longer period of time.

The dissertation distance graph (*rs*: 9% and *b*: 25%) also shows small semi-metric behavior, though larger than the Word Norm and PCP cases. This is also expected since it was extracted from the keywords of all the books referred to in a dissertation. Such a collection of books is necessarily fairly related in order for the dissertation to be a coherent piece. We have discussed in section 6.6 that the semi-metric pairs discovered in this distance graph revealed what was novel in the dissertation. The low numbers of semi-metric pairs reveal that the distance graph is also a fairly complete measurement of the associative semantics implied by the dissertation. This supports the usage of distance functions in the knowledge context structure (section 6.3.3) to characterize the semantic interests of a user in recommendation systems, since a single user tends to collect fairly related documents.

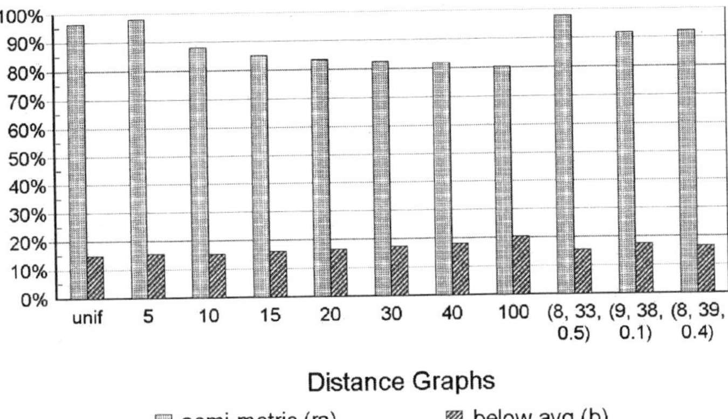

Figure 2. Average values of semi-metric ratios for random distance graphs with 150 vertices. Leftmost distance graph is for the uniform random case. Rightmost three graphs refer to the hyper-exponential distance graphs discussed above, with $(\lambda_1, \lambda_2, p)$. All other distance graphs refer to the various exponential cases identified by λ.

Figure 2 depicts the average percentage of semi-metric pairs in the various random distance graphs with 150 vertices. Table 6 also summarizes the values for random distance graphs with 150 and 500 vertices, and also indicates the standard deviation of these values. In all random cases, we observe high percentages of semi-metric pairs (though not very large values of below average measure b). This shows that in all types of random graphs, most pairs of vertices possess some smaller indirect distance pathway. By contrasting figures 1 and 2 (or Table 6), we notice immediately that the semi-metric behavior of the random distance graphs is similar to that of the ARP distance graph. Nevertheless, we can show that the semi-metric behavior of random graphs, where we do not expect a real semantics to exist at all, is quite different from the behavior of graphs such as ARP where some semantics does exist, even if fractional or incomplete. To better distinguish between random distance graphs and distance graphs such as ARP produced from large collections of documents, we study their semi-metric behavior in more detail in the next subsection.

We end this section by concluding that we compiled and discussed evidence that the percentage of pairs with semi-metric behavior in a distance graph can be a good indicator of how well such graph captures the associative semantics of a DN from where it is derived. On one extreme we have Word Norms, a complete semantic measurement of common words, with low percentages of semi-metric pairs, and on the other, DN such as ARP, a very fractional measurement of keyword semantics, with high percentages of semi-metric pairs. Next we discuss another dimension of semi-metric behavior, and propose a means to classify the nature of the associative semantics entailed in DN.

6.8.3 The behavior of the most semi-metric-pairs: Strength of Latent Associations

The distance graphs analyzed are of different sizes, from 86 keywords (3655 pairs) in the dissertation database, to 500 in the ARP case (124750 pairs). To compare the semi-metric behavior of all these DN of different sizes, we selected 1% of all pairs with highest rs in the respective distance graph D. In other words, we ranked all pairs according to rs, and then selected the top 1%[10]. We chose 1% of all pairs because this is the percentage of semi-metric pairs found in the Word Norm dataset, which displays the smallest number of semi-metric pairs. The Word Norm clearly functions in this analysis as a benchmark since it contains as good an example of a measurement of a population's associative semantics as one can get. This way, we can compare the semi-metric behavior of the other distance graphs against a complete picture of the behavior of a very complete associative semantics. Table 7 lists the numbers of pairs that 1% represents for each dataset.

To obtain a graphic model of semi-metric behavior, we further need to normalize the number of pairs. Thus, for each ranked list of top 1% pairs, we sampled 100 equally spaced (in rank) pairs, except for the dissertation dataset where we expanded the existing 37 pairs to 100 using linear interpolation of the values of *rs*. We denote this ranked, sampled (or expanded) set of pairs as $TRS^{1\%}$. Figure 3 depicts the values of *rs* for the pairs in $TRS^{1\%}$ for each distance graph. Each curve depicts the normalized semi-metric behavior of the top 1% most semi-metric pairs for each distance graph.

Table 7. Number of Pairs in top 1% pairs.

ARP	Dissertation	PCP	ISSN	Random 150	Random 500	Word Norms
1248	37	893	1112	112	1248	112

One thing we immediately notice in figure 3 is that even though both the ARP and uniform random distance networks produce large percentages of semi-metric pairs (figures 1 and 2), the behavior of *rs* is quite different in their $TRS^{1\%}$ sets. The uniform random graphs, except for a very small number of pairs, show very low values of *rs* which quickly decay to close to zero. In fact, almost all of the many semi-metric pairs in uniform random graphs possess a very small value of *rs*, whereas in the ARP case, semi-metric pairs possess a substantially higher value of *rs*.

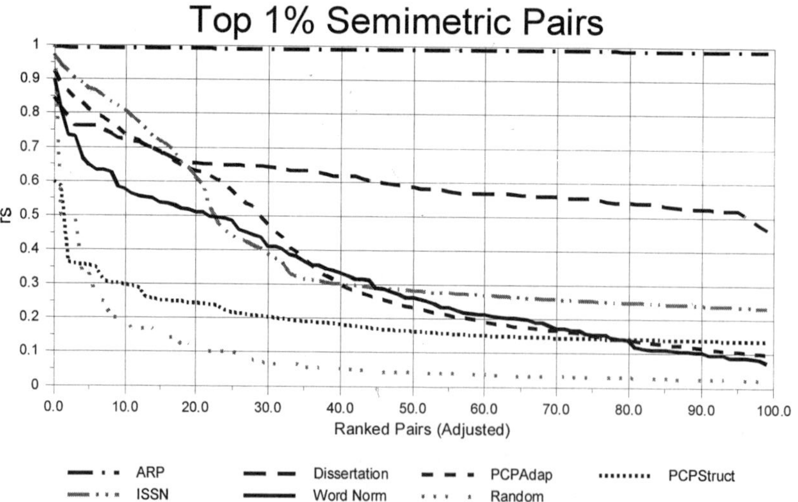

Figure 3. Top 1% semi-metric pairs sampled or expanded to a series of 100 points. Random depicts a uniform random case.

This shows, as expected, that vertices in a uniform random graph are not related in a semantically coherent manner. For most pairs of vertices, there tends to exist a shorter indirect distance (semi-metric path), but which nonetheless tends not to be much shorter

---

[10] Not 1% of the set of semi-metric pairs, but 15 of all pairs in D.

than the direct path, because the distances of the edges in the indirect paths are also computed from a uniformly random proximity distribution, and thus tend not to reduce the distance by much. The longer the indirect path between a pair of vertices, the smaller the probability of it offering a shorter path than the direct distance between the pair[11]. ARP, on the other hand, is clearly not random. Most of its keyword pairs do have shorter indirect paths, but many of these offer substantial distance reductions. This means that there exist plenty of strong latent associations.

Both the ARP and uniform random distance graphs are incomplete as a representation of associative semantics, since both have large percentages of semi-metric pairs (figures 1 and 2), but most of the semi-metric associations in the uniform random distance graphs are very weak, whereas the ARP distance graph contains many strong ones (figure 3).

6.8.4 Quantifying Latent Associations in Document Networks

Using Semi-metric BehaviorWe need now to compare the semi-metric behavior of real distance graphs such as ARP with the more realistic random distance graphs such as the ones derived from exponential and hyper-exponential distributions. In particular, we want to quantify the existence of strong latent associations in distance graphs. To do this, we compute the mean value of rs in $TRS^{1\%}$, which we denote by μ, shown in Table 8 for all distance graphs. We denote by π the ratio of semi-metric pairs (those with $rs > 0$) from all pairs in each distance graph. This value is the percentage of semi-metric pairs, as shown in Table 6, divided by 100. We can now compare the different distance graphs according to μ and π. The first parameter quantifies the existence of strong latent associations, whereas the second quantifies the fractional or incomplete nature of a given distance graph as a representation of associative semantics. Figure 4 plots the values of each distance graph according to these two parameters.

We can clearly see in this figure that the Word Norm distance graph is the least fractional and it contains less latent associations than all the other real distance graphs. As already noted, this graph captures most semantic associations directly and those few latent associations that it entails tend not to be very strong. The same applies to the PCPAdap graph. We can say it is a good representation of the semantics of its user community. The Dissertation distance graph is very semantically complete (small percentage of semi-metric pairs), but it still contains strong latent associations amongst the few semi-metric pairs – the novel associations strongly implied by the collection of books but not made by many of the individual books (see section 6.6).

The PCPStruct and ISSN distance graphs are more fractional than the Dissertation, Word Norm and PCPAdap cases (more semi-metric pairs), but with weaker latent associations than the Dissertation. They are indeed more like random graphs than the previous ones, as they possesses plenty of semi-metric pairs, with only moderately strong latent associations. The ARP distance graph, displays high values of μ and π, showing that while it is a very incomplete representation of associative semantics, as random graphs do, it does contain many strong latent associations. In the case of ARP, this means that many strong latent associations are implied by the literature, but few articles make it explicit, suggesting plenty of room for exploiting novel associations in Science.

---

[11] If we simplify this problem by considering that the distance between two vertices has equal probability of being large or small, then for a path of length 2, the probability of every segment in this path possessing a small distance is 0.25, for a path of length 3 it is 0.125, and for a path of length n it is $1/n^2$. We note that for an indirect path to possess a small distance, every segment must be reasonably small.

Table 8. μ mean value of rs in $TRS^{1\%}$.

Graph	N	parameters	μ	Std.Dev.
PCPAdap	423		0.352776	
PCPStruct	423		0.2007	
ISSN	472		0.399713	
Dissert	86		0.6080235	
ARP	500		0.990388	
Word Norm	150		0.319139	
Uniform	150		0.065874	0.020077
Uniform	500		0.051606	0.0051279
Exponential	150	5	0.166922	0.0166281
Exponential	500	5	0.180608	0.0080763
Exponential	150	10	0.319879	0.0327653
Exponential	500	10	0.286318	0.0036716
Exponential	150	15	0.3938033	0.0208518
Exponential	500	15	0.38278	0.0135159
Exponential	150	20	0.456823	0.0512222
Exponential	500	20	0.455522	0.0095474
Exponential	150	30	0.568661	0.0370173
Exponential	500	30	0.57756	0.0110469
Exponential	150	40	0.648974	0.0419679
Exponential	500	40	0.66449	0.0135768
Exponential	150	100	0.952153	0.0381469
Exponential	500	100	0.988852	0.0084951
Hyper-exponential	150	(8, 39, 0.4)	0.541686	0.0403997
Hyper-exponential	150	(8, 39, 0.4)	0.538308	0.014352
Hyper-exponential	150	(8, 33, 0.5)	0.476169	0.0427201
Hyper-exponential	500	(8, 33, 0.5)	0.469438	0.0038927
Hyper-exponential	150	(9, 38, 0.1)	0.612927	0.0364466
Hyper-exponential	500	(9, 38, 0.1)	0.61674	0.0099022

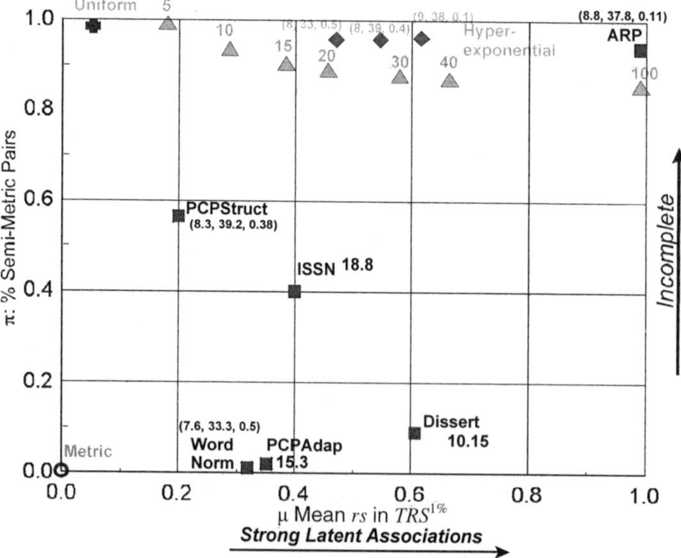

Figure 4. Semi-metric behavior of several distance graphs. Values for random graphs are averages; only random graphs with 500 vertices are shown. The parameters for the exponential and hyper-exponential distributions which characterize the weights of the respective proximity graphs are also shown.

The three types of random graph produces are also plotted in figure 4. Uniform random graphs display a very high percentage of semi-metric pairs (fractional), but very weak latent associations. This behavior is quite distinct from the case of ARP, where we have an equally high percentage of semi-metric pairs, but very strong latent associations. However, the distribution of proximity weights in the real data sets are either exponential or hyper-exponential (see section 6.8.1), so we need to contrast these with more similar random graphs.

We can see in figure 4 that the exponential random graphs create a curve in the space of the two semi-metric parameters μ and π for the parameter λ of the exponential distribution. A non-linear regression of the values of the ratio of semi-metric pairs (π) and mean value of *rs* in $TRS^{1\%}$ (μ) yields the following model for values of λ[12]:

$$\pi = a + \frac{b}{\lambda}$$
$$\mu = c\lambda^2 + d\lambda + e \tag{7}$$

where a, b, c, d, and e are real values shown in table 9 for random graphs of 150 and 500 vertices. We note that the curves for graphs of the two different dimensions are very near.

Table 9. Model of semi-metric behavior of exponential random graphs.

N	a	b	c	d	e
150	0.7903816582	0.9315307064	-0.0000913272	0.01733546	0.1290713052
500	0.8550775455	0.7143364562	-0.0000930467	0.0180254566	0.1147711017

As discussed in section 6.8.1, the weights of the PCPAdapt, ISSN, and Dissertation proximity graphs fit an exponential random distribution with λ = 15.3; 18.8; and 10.15 respectively. All these three distance graphs have different sizes, N = 423, 472, and 86 respectively. We compare the first two distance graphs to random graphs of 500 vertices, and the third to random graphs of 150 vertices[13]. Using formula 8 with the parameters from table 9 (those of 500 vertices for PCPAdap and ISSN, and those 150 vertices for the Dissertation data set), we obtain values of π and μ for random counterparts of these three data sets, listed in table 10.

Table 10. Comparison of real distance graphs to random counterparts.

	μ	π	μ' random	π' random	d	d_{metric}	$d_{uniform}$
Dissert	0.608	0.09	0.2956	0.7913	0.7677	0.6146	1.027822
PCPAdap	0.3528	0.02	0.3688	0.9017	0.8818	0.3534	1.012311
ISSN	0.3997	0.4	0.4208	0.8931	0.4935	0.5655	0.681991
ARP	0.9903	0.94	0.6167	0.9635	0.3743	1.3654	0.939843
Word Norm	0.3191	0.01	0.4762	0.9794	0.9820	0.3193	0.986285
PCPStruc	0.2007	0.56	0.5383	0.9616	0.5247	0.5949	0.451777

As discussed in section 6.8.1, the PCPStruct, ARP, and Word Norm proximity graphs fit a hyper-exponential random distribution with λ_1 = 8.3, λ_2 = 39.2, p = 0.38; λ_1 = 8.8, λ_2 = 37.8, p = 0.11; and λ_1 = 7.6, λ_2 = 33.3, p = 0.5, respectively. Given that a hyper-exponential distribution depends on three parameters, obtaining a model curve such as the one obtained

---

[12] The coefficient of multiple determination (R^2) for this model is 0.9974609914 for π and .9881903595 for μ, for graphs of 150 vertices, and 0.9881136391 for π and 0.9961577382 for μ, for graphs of 500 vertices.

[13] Ideally, we would compute a curve for graphs with exactly the same size of vertices as the real data sets. However, as can be seen in table 8, and also from the parameters derived for formula 8, the behavior of exponential random graphs of 150 and 500 vertices is not very distinct. Thus, our comparison of real distance graphs of size 423 and 472 to a random graph of 500 vertices, and a real graph of 86 vertices to a random graph 150 vertices is acceptable.

for the exponential case would require the generation of a much larger set of random graphs. Thus, we generated hyper-exponential random proximity graphs with parameters similar to those of the real data sets: $\lambda_1 = 8$, $\lambda_2 = 39$, $p = 0.4$; $\lambda_1 = 9$, $\lambda_2 = 38$, $p = 0.1$; and $\lambda_1 = 8$, $\lambda_2 = 33$, $p = 0.5$, respectively. Table 10 also lists the values of π and μ for these cases. These values give us an indication of how far from an equivalent random graph each real distance graph is. Clearly, π and μ give us two distinct qualities of semi-metric behavior, namely, how incomplete the associative semantics contained in a distance graph is and the strength of latent associations it contains. Above, we have already discussed these qualities for each real distance graph. But to quantify semi-metric behavior as a phenomenon, we calculate the Euclidean distance d between a real distance graph and its random counterpart, as shown in table 10. As expected, the ARP, ISSN, and PCPStruct distance graphs are nearer to their random counterparts, than the other graphs. These distances can be visualized in Figure 5.

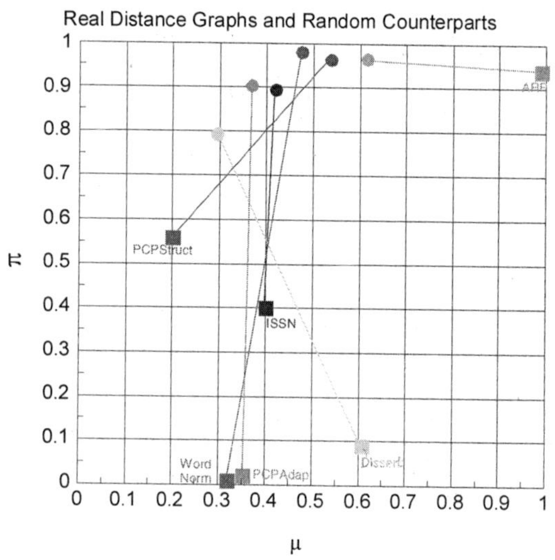

Figure 5. Real distance graphs (squares) and their random counterparts (circles) in μ-π space.

However, interestingly, when we calculate the Euclidean distance to mean uniform random graphs[14], $d_{uniform}$ (shown in table 10), we find that the ISSN and PCPStruct graphs are much nearer to uniform random graphs than ARP. This is a result of the high strength of latent associations in the ARP distance graph, which uniform random graphs do not observe, but which exponential and hyper-exponential random graphs observe in moderate amounts. Notice that both parameters (π and μ) would be null if we had imposed a metric distance (a transitive closure) on the original proximity graphs. Indeed, a metric distance graph would exist at the origin of the plot in figures 4 and 5. Table 10 also lists the distances of every real distance graph to a metric distance graph (the origin): d_{metric}.

6.9 Metric Behavior for Recommendation and Characterization of Document Networks

By utilizing a semi-metric distance function, we have gained a mechanism to classify DN

---

[14]Again, this distance is computed for graphs of 150 vertices for the Dissertation and Word Norm cases, and for graphs of 500 vertices for all other cases.

according to how complete a representation of associative semantics it is, and how strong its latent associations are. Clearly, depending on the application one has in mind, the two parameters π and μ and derivable distances, allow us to better understand a DN under study. We can detect if it reflects the expected semantics of a population, in which case it will behave more like the Word Norm and PCPAdap DN, which are nearer to metric graphs. We can also detect if a semantically complete DN still contains strong latent associations, in which case it will behave more like the Dissertation DN with high values of μ and low values of π. Conversely, a semantically incomplete DN with strong latent associations will behave more like ARP, with high values of both π and μ.

Indeed, the ability to map a semi-metric distance graph in the π/μ space, gives us a mechanism to evaluate adaptive algorithms such as the one used on the PCP Web site and the ISSN data set. Clearly Bollen's algorithm worked well on the PCP web site, as the adapted network is much closer to the Word Norm case, than the original hyperlink structure used to compute PCPStruct. But, for reasons already discussed above, it did not behave as well on the ISSN case, which was not adapted to a complete semantics nor does it entail strong latent associations.

We have compiled and presented evidence that the semi-metric analysis of distance graphs obtained from DN is a methodology useful for both recommendation of documents and chracetrization of different types of DN. Clearly, this analysis needs to be conducted for many more DN to fully develop its power, but we hope to have presented enough compelling evidence here to convince the reader that it is a methodology worth pursuing.

6.10 Integrating Evidence from Different Knowledge Contexts

6.10.1 Describing User Interest with Evidence Sets

Humans use language to communicate categories of objects in the world. But such linguistic categories are notoriously context-dependent (Lakoff 1987, Rocha 1999), which makes it harder for computer programs to grasp the real interests of users. In information retrieval we tend to use keywors to describe the content of documents, and sets of keywords to describe the present interests of a given user at a particular time (e.g. a web search).

One of the advantages of using the knowledge contexts defined in section 6.3 in our recommendation architecture is that the same keyterms can be differently associated in different information resources. Indeed, the distance functions of knowledge contexts allow us to regard these as connectionist memory systems (Rocha 2001a, Rocha 2001b). This way, the same set of keyterms describing the present interests (or search) of a user, is associated with different sets of other keyterms in distinct knowledge contexts. Thus, the interests of the user are also context-dependent when several information resources are at stake.

In this setting, the objective of a recommendation system that takes as input the present interest of a user, is to select and integrate the appropriate contexts, or perspectives, from the several ways the user interests are constructed in each information resource. We have developed an algorithm named *TalkMine* which implements the selective communication fabric necessary for this integration (Rocha 1999, Rocha 2001a, Rocha 2001b).

TalkMine uses an interval valued set structure named *evidence set* (Rocha 1994, Rocha 1999), an extension of a fuzzy set (Zadeh 1965), to model the interests of users defined as categories, or weighted sets of kewords. Evidence sets are set structures which provide interval degrees of membership, weighted by the probability constraint of the Dempster-

Shafer Theory of Evidence (DST) (Shafer 1976). They are defined by two complementary dimensions: membership and belief. The first represents an interval (type-2) fuzzy degree of membership, and the second a degree of belief on that membership. Specifically, an *evidence set A* of *X*, is defined for all $x \in X$, by a membership function of the form:

$$A(x) \rightarrow (\mathcal{F}^x, m^x) \in \mathcal{B}[0, 1]$$

where $\mathcal{B}[0, 1]$ is the set of all possible bodies of evidence $(\mathcal{F}^x, m^x)$ on $\mathcal{I}$, the set of all subintervals of [0, 1]. Such bodies of evidence are defined by a basic probability assignment m^x on $\mathcal{I}$, for every x in X (see figure 6).

Each interval of membership I_j^x represents the degree of importance of a particular element x of X (e.g. a keyterm) in category A (e.g. the interests of a user) *according* to a particular *perspective* (e.g. a particular database), defined by evidential weight $m^x(I_j^x)$. Thus, the membership of each element x of an evidence set A is defined by distinct intervals representing different perspectives.

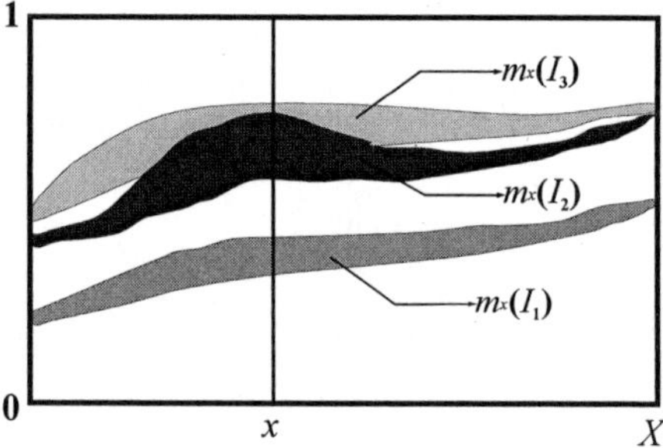

Figure 6. Evidence Set with 3 Perspectives.

The basic set operations of complementation, intersection, and union have been defined for evidence sets, of which fuzzy approximate reasoning and traditional set operations are special cases (Rocha 1997b, Rocha 1999). Measures of uncertainty have also been defined for evidence sets. The total uncertainty of an evidence set A is defined by: $U(A) = (IF(A), IN(A), IS(A))$. The three indices of uncertainty, which vary between 1 and 0, *IF* (*fuzziness*), *IN* (*nonspecificity*), and *IS* (*conflict*) were introduced in (Rocha 1997b). *IF* is based on Yager's (Yager 1979, Yager 1980) and Klir and Yuan's (Klir & Yuan 1995) measure of fuzziness. *IN* is based on the Hartley measure, and *IS* on the Shannon entropy as extended by Klir (Klir 1993) into the DST framework.

6.10.2 Inferring User Interest in Different Knowledge Contexts

Fundamental to the *TalkMine* algorithm is the integration of information from different knowledge contexts into an evidence set, representing the category of topics (described by keywords) a user is interested at a particular time. Thus, the keywords the user employs to describe her interests or in a search, need to be "decoded" into appropriate keywords for each information resource: the perspective of each knowledge context.

The *present interests* of each user can be described by a set of keywords $P^u = \{k_1, \ldots, k_p\}$. Using these keywords and the DST keyword distance function (2) of the several knowledge contexts involved, we want to infer the interests of the user as "seen" from the several knowledge contexts involved.

Let us assume that r knowledge contexts R_t are involved in addition to one from the user herself. The set of keywords contained in all the participating knowledge contexts is denoted by $\mathcal{K}$. d_0 is the distance function of the knowledge context of the user, while $d_1...d_r$ are the distance functions from each of the other knowledge contexts. For each knowledge context R_t and each keyword k_u in the user's present interests $P^u = \{k_1, ..., k_p\}$, a *spreading interest fuzzy set* $F_{t,u}$ is calculated using d_t:

$$F_{t,u}(k) = \max\left[e^{\left(-\alpha d_t(k,k_u)^2\right)}, \varepsilon\right] \forall k \in R_t, t = 1...r, u = 1...p \tag{8}$$

This fuzzy set contains the keywords of R_t which are closer than, to k_u, according to an exponential function of d_t. $F_{t,u}$ spreads the interest of the user in k_u to keywords of R_t that are near according to d_t. The parameter α controls the spread of the exponential function. Because each knowledge context R_t contains a different d_t, each $F_{t,u}$ is also a different fuzzy set for the same k_u, possibly even containing keywords that do not exist in other knowledge contexts. There exist a total of $n = r.p$ spreading interest fuzzy sets $F_{t,u}$ given r knowledge context and p keyterms in the user's present interests.

6.10.3 The Linguistic "And/OR" Combination

Since each knowledge context produces a distinct fuzzy set, we need a procedure for integrating several of these fuzzy sets into an evidence set to obtain the integrated representation of user interests we desire. We have proposed such a procedure (Rocha 2001b) based on Turksen's (Turksen 1996) combination of Fuzzy Sets into Interval Valued Fuzzy Sets (IVFS). Turksen proposed that fuzzy logic compositions could be represented by IVFS's given by the interval obtained from a composition's Disjunctive Normal Form (DNF) and Conjucntive Normal Form (CNF): [DNF, CNF]. We note that in fuzzy logic, for certain families of conjugate pairs of conjunctions and disjunctions, DNF $\subseteq$ CNF.

Using Turksen's approach, the union and intersection of two fuzzy sets F_1 and F_2 result in the two following IVFS, respectively:

$$IV^{\cup}(x) = \left[F_1(x) \underset{DNF}{\cup} F_2(x), F_1(x) \underset{CNF}{\cup} F_2(x) \right]$$
$$IV^{\cap}(x) = \left[F_1(x) \underset{DNF}{\cap} F_2(x), F_1(x) \underset{CNF}{\cap} F_2(x) \right] \tag{9}$$

where, $A \underset{CNF}{\cup} B = A \cup B$, $A \underset{DNF}{\cup} B = (A \cap B) \cup (A \cap \overline{B}) \cup (\overline{A} \cap B)$,

$A \underset{CNF}{\cap} B = (A \cup B) \cap (A \cup \overline{B}) \cap (\overline{A} \cup B)$, and $A \underset{DNF}{\cap} B = A \cap B$ for any two fuzzy sets A and B.

Formulae (9) constitute a procedure for calculating the union and intersection IVFS from two fuzzy sets. $IV^{\cup}$ describes the linguistic expression "F_1 or F_2", while $IV^{\cap}$ describes "F_1 and F_2", – capturing both fuzziness and nonspecificity of the particular fuzzy logic operators employed, as Turksen suggested (Rocha 2001b). However, in common language, often "and" is used as an unspecified "and/or". In other words, what we mean by the statement "I am interested in x and y", is more correctly understood as an unspecified combination of "x and y" with "x or y". This is particularly relevant for recommendation systems where it is precisely this kind of statement from users that we wish to respond to. One use of evidence sets is as representations of the integration of both $IV^{\cup}$ and $IV^{\cap}$ into a linguistic category that expresses this ambiguous "and/or". To make this combination more general, assume that we possess an evidential weight m_1 and m_2 associated with each F_1 and F_2 respectively. These are probabilistic weights ($m_1 + m_2 = 1$) which represent the strength we associate with each fuzzy set being combined. The linguistic expression at stake now becomes "I am interested in x and y, but I value x more/less than y". To combine all this information into an evidence set we use the following procedure:

$$ES(x) = \left\{ \left\langle IV^{\cup}(x), \min(m_1, m_2) \right\rangle, \left\langle IV^{\cap}(x), \max(m_1, m_2) \right\rangle \right\} \qquad (10)$$

Because $IV^{\cup}$ is the less restrictive combination, obtained by applying the maximum operator to the original fuzzy sets F_1 and F_2, its evidential weight is acquired via the minimum operator of the evidential weights associated with F_1 and F_2. The reverse is true for $IV^{\cap}$. Thus, the evidence set obtained from (10) contains $IV^{\cup}$ with the lowest evidence, and $IV^{\cap}$ with the highest. Linguistically, it describes the ambiguity of the "and/or" by giving the strongest belief weight to "and" and the weakest to "or". It expresses: "I am interested in x and y to a higher degree, but I am also interested in x or y to a lower degree".

Finally, formula (10) can be easily generalized for a combination of n fuzzy sets F_i with probability constrained weights m_i:

$$ES(x) = \left\{ \left\langle IV^{\cup}_{F_i/F_j}(x), \frac{\min(m_i, m_j)}{n-1} \right\rangle, \left\langle IV^{\cap}_{F_i/F_j}(x), \frac{\max(m_i, m_j)}{n-1} \right\rangle \right\} \qquad (11)$$

In *TalkMine*, this formula is used to combine the n spreading interest Fuzzy Sets obtained from r knowledge context and p keyterms in P^u as described in section 6.10.2. The resulting evidence set $ES(k)$ defined on $\mathcal{K}$, represents the interests of the user inferred from spreading the initial interest set of keywords in the intervening knowledge contexts using their respective distance functions. The inferring process combines each $F_{t,u}$ with the "and/or" linguistic expression entailed by formula (11). Each $F_{t,u}$ contains the keywords related to keyword k_u in the knowledge context R_t, that is, the perspective of R_t on k_u. Thus, $ES(k)$ contains the "and/or" combination of all the perspectives on each keyword $k_u \in \{k_1, ..., k_p\}$ from each knowledge context R_t.

As an example, without loss of generality, consider that the initial interests of an user contain one single keyword k_1, and that the user is querying two distinct information resources R_1 and R_2. Two spreading interest fuzzy sets, F_1 and F_2, are generated using d_1 and d_2 respectively, with probabilistic weights $m_1 = v_1$ and $m_2 = v_2$, say, with $m_1 > m_2$ to indicate that the user trusts R_1 more than R_2. $ES(k)$ is easily obtained straight from formula (10). This evidence set contains the keywords related to k_1 in R_1 "and/or" the keywords related to k_1 in R_2, taking into account the probabilistic weights attributed to R_1 and R_2. F_1 is the perspective of R_1 on k_1 and F_2 the perspective of R_2 on k_1.

6.11 Distance Functions in Recommendation Systems

The evidence set combination defined in Section 6.10.3 with formulas (10) and (11) is a first cut at detecting the interests of a user in a set of information resources. Our *TalkMine* recommendation algorithm computes a more tuned interest set of keywords, using an interactive conversation process between the user and the information resources being queried. Such conversation is an uncertainty reducing process based on the IR system of Nakamura and Iwai (Nakamura & Iwai 1982), which we extended to Evidence Sets (Rocha 1999, Rocha 2001b).

TalkMine can be understood as an algorithm for obtaining a representation of user interests in several information resources (including other users). It works by combining into an evidence set, the present user interests with all the perspectives derived from each information resource. The resulting Evidence Set is further fine-tuned by an automated conversation process with the user's agent/browser (Rocha 2001b). The combination of perspectives utilizes the evidence set combination defined in section 6.10, which in turn employs the semi-metric distance functions described in this article. The importance of such semi-metric distance functions on their own, is also described in this article. They allow us to both characterize Document Networks for interests and trends (useful for recommendation), as well as offer an avenue to combine user interests in distinct information resources.

In this article we have detailed empirical evidence of the utility of semi-metric distance functions for recommendation processes. In particular, we emphasize that forcing distance functions in recommendation systems to be metric, leads to the loss of important information entailed in DN. Namely, the capacity to identify strong latent associations, trends, and to characterize and compare different DN. We have also offered a mechanism to integrate associations (defined by distances) of items from different DN into a single representation (an evidence set) useful for recommendation processes.

References

Berry, M.W., Dumais, S.T., & Obrien, G.W. (1995). "Using linear algebra for intelligent information-retrieval". *Siam Review*, vol. 37, no. 4, pp. 573-595.

Bollen, J. (2001). *A Cognitive Model of Adaptive Web Design and Navigation - a Shared Kwowledge Perspective.* PhD Dissertation, Free University of Brussels.

Bollen, J. & Heylighen, F. (1998). " A system to restructure hypertext networks into valid user models." *The new review of Hypermedia and Multimedia*, vol. 4, pp. 189-213.

Bollen, J. & Rocha, L.M. (2000). "An adaptive systems approach to the implementation and evaluation of digital library recommendation systems". In *Research and Advanced Technology for Digital Libraries: 4th European Conference, ECDL 2000 Lectures Notes in Computer Science* Springer-Verlag, pp. 356-359.

Bollen, J. & Vandesompel, H. (2000). A recommendation system based on Spreading Activation for SFX. Unpublished Manuscript.

Bollen, J., Vandesompel, H., & Rocha, L.M. (1999). "Mining associative relations from website logs and their application to context-dependent retrieval using spreading activation", in *Workshop on Organizing Web Space (WOWS), ACM Digital Libraries 99* Berkeley, California.

Chakrabarti, S., Dom, B.E., Kumar, S.R., Raghavan, P., Rajagopalan, S., Tomkins, A., Gibson, D., & Kleinberg, J. (1999). "Mining the web's link structure". *Computer*, vol. 32, no. 8, p. 60-AUG.

Galvin, F. & Shore, S.D. (1991). "Distance Functions and Topologies". *American Mathematical Monthly*, vol. 98, no. 7, pp. 620-623.

Herlocker, J.L., Konstan, J.A., Bouchers, A., & Riedl, J. (1999). "An algorithmic framework for performing collaborative filtering", in *Proceedings of the 22nd annual international ACM SIGIR conference on Research and development in information retrieval 1999* ACM Press, New York, NY, USA, pp. 230-237.

Kanehisa, M. (2000). *Post-Genome Informatics* Oxford University Press.

Kleinberg, J.M. (1999). "Authoritative sources in a hyperlinked environment". *Journal of the Acm*, vol. 46, no. 5, pp. 604-632.

Klir, G.J. (1993). "Developments in uncertainty-based information," in *Advances in Computers*, M. Yovits, ed., Academic Press, pp. 255-332.

Klir, G.J. & Yuan, B. (1995). *Fuzzy Sets and Fuzzy Logic: Theory and Applications* Prentice Hall, Upper Saddle River, NJ.

Konstan, J., Miller, B., Maltz, D., Herlocker, J., Gordon, L., & Riedl, J. (1997). "GroupLens - Applying Collaborative Filtering to Usenet News". *Communications of the ACM*, vol. 40, no. 3, pp. 77-87.

Krulwich, B. & Burkey, C. (1996). "Learning user information interests through extraction of semantically significant phrases", in *Proceedings of the AAAI Spring Symposium on Machine Learning in Information Access* Stanford, California, March 1996.

Lakoff, G. (1987). *Women, Fire, and Dangerous Things: What Categories Reveal about the Mind* University of Chicago Press.

Landauer, T.K., Foltz, P.W. & Laham, D. (1998). "Introduction to Latent Semantic Analysis." *Discourse Processes*, vol. 25, pp. 259-284.

Li, P., Burgess, C., & Lund, K. (2000). "The acquisition of word meaning through global lexical co-occurrences", Stanford, CA: Center for the Study of Language and Information, pp. 167-178.

Miyamoto, S. (1990). *Fuzzy Sets in Information Retrieval and Cluster Analysis* Kluwer Academic Publishers.

Nakamura, K. & Iwai, S. (1982). "Representation of Analogical Inference by Fuzzy Sets and its Application to Information Retrieval System", in *Fuzzy Inf and Decis Processes* pp. 373-386.

Nelson, D.L., McEvoy, C.L., & Schreiber, T.A. (1998). The University of South Florida word association, rhyme, and word fragment norms. Ref Type: Internet Communication

Newman, M.E. (2001). "The structure of scientific collaboration networks". *Proc.Natl.Acad.Sci.U.S.A*, vol. 98, no. 2, pp. 404-409.

Rocha, L.M. (1994). "Cognitive categorization revisited: extending interval valued fuzzy sets as simulation tools concept combination", in *Proc.of the 1994 Int.Conference of NAFIPS/IFIS/NASA* IEEE Press, pp. 400-404.

Rocha, L.M. (1997a). *Evidence Sets and Contextual Genetic Algorithms: Exploring Uncertainty, Context and Embodiment in Cognitive and biological Systems,* PhD, State University of New York at Binghamton.

Rocha, L.M. (1997b). "Relative uncertainty and evidence sets: A constructivist framework". *International Journal of General Systems,* vol. 26, no. 1-2, pp. 35-61.

Rocha, L.M. (1999). "Evidence sets: Modeling subjective categories". *International Journal of General Systems,* vol. 27, no. 6, pp. 457-494.

Rocha, L.M. (2001a). "Adaptive recommendation and open-ended semiosis". *Kybernetes,* vol. 30, no. 5-6, pp. 821-851.

Rocha, L.M. (2001b). "TalkMine: a Soft Computing Approach to Adaptive Knowledge Recommendation," in *Soft Computing Agents: New Trends for Designing Autonomous Systems,* Vincenzo Loia & Salvatore Sessa, eds., Physica-Verlag, Springer, pp. 89-116.

Rocha, L.M. & Bollen, J. (2001). "Biologically motivated distributed designs for adaptive knowledge management," in *Design Principles for the Immune System and other Distributed Autonomous Systems,* L.A. Segel & I. Cohen, eds., Oxford University Press, pp. 305-334.

Shafer, G. (1976). *A Mathematical Theory of Evidence* Princeton University Press.

Shore, S.D. & Sawyer, L.J. (1993). "Explicit Metrization". *Annals of the New York Academy of Sciences,* vol. 704, pp. 328-336.

Turksen, I.B. (1996). "Non-specificity and interval-valued fuzzy sets". *Fuzzy Sets and Systems,* vol. 80, no. 1, pp. 87-100.

Watts, D. (1999). *Small Worlds: The Dynamics of Networks between Order and Randomness* Princeton University Press.

Yager, R.R. (1979). "Measure of Fuzziness and Negation .1. Membership in the Unit Interval". *International Journal of General Systems,* vol. 5, no. 4, pp. 221-229.

Yager, R.R. (1980). "On the Measure of Fuzziness and Negation .2. Lattices". *Information and Control,* vol. 44, no. 3, pp. 236-260.

Zadeh, L.A. (1965). "Fuzzy Sets". *Information and Control,* vol. 8, pp. 338-353.

Soft Computing Agents
V. Loia (Ed.)
IOS Press, 2002

Chapter 7

A Modeling Tool for Intelligent-Agent Based Systems: the API-Calculus

Shahram Rahimi
Maria Cobb
Dia Ali
Fred Petry

7.1 Introduction

Software agents offer several unique advantages over the client-server approach. First, the ability to move to the source of activity, i.e. a database server, reduces the additional network overhead involved in remote communication. For instance, by executing a series of database queries locally, intermediate results are not required to be transmitted to the remote system; rather, transmission is delayed until the final query has been executed, thus reducing overall execution time and bandwidth. In conjunction with mobility is the ability to easily deploy software to a remote site. This merely involves instructing the agent to move to the remote site and begin execution. In this manner, a server's functionality may easily and unobtrusively be extended. Another advantage is the autonomous nature of agents. Once an agent has moved off of the client machine to another host, the client machine may safely shut down. Upon restarting, the client machine needs merely to re-establish contact with mobile agent to regain control. Alternatively, the agent may be programmed to periodically attempt to return to its originating site.

Moreover, multiple agents can simultaneously process information stored in multiple data locations. Such agents can communicate and cross-reference distributed data by forming a multi-level system to support the distributed process. All these unique capabilities make agent technology an excellent paradigm for many distributed applications.

For the above reasons, intelligent agents and mobile computations in general are becoming more and more popular. These paradigms are making a wide range of exciting new distributed applications possible. However, beyond the facilitation and basic engineering challenge in design and implementation of agent-based systems, there are several security, validation, verification, and performance related questions that need to be addressed (Serugendo 1998). Here are some questions that need to be answered for any agent-based system:

- security: "How does the system react to malicious agents or malicious hosts?"
- validation: "Does the application perform the correct functionality?"
- verification: "Is the application implemented in a correct way?"
- performance: "Is the performance of the system acceptable in comparision to the other technologies?"

In order to obtain a conclusive answer to these and many other questions, it is necessary to introduce formal modeling methods useful for specifying and verifying such systems. There are several calculi introduced for this purpose, for instance, pi-calculus and its extensions, ambient-calculus and petri nets based tools. These calculi are used to describe and analyze systems consisting of processes and agents in which agents interact among each other, and their configuration or neighborhood is continually changing.

One of the most popular calculi in this category is the pi-calculus (Sangiorgi 1993 and 2001). The pi-calculus is able to describe dynamically changing networks of concurrent processes (Sangiorgi 2001). Several extensions of this popular calculus have been introduced in an effort to complete some of its missing capabilities (Abadi 1997 and 2001, Milner 1993 and 1997, Sangiorgi 1993).

Api-calculus, introduced in this chapter, is one such extension that addresses intelligent, natural grouping and migration aspects of intelligent agents. Moreover, it has the potential for handling the security of agent-based systems.

Api-calculus introduces three new concepts over ordinary pi-calculus and its extensions, higher order and polyadic pi-calculi. By introducing these new concepts, we can address the intelligence, natural grouping and security aspects of mobile agents.

Api-calculus introduces the concept of *knowledge unit*. A knowledge unit consists of a knowledge base and a set of facts. Agents have the capability to add/drop facts to/from the fact list and modify the knowledge base by adding new rules or eliminating existing ones. Each mobile agent is capable of carrying one or more knowledge units and sending and receiving them to/from other agents.

We also introduce the notion of *term*. A term consists of a name, a rule/fact, or a function, where a name can be a channel or a variable. In the standard pi-calculus, names are the only terms.

Moreover, we introduce *milieu*, a new level of abstraction, that is in-between single mobile agents and the system as a whole. Milieu focuses on families of processes. Thus, it addresses related questions such as how we can specify a collection (family) of mobile agents working towards some common goal. Milieu is a closed environment that may consist of none or many agents or other milieus that cooperate to solve a computational problem.

The remaining parts of this chapter are organized as follows. First, the syntax of the api-calculus is described in section 7.2. Then the reduction relations and the axioms of structural congruence are proposed in section 7.3. Next, the abbreviations are discussed in section 7.4. Finally, some concrete knowledge units and milieu illustrative examples are given in sections 7.5 though 7.7.

7.2 Syntax

We begin with the basic definition for the elements of api-calculus:

7.2.1 Term

A term can be a name, fact/rule or a function:

- A name can be a channel or a variable name.
- A term can be a fact or a rule which can be added to a knowledge base, or sent/received to/from a different process.
- A term may be a function. A function may have l parameters. f ranges over the functions of Φ and one matches the arity of f.

Although names, facts and rules have similarities, we find it clearer to keep them separated.
Definition I: Term.

$$R,T \quad \equiv \qquad\qquad \text{(term)}$$
$$x,y,z,... \qquad \text{(name)}$$

$$a, b, c,... \quad \text{(fact or rule)}$$
$$f(x, y, z,...) \quad \text{(functions)}$$

We use variables u, v, w to range over names, facts and rules. Moreover, we use $\vec{u}$ and $\vec{T}$ to abbreviate tuples u_1, u_2, ..., u_l and T_1, T_2, ... T_l respectively. Terms are partitioned into a collection of *subject sorts*, each of which contains an infinite number of terms. We write $R : s$ to mean that term R belongs to the subject sort s. This notation is extended to tuples component wise. *Object sorts*, range over by S, are just sequences over subject sorts, such as $(s_1, s_2,..., s_n)$ or (s). Finally a sorting is a function Sf mapping each subject sort to an object sort. We write $s \mapsto (\vec{s}) \in Sf$, if Sf assigns the object sort $(\vec{s})$ to s. In this case we say that $(\vec{s})$ appears in Sf. By assigning the object sort (s_1, s_2) to the object sort s, one forces the object part of any term in s to be a pair whose first component is a term of s_1 and whose second component is a term of s_2.

7.2.2 Process

In pi-calculus only object sorts of the form $(\tilde{s})$ are allowed and the sortings so obtained are first order, as indicated by the level of bracket, which is limited to one. Api-calculus follows the rules for higher order pi-calculus (HOpi) and is essentially derived by dropping this limitation. Thus, one may enforce processes to be communicated along a name x by declaring $x : s \mapsto (())$ (Sangiorgi 1993). Then an executer, which receives a process as X and executes it can be written as $x(X).X$ expression. Before we continue on this subject let us define the syntax of a process.

Definition II (Process). Api-calculus allows processes to be passed as terms in a communication (as in HOpi). After a process has been transmitted, it can begin its execution. This is a process-passing mechanism. Here is the process definition:

$$
\begin{array}{llll}
P & \equiv & 0 & \text{(no action)} \\
& | & \alpha.P & \text{(action prefix)} \\
& | & P_1 + P_2 & \text{(summation process)} \\
& | & [T = R]P_1 : P_2 & \text{(conditional process)} \\
& | & vxP & \text{(name restriction)} \\
& | & (K_i)P & \text{(knowledge name restriction)} \\
& | & !P & \text{(replication)} \\
& | & D\langle \vec{L} \rangle & \text{(constant)}
\end{array}
$$

Letters P, P_1, P_2,... and Q, Q_1, Q_2,... are used to denote processes. **0** is the no action process. This is the process that does internal computations. α is called an action prefix (definition V). The expression $\alpha.P$ performs the action α and then behaves like P. The summation process $P_1 + P_2$ acts like either P_1 or P_2. Terms are identified by T and R (names, fact/rules, or functions). $[T = R]P_1 : P_2$ is a conditional process, but we should stress that $T = R$ represents equality of T and R, rather than strict syntactic identity. We abbreviate it to $[T = R] : P_1$ when P_2 is **0**. The expression $vx P$ makes a new, private name x (local) then behaves as P process. $(K_i)P$ indicates that K_i is a knowledge unit name local (restricted) to process P, which means that we may have more than one K_i in a multi-agent system (more in examples). $!P$ is the replicated processes (means $P \mid P \mid ...$). For instance $P_1 \mid P_2$ consists of P_1 and P_2 acting in parallel. The components may act independently; also, an output action of P_1 at any output port $\bar{x}$ may synchronize with an input action of P_2 at x, to create a silent, τ, action of the composite agent $P_1 \mid P_2$.

X is a process variable, $\vec{L}$ stands for any tuple of processes or terms (i.e. L_1 is a term or a process), and $\vec{T}$ stands for any tuple of terms. The constant D is defined as $D = (\vec{T})P$. Constants are to be seen as functions whose parameters can be processes or other functions. For example, consider $x(L)$ to be an input prefix which receives a term or a process L from channel x and $\bar{x}L$ to be an output prefix that sends a term or a process L through channel x. Now in $\bar{x}P.Q \mid x(X).X$, once the interaction between the two processes has taken place, the resulting process is $Q \mid P$. Indeed, process $x(X).X$ was waiting for X to be sent along channel x, i.e., it was waiting for a process X defining its subsequent behavior.

If $x : s \mapsto (s_1, s_2)$, then for $x(\vec{T}).P$ and $\bar{x}\vec{T}.P$ (the first one sends term tuple $\vec{T}$ through channel x and the second one receives $\vec{T}$ from channel x; more later) to respect Sf (sorting function, explained above), it must be that $\vec{T} = T_1, T_2$, for some $T_1 : s_1$ and $T_2 : s_2$. Moreover in a matching $[T = R]$ we require that the tested terms T and R belong to the same sort. We also assign an object sort to agents: processes take the sort ( ), whereas if $D \equiv (\vec{T})P$ and $\vec{T} : \vec{s}$, then D, and $(\vec{T})P$ take the sort $(\vec{s})$. Now the requirement on $D\langle \vec{R} \rangle$ is that $\vec{s}$ exists for instance $\vec{R} : \vec{s}$ and $D : (\vec{s})$ (Sangiorgi 1993).

Before we talk about the actions, α , we need to define the concept of knowledge unit.

7.2.3 Knowledge Unit

Definition III (knowledge units). A knowledge unit consists of a knowledge base (rules) and a set of facts. A knowledge unit reacts to any new fact(s) added to its facts list. K_1, K_2, ... represents knowledge units. K^i denotes the set of knowledge units that belong to process i (P_i).

Here is the grammar of knowledge units:

$$
\begin{array}{llll}
K & \equiv & 0 & \textit{(empty knowledge unit)} \\
  & \mid & r & \textit{(a single rule)} \\
  & \mid & K_1 + K_2 & \textit{(knowledge units summation)}
\end{array}
$$

0 is called an empty knowledge unit. An empty knowledge unit is produced if all the rules and facts are deleted from it. A knowledge unit may consist of a single rule. $K_1 + K_2$ is called a knowledge unit summation, which means that both of the knowledge units react to a fact at the same time. This means that K_1 and K_2 join together and act as a single knowledge unit.

7.2.4 Actions

Definition IV (Actions). In addition to send and receive actions in pi-calculus, api-calculus includes knowledge and milieus actions. Moreover, instead of just having 'names' (as in pi-calculus), we may have 'terms' and processes in actions. Knowledge actions consist of knowledge unit calls, receiving knowledge units, sending knowledge units and adding/dropping facts and rules to/from a knowledge unit. Later, we will see that milieus' actions include join and leave milieus. Letters $\alpha_1, \alpha_2, ...$ are used to represent action prefixes. Let A denote the set of all actions in the calculus:

- τ is a no external, but an internal action.

- $x(\vec{L})$ is an input prefix. Variable x stands for a name of an input port (channel) of a process which contains it; $\vec{L}$ stands for any tuple of processes or terms. $x(\vec{L}).P$ inputs arbitrary terms or processes $\vec{L}_1$ at the port x and then behaves like $P\{\vec{L}_1 / \vec{L}\}$. All free occurrences of the names $\vec{L}$ in P are bound by the input action prefix $x(\vec{L})$ in P.

- $\overline{x}\vec{L}$ is an output prefix. A name x is thought of as an output port of a process which contains it; $\overline{x}\vec{L}.P$ outputs the tuple of terms or processes $\vec{L}$ at the port x and then behaves like P.

- $(\vec{K}).P$ makes the tuple of knowledge names $\vec{K}$ private(local) to P.

- $K_i\langle\vec{a}\rangle(\vec{R})$ is a knowledge unit call. Expression $K_i\langle\vec{a}\rangle(\vec{R}).P$ calls the knowledge unit, K_i, passing a list of facts, $\vec{a}$. The result of this call is placed in $\vec{R}$. All free occurrences of $\vec{R}$ in P are bound by the prefix $K_i\langle\vec{a}\rangle(\vec{R})$ in P.

- $x(\vec{K}).P$ is an input prefix which receives a knowledge units, $\vec{K}$, from a process that is sending it through port x. Expression $x(K_1').P$ inputs a knowledge unit, K_1, at the port x and then behaves like $P\{K_1 / K_1'\}$.

- $\overline{x}\vec{K}$ is an output prefix which sends a knowledge unit to a process that is receiving through port x. Expression $\overline{x}K_i.P$ outputs the knowledge unit K_i through port x and then acts like P.

- $K_i(\vec{a})$ is a prefix that adds tuple $\vec{a}$ to the facts list of K_i, if $\vec{a}$ is tuple of facts, or to the rule list of K_i if $\vec{a}$ is a tuple of rules. Expression $K_i(\vec{a}).P$ adds $\vec{a}$ to the facts list or rule base of K_i and then acts like P.

- $\overline{K}_i a$ is a prefix which drops a from the facts list (if a is a fact) or from the rule base (if a is a rule). Expression $\overline{K}_i a.P$ drops a from the facts list or the rule base of K_i and then acts like P.

- *join m.P* makes process P to join milieu m (a closed environment, definition VI) and then acts like P inside of the milieu m.

- *leave m.P* makes process P to leave milieu m and then acts like P outside of milieu m.

Definition V (binding). In each of $x(T).P$ and $vT.P$, the displayed occurrence of T is binding with scope P (as we defined earlier T and R are used to range over terms). An occurrence of a term in process is bound if it is, or it lies within the scope of, a binding occurrence of the term. An occurrence of a name in a process is free if it is not bound. We write *ft(P)* for the set of terms that have a free occurrence in P. For instance,

$$ft((\overline{z}y.0 + \overline{w}T.0) \mid \overline{x}u.0) = \{z, y, w, T, x, u\}$$

and

$$ft(vx((x(z).\overline{z}y.0 + \overline{w}v.0) \mid vu\ \overline{x}u.0)) = \{y, w, v\}$$

The free terms of a process circumscribe its capabilities for action: for a term R, in order for P to send R, to send via R or to receive via R, it must be that $R \in ft(P)$. Thus in order for two processes to interact via a name, that name must occur free in both of them, in one case expressing a capability to send, and in the other a capability to receive. In api-calculus and most other calculus, much can be understood about the behavior of processes by looking closely at how terms occur in them (Sangiorgi 2001).

7.2.5 Milieu

Definition VI (Milieu). The existence of separate locations is represented by a topology of boundaries.A milieu is an environment (a bounded place) in which processes live and computations take place. A milieu in some ways is similar to an ambient, introduced by Cardelli and Gordon in 1998 (Cardelli and Gordon 1998), but unlike ambients, milieus are not basic units of a system; rather, they are an environment where processes can join one another and form a new computational unit.

A milieu is surrounded by a border, which needs to be passed to join or leave it. A whole milieu can move together with its whole content (all the processes inside the milieu). The concept of milieu not only introduces a new level of abstraction to the pi-calculus, but also can be used to address the problem of the natural grouping and the security of the system. Here is the syntax of milieu:

$$M \quad \equiv \quad 0$$
$$M[O]$$
$$M[O_1 \,|\, O_2]$$
$$M_1 + M_2$$
$$\beta.M_1$$

$$\beta \equiv join\ m \mid leave\ m \mid open$$

An empty milieu is declared as 0. Variables $O_1, O_2, \ldots, O_n$ are used to range over processes and milieus. $M[O]$ is a milieu in which process or milieu O exists. A milieu may consist of other milieus or processes acting in parallel, $M[O_1 \,|\, O_2]$. Expression $M_1 + M_2$ indicates that milieu M is composed from the merge of milieus M_1 and M_2. Letter β is a milieu action prefix. Expression $\beta.M$ performs the action β and then acts as M.

$M[O]$ exhibits a tree structure induced by processes and the nesting of milieu brackets, i.e. $M[P_1 | \ldots | P_p | M_1[\ldots]] | \ldots | M_q[\ldots]]$. In api-calculus, process mobility is represented as crossing of milieus' boundaries. It is important to point out that in this calculus interaction between processes is by shared location within a common boundary or outside of any boundaries.

- *join m.M* makes milieu M to join milieu m and then acts like M inside the milieu m.
- *leave m.M* makes milieu M to leave milieu m and then acts like M outside the milieu m.
- *open.M* dissolves the boundaries of milieu M and makes it open up its boards and cease its existence. Then the processes and the milieus, inside the M, act as if they don't belong to M anymore.

7.2.6 Substitution and Convertibility

Here we want to see the effect of applying a substitution σ to a process P. For process P, this is essentially to replace each free occurrence of each term T in P by $T\sigma$. The replacement must, however, be done in such a way that the substitution of a term does not result in unintended capture of variables by binding. For instance, the result of substituting the name z for the name x in the process $y(z).\bar{z}x.0$ should be $y(w).\bar{w}z.0$ for some name $w \neq z$ (Sangiorgi 2001).

For convertibility:

1. If the name w does not occur in the process P, then $P\{w/z\}$ is the process obtained by replacing each free occurrence of z in P by w.
2. In process P, the replacement of $x(T).Q$ by $x(R).Q\{R/T\}$, or the replacement of vT Q by $vw\ Q\{R/T\}$, is a *change of bound terms*, where in each case R does not occur in Q. Processes P and Q are convertible, $P = Q$, if Q can be obtained from P by a finite number of changes of bound names.

For example:

$$y(z).\bar{z}x.0 = y(w).\overline{w}x.0$$

and

$$vy(y(z).\bar{z}x.0 \mid vw\ \bar{y}w.w(v).\bar{x}v.0) = vu(u(y).\bar{y}x.0 \mid vw\ \bar{u}w.w(z).\bar{x}z.0)$$

Here are two examples for substitution:

$$(y(w).\overline{w}x.0)\{z/x\} = (y(w).\overline{w}z.0)$$

and

$$(!vz\ \bar{x}z.0 \mid y(w).0)\{v/x, v/y\} = !vz\ \bar{v}z.0 \mid v(w).0$$

7.3 Reduction

This section defines the reduction relation, $\rightarrow$, on processes and milieus. The assertion $O \rightarrow O'$ expresses that process or milieu O can evolve to process or milieu O' as a result of an interaction, that is, an action within O. Reduction is defined by a family of inference rules, and a relation of structural congruence plays a key role in the definition by allowing manipulation of equations (Sangiorgi 2001).
This section includes two subsections. The first discusses the rules defining reduction informally. The second defines structural congruence and reduction, and gives some examples.

7.3.1 Discussion

Lets start with the following important axiom:

$$\bar{x}L_1.P_1 \mid x(L_2).P_2 \rightarrow P_1 \mid P_2\{L_1/L_2\} \tag{1}$$

The process P, on the left side of the arrow, consists of two components. Among its capabilities are in the one case to send L_1 (a process or a term) via x from P_1, and in the other to receive L_1 via x by P_2. The axiom expresses that P has a reduction arising from an interaction between its components via x, and as effects of this reduction: L_1 is passed from the first component to the second and is substituted for the placeholder L_2 in P_2, and the two prefixes are consumed. In summary P evolves to $P_1 \mid P_2\{L_1/L_2\}$.
There is a second axiom,

$$\tau.P \rightarrow P \tag{2}$$

where we think of the τ prefix as expressing an internal action whose origin is not made explicit. After (1) and (2), we should introduce an important rule called structural rule:

$$\textit{from } O_1 \equiv O_2 \textit{ and } O_2 \to O_2' \textit{ and } O_1' \equiv O_2', \textit{ infer } O_1 \to O_1', \tag{3}$$

where $\equiv$ is the structural-congruence relation defined later.

To complete the inference system defining $\to$, the axioms (1) and (2) and the structural rule (3) are joined by three further rules. The first one is:

$$\textit{from } O_1 \to O_1' \textit{ infer } O_1 \mid O_2 \to O_1' \mid O_2 \tag{4}$$

It expresses that if the component O_1 of the process $O_1 \mid O_2$ has a reduction, then $O_1 \mid O_2$ itself has a reduction, the effect of which is just the effect on O_1. The other component, O_2, is unaffected by the action within O_1. The second one expresses that restriction of a term does not inhibit a reduction in a process:

$$\textit{from } P \to P' \textit{ infer } \nu T\, P \to \nu T\, P' \tag{5}$$

The third rule is just like the second one but for the knowledge units:

$$\textit{from } P \to P' \textit{ infer } (K)\, P \to (K)\, P' \tag{6}$$

This approach for defining reduction – the two axioms (1) and (2), the three rules (4), (5) and (6) and the structural rule (3) – is very simple. It is clear, however, that for approach to capture the richness of process behavior, much of the action must be in the structural-congruence relation, which features so prominently in the crucial structural rule (Sangiorgi 2001).

7.3.2 Structural congruence and reduction

The basis for the definition of structural congruence is a small collection of axioms that allows manipulation of structures. The particular axioms are chosen because they allow just the desired manipulation.

To define structural congruence, we need the notions of context and congruence. Informally, a context differs from a process only in having the *hole* [.] in place of an occurrence of **0**. A context is regarded as a syntactic entity that transforms processes to new processes (Sangiorgi 2001). Formally, therefore, we have:

Definition VII (Context). A context is obtained when the hole [.] replaces an occurrence of **0** in a process structure given by the grammar in *definition II*. Here are some examples for contexts:

$$z\,([.]\mid !z(u).\bar{y}u.0)$$

and

$$x(T).!\nu x\,(\bar{z}x.[.]+y(v).0)$$

If C is a context and P a process, we write $C[P]$ for the process obtained by replacing the [.] in C by P. The replacement is literal, so terms free in P may be bound in $C[P]$. For example, writing C_0 for the first example context above,

$$C_0[!\bar{z}b.0] = \nu z(!\bar{z}b.0 \mid !z(u).\bar{y}u.0)$$

The notion of congruence is very important in the theory of processes in general.

Definition VIII (Congruence). An equivalence relation S on processes is a congruence if $(P,Q) \in S$ implies $(C[P], C[Q]) \in S$ for every context C. Now finally we can define structural congruence:

Table 1. The axioms of structural congruence.

SC 1, Match	$[T = T]\tau.P \equiv \tau.P$
SC 2, Summation Associativity	$O_1 + (O_2 + O_3) \equiv (O_1 + O_2) + O_3$
SC 3, Summation Commutativity	$O_1 + O_2 \equiv O_2 + O_1$
SC 4, Summation Identity	$O_1 + 0 \equiv O_1$
SC 5, Composition Associativity	$O_1 \mid (O_2 \mid O_3) \equiv (O_1 \mid O_2) \mid O_3$
SC 6, Same Process	$O + O \equiv O$
SC 7, Composition Commutativity	$O_1 \mid O_2 \equiv O_2 \mid O_1$
SC 8, Composition Identity	$O \mid 0 \equiv O$
SC 9, Restriction	$\nu T_1 \nu T_2 \, P \equiv \nu T_2 \nu T_1 \, P$
SC 10, Restriction Identity	$T\,0 \equiv 0$
SC 11, Restriction Composition	$\nu T \, (P_1 \mid P_2) \equiv P_1 \mid \nu T \, P_2, \text{ if } T \notin ft(P_1)$
SC 12, Replication	$!P \equiv P \mid !P$

Table 2. The rules of equational reasoning.

Reflexivity	$O = O$
Symmetry	$O_1 = O_2$ implies $O_2 = O_1$
Transitivity	$O_1 = O_2$ and $O_2 = O_3$ implies $O_1 = O_3$
Generality	$P = Q$ implies $C[P] = C[Q]$

Definition IX (Structural Congruence). Structural congruence, $\equiv$, is the congruence on processes that satisfies the axioms in table 1. In other word, processes P and Q are structurally congruent if $P \equiv Q$ can be inferred from axioms listed in table 3 together with the rules of equational reasoning, that is, the rules in table 2.

The axioms of structural congruence allow manipulation of structures. Axiom SC 10 expresses that a restriction can be moved so as to include in or exclude from its scope a process in which the restricted term is not free. It shows that ν is a static binder (Sangiorgi 2001).

For example, suppose:

$$P = \nu x(x(z).\bar{z}a.0 \mid (\bar{x}y.\tau \mid \bar{x}b.0))$$

Then by associativity and commutativity of composition, and identity of τ,

$$P \equiv P_1 = \nu x(((\bar{x}y.0 + 0) \mid (x(z).\bar{z}a.0 + 0)) \mid \bar{x}b.0) \,.$$

In the transformation from P to P_1, two potential interactors have been brought together, and in the form required for axiom of reduction (1) to be applied. Equally,

$$P \equiv P_2 = \nu x(((\bar{x}b.0 + 0) \mid (x(z).\bar{z}a.0 + 0)) \mid \bar{x}y.0) \,,$$

where the other potential sender has been brought into contact with a potential receiver.

Definition X (Reduction): The reduction relation, $\rightarrow$, is defined by the rules in table 3. As an example of applying these rules, let us see how to infer the reductions for the process in the following example:

$$P = vx\,((x(u).Q_1 + y(v).Q_2)\,|\,\bar{x}a.0)\,|\,(\bar{y}b.R_1 + \bar{x}c.R_2)$$

First, $(x(u).Q_1 + y(v).Q_2)\,|\,\bar{x}a$ matches the left side of the REACT rule, so we have $(x(u).Q_1 + y(v).Q_2)\,|\,\bar{x}a \rightarrow Q_1\,|\,0$. Then using STRUCT, RES and PAR we can infer a reduction in P:

$$
\begin{aligned}
&-\,(x(u).Q_1 + y(v).Q_2)\,|\,\bar{x}a \rightarrow Q_1\,|\,0 && REACT \\
&-\,(x(u).Q_1 + y(v).Q_2)\,|\,\bar{x}a \rightarrow Q_1 && STRUCT \\
&-\,vx\,((x(u).Q_1 + y(v).Q_2)\,|\,\bar{x}a \rightarrow vx\,Q_1 && RES \\
&-\,vx\,((x(u).Q_1 + y(v).Q_2)\,|\,\bar{x}a)\,|\,(\bar{y}(b).R_1 + \bar{x}(c).R_2) \rightarrow \\
&\quad vx\,Q_1\,|\,(\bar{y}(b).R_1 + \bar{x}(c).R_2) && PAR
\end{aligned}
$$

Table 3. Reduction Rules.

$$
\begin{array}{c}
\text{TAU: } \tau.P + Q \rightarrow P \\[6pt]
\text{REACT: } (x(\vec{T}).P + P')\,|\,(\bar{x}\vec{R}.Q + Q') \rightarrow P\,|\,Q\{\vec{R}/\vec{T}\} \\[6pt]
\end{array}
$$

$$
\text{PAR: } \frac{O_1 \rightarrow O_1'}{O_1\,|\,O_2 \rightarrow O_1'\,|\,O_2}
\qquad
\text{RES: } \frac{P \rightarrow Q}{vT\,P \rightarrow vT\,Q}
\qquad
\text{RES-K: } \frac{P \rightarrow Q}{(K)P \rightarrow (K)Q}
$$

$$
\text{MIL: } \frac{P \rightarrow Q}{M[P] \rightarrow M[Q]}
$$

$$
\text{STRUCT: } \frac{O_1 \rightarrow O_1'}{O_2 \rightarrow O_2'}\; if\; O_1 \equiv O_2\; and\; O_1' \equiv O_2'
$$

Definition XI (n-hole context). For $n \geq 1$, an n-hole context is obtained when n occurrences of **0** in a process-structure, given by the grammar in definition II, are replaced by the holes $[.]_1$, $[.]_2$, ..., $[.]_n$. If C is an n-hole context then we write $C[P_1, ..., P_n]$ for the process obtained by replacing $[.]_i$ in C by P_i for each i.

7.4 Abbreviations

Before we look at some concrete examples, a number of abbreviations are defined:
1) Sometimes a communication needs to carry no parameter. To model this we presuppose a special name, ε, which is never bound; then we write:

$$\bar{x}.P \;\; in\, place\, of \;\; \bar{x}\varepsilon.P$$

$$x.P \;\; in\, place\, of \;\; x(y).P \qquad (y\; not\; free\; in\; P)$$

2) We shall often omit '.0' in an process, and write for example:

$$\bar{x}y \;\; in\, place\, of \;\; \bar{x}y.0$$

We shall often wish to allow input names to determine the course of computation. Thus, we naturally write:

$$x(v).([v = y_1]P_1 + [v = y_2]P_2 + ...)$$

where usually the names y_i will be distinct. Assuming that v does not occur free in any P_i, we shall abbreviate this to:

$$x : [y_1 \Rightarrow P_1, y_2 \Rightarrow P_2, ...]$$

3) We define some composite prefixes:

$$\bar{x}y_1 ... y_n \ \ means \ \ \bar{x}y_1 ... \bar{x}y_n$$
$$\bar{x}(y_1)...(y_n) \ \ means \ \ \bar{x}(y_1)...\bar{x}(y_n)$$
$$join \ M_1 ... M_n \ \ means \ \ join \ M_1 ... join \ M_n$$
$$leave \ M_1 ... M_n \ \ means \ \ leave \ M_1 ... leave \ M_n$$

4) If a process leave a milieu just to communicate with a second process:

$$l.\bar{x}a.j.P \ \ means \ \ leave \ M.\bar{x}a.join \ M.P$$

if the process needs to leave n milieus to communicate:

$$l''.\bar{x}a.j''.P \ \ means \ \ leave \ M_1...leave \ M_n.\bar{x}a.join \ M_n ... join \ M_1.P$$

7.5 Concrete Examples

In this section, we explore some concrete examples. They are on a small scale, but deal with real applications in computing.

7.5.1 Example 1: An Executor

Let us define: $Exec(x) = x(y).\bar{y}$

Exec(x) may be called an *executor*. It receives, on channel x, a channel which it calls y. It then activates that channel. We can think of y as the trigger of a process which $Exec(x)$ has been called upon to run.

Now for any process P, we should (up to a few initial communications) obtain the same behavior in each of the following cases: (a) We run P directly; (b) We prefix a trigger z to P, and pass z along the link x to the executor $Exec(x)$ (we assume $x, z \notin ft(P)$).

Here is the process which, in the presence of $Exec(x)$, should behave like P:

$$vz(\bar{x}z \mid z.P)$$

A construction like this can be regarded as passing the process P itself as a value along the link x (as we saw earlier). The passing of channels as values has other applications as well. Here is the process, which should be equivalent to P:

$$vx(vz(\bar{x}z \mid z.P) \mid Exec(x)) \tag{7}$$

To see this, first apply axiom SC11 (Restriction Composition) to obtain:

$$vx\,vz(\bar{x}z \mid z.P \mid x(y).\bar{y})$$

Now this by REACT of reduction rules becomes:

$$\tau.vx\,vz(0 \mid z.P \mid \bar{z})$$

Which in turn becomes:

$$\tau.\tau.vx\,vz(0 \mid P \mid 0)$$

which since x and z were chosen not free in P, is equal to:

$$\tau.\tau.P$$

7.5.2 Example 2: Passing Processes as Parameter

Earlier, an example of passing processes was given:

$$vx(\bar{x}P_1.Q \mid x(X).X) \tag{8}$$

We pursue this direct representation of process passing further to draw attention to an important issue of scope. To develop (8), suppose that the executor, after receiving P_1, wishes to run it in parallel with P_2. We would write:

$$vx(\bar{x}P_1.Q \mid x(X).(X \mid P_2)) \tag{9}$$

where we assume that $x \notin fn(P_1, P_2, Q)$. The REACT law would equate this to:

$$\tau.(Q \mid (P_1 \mid P_2))$$

To develop the example further, we now suppose that before transmission a private channel z exists between P_1 and Q; this privacy may be represented as a restriction (z) applied to the sender:

$$vx(vz(\bar{x}P_1.Q) \mid x(X).(X \mid P_2)) \tag{10}$$

Now there are two alternatives for how the transmission of P_1 should treat the private link z. The choice is significant when $z \notin fn(P_2)$, and even more significant when $z \in fn(P_2)$.

In the first alternative, the REACT law would equate (10) with $\tau.(vzQ) \mid (P_1 \mid P_2))$. This shows that the private link z between P_1 and Q is broken by the communication. We can put it differently, in the expression $vz(\bar{x}P_1.Q)$, the restriction vz binds z in Q but not in P (and thus the private link does not in fact exist!). Moreover, if $z \in ft(P_2)$, then z represents a link between P_1 and P_2. This has often been called 'dynamic binding'; the free variables in (the text of) a function parameter are interpreted in the receiving environment. Thomason has adopted dynamic binding in his Calculus of Higher-order Communication Systems

(CHOCS), and has found that many important computational phenomena can thereby be modeled satisfactorily. However, we intend to adopt static binding.

The second alternative is that, by a form of scope extrusion, the generalized expansion law equates (10) to:

$$\tau.\nu z'(Q\{z'/z\} \mid P_1\{z'/z\} \mid P_2))$$

where z' has been chosen not free in P_1, Q or P_2. This alternative preserves the z link between P_1 and Q, and preserves its distinction from any z link possessed by P_2.

7.5.3 Example 3: Basic Process Definitions

Consider writing a process which simply copies a value from one link to another:

$$Copy(y,z) = y(x).\bar{z}x$$

Further, a process $And(x, y, z)$, which produces at z the logical conjunction of the truth values received at x and y, may be defined as follows:

$$And(x,y,z) = x : [T \Rightarrow Copy(y,z), F \Rightarrow \bar{z}F]$$

We may then represent application of a function by composition of processes. Knowing that $True(x) = \bar{x}T$ and $False(x) = \bar{x}F$, it would be easy to prove the simple equations, which justify the above encoding, such as the following:

$$(x)(True(x) \mid Copy(x,y)) = \tau.True(y)$$

$$(x)(y)(True(x) \mid False(y) \mid And(x,y,z)) = \tau.\tau.False(z)$$

7.6 Knowledge Unit Illustrative Examples

In this section, we shall present some examples to demonstrate the basic anatomy of the knowledge units in api-calculus. Moreover, we will demonstrate the use of the new formalism in a system for solving the mapping conflation issue, which includes five intelligent agents.

7.6.1 Example 4: Knowledge Unit Passing

Agent P has a link x to agent Q and wishes to pass knowledge unit K_1 along its link to Q. Process Q is willing to receive it. Thus P may be $\bar{x}K_1.P'$ and Q may be $x(K_1').Q'$ (Figure 1).

A knowledge unit with a private (restricted) name: $\boxed{K_i}$

A knowledge unit with a non-private name: $\boxed{K_i}$

In this case, the transition is:

$$\bar{x}K_1.P' \mid x(K_1').Q' \rightarrow P' \mid Q'\{K_1 / K_1'\}$$

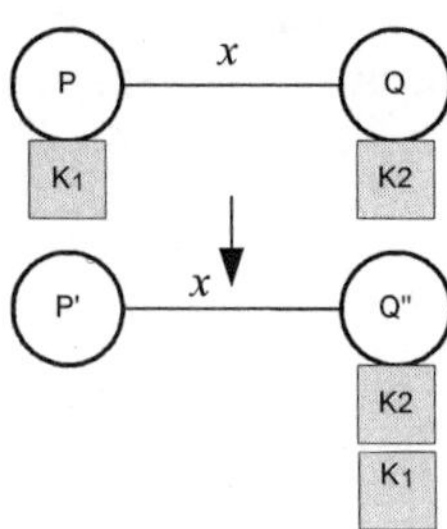

Figure 1. Illustrative example 4

So Q'' in the diagram is $Q'\{K_1 / K_1'\}$. If K_1 was private to agent P', then just a copy of the knowledge unit would be sent.

7.6.2 Example 5: Passing a Copy of Knowledge Unit

As in example one, P has a knowledge unit K_i, but now suppose that this knowledge unit name is private (local). P wishes to pass a copy of K_i to Q along its link x. In this case:

$$(K_1)(\bar{x}K_1.P') \mid x(K_1').Q' \to (K_1)(P' \mid Q'\{K_1 / K_1'\})$$

7.6.3 Example 6: Knowledge Unit Call

In this example, agent P receives a fact, a, from agent Q and then calls knowledge unit K_1 by adding the fact to K_1 facts list and then behaving like P' which in fact is the same as $P\{a/b\}$.

$$x(b).P \mid \bar{x}a.Q \to P\{a / b\} \mid Q\,;$$
$$K_i\langle a\rangle(\bar{y}).P' \to P'$$

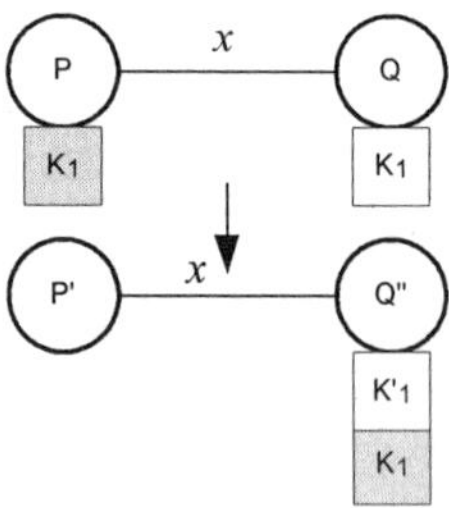

Figure 2. Illustrative example 7, first part.

7.6.4 Example 7: Scope Extrusion

Now let's assume that agent P wishes to send a knowledge unit K_i, which is not a private name, to the agent Q that already has a knowledge unit with the same name (a private name). In this case, agent Q changes its private knowledge unit name, K_1, to K_1' (figure 2).

$$\bar{x}K_1.P' \mid (K_1)(x(K_2).Q') \to P' \mid (K_1')(Q'\{K_1'/K_1\}\{K_1/K_2\})$$

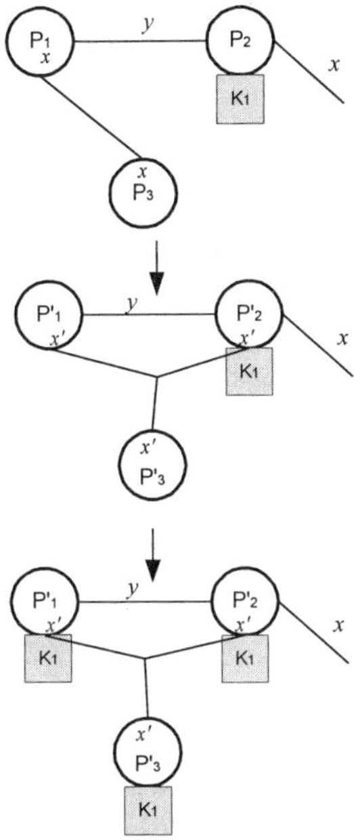

Figure 3. Illustrative example 7, second part.

Now let's consider a group of three agents, P_1, P_2, and P_3. Agent P_1 has a private link, x, to P_3. P_1 also has a non-private link, y, to P_2, which has a non-private link x as well. Agent P_2 would like to pass its knowledge unit K_1 to both P_1 and P_3 at the same time, and both P_1 and P_3 are willing to accept this knowledge unit. K_1 is a private name to agent P_2. In this scenario, agent P_1 may pass channel x to P_2, so P_2 can contact both P_1 and P_3. Because P_2 already has a non-private channel with name x, they (P_1, P_3 and P_2) have to rename the private channel x to x' (figure 3). In this case:

$$vx(\bar{y}x.P_1' \mid P_3) \mid y(z)P_2' \to vx'(P_1' \mid P_3 \mid P_2'\{x'/z\})$$

and

$$x'((K_1)(\bar{x}'K_1.P_2')) \mid x'(K_1').P_1' \mid x'(K_1').P_3 \to$$
$$x'(K_1)(P_2' \mid P_1'\{K_1/K_1'\} \mid P_3\{K_1/K_1'\})$$

It should be emphasized that in case of name duplication, the private name is always the one that changes. This is to be expected, because other agents may use a non-private name in the system and changes to a non-private name may cause system irregularities.

7.6.5 Example 8: An Example of a Small Geographical Conflation System

In this scenario, there are five agents involved (figure 4):

- Manager Agent: P_M
- Conflation Agents: P_{C1} and P_{C2}
- Query/Conversion Agents: P_{Q1} and P_{Q2}

The manager agent divides this specific conflation task to point and line conflations by sending the line conflation knowledge unit, K_L, to P_{C2}, and the point conflation knowledge unit, K_P, to P_{C1}.

The query/conversion agents have responsibility to get the data from two different data sources, one in vector format and the other one in raster format. These agents then convert the data to a proper format and pass it to the conflation agents. Again, it is the manager agent that sends the query agents the proper knowledge units for vector and raster format conversion (K_V and K_R).

Next, the point and line conflation agents (P_{C1} and P_{C2}) perform the conflation process on the data they receive from query agents and pass the results to the manager agent (figure 4). It is particularly in the case of the conflation agents that we will implement the needed extensions required for fuzzy agent mechanisms. Based on our current conflation approach that uses fuzzy logic for the spatial data integration, we can use the formal agent representations developed here to extend the fuzzy spatial techniques to the conflation agents (Higgs and Cottman 1998, Sangiorgi 1999). The overall model is as follows:

(1) Manager Agent sends the knowledge units to conflation and query agents:

$$-\,\bar{x}_1 K_P.\bar{x}_2 K_L.\bar{z}_1 K_V.\bar{z}_2 K_R.P_M' \mid x_1(K_P').P_{C1}' \mid x_2(K_L').P_{C2}' \mid z_1(K_V').P_{Q1}' \mid z_2(K_R').P_{Q2}' \; ;$$

(2) Query/conversion agents call their knowledge units to convert the data format. The knowledge units return the converted data, which is split to points and lines to be sent to point and line conflation agents:

$$-\,K_V'\langle D_{I1}\rangle(\bar{D}_{O1}).P_{Q1} \mid K_R'\langle D_{I2}\rangle(\bar{D}_{O2}).P_{Q2} \; ;$$
$$\bar{D}_{O1} \equiv [D_{P1}, D_{L1}] \;\; and \;\; \bar{D}_{O2} \equiv [D_{P2}, D_{L2}]$$

(3) Next the query agents send their data to conflation agents:

$$-\,\bar{y}_1 D_{P1}.\bar{y}_3 D_{L1}.P_{Q1}' \mid \bar{y}_2 D_{P2}.\bar{y}_4 D_{L2}.P_{Q2}' \mid y_1(D_{P1}').y_2(D_{P2}').P_{C1}' \mid$$
$$y_3(D_{L1}').y_4(D_{L2}').P_{C2}' ;$$

(4) Then the point and line conflation agents (C_P and C_L) call their knowledge units to perform the conflation process:

$$-\,K_P'\langle \bar{D}_P\rangle(D_{FP}).P_{C1}' \mid K_L'\langle \bar{D}_L\rangle(D_{FL}).P_{C2}' \; ;$$
$$\bar{D}_P \equiv [D_{P1}', D_{P2}'] \;\; and \;\; \bar{D}_L \equiv [D_{L1}', D_{L2}']$$

(5) Finally, conflation agents send the results of the conflation process to the manager agent:

$$-\,\bar{x}_1 D_{FP}.P_{C1}' \mid \bar{x}_2 D_{FL}.P_{C2}' \mid x_1(D_{FP}').x_2(D_{FL}').P_M' \; ;$$

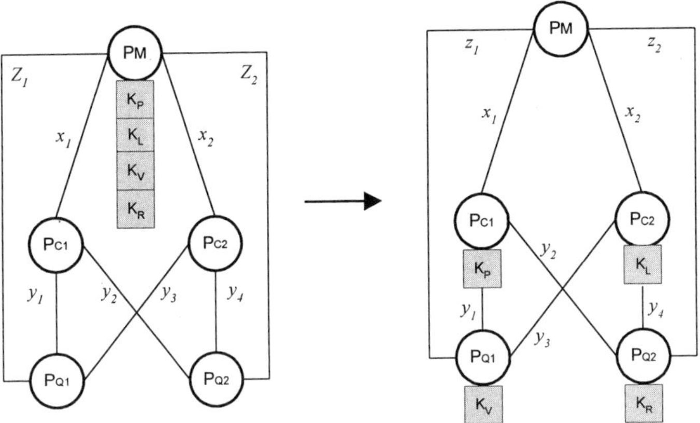

Figure 4. Illustrative example 8.

7.7 Milieu Illustrative Examples

7.7.1 Example 9: Joining and Leaving Milieus

In this example, processes P_1 and P_2 join milieu M_1, and then milieu M_1 joins milieu M_2, which already contains processes Q_1 and Q_2 (figure 5).

$$join\ M_1.P_1\ |\ join\ M_1.P_2\ |\ M_1[0] \to M_1[P_1\ |\ P_2]$$
$$join\ M_2.M_1[P_1\ |\ P_2] \to M_2[Q_1\ |\ Q_2\ |\ M_1[P_1\ |\ P_2]]$$

Now, let's assume that process P_1 leaves milieu M_1 and then milieu M_2:

$$M_2[Q_1\ |\ Q_2\ |\ M_1[leave\ M_1.P_1\ |\ P_2]] \to M_2[Q_1\ |\ Q_2\ |\ M_1[P_2]\ |\ P_1]$$

$$M_2[Q_1\ |\ Q_2\ |\ M_1[P_2]\ |\ leave\ M_2.P_1] \to M_2[Q_1\ |\ Q_2\ |\ M_1[P_2]]\ |\ P_1$$

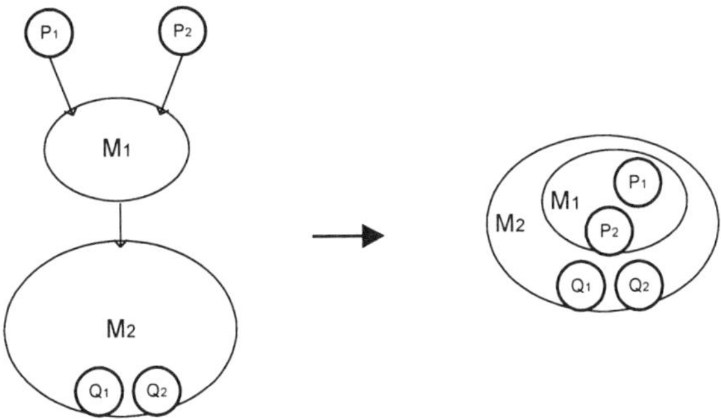

Figure 5. Illustrative example 9.

Process P_1 can leave milieus M_1 and M_2 in one step (as we mentioned earlier):

$$M_2[Q_1 \mid Q_2 \mid M_1[leave\ M_1\ M_2.P_1 \mid P_2]] \rightarrow M_2[Q_1 \mid Q_2 \mid M_1[P_2]] \mid P_1$$

When using join and leave, the sequence of the milieus is important. For instance in the above example, *leave M_1 M_2.P_1* cannot be written as *leave M_2 M_1.P_1* since P_1 would not be able to leave M_2 before leaving M_1.

7.7.2 Example 10: Interaction between Processes

We assume that process P is inside milieu M_1, and milieu M_1 and process Q are inside milieu M_2. Process P would like to send a rule, '*a*', to process Q, which adds '*a*' to its knowledge unit K. As we mentioned earlier, interaction between processes is by shared location within a common boundary or outside of any boundaries. Therefore, for this communication to happen, either process P has to leave milieu M_1 or process Q should join milieu M_2 (figure 6).

$$M_2[Q \mid M_1[leave\ M_1.P]] \rightarrow M_2[Q \mid M_1[0] \mid P]$$

$$M_2[Q \mid M_1[0] \mid P] \rightarrow M_2[Q \mid P \mid M_1[0]]$$

$$M_2[Q \mid P \mid M_1[0]] \rightarrow M_2[x(b).Q \mid \bar{x}aP \mid M_1[0]]$$

$$M_2[x(b).Q \mid \bar{x}aP \mid M_1[0]] \rightarrow M_2[Q\{a/b\} \mid P \mid M_1[0]] \rightarrow$$
$$M_2[K(a).Q \mid P \mid M_1[0]]$$

This example shows that if two processes are not within a common boundary, they have to leave their boundaries to be able to communicate. However, they can join back their boundaries again after the communication takes place. For instance, for the above example, we may write:

$$M_2[x(b).Q \mid M_1[leave\ M_1.\bar{x}a.\,join\ M_1.P]] \rightarrow M_2[Q \mid M_1[P]]$$

This is just like using a socket port to communicate with a remote computer.

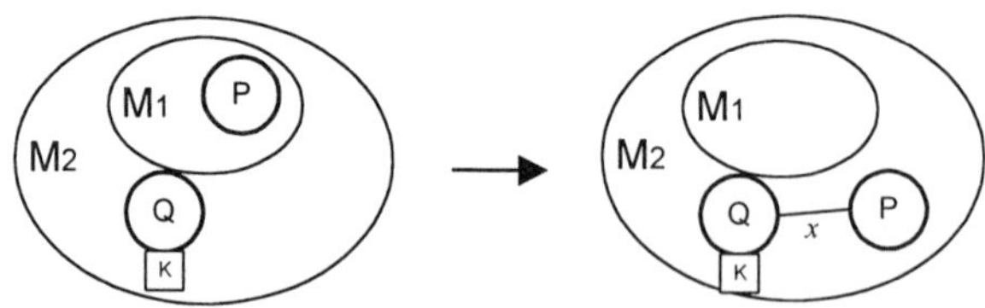

Figure 6. Illustrative example 10.

7.8 Discussion

We introduced three core concepts to the pi-calculus: *Term*, *Knowledge Unit*, and *Milieu*. A *Term* can be a name, fact/rule, or function and can be sent and received by processes. The capability of sending and receiving rules allows agents to teach and learn by updating the knowledge units, which in turn can be sent and received. Furthermore, transmission of functions between processes can be used to model proxies and CORBA based systems.

Knowledge units address the intelligent capabilities of mobile agents. A *knowledge unit* includes a knowledge base (rules) and a set of facts. The knowledge base contains the domain knowledge needed to solve problems, and the set of facts that are used by the knowledge base for production of decisions. Api-calculus also provides the modeling facilities for adding/dropping facts to/from the fact list and modification of the knowledge base as well as facilities for calling the knowledge units and more.

Api-calculus represents the existence of separate locations by a topology of boundaries named *milieu*, a new level of abstraction.

A *Milieu* is an environment (a bounded place) in which processes live and computations take place. Natural groupings can be modeled, using *milieu*. Moreover, milieus and terms may be used to model security in agent-based systems.

In summary, api-calculus is capable of addressing several deficiencies of other agent calculi including migration, intelligence representation, natural grouping and potentially security of the intelligent-agent based systems.

References

Abadi, M., and Gordon, A.D. (1997), "A Calculus for Cryptographic Protocols: The Spi Calculus," *Fourth ACM Conference on Computer and Communications Security*, ACM Press, pp. 36-47.

Abadi, M., and Fournet, C. (2001), "Mobile values, new names, and secure Communication," *Proceedings of POPL'01*, ACM Press.

Amadio, R. M. (1997), "An Asynchronous Model of Locality, Failure, and Process Mobility," *Proceedings the 2nd International Conference on Coordination Languages and Models* (COORDINATION'97).

Asperti, A., and Busi, N. (1996), *Mobile Petri Nets*, tech. report UBLCS-96-10, Laboratory for Computer Science, Univ. of Bologna, Italy.

Belgrave, M. (1999), "The Unified Agent Architecture: A White Paper", http://www.ee.mcgill.ca/~belmarc/uaa_paper.html.

Baumann, J. (1999), *Control Algorithms for Mobile Agent*, doctoral dissertation, Institut für Parallele und Verteilte Höchstleistungsrechner (IPVR), Univ. of Stuttgart.

Benjamin, C.P., and Turner D.N. (1997), *Pict: A programming language based on the pi-calculus*, tech. report CSCI 476, Computer Science Department, Indiana University.

Biberstein, O. (1997), *CO-OPN/2 An Object-Oriented Formalism for Concurrent Processes*, doctoral dissertation, Univ. of Geneva, Geneva, Switzerland.

Boreale, M., and Nicola, R. De (1995), "Testing Equivalence for Mobile Processes," *Information and Computation*, vol. 120, no. 2, pp. 279-303, August.

Cardelli L. (1995), "A Language with Distributed Scope," *Proceeding of 22nd ACM Symposium on Principles of ProgrammingLanguages* (POPL'95), San Francisco, California.

Cardelli L., and Gordon, A. D. (1998), "Mobile Ambients," *proceeding of Foundations of Software Science and Computation Structures* (FoSSaCS), European Joint Conferences on Theory and Practice of Software (ETAPS), Lisbon.

Channon, A.D., and Damper, R.I. (1998), "The evolutionary Emergence of Socially Intelligent Agents", *workshop at the Fifth International Conference of the Society for Adaptive Behavior*, Univ. of Zürich.

Dalmonte, A., and Gaspari, M. (1995), *Modeling Interaction in Agent System*, tech. report UBLCS-95-7, Laboratory for Computer Science, Univ. of Bologna, Italy.

Eisenbach, S., and Paterson, R. (1993), "Pi-calculus Semantics for the Concurrent Configuration Language Darwin," *Proc. Hawaii International Conference on System Sciences.*

Gay, S. (1993), "A Sort Inference Algorithm for the Polyadic Pi-calculus," *In Conference Record of the 20th Symposium on Principles of Programming Languages*, ACM Press.

Higgs, M., and Cottman, B. (1998), "Solving the Interoperability Problem using a Universal Data Access Broker," *Data Eng. Bulletin*, vol. 21, no. 3, pp 34-42.

Lieberman, H., Van Dyke, N.W., and Vivacqua, A.S. (1999), "Let's Browse: A Collaborative Web Browsing Agent," *Proceedings of the 99 International Conference on Intelligent User Interfaces*, Redondo Beach.

Melham, T.F. (1992), *A Mechanized Theory of the Pi-calculus in HOL*, tech. report 244, Univ. of Cambridge Computer Laboratory, Cambridge, UK.

Milner, R. (1993), "The Polyadic Pi-calculus: a Tutorial," *In Logic and Algebra of Specification,* Hamer, Brauer, and Schwichtenberg, Eds., Springer-Verlag, Berlin, Germany, pp. 1- 49.

Milner, R., Parrow, J.G., and Walker, D.J. (1989), *A Calculus of Mobile Processes. Part I and II*, tech report ECS-LFCS-89-86, Edinburgh University.

Milner, R. (1992), "Functions as processes," *Journal of Mathematical Structure in Computer Science,* vol. 2, no 2, pp. 119-141.

Mitaim, S., and Kosko, B. (1997), "Neural fuzzy agents that learn a user's preference map," *Proceeding of 4th ADL conference*, Washington, DC.

Nwana, H.S. (1996), "Software agents: an overview", *Knowledge Engineering Review*, vol. 11, no. 3.

Papastavrou, S., Samaras, G., Pitoura, E. (2000), "Mobile Agents for World Wide Web Distributed Database Access", *IEEE transactions on knowledge and data engineering,* vol. 12, no. 5.

Paprzycki, M., Cobb, M., Ali, D., and Rahimi S. (2001), "Methodology for Spatial Data Integration Agents," *Proceedings of the 27th Summer School on Mathematics in Applications,* Sozopol, Bulgaria.

Perdikeas, M.K., Chatzipapadopoulos, F.G., Venieris, I.S., and Marino, G. (1999), "Mobile agent standards and available platforms", *Computer Networks*, vol. 31.

Rahimi, S., Cobb, M., Ali, D., and Petry, F. (2002), " Intelligence Representation in Agent Systems: an Extended Pi-Calculus," *Proceedings of IEEE International Conference on Fuzzy Systems*, Honolulu, Hawaii.

Rahimi, S., Bjursell, J., Angryk, R., Paprzycki M., Ali, D., Cobb, M. (2001), "An Evaluation of Mobile Agent Environments for Geospatial Knowledge Integration and Management System," *Proceedings of PIONIER*, Poznan, Poland, pp. 267-278.

Rahimi, S., Ali, A., and Ali, D. (2001), "An Investigation on Intelligent Software-Agent Technology," *Proceedings of IEMS and IC&IE joined international conference' 01*, Cocoa Beach, Florida.

Rahimi, S., Cobb, M., Ali, D., Paprzycki, M. (2001), "An Analysis of Intelligence-Enhancing Techniques for Software Agents," *Proceedings of the 5th World Multi-Conference on Systemics, Cybernetics and Informatics*, Orlando, pp. 100-105.

Salomon, R. (1996), "Neural Networks in the Context of Autonomous Agents: Important Concepts Revisited", *Proceedings of the ANNIE'96*, New York.

Sandholm, T. (2000), "A Next Generation Electronic Commerce Server", *Proceedings of International Conference on Autonomous Agents*, Barcelona, Spain.

Sangiorgi, D., and Walker, D. (2001), *The Pi-calculus: a Theory of Mobile Processing*, Cambridge University Press, Cambridge, UK, pp. 11-32.

Sangiorgi, D. (1999), "Asynchronous process calculi: the first- order and higher-order paradigms," *INRIA Sophia-Antipoils*, France.

Sangiorgi, D. (1993), *Expressing Mobility in Process Algebra*, doctoral dissertation, Univ. of Edinburgh, Edinburgh, UK.

Sangiorgi, D. (1993), "From Pi-Calculus to Higher-order Pi- Calculus - and back," *Proceedings of TAPSOFT '93. LNCS 668*, Springer Verlag, pp. 151-166.

Satoh, I., and Tokoro, M. (1992), "A Formalism for Real-Time Concurrent Object-Oriented Computing," *ACM SIGPLAN Notices*, vol. 27, no. 10, pp. 315-326.

Schneider, J.G., and Lumpe M. (1996), *Modeling Objects in PICT*, tech. report IAM-96-004, Univ. of Bern, Institute of Computer Science and Applied Mathematics.

Serugendo, G., Muhugusa, M., and Tschudin, C. (1998), "A Survey of Theories for Mobile Agents," *WWW Journal*, vol. 1, no. 3, pp. 139-153.

Thomsen, B. (1993), "Plain CHOCS. A Second Generation Calculus for Higher Order Processes," *Acta Informatica*, vol. 30, no. 1, pp. 1-59.

Togashi, A., Tsukasaki, S., Kanezashi, F. (2001), "M-pi: A Mobile Agent Calculus with Module Description," *Proceedings of the 5th World Multi-Conference on Systemics,*

Cybernetics and Informatics, Orlando, pp. 338-343.

Walker, D. (1991), "Pi-calculus Semantics for Object-Oriented Programming Languages," *Proceedings of The International Conference on Theoretical Aspects of Computer Science, Lecture Notes in Computer Science*, vol. 526, Springer-Verlag, Amsterdam, Netherlands, pp. 532-547.

Wooldridge, M. (1999), "Intelligent Agents: Theory and Practice", http://www.doc.mmu.ac.uk:80.

Chapter 8

Emergence of Holonic Enterprises from Multi-Agent Systems: A Fuzzy Evolutionary Approach

Mihaela Ulieru

8.1 Introduction

The recent advances in information and networking technologies have enabled global connections unthinkable before. The web is linking our world enabling partnerships otherwise impossible in all areas of our life. From e-Commerce and e-Business to e-Learning and e-Health the economics strategies as well as the routine professional practices have been irreversibly contaminated with the spice of electronic connectivity. Supported by this technological leverage new paradigms have emerged with models that are dynamic, autonomous, self-organizing and proactive, generically coined as 'intelligent'. In particular the novel AI paradigm of distributed intelligence referred to as Multi-Agent Systems (MAS) has challenged the software world and with it the world of information technologies through its ability to enable emulation in Cyberspace of real-world societies with their entities modeled as agents.

The marriage between MAS and the Internet has enabled a parallel world of information to 'live' in the Web Universe emulating our games in all aspects of life, be they economic, financial, business, school or health related, or even just-for-fun in computer games. Paradigm shifts abound in our world, building on the power of distributed intelligence on the web to change the driving forces from competition to cooperation, from individualism to strategic partnering, from power-from-information to authority-from- wisdom, from fear to trust.

Interdisciplinarity is the keyword in the creation of novel paradigms for the connected world. In 2001 Lotfi Zadeh and Masoud Nikravesh have suggested another marriage that has proven successful in the connected world: Fuzzy Logic and the Internet (Nikravesh and Azvine 2001). Endowing the Information Highway with the best tool known so far for handling imprecision is not only a blessing but as well an act of grace in a time when the explosion of unclassified and unsorted information makes it practically unusable. However an extended family has proven more successful in the meantime, as search engines using evolutionary search and neural networks are now learning customer preferences in e-marketing systems (Norvig 2002). History repeats itself again and Fuzzy Logic makes now room to the whole family of computational intelligence on the web: it's *Soft Computing* and the Internet!

Adding reasoning capabilities to search engines (Zadeh 2002) is not the only way the Internet can be helped. If the reasoning is encapsulated in a *software agent* (that is an expert system in its own rights), or better in a society of agents (that is a MAS) who 'live' independently on the web, then the Internet becomes a dynamic environment through which agents move from place to place to deliver their services and eventually to compose them with the ones of other agents, just like people cooperate by exchanging services and/or putting together their competencies in a larger, more complex service.

By suggesting the third marriage, between Soft Computing and Agent Technology, Vincenzo Loia has proven to be a man of vision. Now empowered with the ability of soft computing, virtual communities of agents that emulate our World in Cyberspace are able to deal with the uncertainty intrinsic in the real-life that they mirror.

This third marriage closes the triad: Multi-Agent Systems-Internet-Soft Computing to enable the Web become a Dynamic Service Environment[1] (DSE) supporting emulation of real-life communities in all aspects of life, from business and commerce to education and health. What a leverage for us when the agents acting on our behalf make the best decisions and turn the world around in our favor without us needing to do more then click on the cell-phone to give the final blessing by 'OK'–ing the deal. Or when they can find the best partners to help our company get that highly demanded product on the market sooner then the competitor can manage. This dream turns day-by-day into reality, with every successful implementation of agent technology, with every new application involving distributed intelligence on the soft-computing-empowered web.

This chapter seals the magic MAS-Internet-Soft Computing triad to create a web-centric model endowing virtual communities/societies (generically coined as 'enterprises') with proactive self-organizing properties in an open environment connected via the dynamic Web.

In Section 8.2 we present the *holonic enterprise* (HE) as a paradigm of paradigms embracing holonics, MAS, web-centric, Virtual Enterprise (VE) and the novel business paradigm of co-opetition to enable harmonious workflow/information management in a virtual organization. Section 8.3 presents the HE as an information ecosystem, underlying the functional patterns that generate its fundamental properties. A fuzzy-evolutionary approach which enables the HE with the property of self-organization and evolution in Cyberspace towards the best structure is presented in Sections 8.4 and 8.5. Section 8.6 illustrates on a numerical toy example that the theoretical concepts work.

8.2 The Holonic Enterprise as a Paradigm of Paradigms

In the Web-Centric Economy the Dynamic Systems Environment information infrastructure supports production, binds organizations together and reflects in all other organizational aspects. Specifically, production processes are information rich and the dynamics of the information infrastructure is the tool for carrying it out both at individual locales and across the global environment. The electronic linking implies that work matter (or critical parts of it) is being transferred across virtual locales via the DSE which supports organizational information which in turn can mirror social organization.

The HE has emerged as a business paradigm from the need for flexible open reconfigurable models able to emulate the market dynamics in the networked economy (McHugh *et al.* 1995) which necessitates that strategies and relationships evolve over time, changing with the dynamic business environment. The HE integrates into a unified, versatile model several paradigms that have emerged as a result of the tremendous shift in the business dynamics on the global market enabled by the Internet and communication network technologies.

8.2.1 The Universes' Self-Organizing Structure: Holonics Paradigm

The main idea of the HE model stems from the work of Arthur Koestler (Koestler 1968). Koestler postulated a set of underlying principles to explain the self-organizing tendencies of social and biological systems. He proposed the term *holon* to describe the elements of these systems. This term is a combination of the Greek word *holos*, meaning "whole", with the suffix *-on* meaning "part", as in pro*ton* or neur*on*. This term reflects the tendencies of

---

[1] www.agentcities.org (The Global Agentcities Task Force has the mandate to bring together forces from all continents in a common effort to develop the dynamic infrastructures of tomorrow's 'alive'-Web.)

holons to act as autonomous entities, yet cooperating to form apparently self-organizing hierarchies of subsystems, such as the cell/tissue/organ/system hierarchy in biology.

Starting from the empirical observation that, from the Solar System to the Atom the Universe is organized into self-replicating structures of nested hierarchies intrinsically embedded in the functionality of natural systems, in his attempt to creating a model for self-organization in biological systems, Koestler has identified structural patterns of self-replicating structures, named holarchies. Holarchies have been envisioned as models for the Universe's self-organizing structure in which holons at several levels of resolution in the nested hierarchy (Koestler 1968), (Figure 1) behave as autonomous wholes and yet as cooperative parts for achieving the goal of the holarchy.

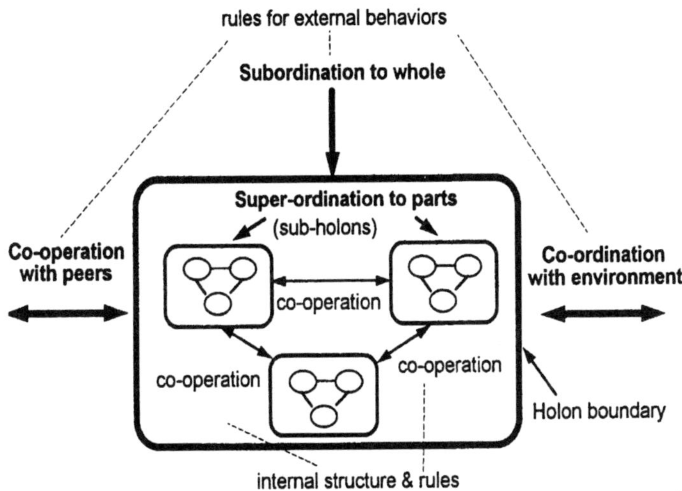

Figure 1. Generic Model of a Holarchy.

In such a nested hierarchy each holon is a sub-system retaining the characteristic attributes of the whole system. What actually defines a holarchy is a purpose around which holons are clustered and subdivided in sub-holons at several levels of resolution according to the organizational dissectibility required. A Confederation is a *political holarchy*, for example having Canada at the highest level of resolution then the provinces at the immediate lower level, and finally the cities at the lowest levels in the hierarchy. Each individual person is regarded as a primitive holon within this social holarchy.

From a software engineering perspective a holon, as a unit of composition retaining characteristic attributes of the whole system (holarchy), can be viewed as a class. Thus the object-oriented paradigm seemed[2] suitable for modeling holarchies as software systems.

Within a holarchy, holons can belong to different clusters simultaneously, displaying *rule-governed behavior*. The rules define a system as a holon with an individuality of its own; they determine its invariant properties, its structural configuration and functional pattern. The greatest challenge faced by holons in a holarchy is 'the whole in the part' dichotomy. As autonomous systems (wholes) holons are animated by autonomy and separation forces while being constraint as parts of the holarchy to work cooperatively with other holons towards the common goal around which the holarchy was formed. The duality autonomy-cooperation as main contradictory forces within a holarchy is balanced by the rules that define the functionality of such a system of semi-autonomous holons (Christensen 1994,

---

[2] HMS – Strategies, Vol. 1 (Deliverable of WP6, March 1994 – Confidential).

Zhang and Norrie 1999). These rules endow the holons with interdependence, namely the capability of integration as parts within the holarchy. Of crucial importance is that rules ensure coordination with local environment that is with the other holons and sub-holarchies. It has been identified -on a manufacturing holarchy (Shu and Norrie 1999)- that the rules organize the holarchies around patterns of functionality, named generically *patterns of holonic collaboration*, Figure 2, which will be further detailed in the context of the HE.

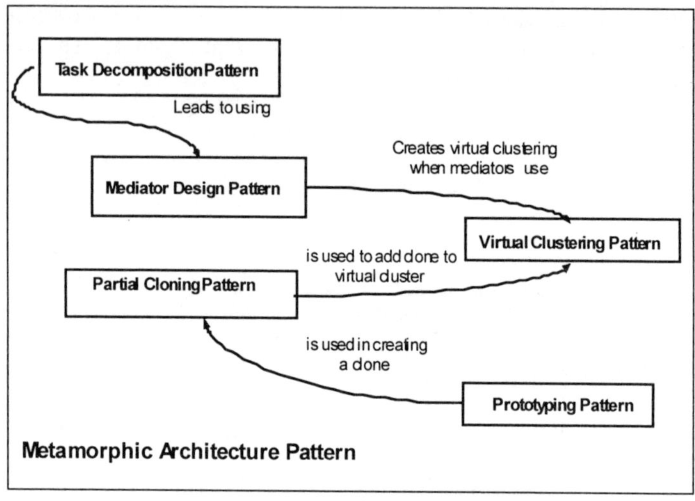

Figure 2. Patterns of Holonic Collaboration

8.2.2 The Universe Encapsulated in Software: Multi-Agent Paradigm

In response to the need for modeling the complexity of interactions in large scale distributed systems, agent technology has emerged (from the AI distributed intelligence task force) as a paradigm for structuring, designing and building software systems that require complex interactions between autonomous distributed (software) components (Woolridge 2001). While the object-oriented paradigm models systems focusing on the structural, static characteristics of their parts which are defined through encapsulation and inheritance, the agent paradigm models systems focusing on the underlining dynamics defined by the *interactions* between their parts. In contrast to the passive way in which objects communicate by invoking methods in one another in a way controlled externally by the user (e.g. from a 'main' program), agents are capable to initiate communication and decide (like a human) when and how to respond to external stimuli (e.g. manifested upon them as requests from other agents). From this perspective the agent paradigm extends the object paradigm in that agents can be regarded as proactive objects (Weiss 1999) that have an internal mechanism which governs their behavior enabling them to initiate action as well as to respond to the outside environment in an autonomous way. With this in mind one can define:

- an intelligent agent as a *software entity* which exhibits, in some significant measure, autonomy, intelligence, and environmental awareness, and which interacts with its environment to achieve internal goals;
- a multi-agent system (MAS) as a software system in which program modules (the individual agents) are given autonomy and intelligence and an underlining coordination mechanism (implementing rules for collaboration, like for holarchies) which enables collaboration between such modules (agents) to attain system objectives

8.2.3 MAS as Software Representations of Holarchies

A software representation of a holarchy thus appears natural as MAS, consisting of autonomous yet cooperative agents. From this perspective a MAS is regarded as a system of agents (software holons) which can cooperate to achieve a goal or objective. The MAS (software holarchy) defines the basic rules for cooperation of the agents (software holons) and thereby limits their autonomy. In this context **autonomy** is defined as the capability of an entity (agent/holon) to create and control the execution of its own plans and/or strategies while **cooperation** - as a process whereby a set of entities (agents/holons) develop mutually acceptable plans and execute them.

The debate on clarifying the difference between holons and agents is an ongoing issue in the research communities using these paradigms. Given the essentially different path on which each concept was developed the question itself is inappropriate. Holarchies (Koestler 1968) have been envisioned as models for the Universe's self-organizing structure (Section 8.2.1). On the other side, agents have been envisioned as a software paradigm aiming to expand the limitations of the static object model with proactive capabilities of autonomy and environmental awareness, the emphasis being on the *interaction* between software components rather then on their structure. In the sequel we briefly present the main characteristics of the holonic and MAS paradigms (Woolridge 2001).

Thus, holonics is an *organizational paradigm* (inspired by the self-organizing properties of natural systems) which models organizations as nested clusters (holons) of sub-organizations (sub-holons) driven towards a common purpose by collaborative rules. The rules act as forces that coordinate interactions between sub-holons working together towards to common purpose. MAS is a *software paradigm* which aims to represent dynamical systems in software by focusing on the interactions between their parts (modeled as software agents).

The common denominator between holonics and MAS as paradigms is obviously the focus on the dynamics of the interactions, however in a MAS there is no pre-assigned condition that the interactions should be driven by cooperative forces, while in a holonic system this is a precondition for the existence of the holarchy per se (the glue that binds the holarchy together driving it towards the common goal.) It is this 'team-spirit' that characterizes a holarchy, in that all its component parts at all levels of resolution work together towards achieving the goal in an optimal manner. This 'togetherness' drives the self-organizing power that configures all the sub-holons to optimize the interactions within the holarchy to reach the common goal with maximum efficiency. On the other side in a MAS agents may interact based on competitive rather than cooperative rules (e.g. electronic markets or other competitive/conflicting environments such as military scenarios; competing over resources or societal/political disputes, etc.) – which is excluded as a possibility in a holarchy.

Organizational hoarchies are real-world entities (as we exemplified before Canada as a Confederation being a political holarchy. Other examples are: a global enterprise is a collaborative purpose-driven/market-driven holarchy; a distributed manufacturing system is a production-driven holarchy, the organism is a survival-driven holarchy, The Universe is an evolution-driven holarchy.

As elements of such organizational holarchies, holons per se are by no means software entities. Thus a 'comparison' with agents does not really make sense. In the manufacturing domain (Ulieru *et al.* 2000) however holons have been considered to be software and physical entities alike, in a co-habitation nature-software expressed through the concept of 'partial cloning' of a physical entity (either a human or a manufacturing machine/robot) as software entity which encapsulates those characteristics abstracted from the real entity needed in the particular collaborative context of the holarchy. Thus one distinguishes two ontological levels in a manufacturing holarchy, Figure 3: a physical one (humans and machines cooperating to fulfill the production needs optimally) and a logical (software) one, which emulates the physical one through software entities (objects or agents) to enable the coordination of production through intelligent control procedures (Brennan 2000). The software representation of the manufacturing holarchy enables emulation of production with distribution of the scheduled tasks on the various software agents 'cloning' the physical machines and once an optimal configuration solution has been reached the appropriate control law is deployed from the software agent on the appropriate physical machine at the appropriate time[3] (Zhang and Norrie 1999).

An intrinsic issue in manufacturing holarchies is thus co-habitation physical holons – software agents. In such a manufacturing co-habitation context the concepts of holon and agent merge and software agents are regarded as holons (but not vice versa, of course). From this perspective, as a software paradigm MAS appears to be an excellent tool for emulating holarchies. A MAS which emulates a holonic system will consists of agents driven by a coordination mechanism designed according to the rules for cooperation of the respective holarchy. With this in mind it is easy to point that software holarchies are specialized MAS that define the interaction between their agents based on the underlining cooperative holonic model. Such software 'holons' appear to be specialized agents that have a particular structure and holonic properties, that is they are decomposable into sub-agents which work cooperatively towards a common goal of the holarchy.

8.2.4 The Web as a Living Organism: Global Enterprises as Holarchies

The tremendous progress of information and communication technologies has transformed our World to an extent to which real-life entities virtually "exist" in a parallel Universe of information. The World Wide Web connects by invisible links these entities through their virtual "clones" forming "societies" in which the virtual entities (mostly modeled as software agents) have their own "life" interacting with an autonomy of their own. Implementing an organizational holarchy (real life system) into software using the MAS paradigm opens the perspective of regarding the Web as a "living organism" consisting of a society of agents that emulates different contexts of the world cloned in software according to the abstractions needed for the specific contextual purpose that determines the holarchy.

In such holarchies enterprises can be partially "cloned" as agents to interact and form global virtual organizations. Two main paradigms have emerged supported by this technological development.

8.2.4.1 The Web-Centric Paradigm: Glue in Virtual Organizations

The use of the World Wide Web in business has radically altered expectations regarding the appropriate infrastructure for enterprise systems. The Web-Centric Enterprise[4] (Hornberger 2001) is a novel business model that provides a foundation on which companies can build processes and procedures to create products for their customers within the context of today's market dynamics in which systems need to be able to accommodate unique customer requirements, both upon initial implementation and over time. Unlike existing point solutions that focus on a single-department or activity product, such as data management or product-design-and-manufacturing, the Web-Centric model addresses product and process life cycle management across the extended enterprise regarded as a global organization. At the core of the Web-Centric Enterprise model is a breakthrough in information technology infrastructure conceptualization, namely the internet-enabled

---

[3] http://www.holobloc.com/.
[4] http://www.hourgroup.com/e-energy/reg2001.html

software infrastructure acting as a worldwide open DSE (footnote 1). Such an integrated framework enables sharing of information, services and applications among suppliers, employees, partners and customers via:

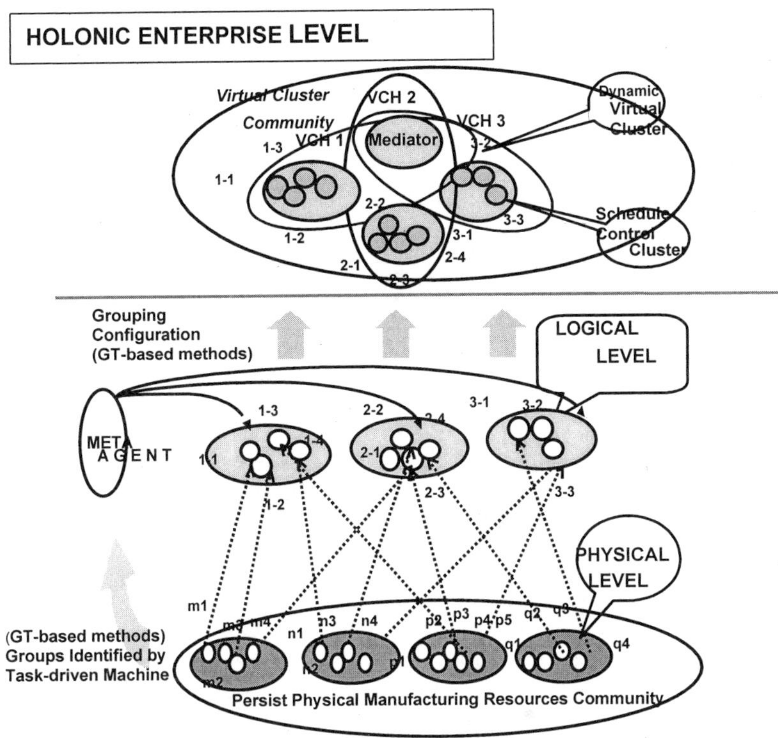

Figure 3. Logical and Physical Level in a Holonic Enterprise

- Deployment of automated, intelligent software services (e.g., internet-enabled negotiations, financial transactions, advertising and bidding; order placement/delivery, automatic order tracking and reporting, etc.)
- Complex interactions between such services (e.g., compliance policies; argumentation and persuasion via complex conversation protocols, bargaining, etc.);
- Dynamic discovery and composition of services to create new compound value added services (e.g., dynamic virtual clustering of synergetic partnerships of collaborative organizations aiming to achieve a common goal, finding and accessing an unknown service that is available on the Web, matching of different templates from different sources to design a product optimally, etc.).

Such a dynamic Web synergistically glues different dispersed organizations/resources into an added value holarchy capable to accomplish more then the sum of each individual organization/resource could.

8.2.4.2 Bringing The World Together: The Virtual Enterprise (VE) Paradigm

A virtual organization or company is one whose members are geographically apart, usually working by electronic linking via computers while appearing to others to be a single, unified organization with a real physical location. Within a virtual organization work cannot be completed without support of an information technology infrastructure in linking the parts.

The VE (VE) paradigm differs from the Web-centric paradigm in that a VE is a distinct organizational form, not just a property of any organization. Thus, Web-centric organizations that can use communications extensively, but not in a way critical in fulfilling the goal of the organization (e.g., a multinational corporation with dispersed parts being on the same satellite network whose use, however, is not critical for completing the production process) are not VE. In today's global economy in which enterprises put together their competitive advantage to leverage a higher purpose otherwise impossible to achieve the VE is an appropriate model for strategic partnerships. Such a strategic partnership model calls for new perspectives on competition in the global open internet-enabled economy.

8.2.5 Balancing Autonomy and Cooperation in the Networked Economy: The Co-opetition Paradigm

The new economy mandates the shift from industrial age, "brick and mortar" strategic thinking to an emphasis on new alliances and a rethinking of traditional partnerships. Alliances and partnerships can be formed in ways that increase value for all players. The concept of co-opetition (Brandenburger and Nalebuff 1996) builds on the duality inherent in all relationships with respect to win-win and win-lose interactions. The success of most businesses is dependent on the success of others, yet they must compete to capture value created in the market and protect their own interests. The main issues to be addressed when developing a business strategy based on co-opetition are:
-   Who are the players in the network and how can they collaborate to maximize value?
-   Which relationships are complementary in nature (which companies can add value to what they provide)?
-   Which players are competitors, and are there mutually beneficial ways to create value?
-   What should they do to leverage relationships with customers and suppliers?
-   What can they do to sustain their competitive advantage over time?

From this perspective we can regard the global enterprise as a holarchy whose holons interact according to co-opetition rules implemented as strategies for negotiation, collaboration, cooperation and other coordination mechanisms defining the patterns of holonic collaboration according to which the holarchy functions.

8.3 The Holonic Enterprise as an Information Ecosystem

Considering VEs as holarchies of web-glued enterprises, which are modeled as MAS - naturally leads to the concept of HE, Figure 4. Thus a HE is a holarchy of collaborative enterprises, where each enterprise is regarded as a holon and is modeled by a software agent with *holonic* properties, so that the software agent may be composed of other agents that behave in a similar way but perform different functions at lower levels of resolution. There are three levels of resolution within the HE holarchy (Ulieru *et al.* 2002):

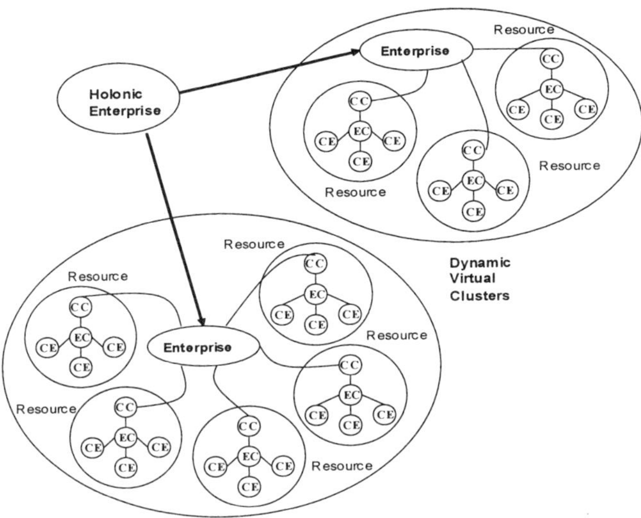

Figure 4. Holonic Enterprise as an Information-Ecosystem

8.3.1 Inter-enterprise, global collaboration level

At this level several holon-enterprises cluster into a collaborative holarchy to produce a product or service. The clustering criteria support maximal synergy and efficiency. Traditionally this level was regarded as a mostly static chain of customers and suppliers through which the workflow and information was moving from the end customer that required the product to the end supplier that delivered it. In the HE the *supply chain* paradigm is replaced by the *collaborative holarchy* paradigm. With each collaborative partner modeled as an agent that encapsulates those abstractions relevant to the particular cooperation, a dynamic virtual cluster emerges that can be configured on-line according to the collaborative goals.

8.3.2 Intra-enterprise level

Once each enterprise has undertaken responsibility for the assigned part of the work, it has to organize in turn its own internal resources to deliver on time according to the coordination requirements of the collaborative cluster. Planning and dynamic scheduling of resources at this level enable functional reconfiguration and flexibility via (re)selecting functional units, (re)assigning their locations, and (re)defining their interconnections (e.g., rerouting around a broken machine, changing the functions of a multi-functional machine). This is achieved through a replication of the dynamic virtual clustering mechanism having now each resource within the enterprise cloned as an agent that abstracts those functional characteristics relevant to the specific task assigned by the collaborative holarchy to the partner.

8.3.3 Basic resource level

To enable the resource management through the DSE each resource (machine; human; information entity) is cloned as an agent that abstracts those parameters needed for the configuration of the holonic production system.

Thus the HE paradigm links the three levels of a global collaborative organization to build a web-centric ecosystem partnering in which the workflow is harmoniously managed through the dynamic information infrastructure (the logical level in Figure 3) that links the resources of all involved organizations (the physical level in Figure 3).

8.3.4 Patterns of Holonic Collaboration

The coordination backbone for a HE is based on the patterns of holonic collaboration (Figure 2). They follow the design patterns for adaptive MAS identified in (Shu and Norrie 1999). The overall architecture of the HE builds on the Metamorphic Architecture Pattern (Maturana and Norrie 1996) that replicates at all levels. This pattern works by synergetic integration of two other patterns

- **Dynamic Virtual Clustering** This pattern is facilitated by the general layered architecture of the HE. The dynamic virtual clustering pattern plays a crucial role in that it embeds the self-organizing properties of a HE. The main responsibility of this pattern is to configure the enterprise to minimize cost enabling for flexible, re-configurable structures. At all levels of the HE, task propagation occurs by a process of virtual cluster (or holarchy) formation. It is debatable if this pattern should be implemented by mutual adjustment mechanisms (in a totally decentralized manner which would leave room for maximum autonomy in the holarchy) or via a mediator - Figure 3 (Maturana and Norrie 1996). This implementation (which is suitable for manufacturing holarchies) places the control of the holarchy into a mediator agent and by this reduces the degree of autonomy of the individual holons in the HE.
- **Mediator Agent Pattern** supporting the decision-making process that creates and (re)-configures the dynamic virtual clusters of collaborative entities, eventually by adding/removing entities to/from the holarchy.
- **Partial Cloning Pattern.** This pattern defines which of the enterprise's characteristics (attributes and functionality) we need to abstract into agents at each level when modeling the HE as a collaborative multi-agent system.
- **Task Decomposition-Distribution Pattern.** This pattern is enhanced with capability to distribute harmoniously among the participants, the overall task assigned to the collaborative holon, at each level. The main mechanisms by which this pattern works are:
- *task distribution among the cluster's entities* (outside-in view from the mediator "down" into each collaborative partner at that level) and
- *task deployment within each entity* (inside-out view – from the entity, regarded as a holon with distributed resources available to it for accomplishing the assigned task, to the mediator).
- **Ontology Pattern.** This consists of two kind of ontologies:
- for **'peer-to-peer'** communication within each level (that is **'inter-agent' communication among entities that form a cluster);**
- for **'inter-level' communication** that enables deployment of tasks assigned at higher levels (by the mediator) on lower level clusters of resources as well as reporting (from the lower level to the higher) of emergency situations for which rescheduling/re-planning reconfiguration are required.

For more details on the flow of information among the three levels of the HE as well as on the interaction between the physical and logical level please see (Ulieru *et al.* 2002).

In the sequel we propose a fuzzy-evolutionary approach that implemented within the mediator - Figure 3 (Maturana and Norrie 1996) - stabilizes the HE in an optimal structure by first configuring it through optimal clustering of the existing resources via fuzzy entropy minimization (Section 8.4) then by expanding the search on the dynamic Web for even better resources to iteratively replace the old ones (Section 8.5).

8.4 Emergence of Holonic Enterprises from Virtual Enterprises: The Natural Order is Holonic

The first part of this approach is an implementation of the dynamic virtual clustering pattern that optimizes the information and resource management across the HE to fulfill in the most efficient way the holarchy goal. The main idea is to minimize the entropy in the information spread across the VE (modeled as a multi-agent system) – such that each holon maximizes its knowledge of the task it is assigned, in order to best accomplish it. This naturally leads to the (self)organization of the VE in a holarchy (which defines a HE).

We consider the holarchy having its resources predefined and represented as software agents at the logical level of the HE. At this level the holarchy is regarded as a MAS. Our purpose is to organize the HE such that it can accomplish the goal (say manufacturing of a certain product) with minimal cost. This calls for all the resources to be loaded at optimal capacity through a harmonized flow of information and material across the HE. Given that we aim to attain and preserve this perfect order in the holarchy it seems natural to attempt this by minimizing the entropy measuring the degree of order in the information spread across the holarchy's resources.

To enable a mathematical formalism that can support this purpose we regard a MAS as a dynamical system in which agents exchange information and organize it through reasoning into knowledge about the assigned goal (Ulieru and Ramakhrishnan 1999). Optimal knowledge at the holarchy's highest level of resolution (inter-enterprise level) corresponds to an optimal level of information organization and distribution among the agents within all levels of the holarchy. We consider the entropy as a measure of the degree of order in the information spread across the multi-agent system modeling the holarchy. One can envision the agents in the MAS as being under the influence of an information "field" which drives the agent interactions towards achieving "equilibrium" with other agents with respect to this entropy[5].

This information is usually uncertain, requiring several ways of modeling to cope with the different aspects of the uncertainty. Fuzzy set theory offers an adequate framework for dealing with this uncertainty (Klir and Folger 1988). Therefore we will use the generalized fuzzy entropy (Zimmermann 1991) to measure the degree of order in the information spread across the holarchy. The generalized fuzzy entropy is the measure of the "potential" of this information field and *equilibrium* for the agents under this influence corresponds to an optimal organization of the information across the MAS with respect to the assigned goal's achievement (Ulieru and Ramakhrishnan 1999). When the circumstances change across the holarchy (due to unexpected events, such as need to change a partner that went out of business, machine break-down, raw materials unavailable, etc.) the equilibrium point changes as well inducing a new re-distribution of information among the agents with new emerging agent interactions.

We start with the assumption that only the set of resources available for the holarchy formation is given (that is we know the enterprises that will collaborate to accomplish the pre-set goal) and we aim to organize these enterprises such that their resources are optimally used to accomplish the goal most efficiently (minimal cost and time). In short we have a VE with several distributed partners linked via the dynamic Web and we want to

---

[5] The information 'field' acts upon the agents much in the same manner as the gravitational and electromagnetic fields act upon physical and electrical entities respectively.

organize it such that it accomplishes a certain goal optimally. In the sequel we will prove mathematically that the optimal organizational structure of the distributed partners' resources is a holarchy, so a HE enterprise emerges from the VE.

8.4.1 A Framework for Capturing Uncertainty in MAS

Denote by $\mathcal{A}_N = \{a_n\}_{n \in \overline{1,N}}$ the set of $N \geq 1$ agents that belong to the MAS modeling a VE. Based only on the initial uncertain information, one can build a family $\mathcal{P} = \{\mathcal{P}_k\}_{k \in \overline{1,K}}$, containing $K \geq 1$ collections of clustering configurations, for a preset global goal (Figure 3). Each $\mathcal{P}_k$ ($k \in \overline{1,K}$) can be referred to as a *source-plan* in the sense that it can be a source of partitions for a MAS plan. Thus, a source-plan is expressed as a collection of $M_k \geq 1$ different clustering configurations in which the agents team-up to accomplish the enterprise goal: $\mathcal{P}_k = \{P_{k,m}\}_{m \in \overline{1,M_k}}$. The only available information about $\mathcal{P}_k$ is the *degree of occurrence* associated to each of its clustering configurations (Figure 3), $P_{k,m}$, which can be assigned as a possibility measure (Dubois and Prade 1988), $\alpha_{k,m} \in [0,1]$. Thus, the corresponding degrees of occurrence are members of a two-dimension family $\{\alpha_{k,m}\}_{k \in \overline{1,K}; m \in \overline{1,M_k}}$, which quantifies all the available information about the MAS modeling the VE.

We aim to construct a measure of uncertainty, V (from "<u>v</u>agueness") (Klir and Folger 1988), fuzzy-type, real-valued, defined on the set of all source-plans of $\mathcal{A}_N$ and optimize it in order to select the *least vague* source-plan from the family $\mathcal{P} = \{\mathcal{P}_k\}_{k \in \overline{1,K}}$:

$$\mathcal{P}_{k_0} = \underset{k \in \overline{1,K}}{\arg\text{opt}} V(\mathcal{P}_k) \text{, where } k_o \in \overline{1,K} \tag{1}$$

The cost function V required in problem (1) will be constructed by using a *measure of fuzziness* (Klir and Folger 1988). We present hereafter the steps of this construction.

8.4.2 Modeling Agent Interactions via Fuzzy Relations

We model agent interactions through fuzzy relations considering that two agents are in relation if they exchange information. As two agents exchanging information are as well in the same cluster one can describe the clustering configurations by means of these fuzzy relations. The family of fuzzy relations, $\{\mathcal{R}_k\}_{k \in \overline{1,K}}$, modeling the clustering possibility over the MAS agents($\mathcal{A}_N$) is built using the possibility measures $\{\alpha_{k,m}\}_{k \in \overline{1,K}; m \in \overline{1,M_k}}$ and the family of source-plans $\{\mathcal{P}_k\}_{k \in \overline{1,K}}$. Consider $k \in \overline{1,K}$ and $m \in \overline{1,M_k}$ arbitrarily fixed.

In construction of the fuzzy relation $\mathcal{R}_k$, one starts from the observation that associating agents in clusters is very similar to grouping them into *compatibility* or *equivalence classes*, given a (binary) crisp relation between them. The compatibility properties of reflexivity and symmetry are fulfilled for covers (overlapped clusters), whereas the equivalence conditions of compatibility and transitivity stand for partitions. The corresponding crisp relation denoted by $R_{k,m}$, can be described by the statement: *two agents are related if they belong to the same cluster*. The facts that a and b are, respectively *are not* in the relation $R_{k,m}$ (where $a, b \in \mathcal{A}_N$) are expressed by "$a R_{k,m} b$" and "$a \neg R_{k,m} b$" respectively. The relation $R_{k,m}$ is a $N \times N$ matrix $H_{k,m} \in \mathfrak{R}^{N \times N}$ - the *characteristic matrix* which completely specifies the configuration $P_{k,m}$. Consequently, we can construct an elementary fuzzy (binary) relation $\mathcal{R}_{k,m}$ whose membership matrix is expressed as the product between the characteristic matrix $H_{k,m}$, and the degree of occurrence $\alpha_{k,m}$, that is: $\alpha_{k,m} H_{k,m}$. This fuzzy relation of $\mathcal{A}_N \times \mathcal{A}_N$ is also uniquely associated to $P_{k,m}$. If $k \in \overline{1,K}$ is kept fixed, but m varies in the range $\overline{1,M_k}$, then a family of fuzzy elementary relations is generated: $\{\mathcal{R}_{k,m}\}_{m \in \overline{1,M_k}}$. Naturally, $\mathcal{R}_k$ is then defined as the fuzzy union. Thus a bijective map associating a family of source plans $\mathcal{P} = \{\mathcal{P}_k\}_{k \in \overline{1,K}}$ to a fuzzy relation measuring their possibility of occurrence $\mathcal{R} = \{\mathcal{R}_k\}_{k \in \overline{1,K}}$, can be built:

$$T(\mathcal{P}_k) = \mathcal{R}_k \ , \ \forall k \in \overline{1,K} \tag{2}$$

8.4.3 Fuzzy Entropy as a Measure of Order in MAS

A measure that evaluates "the fuzziness" of a fuzzy set by taking into consideration both the set and its (fuzzy) complement is the *Shannon measure*, derived from the generalized Shannon's function:

$$\left[\begin{array}{l} S : [0,1]^M \rightarrow \mathfrak{R}_+ \\[2mm] (x_1,...,x_M) \mapsto S(x) \overset{def}{=} -\sum_{m=1}^{M} \left[x_m \log_2 x_m + (1-x_m) \log_2 (1-x_m) \right]. \end{array} \right. \tag{3}$$

If the argument of this function is a probability distribution, it is referred to as *Shannon entropy*. If the argument is a membership function defining a fuzzy set, it is refereed to as *(Shannon) fuzzy entropy* (Zimmermann 1991). Denote the fuzzy entropy by S_μ. Then, according to equation (3), S_μ is expressed for all $k \in \overline{1,K}$ by:

$$S_\mu(\mathcal{R}_k) = -\sum_{i=1}^{N}\sum_{j=1}^{N} \mathcal{M}_k[i,j] \log \mathcal{M}_k[i,j] - \sum_{i=1}^{N}\sum_{j=1}^{N} \left[1 - \mathcal{M}_k[i,j]\right] \log \left[1 - \mathcal{M}_k[i,j]\right]. \tag{4}$$

Although a unique maximum of Shannon fuzzy entropy (4) exists, we are searching for one of its minima that corresponds to a most efficient resource clustering in the VE. The required measure of uncertainty, V, is obtained by composing S_μ in (4) with T in (2), that is: $V = S_\mu \circ T$. Since T is a bijection, the optimization problem (1) is equivalent with:

$$\mathcal{P}_{k_0} = T^{-1}(\arg\min_{k \in \overline{1,K}} S_\mu(\mathcal{P}_k)) \text{ , where } k_o \in \overline{1,K} . \tag{5}$$

8.4.4 Building the Optimal Configuration of the Multi-Agent System modeling the VE

$\mathcal{P}_{k_0}$ is the least fuzzy (minimally fuzzy), i.e. the least uncertain source-plan. The fuzzy relation encoding the agent clustering to fulfill the VE goal according to this optimal plan, $\mathcal{R}_{k_0}$ is useful in the reverse construction of a *least uncertain plan*, as follows. Once one pair ($\mathcal{P}_{k_0}$, $\mathcal{R}_{k_0}$) has been selected by solving the problem (5), a corresponding source-plan should be identified.

The α-cuts of $\mathcal{R}_{k_0}$ are the crisp relations $R_{k_0,\alpha}$, for degrees of membership $\alpha \in [0,1]$. The characteristic matrix elements of $R_{k_0,\alpha}$ are defined by:

$$H_{k_0,\alpha}[i,j] \stackrel{def}{=} \begin{cases} 1 \text{ , if } M_{k_0}[i,j] \geq \alpha \\ 0 \text{ , otherwise} \end{cases} , \forall i,j \in \overline{1,N} \tag{6}$$

Each matrix $H_{k_0,\alpha}$ in (6) describes a unique clustering configuration of agents over $\mathcal{A}_N$. Thus, two categories of source-plans emerge: *equivalence* or *holonic source-plans* (when $\mathcal{R}_{k_0}$ is a similarity relation) and *compatibility source-plans* (when $\mathcal{R}_{k_0}$ is only a proximity relation).

- When $\mathcal{R}_{k_0}$ is a *similarity relation*, then clusters are associated in order to form new clusters, and a nested hierarchy emerges that organizes the MAS modeling the VE into a holarchy (that is a HE emerges from the VE[6]).

- When $\mathcal{R}_{k_0}$ is only a *proximity* relation, tolerance (compatibility) classes can be constructed as collections of eventually overlapping clusters (covers). This time, the fact that clusters could be overlapping (i.e. one or more agents can belong to different clusters simultaneously) reveals the capacity of some agents to play multiple roles by being involved in several tasks at the same time while the holonic properties of the organization are still preserved.

This proves that the optimal organizational structure in a virtual organization is a holarchy.

8.4.5 Virtual Clustering Mechanism

The procedure by which the virtual clustering pattern can be designed to ensure an optimal clustering of resources for most efficient goal accomplishment by the virtual organization is:

---

[6] a (unique) similarity relation can be constructed starting from the proximity relation $\mathcal{R}_{k_0}$, by computing its *transitive closure*. Thus, the potential holonic structure of MAS can be revealed, even when it seems to evolve in a non-holonic manner.

$\boxed{\text{START}}$

- Initial data: the number of agents: N; the collection of K source-plans: $\mathcal{P} = \{\mathcal{P}_k\}_{k \in \overline{1,K}}$; the occurrence degrees (possibility measures): $\{\alpha_{k,m}\}_{k \in \overline{1,K}; m \in \overline{1,M_k}}$.

- For $k \in \overline{1,K}$:
  - For $m \in \overline{1,M_k}$:

  a.   Construct the characteristic matrix $H_{k,m}$ associated to configuration $P_{k,m}$ (Section 8.4.2).

  b. Multiply $H_{k,m}$ by $\alpha_{k,m}$ ($H_{k,m} \leftarrow \alpha_{k,m} H_{k,m}$).

  - Construct the membership matrix of fuzzy relation $\mathcal{R}_k$ by:

$$\mathcal{M}_k = \max_{m \in 1, M_k} \bullet \{H_{k,m}\}.$$

[where "max$\bullet$"acts on matrix elements and not globally, on matrices.]

- Compute the vagueness of $\mathcal{R}_k$ (by using the symmetry, Section 8.4.3):

$$S_\mu(\mathcal{R}_k) = -2 \sum_{i=1}^{N} \sum_{j=i+1}^{N} \mathcal{M}_k[i,j] \log \mathcal{M}_k[i,j] - 2 \sum_{i=1}^{N} \sum_{j=i+1}^{N} \left[1 - \mathcal{M}_k[i,j]\right] \log\left[1 - \mathcal{M}_k[i,j]\right].$$

- Solve the problem: $\mathcal{R}_{k_0} = \arg\min_{k \in \overline{1,K}} S_\mu(\mathcal{R}_k)$.

- List the Solution: The least vague source-plan is $\mathcal{P}_{k_0}$.
- Other alternatives desired?

$\boxed{\text{Yes}}$

  - Construct $\mathcal{Z}_{k_0}$ - the transitive closure of $\mathcal{R}_{k_0}$:

  c.   Set $\mathcal{M}_{k_0}^{\mathcal{R}} = \mathcal{M}_{k_0}$.

  d.   Compute: $\mathcal{M}_{k_0}^2 = \max \bullet \{\mathcal{M}_{k_0}^{\mathcal{R}}, \left(\mathcal{M}_{k_0}^{\mathcal{R}} \circ \mathcal{M}_{k_0}^{\mathcal{R}}\right)\}$.

  e.   If $\mathcal{M}_{k_0}^{\mathcal{R}} \neq \mathcal{M}_{k_0}^2$,

  Then: replace the matrix $\mathcal{M}_{k_0}^{\mathcal{R}}$ by $\mathcal{M}_{k_0}^2$ ($\mathcal{M}_{k_0}^{\mathcal{R}} \leftarrow \mathcal{M}_{k_0}^2$) and jump to step d.

  Else: $\mathcal{M}_{k_0}^2$ is the membership matrix of the transitive closure $\mathcal{Z}_{k_0}$.

  - If $\mathcal{M}_{k_0} \neq \mathcal{M}_{k_0}^2$

  Then: $\mathcal{R}_{k_0}$ is just a proximity relation and a compatibility source-plan $\mathcal{P}_{k_0}^C$ is obtained by computing its α-cuts.

Else: $\mathcal{Z}_{k_0}$ is a similarity relation and a holonic source-plan $\mathcal{P}_{k_0}^{H}$ is obtained by computing the corresponding α -cuts.

Designing the virtual clustering pattern by this procedure endows the VE with self-organizing properties that ensure emergence of the optimal holonic structure once the resources are known (that is once the distributed partners have committed to the common goal and allocated the resources they want to put in to accomplish it.) Thus the above procedure ensures emergence of an optimal HE from any predefined virtual organization.

However one more step is required to cope with the high dynamics of today's Web-centric economy, namely capability to include new partners in the virtual organization. The next section addresses this issue.

8.5 Evolution of the HE in Cyberspace Towards the Best Structure

In the open environment created by the dynamic Web opportunities for improvement of an existing virtual organization arise continuously. New partners and customers alike come into the virtual game bidding their capabilities and money to get the best deal. Staying competitive in this high dynamics requires openness and ability to accommodate chance rapidly through a flexible strategy enabling re-configuration of the organization to be able to respond to new market demands as well as to opportunities (e.g. in playing with a better partner when needed.) In response to this need we have designed an evolutionary search strategy that enables the virtual organization to continuously find better partners fitting the dynamics of its goals as they change according to the market dynamics.

8.5.1 An Evolutionary Search Model for New Agents that Fit Better the HE Objective

We regard 'the living Web' (Subsection 8.2.5) as a genetic evolutionary system. The selection of the agents (partners) that best fit the holarchy's objective is done in a similar way to the natural selection by 'survival of the fittest' through which the agents/partners that best suit the HE with respect to the goal accomplishment are chosen from the offers available on the Web. In this search model the mutation and crossover operators (p_m and p_c) represent probabilities of finding 'keywords' (describing the attributes required from the new partners searched for) inside the search domain considered. Our construction is based on the observation that the search process on an agent domain[7] (Ulieru *et al.* 2001) containing information about a set of agents that "live" on the Web - e.g. a directory "look-up"-like table of "yellow page" agents describing the services that the possible partners offer (Ulieru *et al.* 2000) - is analogous to the genetic selection of the most suitable ones in a population of agents meant to "fit" the virtual organizations' goals.

---

[7] See the FIPA architecture standard at www.fipa.org

The main idea is to express the fitness function (measuring how well the new agent fits the holarchy's goal) in terms of the fuzzy entropy (4):

$$F = S_\mu \tag{7}$$

With this, minimizing the entropy across the extended MAS (which includes the agents from the search domain) according to HE goal-reach optimization equates optimizing the fitness function which naturally selects the best agents fitting the optimal organizational structure of the HE. In the sequel we present the mathematical formalism for this evolutionary search.

8.5.2 A Fuzzy Measure for Search Relevance Evaluation

The first step in our construction is to define a measure of relevancy for the search of new agents, based on which partners that better fit the HE goal-reach optimum can be found on the Web to replace the existing ones that are less suitable. That is:

$$S_\mu{}' < S_\mu \tag{8}$$

where $S_\mu{}'$ is the entropy for the HE with the new partners and S_μ - for the initial HE. According to (7), (8) collapses into

$$F' < F \tag{9}$$

(where F' is the fitness function for the HE with new partners) meaning that the new partners better fit the system's goal-reach.

In the previous Section we have proven that minimizing S_μ leads to a fuzzy relation that encodes the best clustering configuration for the HE. This fuzzy relation being either a proximity or a similarity measure it is intuitive to consider it as a good measure for the relevancy of the new agents to the HE goal-reach. Defining for example the fuzzy relation $\mathcal{R}_k$ in (2) as a preference relation encoding, e.g. the desire of agents to work cooperatively, gives a relevancy measure that perfectly fits the purpose of the search for better partners. That is – when agents are found for which the preference is higher then for the existing ones, they should replace the old ones. This increases the membership values of the preference relationship, which indicates that the relevance relative to our search is higher. So defining $\mathcal{R}_k$ as a preference relationship, leads to the following definition of the relevancy measure **R**:

$$\mathbf{R} = \mathcal{R}_{k_0} = \arg\min_{k\in\overline{1,K}} S_\mu(\mathcal{R}_k) \tag{10}$$

From (10) it results that the higher the preference, the smaller the entropy (and accordingly the fitness (7) of the new agents into the holarchy).

8.5.3 The Dynamic Web Regarded as an Evolutionary System

With this we are ready to present the algorithm that searches for better partners in Cyberspace. We initialize the search process as follows:

(a) The initial population (*phenotype*) consists of the existing agents in the HE before the search.

(b) Calculate **R** for the phenotype
(c) Rank the preferences and determine the optimal source plan (5) by computing the corresponding α-cuts.
(d) The preferences for the optimal source plan represented as binary strings constitute the *genotype*. They encode all the relevant information needed to evolve the HE towards a better structure by selecting better agents while searching on an expanded domain.
(e) The phenotype evolves by reproduction according to how the probabilities of mutation and crossover (p_m and p_c) affect the genotype (Fogel 1998). Each chromosome of the population (in the genotype) will be randomly affected.

We define p_m and p_c to be the probabilities of finding agents in Cyberspace that better fit the HE context. Such agents will have higher preferences (10) then the ones in the phenotype. Michalenicz (Michalenicz 1992) has proven experimentally that e.g. choosing $p_m \leq 1\%$, $p_c = 20 \div 30\%$ leads to convergence of the genetic algorithm. With this the evolutionary search, Figure 5, is done as follows:

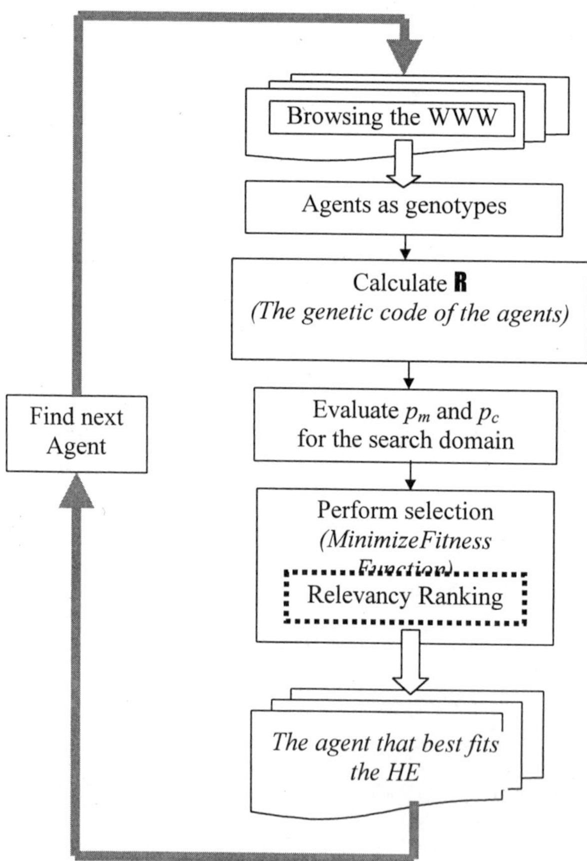

Figure 5. The dynamic search in Cyberspace

(f) Define the goal of the search as maximizing **R** that is: select those agents for which preferences are higher then the highest existing ones, and replace by them the agents with lowest preferences.

(g) Define the search domain, e.g. a standard FIPA agent domain (see footnote 7)[8].

(h) The search process on the chosen agent domain is done by genetic selection of the agents that have highest preferences -using to any classical genetic algorithm (Fogel 1998).

(i) Once the agent domain has been entirely explored a new search is carried on for the next agent domain recommended by the yellow page agent.

The essence of this evolutionary search process stems from the recursive modification of the chromosomes in the genotype in each generation while monitoring the fitness function (7). At each iteration (that is whenever a new agent domain s searched) all members of the current generation (that is the existing agents in the holarchy and the new ones searched for) are compared with each other in terms of the preference measures. The ones with highest preferences are placed at the top and the worst are replaced with the new agents. The subsequent iteration resumes this process on the partially renewed population. In this way the openness to new opportunities for continuous improvement in the HE constituency is achieved and with this the emergence of an optimal structure for the holarchy. Embedding this strategy in the mediator (Figure 3) endows the HE with the capability to continuously evolve towards a better and better structure by bringing to the table better and better partners as they are found.

In the sequel we illustrate on a numerical example how the proposed fuzzy-evolutionary approach works.

8.6 Simulation Results

8.6.1 Emergence of HE structure from MAS

Consider a MAS consisting of $N = 7$ agents for which the following roles have emerged after the vagueness minimization procedure (Subsection 8.4.5) was run: (a_4) – manager of the overall assigned task, (a_2 and a_3) – workers accomplishing the tasks operations by using four resource agents (a_1, a_5, a_6 and a_7), Figure 6. Starting with very parsimonious information about clusters created by couples of agents, each preference is assigned to a pair of agents. Although this information is extremely vague, we will be able to construct compatibility and holonic plans.

The MAS is considered initially as a system about which we do not know anything. We can stimulate it by setting some goals and letting it reach them. When the goals have been inputted, the observed output is the succession of agent clusters that occur each time the MAS transitions from the initial state to the final one (when the optimal holonic structure emerges). In order to get the best response from the MAS (in terms of having it go through as many states as possible), we have stimulated it with a set of goals equivalent to the "white noise" in systems identification (Söderström and Stoica 1989) - i.e. a class of goals, as large as possible, that might be set for the system. By inputting these goals one by one (or in a mixed manner - if this is possible), we can count the number of occurrences for each cluster. By normalizing the numbers (i.e. dividing them by their sum) one obtains the

occurrence degrees of each cluster, i.e. the numbers $\{\alpha_{k,m}\}_{k\in\overline{1,K};m\in\overline{1,M_k}}$ that are, in fact,

occurrence frequencies of clusters. For these simulation experiments, quasi-random (Gauss type) numbers were generated as occurrence degrees. After ~200 simulations (we used MATLAB), the final holonic clustering patterns emerged. Moreover, some information about the nature of the agents - i.e. whether they are knowledge agents, or yellow-page

---

[8] The agent domain can be chosen by a yellow page agent [11].

agents or interface agents, etc. (Ulieru *et al.* 2000) - were revealed without any a priori knowledge about the agent's type.

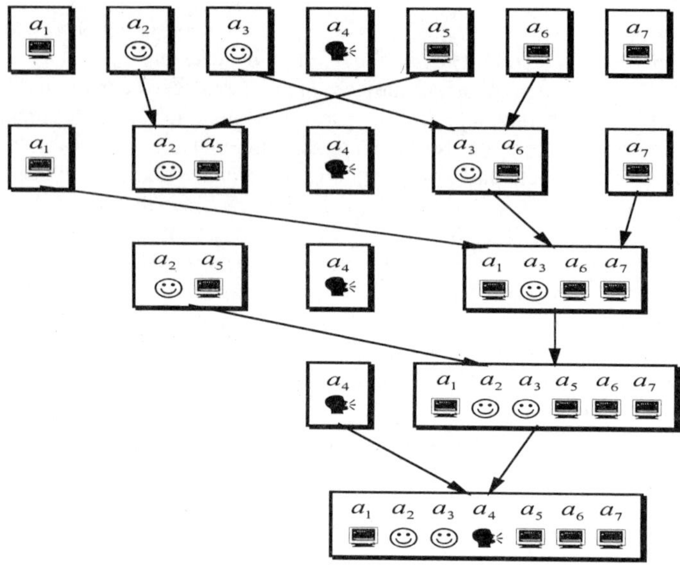

Figure 6. The emerged Holonic Enterprise

Every degree of occurrence is associated with only one pair of agents. Although this information is extremely vague, compatibility and holonic plans are built.

Since $N = 7$, there are maximum $C_7^2 = 21$ possible couples between agents. Each couple of agents has a certain degree of occurrence, but, in general, it is not necessary that all 21 couples appear during the MAS evolution. A null degree of occurrence will be assigned to every impossible couple. However, in this example, all 21 couples were graded by non-null values, in order to avoid triviality.

Starting from this vague information, one constructs first the corresponding fuzzy relation $\mathcal{R}$ between the 7 agents. None of the occurrence degrees has disappeared in $\mathcal{R}$.

$$
\mathcal{M}_{\mathcal{R}}:
\begin{array}{ccccccc}
1.0000 & 0.5402 & 0.6343 & 0.1877 & 0.3424 & 0.2001 & 0.4863 \\
0.5402 & 1.0000 & 0.3561 & 0.4797 & 0.7651 & 0.2092 & 0.2794 \\
0.6343 & 0.3561 & 1.0000 & 0.4780 & 0.1389 & 0.6858 & 0.6414 \\
0.1877 & 0.4797 & 0.4780 & 1.0000 & 0.3191 & 0.4888 & 0.3347 \\
0.3424 & 0.7651 & 0.1389 & 0.3191 & 1.0000 & 0.2784 & 0.4291 \\
0.2001 & 0.2092 & 0.6858 & 0.4888 & 0.2784 & 1.0000 & 0.1666 \\
0.4863 & 0.2794 & 0.6414 & 0.3347 & 0.4291 & 0.1666 & 1.0000
\end{array}
$$

Since this relation is only a proximity one, we generate its transitive cover $\mathcal{Q}$:

$$
1.0000 \quad 0.5402 \quad 0.6343 \quad 0.4888 \quad 0.5402 \quad 0.6343 \quad 0.6343
$$

$$\mathcal{M}_2: \begin{array}{ccccccc} 0.5402 & 1.0000 & 0.5402 & 0.4888 & 0.7651 & 0.5402 & 0.5402 \\ 0.6343 & 0.5402 & 1.0000 & 0.4888 & 0.5402 & 0.6858 & 0.6414 \\ 0.4888 & 0.4888 & 0.4888 & 1.0000 & 0.4888 & 0.4888 & 0.4888 \\ 0.5402 & 0.7651 & 0.5402 & 0.4888 & 1.0000 & 0.5402 & 0.5402 \\ 0.6343 & 0.5402 & 0.6858 & 0.4888 & 0.5402 & 1.0000 & 0.6414 \\ 0.6343 & 0.5402 & 0.6414 & 0.4888 & 0.5402 & 0.6414 & 1.0000 \end{array}$$

$\mathcal{Z}$ is a similarity relation between agents. In the membership matrix $\mathcal{M}_2$ only 6 non-unitary largest occurrence degrees remain (as the smallest 15 are eliminated by the procedure).

Two types of source-plans result: one emerging from $\mathcal{R}$ and including (tolerance) covers (with overlapped clusters) and another – from $\mathcal{Z}$, including partitions (with disjoint clusters), as follows.

First 5 tolerance covers generated by the proximity relation $\mathcal{R}$:

Characteristic matrix

($\alpha = 1.0000$)	Clusters:
1 0 0 0 0 0 0	{a1}
0 1 0 0 0 0 0	{a2}
0 0 1 0 0 0 0	{a3}
0 0 0 1 0 0 0	{a4}
0 0 0 0 1 0 0	{a5}
0 0 0 0 0 1 0	{a6}
0 0 0 0 0 0 1	{a7}

Characteristic matrix

($\alpha = 0.7651$)	Clusters:
1 0 0 0 0 0 0	{a1}
0 1 0 0 1 0 0	{a2,a5}
0 0 1 0 0 0 0	{a3}
0 0 0 1 0 0 0	{a4}
0 1 0 0 1 0 0	
0 0 0 0 0 1 0	{a6}
0 0 0 0 0 0 1	{a7}

Characteristic matrix

($\alpha = 0.6858$)	Clusters:
1 0 0 0 0 0 0	{a1}
0 1 0 0 1 0 0	{a2,a5}
0 0 1 0 0 1 0	{a3,a6}

0 0 0 1 0 0 0   {a4}

0 1 0 0 1 0 0

0 0 1 0 0 1 0

0 0 0 0 0 0 1   {a7}

Characteristic matrix

($\alpha = 0.6414$)   Clusters:

1 0 0 0 0 0 0   {a1}

0 1 0 0 1 0 0   {a2,a5}

0 0 1 0 0 1 1   {a3,a6,a7}

0 0 0 1 0 0 0   {a4}

0 1 0 0 1 0 0

0 0 1 0 0 1 0   {a3,a6}

0 0 1 0 0 0 1   {a3,a7}

Characteristic matrix

($\alpha = 0.6343$)   Clusters:

1 0 1 0 0 0 0   {a1,a3}

0 1 0 0 1 0 0   {a2,a5}

1 0 1 0 0 1 1   {a1,a3,a6,a7}

0 0 0 1 0 0 0   {a4}

0 1 0 0 1 0 0

0 0 1 0 0 1 0   {a3,a6}

0 0 1 0 0 0 1   {a3,a7}

Partitions generated by the similarity relation $\mathcal{2}$:

Characteristic matrix

($\alpha = 1.0000$)   Clusters:

1 0 0 0 0 0 0   {a1}

0 1 0 0 0 0 0   {a2}

0 0 1 0 0 0 0   {a3}

0 0 0 1 0 0 0   {a4}

0 0 0 0 1 0 0   {a5}

0 0 0 0 0 1 0   {a6}

0 0 0 0 0 0 1   {a7}

Characteristic matrix

($\alpha = 0.7651$)   Clusters:

1 0 0 0 0 0 0   {a1}

0 1 0 0 1 0 0   {a2,a5}

```
0 0 1 0 0 0 0          {a3}
0 0 0 1 0 0 0          {a4}
0 1 0 0 1 0 0
0 0 0 0 0 1 0          {a6}
0 0 0 0 0 0 1          {a7}
```
Characteristic matrix
```
( α = 0.6858)          Clusters:
1 0 0 0 0 0 0          {a1}
0 1 0 0 1 0 0          {a2,a5}
0 0 1 0 0 1 0          {a3,a6}
0 0 0 1 0 0 0          {a4}
0 1 0 0 1 0 0
0 0 1 0 0 1 0
0 0 0 0 0 0 1          {a7}
```

Characteristic matrix
```
( α = 0.6414)          Clusters:
1 0 0 0 0 0 0          {a1}
0 1 0 0 1 0 0          {a2,a5}
0 0 1 0 0 1 1          {a3,a6,a7}
0 0 0 1 0 0 0          {a4}
0 1 0 0 1 0 0
0 0 1 0 0 1 1
0 0 1 0 0 1 1
```

Characteristic matrix
```
( α = 0.6343)          Clusters:
1 0 1 0 0 1 1          {a1,a3,a6,a7}
0 1 0 0 1 0 0          {a2,a5}
1 0 1 0 0 1 1
0 0 0 1 0 0 0          {a4}
0 1 0 0 1 0 0
1 0 1 0 0 1 1
1 0 1 0 0 1 1
```

Characteristic matrix
```
( α = 0.5402)          Clusters:
1 1 1 0 1 1 1          {a1,a2,a3,a5,a6,a7}
1 1 1 0 1 1 1
1 1 1 0 1 1 1
0 0 0 1 0 0 0          {a4}
1 1 1 0 1 1 1
1 1 1 0 1 1 1
1 1 1 0 1 1 1
```
Characteristic matrix
```
( α = 0.4888)          Clusters:
1 1 1 1 1 1 1          {a1,a2,a3,a4,a5,a6,a7}
1 1 1 1 1 1 1
```

$$
\begin{array}{ccccccc}
1 & 1 & 1 & 1 & 1 & 1 & 1 \\
1 & 1 & 1 & 1 & 1 & 1 & 1 \\
1 & 1 & 1 & 1 & 1 & 1 & 1 \\
1 & 1 & 1 & 1 & 1 & 1 & 1 \\
1 & 1 & 1 & 1 & 1 & 1 & 1
\end{array}
$$

The MAS evolution starts from the highest degree of occurrence (which is of course 1) and completes when the smallest degree is reached. Assuming that $\mathcal{R}$ is optimal, two source-plans (different from the initial one) could be generated: one emerging from $\mathcal{R}$ and including (tolerance) covers (with overlapped clusters) and another from $\mathcal{Q}$, including partitions (with disjoint clusters). By ordering in decreasing order of their 6 occurrence degrees the configurations derived from $\mathcal{Q}$, a real plan can be derived, Figure 6. (The Shannon fuzzy entropy of the fuzzy relation $\mathcal{R}$ has the value $S_\mu(\mathcal{R}) = 36.6784$).

The following holonic behavior can be observed for the equivalence source-plan: clusters associate together in order to form larger clusters and, finally, the whole agents set is grouped in one single cluster. Analyzing the preferences in $\mathcal{M}_\mathcal{R}$ we observe that the manager is tempted to work in association with the executive a_2 (**0.4797**) rather than with a_3 (**0.4780**), but also is oriented to solve problems by himself using the resource a_6 (**0.4888**).

A possible scenario unfolds like this. First, the manager states a goal. Immediately, the executives a_2 and a_3 reach for resources a_5, and, respectively, a_6 that they prefer to work with mostly (this information is as well encoded in $\mathcal{M}_\mathcal{R}$). The executive a_3 realizes that he needs more resources and he starts to use both a_1 and a_7 (therefore, maybe, the manager prefers a_2). The next step shows that the two executives associate together (including their resources) in order to reach the goal. The manager joins them only in the final phase, when the goal is reached – to give the final approval.

Our experiments have proven that the method works even in the most general case when we have the most parsimonious knowledge about the system. If enough is known about the agents to build the preference relation from the start, the method will obviously work better.

8.6.2 Evolution towards optimal structure in Cyberspace

We consider for the search an agent domain of 100 agents. The search goal is to optimize the constituency of the HE emerged in the previous Subsection.

For the evolutionary search we use mutation and crossover as follows:

- Mutation - the genetic operator that alters one ore more gene values in a chromosome from its initial state, which can result in entirely new gene values being added to the gene pool. There are different mutation mechanisms but we use the procedure that that simply inverts value of the uniform random chosen gene between the user-specified upper and the lower bounds for that gene.
- Crossover - the genetic operator that combines (mates) two chromosomes (parents) to produce a new chromosome (offspring) can as well be implemented through various mechanisms. We use here the procedure that randomly selects a crossover break point within a chromosome then interchanges the two parent chromosomes at this point to produce two new offspring.
- After binary encoding of the relevancy measures (10) (illustrated in Figure 7 before the encoding) we have evaluated the probabilities of mutation and crossover over the entire agent search domain. Table 1 illustrates the genetic alterations for ten agents

(that is the initial 7 and the first 3 found relevant in the search domain of 100 agents. "Agent#1: mutation – gene#1 -> Agent#2" means: "if a mutation is yelling on the first gene of the preference genotype of Agent #2 then this is replaced by Agent#1".

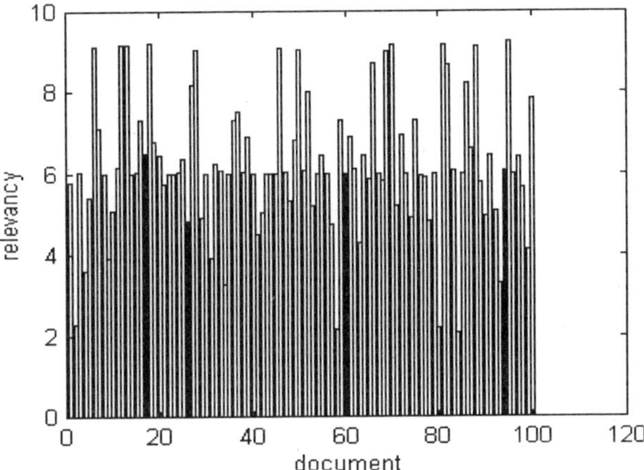

Figure 7. Relevancy measures for the 100 agents in the search domain

Table 1. The observed genetic alteration for mating 3 agents in
the search domain with the 7 agents in the HE

Agent#2: mutation - gene#1 → Agent#1
Agent#3: mutation - gene#4 → Agent#4
Agent#5: mutation - gene#1 → Agent#7
Agent#2: mutation - gene#3 → Agent#10
Agent#1, Agent#8: crossover– gene#2 → Agent#4, New
Agent#4, Agent#9: crossover– gene#2 → Agent#1, New
Agent#4, Agent#9: crossover– gene#4 → New, New
Agent#6, Agent#10: crossover– gene#3 → Agent#7, New
Agent#1, Agent#2: crossover– gene#1 → Agent#1, Agent#2
Agent#5, Agent#10: crossover – gene#4 → Agent#7, New
Agent#8, Agent#9: crossover – gene#1 → New, New
Agent#8, Agent#9: crossover – gene#4 → New, New
Agent#3, Agent#4: crossover– anyone → Agent#3, Agent#4
Agent#9, Agent#10: crossover– gene#3 → Agent#1, New
Note: the crossovers between all chromosomes from gene#5 and gene#6 as break points lead to reproduce themselves. Their number is $45 \times (21 + 7) = 1260$

We ran this model by adapting a more general program for automatic location problems (Ionita 1997).

The total possible crossovers:

$$C_m^n = \frac{m!}{n! \times (m-n)!}$$

-    the number of possible couples for the 10 agents in Table 1 is:

$$C_{10}^2 = \frac{10!}{2! \times (10-2)!} = 45$$

- the possible number of crossovers between two chromosomes of 7 genes each:

$$\sum_{p=1}^{5} C_7^p = C_7^1 + C_7^2 + C_7^3 + C_7^4 + C_7^5 =$$

$$= \frac{7!}{1! \times 6!} + \frac{7!}{2! \times 5!} + \frac{7!}{3! \times 4!} + \frac{7!}{4! \times 3!} + \frac{7!}{5! \times 2!} =$$

$$= 7 + 21 + 35 + 35 + 21 = 119$$

The total possible crossovers is thus 45 x 119 = 5355. Based on estimation from Table 1 the probability to meet part of them in our population of ten agents is given by

$$p_c = \frac{1267}{5355} = 0.2366 \qquad (23.66\%)$$

Each chromosome has 7 genes. Thus:

$$no.\ of\ mutations\ =\ 7\ genes \times 10\ cromosomes\ =\ 70$$

From among them, only four occur in a population of ten agents (Table 1), so we can estimate a probability of mutation:

$$p_m = \frac{4}{70} = 0.0571 \qquad (5.71\%)$$

Applying a genetic search with these probabilities over three different agent domains (each of 100 agents) has converged towards the optimum in about 200 generations, Figure 8 (here expressed in a normalized manner, considering the mean values of the fitness function for each search.)

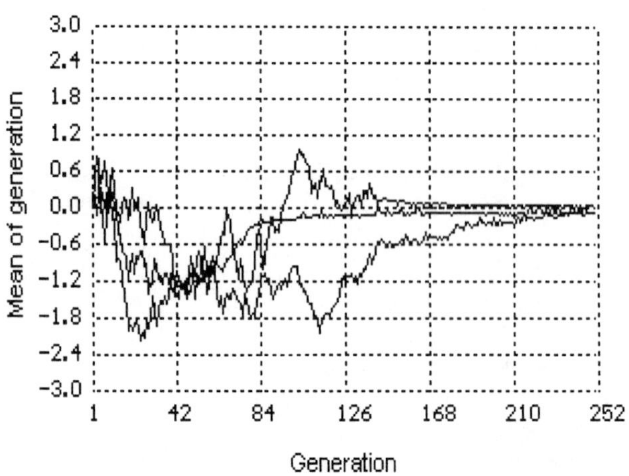

Figure 8. Convergence of the HE structure towards optimum

Embedding this dynamic evolutionary search strategy in the design of the Mediator Pattern enables the HE to continuously evolve in Cyberspace by improving its constituency through addition of better and better partners as they are found to better fit the achievement of its dynamic goals. Once the HE has changed its constituency (through either addition of new partners and/or exclusion of old ones) it will self-organize via the fuzzy entropy minimization by which the dynamic virtual clustering mechanism works, to reach again the optimal holarchic structure that best suits the goal-achievement.

8.7 Conclusion: Towards the Evolutionary, Self-Organizing Cyberspace

As result of the process of evolution driven by the law of synergy, emergence endows the dynamics of composite systems with properties unidentifiable in their individual parts. The phenomenon of emergence involves on one side *self-organization* of the dynamical systems such that the synergetic effects can occur and on the other side interaction with other systems from which the synergetic properties can *evolve* in a new context.

The fuzzy-evolutionary approach introduced in this chapter mimics emergence in natural systems as follows. On one side it induces self-organizing properties by minimizing the entropy measuring the information spread across the dynamical system such that equilibrium is reached in an optimal interaction between the system's parts to reach the system's objectives most efficiently. On the other side it enables system's evolution into a better one by enabling interaction with external systems found via genetic search strategies (mimicking mating with most fit partners in natural evolution) such that the new system's optimal organizational structure (reached by minimizing the entropy) is better then the one before evolution.

MAS enable cloning of real-life systems into autonomous software entities with a 'life' of their own in the dynamic information environment offered by today's Cyberspace. Applying the proposed fuzzy-evolutionary approach to the virtual societies "living" on the dynamic Web endows them with behavioral properties characteristic to natural systems. The HE paradigm provides a framework for information and resource management in global virtual organizations by modeling enterprise entities as software agents linked through the internet (Ulieru *et al.* 2002). In this parallel universe of information, enterprises enabled with the proposed emergence mechanism can evolve towards better and better structures while at the same time self-organizing their resources to optimally accomplish the desired objectives.

Encapsulating the dynamic evolutionary search strategy in the mediator and designing the virtual clustering mechanism by the fuzzy entropy minimization strategy proposed here empowers the HE with self-adapting properties and moreover enables it to evolve like a social organism in Cyberspace, by mating its components with new partners as they are discovered in a continuous incremental improvement search process.

Our current work focuses on the application of this strategy to the design of internet-enabled soft computing holarchies for telemedicine - e-Health, telehealth and telematics (Ulieru 2002a).

Acknowledgements

The author's highest gratitude goes to Professor Douglas Norrie, Leader of the Intelligent Systems Group (ISG) at the University of Calgary without whose vision and inspiration this work would have reached but the level of good intentions. Special thanks to Dr. Dan Stefanoiu for his contribution to the mathematics comprised in the holonic clustering mechanism and to Dr. Silviu Ionita for his insights into the evolutionary search in Cyberspace. The contributions of all ISG members to the development of the metamorphic architecture concepts over the past 10 years are priceless.

References

Brandenburger, A. M. and Nalebuff, B. J., (1996), *Co-opetition*, Doubleday NY.

Brennan, R. (2000), "Performance comparison and analysis of reactive and planning-based control architectures for manufacturing", *Robotics and Computer Integrated Manufacturing 16(2-3),* pp. 191-200.

Christensen, J.H. (1994), "Holonic Manufacturing Systems: Initial Architecture and Standards Directions", *Proceedings of the First European conference on Holonic Manufacturing systems*, European HMS Consortium, Hanover, Germany.

Dubois, D. and Prade, H. (1988), *Possibility Theory*, Plenum Press NY, ISBN 0-306-42520-3.

Fogel, D. (1998) *Evolutionary Computation*: The Fossil Record, IEEE Press, May 1998, ISBN: 0780334817.

Hornberger, R. (2001), "Adapting to the Net Economy", Presentation at the *Energy E-Business Reality Workshop*, Calgary, Alberta.

Ionita, S. (1997), *Genetic Algorithms for Control Engineering Applications* (in Romanian), ECIT-97, Pitesti, Romania, 21-22 Nov. 1997, p. 77-84.

Klir, G. and Folger, T. (1988), *Fuzzy sets, Uncertainty, and Information*, Prentice Hall.

Koestler, A. (1968), *The Ghost in the Machine*, MacMillan.

Maturana, F. and Norrie D.H. (1996), "Multi-agent Mediator Architecture for Distributed Manufacturing", *Journal of Intelligent Manufacturing*, 7, pp.257-270.

McHugh, P., Merli, G. and Wheeler W.A. (1995), *Beyond Business Process Reengineering: Towards the HE*, John Wiley 1995, ISBN 0-471-95087-4.

Michalenicz, Z. (1992), *Genetic Algorithms + Data Structures = Evolution Programs*, Springer Verlag.

Nikravesh, M and Azvine, B. (Eds.) (2001) *New Directions in Enhancing the Power of the Internet*, UC Berkeley Electronics Research Laboratory, Memorandum No. UCB/ERL M01/28, August 2001.

Norvig, P. (2002), "Building a Better Search Engine", *Distinguished Lecture Series, University of California at Berkeley*, Jan 31, 2002. (http://buffy.eecs.berkeley.edu/Seminars/2002/Jan/020131.norvig.html).

Shu, S. and Norrie, D.H. (1999), "Patterns for Adaptive Multi-Agent Systems in Intelligent Manufacturing", *Proceedings of the 2nd International Workshop on Intelligent Manufacturing Systems* (IMS'99), Leuven, Belgium, September 22-24, pp. 67-74.

Söderström, T. and Stoica, P. (1989), *System Identification,* Prentice Hall, London.

Ulieru, M. and Ramakhrishnan S. (1999), "An Approach to the Modeling of Multi-Agent Systems as Fuzzy Dynamical Systems", *Advances in Artificial Intelligence and Engineering Cybernetics, Vol. V: Multi-Agent Systems/Space-Time Logic/Neural Networks* (George Lasker, Ed.), IIAS-68-99, ISBN 0921836619.

Ulieru, M., Norrie, D.H., Kremer, R. and Shen, W. (2000), "A Multi-Resolution Collaborative Architecture for web-Centric Global Manufacturing", *Information Science*, volume 127, Journal no. 7669, ISSN # 0020-0255.

Ulieru, M, Cobzaru, M. and Norrie, D. (2001), "A FIPA-OS Based Multi-Agent Architecture for Global Supply-Chain Applications", *Proceedings of IPMM 2001 International Conference on Intelligent Processing and Manufacturing of Materials*, July 29-August 3, 2001, Vancouver, BC.

Ulieru, M., Walker, S. and Brennan, R. (2002), "The Holonic Enterprise, A Model for Internet-Enabled Global Supply Chain and Workflow Management", *Journal of Integrated Manufacturing Systems – Special Issue on Enabling Supply Chain Integration using Internet Technologies* (McIvor Editor).

Ulieru, M. (2002a), "Internet-Enabled Soft Computing Holarchies for e-Health Applications", Invited Chapter in *Fuzzy Logic and the Internet* (Zadeh, L.A. and M. Nikravesh, Eds.), Physica Verlag.

Weiss, G. (Editor) (1999), *Multiagent Systems, a Modern Approach to Distributed Artificial Intelligence*, The MIT Press, Cambridge, Massachusetts.

Woolridge, M. (Editor) (2001), "Foreword" to the *Proceedings of the Workshop on Agent-Oriented Software Engineering, International Conference Autonomous Agents 2001*, Montreal, Canada.

Zadeh, L.A. (2002), "A Prototype-Centered Approach to Adding Deduction Capability to Search Engines - The Concept of Protoform", Key Note Address at the 3rd World Congress on Computational Intelligence (WCCI 2002), Honolulu, Hawaii, May 12-17, 2002.

Zhang, H., and Norrie, D.H. (1999), "Holonic Control at the Production and Controller Levels", *Proceedings of the 2nd International Workshop on Intelligent Manufacturing Systems*, Leuven, Belgium, pp. 215-224.

Zimmermann, H-J (1991), – *Fuzzy Set Theory And Its Applications*, Kluwer Academic.

Soft Computing Agents
V. Loia (Ed.)
IOS Press, 2002

Chapter 9

Emergent Coordination among Fuzzy Reinforcement Learning Agents

David Vengerov
Hamid R. Berenji
Alex Vengerov

9.1 Introduction

Agent-based modeling is a new direction in Artificial Intelligence (AI) that has become very important in the last decade. The reason for this trend is the growing maturity of AI techniques and a corresponding interest in applying them to increasingly more complex real world problems. Simultaneously, appearance of the information-rich environment of computer systems and networks provided new challenges for AI applications. The complexity of these domains made it apparent that no single centralized algorithm can process all the required information and keep track of various changes that are constantly taking place.

Distributing the processing load among cooperating computing units emerged as the natural solution to this problem. Each unit (agent) in this approach can be designed quickly and inexpensively, as it needs to possess only a limited processing capability. The direct benefits of distributed modeling are robustness, fault tolerance, parallelism and scalability of the solution. In addition to distributing the computing power, the multi-agent methodology allows to tackle complex problems arising in computer networks, where data is naturally distributed and no single entity can have a complete view of the whole network.

Some applications require agents not only to passively extract the required information from the environment but also to change the environment through their actions. Traditionally, such applications have been approached with the techniques of automatic control. However, the automatic control theory assumes a single controller and a full knowledge of the problem structure. In the complex setting of uncertain information-rich environments with multiple agents, the optimal action policy cannot be derived analytically and has to be learned through direct interaction with environment.

Reinforcement learning provides a framework for learning optimal policies in complex and uncertain environments. Unlike the framework of supervised learning, where the "correct" action is known for every situation and the agent adjusts its policy to decrease the error between its action and the correct action, the reinforcement learning agents only receive some reward or punishment after taking each action. In fact, the reinforcements do not even have to come at the end of every action and can be delayed until the end of the learning episode.

In many domains to which we would like to apply reinforcement learning, most states will be encountered only once. This will almost always be the case when the state or action spaces are very large or continuous. The only way to learn anything at all in these domains is to generalize the learning experience from previously experienced states to the ones that have never been seen. In particular, most of the reinforcement learning algorithms rely on computing a *value function*, which evaluates individual states or the benefit of taking a particular action in a given state. The task then becomes to infer the value of a new state based on the values assigned to similar states. This kind of inference has to happen in a noisy, partially known environment, whose characteristics might be changing over time. *Soft computing* is the suite of techniques that are very well positioned for this task.

The concept of soft computing brings formal recognition to computational methods capable of finding robust low cost solutions in the face of imprecision and uncertainty. The main constituent components of soft computing are Genetic Algorithms, Fuzzy Logic, and Neural Networks. Genetic algorithms were designed to model the evolutionary adaptation of large populations over time. Fuzzy Logic and Neural Networks were motivated by investigation of symbolic and connectionist reasoning happening in the human mind. These two techniques are becoming increasingly more popular for solving practical problems that require learning and inference under uncertainty.

More formally, the type of inference needed for learning state evaluations is called *function approximation*, and it has been studied extensively in statistical learning. The two main kinds of statistical approximation architectures are local and global, with fuzzy rules falling into the first category and neural networks falling into the second one. Local architectures are very efficient for state vectors in low dimensions but they suffer from the "curse of dimensionality". Global architectures can be applied to large-dimensional problems, but they have to be trained using nonlinear programming methods, which suffer from the exponential growth of local optima as the input dimension increases. Also, the results of learning cannot be easily examined and interpreted by the modeler. In this chapter we will present an agent architecture based on local fuzzy rules. However, our results on coordination in multi-agent systems do not depend on the details of individual learning algorithms and can work just as well with global function approximation.

Coordination of actions among multiple agents working in the same environment is essential. In many situations, each individual agent simply cannot accomplish the desired task and a coordinated effort of several agents is required. Also, when there is a contention for a common resource among the agents, coordination of actions can greatly increase the efficiency of a multi-agent team. When the environment is dynamic and uncertain, coordination among agents has to be adaptive. That is, agents have to allocate dynamically the consumption of common resources and tasks within the team based on the state of each agent and on the state of the environment.

In Section 9.2 we present our architecture for a fuzzy rulebase agent. We discuss the difference between *crisp* rules used in traditional expert systems and *fuzzy* rules. We then present a mathematical model of a fuzzy rule and show how the conclusions of such rules are combined to produce the final output of the fuzzy rulebase.

Section 9.3 describes the general framework of reinforcement learning. We discuss the importance of generalizing the learning experience across similar states in large or continuous states spaces. We discuss the possible function approximation architectures that can be combined with reinforcement learning for this purpose and highlight the benefits of fuzzy rulebases. We then present a Fuzzy Q-learning algorithm that we use for tuning parameters of fuzzy rulebases.

Section 9.4 starts by discussing possible approaches to multi-agent coordination. We then highlight the importance of *emergent coordination* in uncertain, a priori unknown domains. Based on these considerations, we present an emergent multi-agent coordination (EMAC) architecture. In EMAC, instead of having each agent directly interact and coordinate its actions with all other agents, agents are continuously creating an integrated representation of the multi-agent team. This information is then passed back to each individual agent, which learns how to interpret this integrated global vision in the context of its local environment. As an agent adjusts its local behavior, the integrated representation of the multi-agent team is also slightly changed, which in turn changes the behavior of individual agents.

An overview of related work is given in Section 9.5. We discuss both the abstract coordination models and those that have been proposed in the context of multi-agent reinforcement learning.

In Section 9.6 we briefly describe the problem of distributed dynamic web caching, which will be used as a testing domain for the EMAC architecture. In particular, we focus on the issue dynamic content re-distribution strategies for matching the changing pattern of user requests. The section concludes by presenting an agent-based view of this problem.

Section 9.7 describes the agent-based simulator we designed for the dynamic content redistribution problem. It also describes how the EMAC architecture is instantiated in the domain of fuzzy reinforcement learning, resulting in the EMAC-FRL architecture. Section 9.8 presents simulation results and discussion. Section 9.9 concludes the paper.

9.2 Fuzzy rulebase agent architecture

In this section we present an architecture for a fuzzy rulebase agent. Rule based expert systems for automated decision making have been used successfully in Artificial Intelligence since 1970's, with MYCIN being one of the first ones (Shortliffe 1976). Such systems can easily encode the domain knowledge of human experts using IF-THEN rules, which reflect the way human logic works.

However, a closer look at human decision making revealed that humans do not use *crisp* measurement-based rules, such as

IF (distance to a red stop light is 13m) THEN (press the break pedal with 5.8N of force).

Instead, humans use *fuzzy, perception-based* rules, such as:

IF (distance to a red stop light is SMALL) THEN (press the break pedal HARD)

IF (distance to a red stop light is LARGE) THEN (press the break pedal SOFTLY),

with SMALL and HARD being fuzzy perception labels. They are fuzzy in a sense that a given distance can belong to several perception labels simultaneously to different degrees. For example, a distance of 13m can be SMALL to a degree of 0.9 and large to a degree of 0.1. Consequently, the first fuzzy rule is used to a degree of 0.1 and the second fuzzy rule is used to a degree of 0.1, with the final action being a force that is HARD to a degree of 0.9 and SOFT to a degree of 0.1. As the distance from a red stop light increases, the resulting force with which the break pedal is pressed decreases smoothly.

Perception-based reasoning will be an important capability of future intelligent systems (Zadeh 1999). One of the key aspects of this theory is granulation, which will allow agents to process imprecise information in large complex state spaces. The ability to manipulate perceptions is a major strength of the remarkable human brain. In a typical decision making problem, the human brain focuses on the problem domain and forms an initial perception of the task at hand. As more information becomes available, the initial perception is refined gradually or changed drastically depending on the new sensory inputs. For example, when attending a multi-media lecture, our perception of the subject of the talk changes as our brains learn more and more by fusing the contents of the speaker's multi-media presentation.

Proposed by Lotfi Zadeh (Zadeh 1999), the Computational Theory of Perceptions (CTP) is based on Computing with Words (CW), where *granulation* plays a critical role for data compression. The set of antecedents defines a granule of the state space for which an action is recommended. In other words, new units of computation – fuzzy granules – are used. Fuzziness of the granules means that a given point in the state space can belong to several fuzzy granules to different degrees.

More formally, a fuzzy rulebase is a function f that maps an input vector s in R^K into an output vector a in R^m. This function is represented by a collection of fuzzy rules. A fuzzy rule i is a function f_i that maps an input vector s in R^K into a scalar a in R. We have used the following fuzzy rules in our agent design:

Rule i: IF s_1 is S_1^i and s_2 is S_2^i and ... and s_K is S_K^i THEN a is $\bar{a}^i$,

where S_j^i are the input labels in rule i and $\bar{a}^i$ are tunable coefficients. Each label is a membership function $\mu : R \to R$ that maps its input into a degree to which this input belongs to the fuzzy category (linguistic term) described by the label.

In general, a fuzzy rulebase function $f(s)$ with M rules can be written as:

$$a = f(s) = \frac{\sum_{i=1}^{M} \bar{a}^i w^i(s)}{\sum_{i=1}^{M} w^i(s)}, \tag{1}$$

where $\bar{a}^i$ is the output recommended by rule i and $w^i(s)$ is the weight of rule i. We used the product inference for computing the weight of each rule: $w^i(s) = \prod_{j=1}^{K} \mu_{S_j^i}(s_j)$.

Fuzzy rulebases can be used for developing heterogeneous rule-based intelligent agents with different expertise. For example, a knowledge-rich agent may include a large number of rules allowing it to deal with a great variety of situations, while a more operational or action-rich agent may have fewer rules but be more specialized in executing some specific tasks. Alternatively, agents can have the same number of rules but have them cover different situations that can arise, providing expertise in different aspects of autonomous missions.

The fuzzy rulebase approach to agent design has several unique advantages:

1. General human knowledge of the proper agent reactions in various situations can be easily imparted to agents in the form of an initial policy. This knowledge is naturally formulated in terms of rules, which can be used as a starting point for further refinement during agent learning.

2. Final rules at the end of a learning period can be easily understood and corrected by human experts. Thus, these rules can be telecommunicated to a human expert, who can then make a decision whether the robotic agent is ready for a real mission, whether it needs to continue learning, or whether it should be re-initialized and start learning from scratch.

3. By combining the so-called "actor-critic" reinforcement learning algorithm with fuzzy rule bases, the learning process of each agent is guaranteed to converge to optimality. A proof of this FRL convergence result is given in (Berenji and Vengerov 2001).

9.3   Reinforcement learning for tuning fuzzy rulebases

Reinforcement learning is the natural technique to be used for tuning the parameters of fuzzy rulebases in complex, uncertain, previously unexplored environments. In this technique an agent learns what to do – how to map situations to actions – so as to maximize a numerical reward signal. The agent is not told which actions to take, as in most forms of machine learning, but instead must discover which actions yield the most reward by trying them. In the most interesting and challenging cases, actions may affect not only the immediate reward, but also the next situation and, through that, all subsequent rewards. These two characteristics – trial-and-error search and delayed reward – are the two most important distinguishing features of reinforcement learning (Sutton and Barto 1998).

In many tasks to which we would like to apply reinforcement learning, most states will be encountered only once during learning. This will almost always be the case when the state or action spaces include continuous variables or large number of sensors, such as a visual image. The only way to learn anything at all on these tasks is to generalize the learning experience across similar states. As was mentioned in the introduction, we will be using fuzzy set theory for such a generalization.

9.3.1   Fuzzy Q-learning

In our simulations we have combined the Q-learning algorithm of Watkins (Watkins 1989) with fuzzy logic function approximation. The Q-values are generalized across states by using a function approximation architecture $Q(x, a, r)$ for approximating $Q(x, a)$, where r is the set of all learned parameters arranged in a single vector. The basic parameter updating rule used by Q-learning for such an architecture is presented in (Bertsekas and Tsitsiklis 2000):

$$r_t \leftarrow r_t + \alpha \delta_t \nabla_{r_t} Q(x_t, a, r_t), \tag{2}$$

where α is the learning rate and δ_t is the Bellman error used in the corresponding learning rule for the look-up table case:

$$Q(x_t, a) \leftarrow Q(x_t, a) + \alpha \delta_t. \tag{3}$$

In the look-up table version of discounted Q-learning, update for δ_t takes the following form:

$$\delta_t = g(t) + \gamma \max_a Q(x_{t+1}, a) - Q(x_t, a). \tag{4}$$

In the general version of discounted $Q(\lambda)$-learning, equation (2) becomes:

$$r_t \leftarrow r_t + \delta_t \sum_{\tau=T_0}^{t} (\alpha\lambda)^{t-\tau} \nabla_{r_t} Q(x_t, a, r_t), \tag{5}$$

where T_0 is the time when the current episode began and δ_t is given by equation (4).

The analytical expression for approximating the Q-value using a fuzzy rulebase is:

$$Q(x, a) = \sum_{k=0}^{K} q(k, a)\mu_k(x), \tag{6}$$

where $q(k, a)$ is the Q-value of taking the action a in the k-th fuzzy state s_k and $\mu_k(x)$ is the degree of membership of state x to s_k. If the action space is continuous, then equation (6) still applies after changing $\mu_k(x)$ to $\mu_k(x, a)$.

With $Q(x, a)$ given by equation (6), $\nabla_{r_t} Q(x_t, a, r_t)$ becomes $\mu_k(x_t)$. Thus, equations (2) and (5) can now be rewritten as matrix equations with each component given by:

$$q(k, a) \leftarrow q(k, a) + \alpha \delta_t \mu_k(x_t). \tag{7}$$

$$q(k, a) \leftarrow q(k, a) + \alpha \delta_t \sum_{\tau=T_0}^{t} (\alpha\lambda)^{t-\tau} \mu_k(x_t). \tag{8}$$

The above equations have a natural interpretation in the realm of fuzzy state aggregations: the Q-value of a fuzzy state-action pair (s_k, a) gets updated proportionally to its contribution to the Q-value of the state-action pair (x_t, a) in equation (6).

If the average cost formulation is used instead of the discounted cost formulation, then equations (7) and (8) still hold, except that δ_t in these equations is given by (Sutton and Barto 1998):

$$\delta_t = \sum_{\tau-0}^{T} \gamma^{\tau-t} g(\tau) - Q(x_t, a) - \rho_t \tag{9}$$

for off-line Q-learning, and by

$$\delta_t = g(t) + \gamma \max_a Q(x_{t+1}, a) - Q(x_t, a) - \rho_t \tag{10}$$

for on-line Q-learning. The quantity ρ represents the average reward per time step of the policy learned so far, to which the average reward from every state-action pair is compared. The quantity ρ is updated at every iteration according to

$$\rho_t \leftarrow \rho_t + \alpha \delta_t. \tag{11}$$

In the next sections we will show how the fuzzy Q-learning algorithms can be used in domains requiring coordination among fuzzy rulebase agents.

9.4   Multi-agent coordination

An essential form of interaction in multi-agent systems is that of distribution of tasks or resources among the individuals.

As summarized in (Ferber 1999), the main traditional approaches to task distribution are:

1. *Imposed allocation*: the superior agent tells other agents which tasks to perform.

2. *Allocation by trader*: special agents - traders or brokers - gather requests and bids for service and match them together for execution.

3. *Allocation by acquaintances*: assumes an acquaintance network where agents are aware of the capabilities of their neighbors. The requests for service propagate through this network until a match has been found.

4. *Allocation by contract net*: an auction-like protocol is used to communicate between the clients and the servers. At first, clients openly post descriptions of tasks to be performed. On the basis of these descriptions each server draws up a proposal describing the service it can render and its price. Each client receives the proposals, evaluates them, and awards the contract to the best bidder.

Allocation methods described above assume a predefined communication structure, which all agents have to follow. This approach works well in simple, structurally stable environments. In contrast, the emergent allocation methods use a principally different communication method that is signal-based rather than message-based. Signals do not have semantics and can be interpreted differently by different receivers depending on their context. In the emergent allocation method, agents learn the value of these signals in the context of their local environments. Emergent allocation and signal-based communication methods are beginning to receive more and more attention now, as researchers are turning to modeling complex systems embedded in uncertain and nonstationary environments.

9.4.1   Two-level emergent coordination model

In this section we describe our vision of emergent multi-agent coordination (EMAC), which builds on the work presented in (Vengerov 2002, Vengerov 2002b). The proposed EMAC model contains two processing levels. At the local level, agents learn to behave optimally in a given environment. In the process, agents collect information about their local neighborhoods, thereby forming local visions of the environment. After some time of individual learning, each agent passes this information to the global level, where it is integrated with information collected by other agents. The resulting information represents a global vision of the environment, which agents use in their decision-making throughout the next individual phase. In the terminology of the previous section, agents learn to assign a context-dependent interpretation to the global state of the environment.

Agents coordinate their actions in the proposed EMAC architecture by merging and possibly evolving individual visions at the global level. This allows the modeler to analyze pure coordination at the global level separately from the low-level details of individual tactical behavior. The following mathematical description of the EMAC architecture clarifies its dynamic nature. Let y_t be the output of the global level at time t, and x_t be the vector of local visions accumulated by agents during one phase of individual learning. Then the EMAC architecture is described by the following co-evolutionary equations:

$$x_{t+1} = f(x_t, y_t) \tag{12}$$

$$y_{t+1} = g(y_t, x_{t+1}), \tag{13}$$

where f and g govern the dynamics of the local and global levels respectively.

An important benefit of the EMAC architecture is its scalability. Instead of each agent trying to communicate directly with all other agents, agents only consider a single variable encoding the information about the states of other agents. Therefore, increasing the number of agents in this model does not increase the computational load of each agent.

Another advantage of the EMAC architecture is that it utilizes the benefits of both centralized and decentralized approaches to decision making in multi-agent systems. In the centralized approach, some central planning agency performs optimization and determines the actions each agent should take in order to maximize the team benefit. This approach is very efficient in simple problems, but fails to find even adequate solutions in more complex domains. Also, while satisfying the high-level strategic goals of the team, this approach ignores the low-level tactical goals of individual members. In the decentralized approach, each agent acts to maximize its own benefit, and the global behavior emerges from superposition of individual behaviors. This approach is more robust but is potentially very inefficient, since agents learn to accomplish their tactical goals while ignoring the strategic goals of the team. In the EMAC architecture, agents receive the global information as a part of their state vector, and then *learn* the degree to which it should be utilized in the context of their local environments.

The above description of the proposed coordination architecture is most general. The next level of refinement gives more details about what individual visions are and how they can be merged. An individual vision is that part of each agent's state vector that can provide helpful information for future actions of other agents. In problems where agents are distributed over a metric space, awareness of location of other agents can already bring some improvements to the team behavior. The merging process can then be performed using some feature extraction architecture to compactly encode the locations of other agents. In many situations, agents further away have less impact on behavior of a given agent. Therefore, assigning a certain potential to each agent and letting that potential decay with distance will result in a potential surface whose gradient can serve as the required feature encoding locations of other agents. This approach to implementing the two level architecture is explained more fully in the subsequent sections.

9.5   Relationship to other work

In the last decade, researchers in a wide variety of disciplines became increasingly more interested in phenomena such as evolution of complexity, self-organization, and chaos. This research was sparked by earlier observations of emergent structure in physical systems (e.g. (Prigogine and Nicolis 1997)). In the early 1990's, the field of Artificial Life (AL) emerged from Artificial Intelligence by uniting researchers interested in studying emergent phenomena in biological and social systems. The researchers in this field rely heavily on computational models to simulate and get insights into various aspects of biological and social evolution. The complexity of the AL models varies greatly, from the very simple ones such as John Conway's "Game of Life" to extremely complex models such as the artificial society developed by Epstein and Axtell (Epstein and Axtell 1996).

Researchers in artificial life concern themselves primarily with studying global patterns that emerge in the course of evolution of multi-agent systems. Similarly, the main effort in computational economics is directed at simulating emergence of interaction between individual agents on the market without studying explicitly how individuals can use the emergent global patterns for a more efficient behavior. The novelty of the proposed EMAC architecture is that it implements a feedback from the emerging global pattern of team behavior to learning in individual agents. This feedback allows us to design distributed models that can adapt to their environments more efficiently.

Some analogies can be drawn between the two-level processing in the EMAC coordination model and the learning algorithms such as policy iteration methods (Howard 1960) and actor-critic algorithms (Barto *et al.* 1983). In these algorithms an agent starts with evaluating an initial policy using either a complete model of environment or actual exploration experiences. Then, this policy is modified to perform better given the received evaluations. After that, the modified policy gets evaluated again, and the cycle repeats. In the EMAC architecture, each agent starts by evaluating its local environment with some initial idea of the global team structure. These evaluations are then merged and updated at the global level. The new updated information is passed to individual agents who again start evaluating their local environments, but now with the new information about the global team structure.

Other approaches to describing learning in adaptive environments that are more broadly applicable but are also more informal than the algorithms mentioned above have also been proposed. For example, Marvin Minsky in his book The Society of Mind (Minsky 1986) notes that "nothing can mean anything except within some larger context of ideas." Hence, all learning has to be done in context, and as an example Minsky proposes the following cyclical process for how human mind recognizes objects. Certain clues about an object excite several contexts that are most closely associated with the mind's current state. The mind then considers each of these contexts and checks whether the extra features that are associated with them are found in the object. The context that has the best match to the current object is chosen as the next interpretation of the object. This cycle continues until it either stabilizes on a certain interpretation or until the mind gives up.

The cycle proposed by Minsky is an instance of a so-called "hermeneutic cycle". Hermeneutics is the science of understanding the meaning of information, which has its roots in understanding of written texts. In the hermeneutic cycle, the information received by an observer evokes a possible context in the observer's mind. This context allows the observer to interpret the information in a somewhat different light, which then evokes a possibly different context, and so on. This cycle can also be applied to conversations between agents, where they are trying to converge to a common understanding of a certain issue. In this case, an interpretation proposed by one agent evokes a certain context in the second agent, which then suggests a new interpretation to the second agent. This interpretation is then conveyed back to the first agent, and the cycle continues.

The recently developed theory of autopoiesis (Maturana and Varela 1980) uses a more formal systems-theoretic perspective to describe these interactions. An autopoietic system is a system whose organization is maintained as a consequence of its own operations. Any autopoietic system exists in a medium with which it interacts and, as a result of that interaction, its trajectory in the state-space changes, although its operation as a dynamic system remains closed. If as a result of these interactions the system undergoes plastic changes of structure without disintegration or loss of its autopoiesis, then the system is said to undergo a process of structural coupling with the medium. If the medium is also a structurally plastic system then both systems may become structurally interlocked, mutually selecting their plastic changes. More connections with the theory of autopoiesis and inter-agent communication can be found in (Di Paolo 1998).

The autopoietic view of adaptation requires a departure from the idea that adaptation can be measured by observer-independent scales and that evolution proceeds in accordance with those measures. The mutual adaptation of a system and its environment has been termed "coevolution" in Artificial Life, and many simple computational models of this process have been created. The most famous one is the predator-prey model: a predator learns to capture its prey and the prey learns to avoid the predator (e.g. (Cliff and Miller 1996)). Co-evolutionary models have also been applied to multi-agent games (e.g. (Akiyama and Kaneko 1995)). However, the main effort of coevolutionary modeling in Artificial Life has been directed at simulating behaviors of individual agents that emerge in the course of coevolution rather than studying explicitly how the emerged global patterns affect the behavior of individual agents.

Some researchers have recently experimented with multi-agent coordination in stochastic decision problems that require the use of reinforcement learning algorithms (e.g. (Weiss 1998, Sen and Sekaran 1998, Arai *et al.* 2000)). However, agents in these architectures were not directly aware of each other or the of the multi-agent team. Instead, agents learned to implicitly coordinate their actions by using the environmental reinforcement signal, which reflects the actions of other agents.

For example, Sen and Sekaran (Sen and Sekaran 1998) have used reinforcement learning to coordinate actions between two agents in a simple resource sharing problem. However, they assumed that one agent has already applied some load distribution over a fixed time period, and the other agent is learning to distribute its load on the system without any knowledge of the current distribution. Therefore, the second agent is aware of the actions of the first one only through the reinforcement signal reflecting the state of the environment.

Weiss (Weiss 1998) uses multi-agent reinforcement learning to solve a job assignment problem. In his formulation, different agents can have different execution times for the same job. However, Weiss uses a very simple coordination strategy, where a job that can be executed by several available agents is always assigned to the agent with the shortest execution time for this particular job.

Arai and Sycara (Arai *et al.* 2000) have used multi-agent reinforcement learning for solving a pursuit game with multiple hunters and preys. However, no explicit coordination algorithm was used and agents had no knowledge about each other. As a result, the learned policy started converging in terms of its performance only after about 500,000 time steps, which is impractical in most real world problems.

9.6   Distributed Dynamic Web Caching

With the exponential growth of hosts and traffic workload on the Internet, web caching has been recognized as the only viable solution for alleviating web server bottlenecks and reducing traffic over the Internet. Recently, there has been an increasing deployment of content distribution networks (CDNs) that offer hosting services to Web content providers. CDNs consist of servers distributed throughout the Internet that replicate provider content for better performance and availability than those in the older centralized approach. Existing work on CDNs has focused on techniques for efficiently redirecting user requests to appropriate CDN servers in order to reduce request latency and balance the load. However, little attention has been given so far to the more complex issue of dynamic re-distribution strategies for Web content in order to match the changing pattern of user requests (Qiu *et al.* 2001, Barish and Obraczka 2000).

As a testing example for EMAC architecture, we use the problem of distributed dynamic web caching in the Internet. This problem is of a great importance for the future of the Internet, with companies such as Akamai building large commercial infrastructures for intelligent content redistribution. We present a simulation study and analysis of the issues that arise when content agents are trying to achieve the conflicting objectives of moving toward the highest demand area and achieving a good team-wide coverage of the overall network.

In our simulation study, we use the following general formulation of the distributed dynamic content distribution in some content distribution network (CDN). The changing levels of demand for a certain information item at all locations in the CDN create a demand surface superimposed on the CDN. Agents that represent information content are moving to position themselves at the highest points on this demand surface. They get rewarded at each time step based on the amount of demand they have satisfied. As more agents begin to service a certain area, the demand in that area slowly gets satisfied, and each agent begins to produce less and less benefit with time. We model this effect by having the demand surface slowly sink under each agent. If many agents stay for a long time in the same area, they will eventually satisfy all the demand there and will

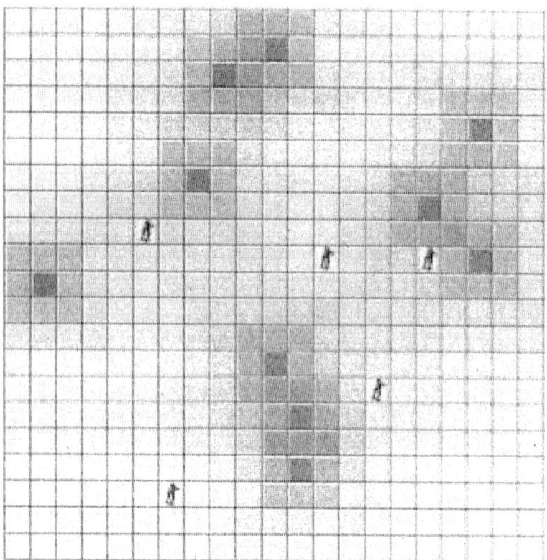

Figure 1: A potential surface model of the tile world

become useless, receiving little or no reward. Thus, there is a natural tradeoff present for agents in our model between satisfying the individual desire of moving to the highest demand area and satisfying the team goal of proportional coverage of all areas in the CDN.

9.7   Description of the simulator and coordination mechanism

We used a 2-D tileworld for simulating the most important features of the dynamic content redistribution problem. Our tileworld consists of demand sources and agents in some locations. The number of demand sources in the tileworld is kept constant. To ensure that agents learn a topology-independent coordination strategy, we allow each demand source to disappear at any time step with probability $1/MeanLife$ and reappear at a randomly chosen location. Newly appearing sources have a height (demand value) distributed uniformly between 0 and $MaxVal$. Each demand source j contributes the following amount to the demand potential of location i in the world:

$$P_{ij} = \frac{V_j}{1 + d_{ij}^2},\tag{14}$$

where V_j is the value of the jth demand source and d_{ij} is the distance between the source and the considered location. The total potential of each location is computed as $P_j = \sum_i P_{ij}$. A graphical representation of this tile world is shown in Figure 4, with darker locations having a higher demand potential.

At every time step, the value of each source decreases by the amount of the total reward extracted by all agents from this source. An agent at location i extracts the reward from source j equal to P_{ij}. At every time step, agents choose which of the 8 neighboring locations they should move to. The goal of each agent is to maximize its average reward per time step. During the training process, agents learn to evaluate locations in the world. The value of each location is the average reward per time step that can be obtained starting from that location and making the optimal choices thereafter.

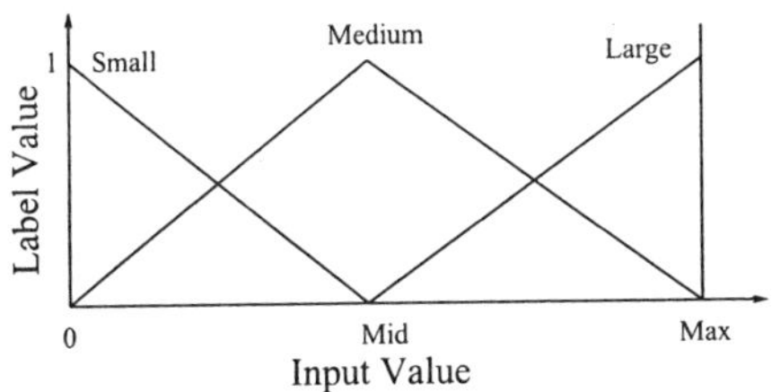

Figure 2: Fuzzy input labels used for each input variable.

When acting independently, agents evaluate each location based only on its demand potential. Then they move to one of the 8 surrounding locations with probability proportional to Q-values assigned to those locations. If an agents does not use any exploration and moves to the adjacent location with the highest potential, then the search procedure becomes equivalent to using the local gradient information for finding the highest point of the demand landscape. However, as our experiments show, using the gradient information can lead to individually optimal but socially suboptimal decisions.

In many domains, agents have only local visions of their environment. We simulate this by assigning a sensory radius to each agent. Only the demand sources within that radius can be used to compute the potentials of the surrounding locations.

In the process of emergent coordination agents store the global vision of the environment in a single active blackboard. After submitting their locations to the blackboard, agents can request from it the value of the agent potential at any location in the tileworld. The agent potential is computed just like the demand potential, except that all agents are assigned the same value. The value of the agent potential at the considered location is used as an extra input variable for coordinating agents. Hence, in the spirit of emergent allocation methods described in the introduction, agents learn to assign appropriate context-dependent meaning to this variable.

The value of each input variable has been fuzzified into three labels: SMALL, MEDIUM, and LARGE. The shapes of these labels are shown in Figure 2. Hence, independent agents needed to learn the Q-values of three fuzzy rules while coordinating agents needed to learn the value of nine fuzzy rules. A sample fuzzy rule j for computing the Q-value of moving to location L_i by a coordinating agent is:

IF (demand potential at L_i is LARGE) AND (agent potential at L_i is SMALL) THEN (Q-value of moving to L_i is Q_j^i).

The final Q-value of moving to location L_i is given by equation (6): $Q^i = \sum_j \mu_j^i Q_j^i$, where μ_j^i is the degree to which fuzzy rule j applies for describing the location i. We compute μ_j^i using product inference by multiplying the label value of the demand potential by that of the agent potential.

After moving to a new location, each agent computes the Q-value of the previous location using equations (7) and (10). The agent then distributes ΔQ among the conclusions of the fuzzy rules according to the Q-value each of them has contributed in equation (6).

Ferber (Ferber 1999) notes that all approaches to reactive coordination in signal-based communication systems, in essence, come down to the following techniques:

1. Use of potential fields or, more generally, vector fields to determine the movement of agents.

2. Use of marks to coordinate the action of several agents, which make it possible to use the environment as a flexible, robust, and simple communication system.

An example of the usage of the first technique is obstacle avoidance in mobile robots. In this technique robots assign decaying potentials to obstacles or other robots and follow the isopotential curves to avoid them. Alternatively, robots might assign repelling potentials to the obstacles and an attracting potential to the goal and move along the potential gradient. Marked environments are often used for global coordination tasks, where agents change the environment by leaving some marks along their paths. These marks can be used for constructing maps of unknown environments or indicating some actions that need to be performed at certain locations. For example, ants leave scented marks on their paths, so that other ants will be able to follow well-established routes to food sources.

The implementation of the EMAC-FRL architecture in the domain of distributed dynamic load balancing makes use of both of these techniques simultaneously. Agents mark environment by their presence, and the value of local movements is computed based on the potential surface created by other agents. However, the difference from the standard approach of marked environments is that agents create marks in an abstract space of potential fields that omits details not essential for interaction and makes the marks more apparent.

9.8   Results and Discussion

We conducted experiments in a 20-by-20 tileworld with 10 demand sources and 5 agents. Agents were trained for 1000 time steps and then tested for another 100 time steps. In these experiments, $MeanLife = 50$ and $MaxVal = 100$.

We experimented with two scenarios: unlimited sensory radius and a sensory radius equal to 5 units of distance. In both scenarios, all else being equal, coordinating agents learned to prefer locations with a smaller agent potential over those with a larger agent potential. That is, coordinating agents learned to avoid each other and ensure a good coverage of the environment. As a result, in both scenarios, agents combining Q-learning with our coordination mechanism obtained 50-100% better performance than agents using individual Q-learning or those choosing the direction of motion at random.

This is a significant result for our domain, since the domain is biased against agents using individual learning. This bias is best observed in simulations when agents used a limited sensory radius. In this case, independent agents obtained WORSE performance than agents choosing the direction of motion at random.

In order to explain the above phenomenon, we measured the average spread of agents in the tileworld. As expected, we found that the average spread of coordinating agents that learn to avoid each other is greater than that of random agents. However, we found that the average spread of independent agents with a limited sensory radius is much smaller than that of random agents. This can be explained by the fact that when independent agents happen to come near each other, all of them usually observe the same highest demand source hill, and consequently they all climb it, getting even closer together. As a result of this closeness, that area of the tileworld sinks quickly, and agents are left in a flat area with little reward per time step.

In many real-world situations involving a group of decision makers, the most individually rewarding behavior in the short term puts too much demand on some common resource, which decreases the average future reward available to each agent in the group. The only big difference among different types of such scenarios is the length of the delay before observing the decrease in the average group reward.

In our experiments, each agent depletes the common resource exactly by the amount of its individual reward. Therefore, the delay between the decision of pursuing a certain opportunity and the punishment that comes after the opportunity is depleted depends on the amount of the common resource at the opportunity. The amount of the common resource at the opportunity was randomly distributed between 0 and 100, which means that the maximum delay value when all 5 agents are exploiting a single opportunity is 20 time steps and the minimum is 1 time step. We used a discounting factor of 0.9, with $0.9^{20} = 0.12$. Therefore, as the delay value increases above 20, the optimal strategy almost stops taking into consideration the disappearing nature of the common resource.

Thus, we can claim that the computational aspects of the environment that define the learning problem for the fuzzy reinforcement learning agents in our experiments correspond to those found in a complete range of realistic scenarios, covering the spectrum between needing to care only about individual benefit (when the common resource does not disappear) and caring only about the choices of other agents (when the common resource disappears as soon as any agent begins to exploit it). This makes the success of our fuzzy reinforcement learning agents to be an important result extending beyond our tileworld.

9.9   Conclusions

In this chapter we showed how to structure fuzzy rulebase agents for decision making in complex, uncertain environments. We also presented a reinforcement learning algorithm that can be used for tuning the parameters of a fuzzy rulebases. We then described a general Emergent Multi-agent Architecture for action Coordination (EMAC) and instantiated it for the case of fuzzy reinforcement learning agents acting in a metric space, obtaining EMAC-FRL.

EMAC-FRL allows the multi-agent team continually redistribute its members in the environment in proportion to the instantaneous demand for service present in each area of the environment. A simulation study of EMAC-FRL demonstrates its benefit in the challenging and practical domain of dynamic web caching, where teams of non-coordinating FRL agents obtain very poor results.

An important feature of the EMAC-FRL architecture is that the extent of coordination in EMAC-FRL is adaptive to the local state of the environment. Hence, this architecture allows a multi-agent system to adjust dynamically the balance between centralized and decentralized behavior, accomplishing both strategic and tactical goals. The simulation results and analysis conducted in our work demonstrates the effectiveness of this approach to emergent multi-agent coordination.

References

Akiyama, E. and Kaneko, K. (1995), "Evolution of cooperation, differentiation, complexity, and diversity in an iterated three-person game." *Artificial Life*, vol. 2, pp. 293-304.

Arai, S., Sycara, K. and Payne, T.R. (2000), "Multi-agent Reinforcement Learning for Scheduling Multiple-Goals," *Proceedings of the Fourth International Conference on Multi-Agent Systems*.

Arthur, W.B. (1994), "Inductive reasoning and bounded rationality," *American Economic Review*, vol. 84, pp. 406-411.

Bambos, N. (1998), "Toward Power-Sensitive Network Architectures in Wireless Communications: Concepts, Issues and Design Aspects." *IEEE Personal Communications Magazine*, vol. 5, no. 3, pp. 50-59.

Bambos, N., Chen, S. C. and Pottie, G. J. (1995), "Radio link admission algorithms for wireless networks with power control and active link quality protection." *Proceedings of IEEE INFOCOM*, Boston.

Bambos, N. and Kandukuri, S. (2000), "Power controlled multiple access (PCMA) in wireless communication networks." *Proceedings of IEEE INFOCOM*, Tel-Aviv, Israel.

Barish, G. and Obraczka, K. (2000), "World wide web caching: Trends and techniques." *IEEE Communications Magazine*, vol. 38, no. 5, pp. 178-184.

Barto, A. G., Sutton, R. S. and Anderson, C. W. (1983) "Neuronlike elements that can solve difficult learning control problems." *IEEE Transactions on Systems, Man, and Cybernetics*, vol. 13, pp. 835-846.

Berenji, H.R. and Vengerov, D. (1999), "Cooperation and Coordination Between Fuzzy Reinforcement Learning Agents in Continuous State Partially Observable Markov Decision Processes," *Proceedings of the 8th IEEE International Conference on Fuzzy Systems (FUZZ-IEEE '99)*, pp. 621-627.

Berenji, H.R. (1992), "An architecture for designing fuzzy controllers using neural networks", *International Journal of Approximate Reasoning*, vol. 6, no. 2, pp. 267-292.

Berenji, H. R. and Khedkar, P. (1992), "Learning and tuning fuzzy logic controllers through reinforcements", *IEEE Transactions on Neural Networks*, vol. 3, no. 5, pp. 724-740.

Berenji, H.R. and Vengerov, D. (2001), "On convergence of fuzzy reinforcement learning," *Proceedings of the 10th IEEE International Conference on Fuzzy Systems (FUZZ-IEEE)*.

Bertsekas, D. and Tsitsiklis, J.N (2000), *Neuro-Dynamic Programming*, Athena Scientific.

Bonarini, A. (1996), "Delayed Reinforcement, Fuzzy Q-Learning and Fuzzy Logic Controllers." In Herrera, F., Verdegay, J. L. (Eds.) *Genetic Algorithms and Soft Computing*, (Studies in Fuzziness, 8), Physica-Verlag, Berlin, D, pp. 447-466.

Challet, D. and Zhang, Y.-C. (1997), "Emergence of Cooperation and Organization in an Evolutionary Game," *Physica A* 246, p.407.

Chavez, A. and Maes, P. (1996), "Kasbah: An Agent Marketplace for Buying and Selling Goods," *Proceedings of the First International Conference on the Practical Appication of Intelligent Agents and Multi-Agent Technology*, London, UK.

Cliff, D. and Miller, G. F. (1996), "Co-evolution of pursuit and evasion 2: Simulation methods and results." In Maes, P., et al., eds., *From Animals to Animats IV*, pp. 506-515, MIT Press.

De Jong, E.D. (1997), "Multi-Agent Coordination by Communication of Evaluations." *Proceedings of the 8th European Workshop on Modelling Autonomous Agents in a Multi-Agent World (MAAMAW)*.

Di Paolo, E. A. (1998), "An investigation into the evolution of communication," *Adaptive Behavior*, vol. 6, no. 2, pp. 285-324.

Durfee, E.H., Mullen, T., Park, S., Vidal, J.M., and Weinstein, P. (1998), "The dynamics of the UMDL service market society." In Matthias Klusch and Gerhard Weiss, editors, *Cooperative Information Agents II*, LNAI, pages 55-78. Springer.

Epstein, J.M. and Axtell, R. L. (1996), *Growing Artificial Societies: Social Science from the Bottom Up*, MIT press.

Fagiolo, G. (1998), "Spatial Interactions in Dynamic Decentralised Economies," in Cohendet P., Llerena, P., Stahn, H. and Umbhauer, G. (Eds.), *The Economics of Networks: Interaction and Behaviours*, Berlin - Heidelberg, Springer Verlag.

Fagiolo, G. (1999), "Endogenous Growth in Open-Ended Economies with Locally Interacting Agents," mimeo, University of Wisconsin at Madison and European University Institute, Florence, Italy.

Ferber, J. (1999), *Multi-agent Systems: An Introduction to Distributed Artificial Intelligence.* Addison-Wesley, Harlow, England.

Foschini, G. J. and Miljanic, Z. (1993) "A simple distributed autonomous power control algorithm and its convergence." *IEEE Transactions on Vehicular Technology*, vol. 42, no. 4, pp. 641-646.

Hanks, S., Pollack, M.E. and Cohen, P. (1993), "Benchmarks, Testbeds, Controlled Experimentation, and the Design of Agent Architectures," *AI Magazine*, 14(4), pp. 17-42.

Hardin, G. (1968), "The Tragedy of the Commons," *Science*, 162, pp. 1243-1248.

Howard, R. (1960), *Dynamic Programming and Markov Processes.* MIT Press, Cambridge, MA.

Ishibuchi, H., Nakashima, T., Miyamoto, H., and Oh, C. H. (1997), "Fuzzy Q-learning for a Multi-Player Non-Cooperative Repeated Game", *Proceedings of 1997 IEEE International Conference on Fuzzy Systems*, pp. 1573-1579.

Jain, S. and Krishna, S. (1998), "Emergence and Growth of Complex Networks in Adaptive Systems," Centre for Theoretical Studies, Indian Institute of Science, Available electronically from http://xyz.lanl.gov/abs/adap-org/9810005.

Jonard, N. and Yildizoglu, M. (1998), "Interaction of Local interactions," in Cohendet et al. (eds) *The Economics of Networks. Interaction and Behaviours*, Springer Verlag.

Kirman, A. P. (1983), "Communication in markets: a suggested approach," *Economic Letters*, vol. 12, pp. 101-108.

Kirman, A. P. (1997), "The economy as an evolving network," *Journal of Evolutionary Economics*, vol. 7, pp. 339-353.

Konda, V.R. and Tsitsiklis, J.N. (2000), "Actor-critic algorithms," *Advances in Neural Information Processing Systems*, vol. 12.

Krugman, P. (1997), "How the Economy Organizes Itself in Space: A Survey of the New Economic Geography," in Arthur, Durlauf, and Lane (eds) *The Economy as an Evolving Complex System II*, Addison-Wesley.

MacLennan, B. J. (1999), "The Emergence of Communication through Synthetic Evolution," In Vasant Honavar, Mukesh Patel, and Karthik Balakrishnan (eds.), *Advances in Evolutionary Synthesis of Neural Systems*, MIT Press.

Maturana, H. and Varela, F. J. (1980), *Autopoiesis and Cognition: The Realization of the Living.* D. Reidel Publishing, Dordrecht, Holland.

Minsky, M. (1986), *The Society of Mind.* Simon and Schuster, New York.

Mitra, D. (1993), "An asynchronous distributed algorithm for power control in cellular radio systems." *Proceedings of 4th WINLAB Workshop*, Rutgers University, NJ, 1993.

Palmer, K. (1997), "The Ontological Foundations of Autopoietic Theory," http://server.snni.com/ palmer/tutor.htm.

Prigogine, I. and Nicolis, G. (1977), *Self-Organization in Non-Equilibrium Systems: From Dissipative Structures to Order Through Fluctuations*, J. Wiley & Sons, New York.

Qiu, L., Padmanabhan, V. and Voelker, G. (2001), "On the placement of Web server replicas," *Proceedings of IEEE INFOCOM*, Anchorage, Alaska.

Sen, S. and Sekaran, M. (1998), "Individual learning of coordination knowledge," *Journal of Experimental & Theoretical Artificial Intelligence*, vol. 10, pp. 333-356.

Seo, H.-S., Youn, S.-J., and Oh, K.-W. (2000), "Fuzzy Reinforcement Function for the Intelligent Agent to Process Vague Goals," *Proceedings of The 19th International Meeting of the North American Fuzzy Information Processing Society (NAFIPS)*, pp. 29-33.

Shortliffe, E.H., ed. (1976), *MYCIN: Computer-Based Medical Consultations*, Elsevier, New York.

Steels, L. (1997), "Synthesising the origins of language and meaning using co-evolution, self-organisation and level formation." In: Hurford, J., C. Knight and M. Studdert-Kennedy (eds.) *Evolution of Human Language*. Edinburgh Univ. Press. Edinburgh.

Sutton, R.S. and Barto, A.G. (1998), *Reinforcement Learning: An Introduction*. MIT Press.

Tesfatsion, L. (2000), "Agent-Based Computational Economics: A Brief Guide to the Literature," Discussion Paper, Economics Department, Iowa State University, prepared for the *Reader's Guide to the Social Sciences*, Fitzroy-Dearborn, London, UK.

Tsitsiklis, J. N. and Van Roy, B. (1996), "Feature-Based Methods for Large-Scale Dynamic Programming," *Machine Learning*, vol. 22, pp. 59-64.

Vengerov, A. (2002) *Application of Holistic Engineering to Sensitive Systems Analysis and Design: Example of E-Business*. Xlibris Corp.

Vengerov, A. (2002b), "Toward integrated pattern-oriented and case based design framework in complex multi-agent system development for e-business environment." To appear in *Proceedings of the Fifth Annual International Conference of American Society of Business and Behavioral Sciences (ASBBS)*, London.

Watkins, C. J. C. H. (1989), *Learning from Delayed Rewards*. PhD thesis, King's College, Cambridge, UK.

Weiss, G. (1998), "A multiagent perspective of parallel and distributed machine learning." *Proceedings of the 2nd International Conference on Autonomous Agents*, pp. 226-230.

Yates, R. (1995) "A framework for uplink power control in cellular radio systems." *IEEE Journal on Selected Areas in Communication*, vol. 13, no. 7, pp. 1341-1347.

Zadeh, L. (1999) "From Computing with Numbers to Computing with Words – From Manipulation of Measurements to Manipulation of Perceptions," *IEEE Transactions on Circuits and Systems*, vol. 45, pp. 105-119.

Soft Computing Agents
V. Loia (Ed.)
IOS Press, 2002

Chapter 10

On Dynamic Domination for Fuzzy Causal Networks

Jian Ying Zhang
Zhi-Qiang Liu

10.1   Introduction

In general, among other features, a software agent should have the following major characteristics: autonomy, personalizability, discourse, cooperation, and anthropomorphism, which enable it to carry out tedious tasks intelligently on behalf of the user or the system in dynamic, networked environments. Although the idea of a virtual agent goes back to the late fifties, it is only recently have we seen significant research and development. This is to a large extent the result of the explosive usage of the Internet and numerous applications in the Internet, e.g., e-commerce, network resource management, information gathering, etc. As the human agent, the software agent must rely on causal inference in its reasoning process. For instance, when the software agent is asked to negotiate prices for power supply, it must know the causal relationship of demand and supply, the effect of a "good" price on the power company's *bottom line*, and how the market would respond.

Recently, fuzzy causal networks (FCNs)[1] have found many interesting applications in developing agent-based intelligent systems (Miao, Liu, Miao and Goh 2002). FCN is useful in decision-support applications that require causal reasoning (Loia 2002). We can use FCNs to model many real-world applications, e.g., plant control (Gotoh 1989), strategic planning (Tsadiras, Margaritis and Mertzios 1995), fault detection (Ndousse and Okuda 1996, Pelaez and Bowles 1996), clinical diagnosis (Innocent 1999), virtual world (Dickerson and Kosko 1993), policy and stock investment analysis (Lee *et al.* 1994, Perusich 1996), to mention a few.

In general, it is difficult to study structural and internal properties of huge FCNs. Recently, some researchers have made initial attempts. For example, Tsadiras and Maragritis have studied the transition and convergence properties of FCNs (Tsadiras and Margaritis 1995, Tsadiras and Margaritis 1997); Liu *et al.* have systematically analyzed inference mechanisms of FCNs (Liu 2000, Miao and Liu 2000) and proposed a dynamic cognitive network as an extension of FCNs (Miao, Liu, Siew and Miao 2001, Miao and Liu 1999). More recently, Liu *et al.* proposed a dynamic causal algebra (Liu and Zhang 2001) and a quotient space theory (Zhang, Liu and Zhou 2001, Zhang and Liu 2001) in FCNs. These results provide a feasible and effective framework for the analysis and design of FCN in complex real-world applications. One of the important issues is to determine the initial set of vertices and their values in FCNs. Most researchers in the literature randomly set a few vertices active at time t (with the remaining being vertices inactive at t) as the initial condition of the FCN (Kosko 1988, Kosko 1993, Liu and Zhang 2001, Miao and Liu 2000, Zhang, Liu and Zhou 2001). However, there is no such a restriction in the original definition of FCNs. In fact, a proper initial condition plays a crucial role in obtaining an accurate and reliable inference pattern. Liu *et al.* presented a recursive formula to calculate inference patterns in FCNs in terms of *key* vertices (Liu 2000, Miao and Liu 2000).

---

[1]Since such maps are networks that consist of *causally* linked vertices (nodes), we prefer to call them fuzzy causal networks.

As an initial attempt, in this chapter, we propose a dynamic domination theory for FCNs. Domination in graph theory has been widely studied by mathematicians; for example for basic concepts and results (Chen and Zhou 1999, Haynes, Hedetniemi and Slater 1998, Zhou 1996). Kelleher used the properties of dominating set in graphs to find a structurally equivalent set in social networks (Kelleher 1985, Kelleher and Cozzens 1988). Das *et al.* used an approximation to the minimum connected dominating set of the ad hoc network topology as the virtual backbone for mobile packet-radio networks (Das and Bharghavan 1997). Tasi *et al.* provided a communication model based on the concept of dominating sets to efficiently implement broadcast in all-port wormhole-routed 3D mesh networks (Tsai and Mckinley 1994, Tsai and Mckinley 1997). However, to the best of our knowledge, there is lack of study of domination properties in FCNs.

This chapter is organized as follows. Section 10.2 presents some basic concepts of FCNs. In Section 10.3, we give the definitions of dynamic dominating set and minimal dynamic dominating set in FCNs and investigate their properties and potential applications. Section 10.4 shows a mock-up FCN that model a university's policy-making process and applies our theory to the university FCN. In Section 10.5, we study related subsets with a focus on the investigation of effective dynamic dominating sets for FCNs. Section 10.6 provides the simulation result. In the last section, we give a short summary and propose some possible directions for further study.

10.2   Basic Concepts and Preliminaries

We use $(\mho, w_\mho, \phi_\mho)$ to denote an FCN, where $\mho = (V, E)$ with V the set of vertices and E the set of arcs (directed edges), $w_\mho$ is the weight function (adjacency matrix) of the FCN defined by $w_\mho = (e_{ij})$ with $e_{ij} \in [-1, 1]$ the strength of the i-th vertex v_i has on the j-th vertex v_j, for $i, j = 1, \ldots, n$, and $\phi_\mho$ is the state function defined by $\phi_\mho(t) = (x_1(t), \ldots, x_n(t))$ with $x_i(t) \in [0, 1]$ the state of vertex v_i at time t, for $i = 1, \ldots, n$, n is defined as the size of the FCN representing the number of vertices in the FCN. As usual the FCN is denoted as $\mho$, but we should keep in mind the weight function $w_\mho$ and state vector function $\phi_\mho$. According to the value of $x_i(t)$, we divide the vertices v_i into two categories: active and inactive. If $0 < x_i(t) \leq 1$, then v_i is called active at t; if $x_i(t) = 0$, then v_i is called inactive at t. For the convenience of study and without loss of generality, throughout this paper we assume that $\mho$ contains no loops (arcs from a vertex to itself) and multiple directed arcs (distinct arcs with the same initial and terminal vertices). In order to present our dynamic domination theory for FCNs and investigate their properties, we introduce several basic concepts and prove some major properties related to these basic concepts. In the following, we give the definition of one vertex dominating another in FCNs.

Definition 10.2.1 *Let $\mho$ be an FCN, let v_i, v_j be any two vertices of $\mho$. We say v_i dominates v_j at time t, or v_j is dominated by v_i at t, if and only if the following two conditions hold:*

(a) *v_i is active at t, that is, $0 < x_i(t) \leq 1$;*

(b) *there exists an arc (v_i, v_j) from v_i to v_j.*

Next we give some basic concepts related to any vertex v and any subset S in $\mho$, which are essential for the dynamic domination theory in FCNs.

Let v be any vertex of $\mho$ (see Figure 1). We use

$$N^-(v) = \{u \mid u \in V, (u, v) \in E\}$$

$$N^+(v) = \{u \mid u \in V, (v, u) \in E\}$$
$$N(v) = N^+(v) \cup N^-(v) \cup \{v\}$$

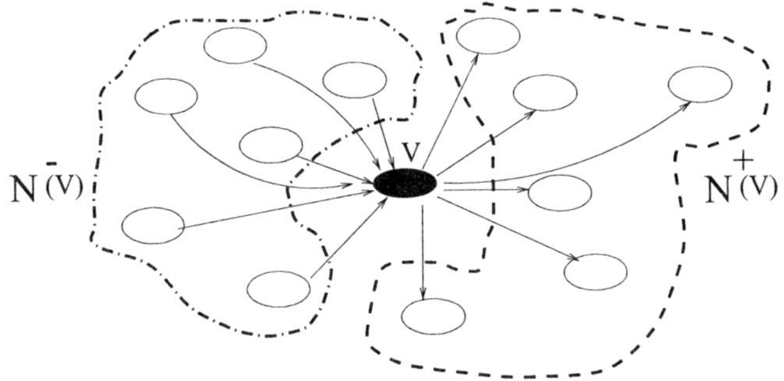

Figure 1. Vertex v and its in-neighborhood $N^-(v)$ and out-neighborhood $N^+(v)$

to denote the in-neighborhood, out-neighborhood and neighborhood of v. A vertex $u \in \mho$ is called an in-neighbor of v if $u \in N^-(v)$, an out-neighbor of v if $u \in N^+(v)$, and a neighbor of v if $u \in N(v)$.

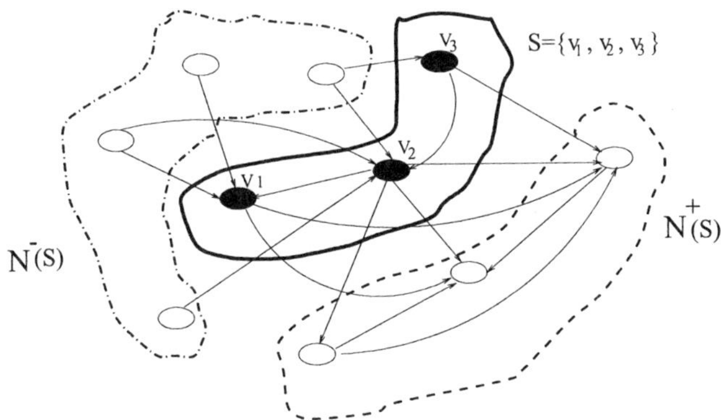

Figure 2. Subset S and its in-neighborhood $N^-(S)$ and out-neighborhood $N^+(S)$

Similarly, for any subset $S \subseteq V$ of $\mho$, we use

$$N^-(S) = \sum_{v \in S} \{u \mid u \in V - S, \ (u, v) \in E\}$$

$$N^+(S) = \sum_{v \in S} \{u \mid u \in V - S, \ (v, u) \in E\}$$

$$N(S) = N^+(S) \cup N^-(S) \cup S$$

to denote the in-neighborhood, out-neighborhood and neighborhood of S as shown in Figure 2.

10.3 Dynamic Domination for FCNs

10.3.1 Dynamic Dominating Set

We give the formal definition of the dynamic dominating set in FCNs at t as follows.

Definition 10.3.1 *Let $\mho$ be an FCN with n vertices, let S be any subset of V, and let $x_i(t)$ be the state of the vertex v_i at time t, for $i = 1, \ldots, n$. Then $S = S(t)$ is called a dynamic dominating set of $\mho$ at t if and only if the following two conditions hold:*

(a) *every vertex $v_i \in S$ is active at t, that is, $0 < x_i(t) \le 1$;*

(b) *for any vertex $v_i \in V - S$, v_i is dominated by at least one vertex of S at t.*

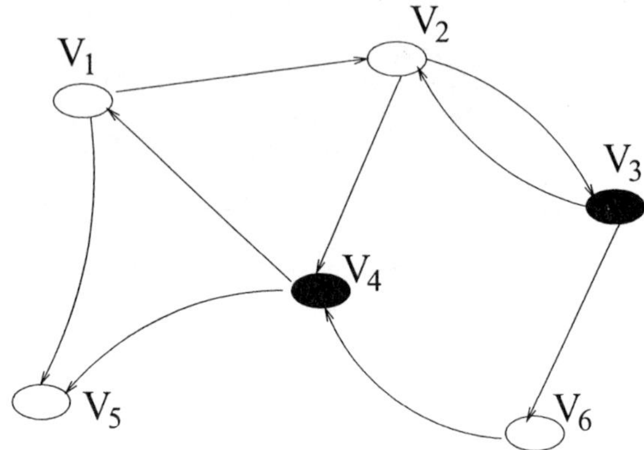

Figure 3. A minimal dynamic dominating set in an FCN.

As an example, we consider the simple FCN $\mho$ shown in Figure 3. We assume that every vertex in $\mho$ is active at t. In this example, v_3 dominates v_2, v_6, and v_4 dominates v_1, v_5. Hence $S(t) = \{v_3, v_4\}$ is a dynamic dominating set of $\mho$ at t. For subset S to be a dynamic dominating set of $\mho$ at t, it is necessary that every vertex in S is active at t. Since the states of vertices of $\mho$ are updated when the vertices receive a series of external input stimuli (Liu 2000, Miao, Liu, Siew and Miao 2001, Zhang, Liu and Zhou 2001), a dynamic dominating set at t may become a non-dominating set at $t + i$, and vice versa. The dynamic nature of such dynamic dominating sets reflects many real scenarios. For instance, in a limited-liability company there are share holders. The share holders with large shares at t form a dominating set that plays a *dominating* role in the operation, capital turnover, and decision-making in the company. However, the turbulent stock market frequently changes the members in the so-called major players club, which means that someone who belongs to the dynamic dominating set at t may be driven out this subset at $t + i$, on the other hand there may also be new comers joining the dominating set at $t + i$. In general, domination in FCNs can be described as a dynamic dominating process that consists of a series of dynamic dominating sets at different t. Such a dynamic dominating process can be represented as follows:

$$(S(t) \mid t = 0, 1, 2, \ldots) = (S_0, S_1, S_2, \ldots)$$

where $S_i = S(t)$ is a dynamic dominating set of $\mho$ at t. When studying this kind of dynamic dominating process, we can regard $S(t)$ as an instantaneous dominating set, which implies that $S(t)$ can be regarded as a cross section of the whole dynamic dominating process. Understanding this kind of *instantaneous* dominating set and related properties will enable us to study the behavior of this dynamic dominating process and its trend with t, so that we will be able to predict more accurately the future from the current events or make reasonable decisions in complex situations. In the following, we present a proposition that describes different aspects of $S(t)$.

Proposition 10.3.2 *Let $\mho = (V, E)$ be an FCN. Let $\{S(t) \mid t = 0, 1, 2, \ldots, \}$ be a dynamic dominating process of $\mho$. Then the following properties hold for any t:*

(1) *for every vertex $v \in V - S(t)$, v is dominated by at least one vertex of $S(t)$;*

(2) $N^+(S(t)) \cup S(t) = V$;

(3) *for every vertex* $v \in V - S(t)$, $|N^-(v) \cap S(t)| \geq 1$.

Proof (1) The result is obvious.

(2) It is obvious that $N^+(S(t)) \cup S(t) \subseteq V$. On the other hand, for any $v \in V$, either $v \in S(t)$ or $v \in V - S(t)$. In the latter case, from the definition of $S(t)$ we know that v is dominated by at least one vertex in $S(t)$, hence $v \in N^+(S(t))$. These imply that $V \subseteq N^+(S(t)) \cup S(t)$. Therefore $N^+(S(t)) \cup S(t) = V$.

(3) For any $v \in V - S(t)$, since $S(t) \subseteq V$ is a dynamic dominating set of $\mho$, v is dominated by at least one vertex in $S(t)$, which means that $N^-(v)$ contains at least one element in $S(t)$. Therefore, $|N^-(v) \cap S(t)| \geq 1$. $\qquad\square$

10.3.2 Minimal Dynamic Dominating Set

We notice that, for an arbitrary FCN $\mho$, if $S(t)$ is a dynamic dominating set of $\mho$, then every superset $S' \supseteq S(t)$ that satisfies $S' \subseteq V$ and any vertex in S' is active at t, is also a dynamic dominating set of $\mho$ at the same t. On the other hand, not every subset $S'' \subseteq S(t)$ is necessarily a dynamic dominating set of $\mho$. We are more interested in studying a minimal dynamic dominating set of $\mho$ at t that is defined as follows.

Definition 10.3.3 *Let $\mho$ be an FCN, and let $S(t)$ be a dynamic dominating set of $\mho$. Then $S(t)$ is called a minimal dynamic dominating set of $\mho$ at t if and only if for any subset $S' \subset S(t)$, S' is a non-dominating set of $\mho$. That is, there exists at least one vertex $v \in V - S'$ that is not dominated at t by any vertex $u \in S'$.*

The study of minimal dynamic dominating set of FCNs at t is useful in modeling real-world applications. For instance, suppose that one exploration society, say, the National Geographic Society, plans to send some people to explore the South Pole. In the first instance, the society chooses those people within the society who have the required expertise so that they can obtain valuable information effectively. This means that people selected to be on the exploration team have to be currently active experts. On the other hand, in order to save costs, the society may have to choose as *few* people as possible. In this exercise, the society is in fact building up a dynamic dominating set that consists of a few, currently active and experienced experts in the society. This is a problem of finding a minimal dynamic dominating set in an FCN at t. Similarly, we can use minimal dynamic dominating set in FCNs at t to model many other real-world applications involving the placement of a minimal number of objects, such as hospitals, schools, fire stations, post offices, police stations, warehouses, service centers and so on, or the placement of undesirable objects, such as toxic wastes, nuclear reactors, airports.

We now extend Ore's idea (Haynes, Hedetniemi and Slater 1998) to FCNs and prove a basic property associated with the minimal dynamic dominating set in FCNs at t.

Theorem 10.3.4 *Let $\mho$ be an FCN, let $S(t)$ be a dynamic dominating set of $\mho$ as in Definition 10.3.1. Then $S(t)$ is a minimal dynamic dominating set of $\mho$ if and only if for every vertex $u \in S(t)$, one of the following two conditions holds:*

(a) $N^-(u) \subseteq V - S(t)$,

(b) *there exists a vertex* $v \in V - S(t)$ *for which* $N^-(v) \cap S(t) = \{u\}$.

Proof Suppose that $S(t)$ is a minimal dynamic dominating set of $\mho$. Then $S(t)$ satisfies the following two conditions: every vertex in $S(t)$ is active at t; and for every vertex $u \in S(t)$, $S(t) - \{u\}$

is a non-dominating set. The latter condition means that there exists at least one vertex $v \in V - (S(t) - \{u\})$ such that v is not dominated by any vertex in $S(t) - \{u\}$, which imply that v satisfies $v = u$ or $v \in V - S(t)$. In the former case, we can obtain immediately that $N^-(u) \subseteq V - S(t)$. In the latter case, since v is not dominated by $S(t) - \{u\}$ but is dominated by $S(t)$, vertex v is dominated only by one vertex $u \in S(t)$, that is, $N^-(v) \cap S(t) = \{u\}$.

Conversely, suppose that $S(t)$ is a dynamic dominating set of $\mho$ such that for every vertex $u \in S(t)$, one of the stated conditions holds. We need to prove that $S(t)$ is a minimal dynamic dominating set of $\mho$. Suppose otherwise, then there exists at least one vertex $u \in S(t)$, such that $S(t) - \{u\}$ is a dynamic dominating set of $\mho$. Hence, u is dominated by at least one vertex in $S(t) - \{u\}$, that is, condition (a) does not hold. Also, if $S(t) - \{u\}$ is a dynamic dominating set, then every vertex in $V - S(t)$ is dominated by at least one vertex in $S(t) - \{u\}$, that is, condition (b) does not hold for u. Thus neither condition (a) nor (b) holds, which contradicts our assumption that at least one of these conditions holds. This contradiction shows that $S(t)$ is a minimal dynamic dominating set of $\mho$, as required. $\square$

Suppose that every vertex in an FCN is active at t, then the FCN has at least one minimal dynamic dominating set at t, even has several minimal dynamic dominating sets at t. We can use the following regular division algorithm (Liu 2000) to find one of such dynamic subsets.

Algorithm 10.3.5 *1. Set $S(t) = \emptyset$.*
2. Choose any vertex $v \in V - S(t)$, mark v.
3. Calculate the out-neighborhood $N^+(v)$ of v.
4. Set $S(t) = S(t) \cup \{v\}$.
5. Set $V = V - N^+(v)$, if $V = \emptyset$, stop, otherwise go to step 2.

The dynamic subset $S(t)$ obtained by using this algorithm is a minimal dynamic dominating set of $\mho$ at t. We can demonstrate this by a simple FCN with 9 vertices shown in Figure 4. Assume that every vertex in this FCN is active at t, that is, $0 < x_i(t) \leq 1$. Then we can obtain a minimal dynamic dominating set of $\mho$ by the following procedure.

- Let $S(t) = \emptyset$. Choose any vertex $v \in V - S(t)$, for example v_1, and mark $v = v_1$. We then have $N^+(v) = \{v_2, v_5, v_6\}$, $V = V - N^+(v) = \{v_1, v_3, v_4, v_7, v_8, v_9\}$, $S(t) = S(t) \cup \{v\} = \emptyset \cup \{v_1\} = \{v_1\}$; we further obtain $V - S(t) = \{v_3, v_4, v_7, v_8, v_9\}$.
- Repeat the same steps above, choose any other vertex $v \in V - S(t)$, for example v_8, mark $v = v_8$, we obtain $N^+(v) = \{v_5, v_9\}$, $V = V - N^+(v) = \{v_3, v_4, v_7\}$, $S(t) = S(t) \cup \{v\} = \{v_1\} \cup \{v_8\} = \{v_1, v_8\}$l; further, $V - S(t) = \{v_3, v_4, v_7\}$.
- We find that v_3, v_4, v_7 are three isolated vertices, so they can be added directly to $S(t)$. Therefore the subset $S(t) = \{v_1, v_3, v_4, v_7, v_8\}$ is a minimal dynamic dominating set of the FCN at t.

Although Algorithm 10.3.5 presented above is easy to construct, unfortunately it requires $O(2^n)$ steps in the worst case; that is, it has an exponential complexity in the size of the FCN. We really would like to know whether there *exists* an algorithm for finding a minimal dynamic dominating set for an arbitrary FCN, which is significantly faster than Algorithm 10.3.5 that tries all possible vertices of the FCN. To the best of our knowledge, this has not been investigated in the context of fuzzy causal inference networks.

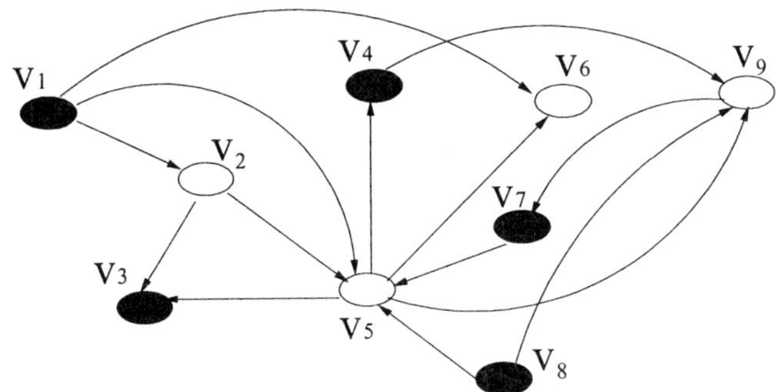

Figure 4. A minimal dynamic dominating set in an FCN

We can extend Garey and Johnson's ideas (Garey and Johnson 1979) to FCNs and give the following basic complexity result concerning dynamic dominating set in FCNs at t. For an arbitrary FCN $\mho$, the graphic structure of $\mho$ is a directed graph in the usual sense (Haynes, Hedetniemi and Slater 1998). Therefore the proof of the following theorem is similar to that of (Garey and Johnson 1979) and hence omitted.

Theorem 10.3.6 *Let $\mho$ be an arbitrary FCN. Then the problem of finding a dynamic dominating set of $\mho$ at t with minimum size is NP-complete.*

10.4 An Illustrative Example

When we use FCN to model real-world applications, we usually aim at determining the impact an initial condition has on the whole FCN, so that we can provide decision support or causal discovery to decision makers. In the literature, most researchers set some vertices active at t (the remaining vertices inactive at t) as the initial condition of the FCN, and then calculate inference patterns (Kosko 1988, Kosko 1993, Liu and Zhang 2001, Miao and Liu 2000, Zhang, Liu and Zhou 2001). The inference process can be summarized as follows (Liu and Zhang 2001, Zhang, Liu and Zhou 2001). Assume that $\phi_\mho(t)$ is the initial state of $\mho$. When $\phi_\mho(t)$ receives a series of external input sequences, its next state $\phi_\mho(t+1)$ will be updated by the following formula:

$$\phi_\mho(t+1) = f_T(\phi_\mho(t) \times W_\mho), \tag{10.1}$$

where $W_\mho$ is the adjacency matrix of $\mho$ shown as follows

$$W_\mho = \begin{pmatrix} \cdots & \cdots & \cdots \\ \cdots & e_{ij} & \cdots \\ \cdots & \cdots & \cdots \end{pmatrix} \tag{10.2}$$

where the ith row of $W_\mho$ lists the values e_{ik} $(k = 1, \ldots, n)$ emitting from v_i, and the jth column lists the values e_{kj} $(k = 1, \ldots, n)$ directing to v_j.

$$T = (T_1, \ldots, T_n),$$

where T_i is given threshold at the i-th vertex v_i, $1 \le i \le n$.

$$\phi_\mho(t) \times W_\mho = (\mu_1, \ldots, \mu_n),$$

where μ_i is the total inputs of v_i defined by $\mu_i = \sum_{k=1}^{n} e_{ki} \cdot x_k(t)$.

$$f_T(\phi_\mho(t) \times W_\mho) = (f_{T_1}(\mu_1), \ldots, f_{T_n}(\mu_n)),$$

where $f_{T_i}(\mu_i)$ is a vertex function (Dickerson and Kosko 1993), which in the literature takes a binary value 1 or 0 shown as follows.

Definition 10.4.1 (Liu 2000) *Given a threshold T_i for the i-th vertex v_i, the vertex function f_{T_i} of v_i is defined by*

$$f_{T_i}(\mu_i) = \left\{ \begin{array}{ll} 1, & \text{if } \mu_i > T_i \\ 0, & \text{if } \mu_i < T_i. \end{array} \right. \tag{10.3}$$

Setting a proper vertex active at t as the initial condition of the FCN plays a critical role in obtaining a reliable inference pattern. On the other hand, from the inference process above, we can see that there is no such a restriction in setting an initial condition. We suggest to set all active vertices in a minimal dynamic dominating set of the FCN at t as the initial condition. According to formula (10.1), the inference pattern can be determined by the vertices of this minimal dynamic dominating set at t. In some sense, it is good enough if we focus our attention on this minimal dynamic dominating set at t to simplify the analysis and design of FCN. To demonstrate the advantage of our theory, we apply this mechanism to analyzing a mock-up FCN for policy making at a university shown in Figure 5. Assume that the decision makers at the university have made some policies to improve teaching and research quality of the university. From time to time, the administration (decision makers) collects feedbacks from the staff, so that it can modify and adjust its policies based on the feedbacks collected. In this case, it is very difficult for the decision makers to deal directly with individual staff. We may construct an

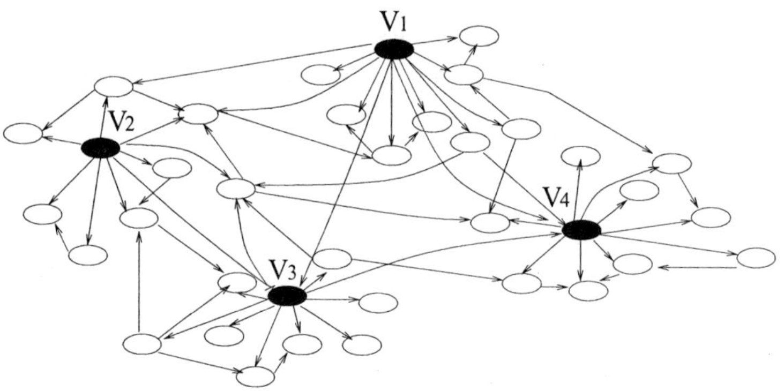

Figure 5. A university network setting current heads of the departments as a minimal dynamic dominating set.

FCN for this problem and use the dynamic dominating set theory to obtain a reliable inference pattern. We first define an FCN for decision makers. Let v_i stand for a staff member of the university. For simplicity we use the same notation to denote the feedback given by v_i to the policies. Let e_{ij} stand for the causal strength from staff v_i to staff v_j. Then $\mathcal{U} = (V, E)$ is an FCN standing for the university network, where $V = \{v_i \mid v_i$ is a staff member of the university$\}$ and $E = \{e_{ij} \mid e_{ij}$ is the causal strength from v_i to $v_j\}$. We take the vertex state value $x_i(t)$ as 1 or 0, which means that the staff has response or no response to the policies. Secondly, assume that the university consists of different departments and the head in each department dominates individual staff in his (or her) department. Finally, the heads from all departments at the university form a minimal dynamic dominating set at t. When the administration at the university is to collect feedbacks from individual staff, initially it needs only to set all active vertices of the minimal dynamic dominating set at t as the initial condition of the FCN. That is, when all vertices of the minimal dynamic dominating set at t receive a series of external input stimuli from the administration, the inference pattern can be obtained by applying formula (10.1) recursively. We can obtain the specific inference pattern using the following procedure:

- Use an FCN $\mho$ to model the university network;
- Find a minimal dynamic dominating set $S(t)$ of $\mho$ at t that consists of all current heads from the departments;
- Set all active vertices in $S(t)$ as the initial condition of $\mho$;
- Calculate inference pattern by using formula (10.1).

We have to emphasize that element in $S(t)$ varies with t, which implies that some head at t may be replaced by someone else at $t + i$. When decision makers at the university would like to collect feedbacks at $t + i$, they should set all active vertices in $S(t + i)$ as the initial condition of the FCN, and predict the impact the initial condition has on the *same* FCN. There are three obvious advantages in using our theory to analyze real-world applications. Firstly, in calculating inference patterns, we set all active vertices of this minimal dynamic dominating set at t as an initial condition of the FCN, which can more effectively describe the dynamic behaviors of FCNs. Secondly, with the minimal dynamic dominating set of $\mho$ at t we can decompose the FCN, which makes design and analysis of large FCNs easier. Finally, using the new inference procedure described we can obtain more reasonable and reliable inference patterns.

10.5　Effective Dynamic Dominating Set

So far, we have presented the dynamic domination theory for FCNs and have investigated their properties and potential applications. In this section, we study related dynamic subsets with a focus on the effective dynamic dominating set. We present some basic concepts first.

Definition 10.5.1 *Let $\mho = (V, E)$ be an FCN, let $S \subseteq V$ be a subset of $\mho$. Then*

(a) $S = S(t)$ is an independent dynamic set of $\mho$ at t if and only if every vertex $v_i \in S$ is active at t, that is, $0 < x_i(t) \leq 1$. And any two vertices $u, v \in S$ satisfy $(u, v) \notin E$ and $(v, u) \notin E$.

(b) $S = S(t)$ is an absorbent dynamic set of $\mho$ at t if and only if every vertex $v_i \in S$ is active at t, that is, $0 < x_i(t) \leq 1$. And any vertex $u \in V - S$ dominates at least one vertex $v \in S$.

(c) $S = S(t)$ is an isolate dynamic set of $\mho$ at t if and only if every vertex $v_i \in S$ is active at t, that is, $0 < x_i(t) \leq 1$. And S is both an independent dynamic set and an absorbent dynamic set of $\mho$ at t.

Definition 10.5.2 *Let $\mho = (V, E)$ be an FCN, let $S \subseteq V$ be a subset of $\mho$. Then $S = S(t)$ is called an effective dynamic dominating set (EDDS) of $\mho$ at t if and only if the following three conditions hold:*

(a) Every vertex $v_i \in S$ is active at t, that is, $0 < x_i(t) \leq 1$.

(b) Any vertex $v \in V - S$ is dominated by at least one vertex $u \in S$.

(c) There exists at least one vertex $v \in V - S$ such that v dominates a vertex $w \in S$.

We are interested in studying such dynamic subsets at t due to their close relationships to many real-world applications. For example, the game theory (Neumann and Morgenstern 1944), logic (Berge and Rao 1977) and facility location (Haynes, Hedetniemi and Slater 1998) are closely related to the dynamic subsets defined in Definition 10.5.1. We provide a few fundamental results associated with the dynamic subsets, one of which is inspired by Berge's idea (Haynes, Hedetniemi and Slater 1998).

The proof of the following lemma is similar to that of (Haynes, Hedetniemi and Slater 1998, Theorem 7.63) and hence is omitted.

Lemma 10.5.3 *Let $\mho = (V, E)$ be an FCN, and let $S(t)$ be an isolate dynamic set of $\mho$ at t. Then $S(t)$ is a maximal independent dynamic set and a minimal absorbent dynamic set of $\mho$ at t.*

Theorem 10.5.4 *Let $\mho = (V, E)$ be an FCN. Suppose that $S(t)$ is a dynamic dominating set and an absorbent dynamic set of $\mho$, then $S(t)$ must be an EDDS of $\mho$. Conversely, suppose that $S(t)$ is an EDDS of $\mho$, then $S(t)$ must be a dynamic dominating set of $\mho$, but it may not be an absorbent dynamic set of $\mho$.*

Proof Assume that $S(t)$ is a dynamic dominating set of $\mho$, then it must satisfy the condition (a) of Definition 10.5.2. Assume that $S(t)$ is also an absorbent dynamic set of $\mho$, then for any vertex $u \in V - S(t)$, u dominates a vertex $v \in S(t)$, it certainly satisfies the condition (b) of Definition 10.5.2. Therefore, $S(t)$ must be an EDDS of $\mho$.

Conversely, assume that $S(t)$ is an EDDS of $\mho$, then $S(t)$ satisfies the conditions (a) and (b) of Definition 10.5.2, it is certainly a dynamic dominating set of $\mho$. On the other hand, we have found a simple FCN with 8 vertices shown in Figure 6, where $S(t) = \{v_2, v_4, v_6\}$ is an EDDS of $\mho$, but there exists a vertex $v_8 \in V - S(t)$, such that v_8 does not dominate any vertex $v \in S(t)$. Hence, $S(t)$ is not an absorbent dynamic set of $\mho$.   □

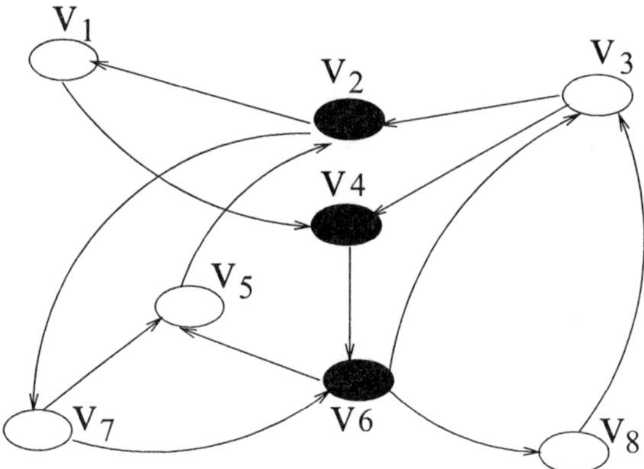

Figure 6. An effective dynamic dominating set in an FCN.

As we know that FCNs are for decision support and causal discovery (Liu and Zhang 2001). For complex real-world applications, the software agent must be able to learn, to reason, to adjust, and to react in the way consistent with that by humans. Usually this goal can be reached by determing the impact an initial condition has on the whole FCN and by collecting feedback (directed cycles). A directed path $P(u, v)$ from a vertex u to another vertex v in FCNs has been defined (Liu and Zhang 2001) as a sequence $v_1, v_2, \ldots, v_r$ of distinct vertices of $\mho$, such that $v_1 = u, v_r = v$ and (v_i, v_{i+1}) is an arc of $\mho$ for each $i = 1, \ldots, r - 1$. Sometimes such a directed path is denoted by $P(u, v) = (v_1, v_2, \ldots, v_r)$. The indirect effect (Liu and Zhang 2001) of vertex u dominates vertex v at t via the directed path $P(u, v)$ is

$$I_P(t) = I_{(v_1, v_2, \ldots, v_r)}(t) = \prod_{i=1}^{r-1} x_i(t) \cdot e_{i\ i+1}. \qquad (10.4)$$

And the definition of feedback is defined as follows.

Definition 10.5.5 *Let $\mho$ be an FCM, and let u be any vertex in $\mho$. Then a piece of feedback is defined as a directed cycle $P(u, u)$ from a vertex u to the same vertex u via a series of distinct vertices $v_1, v_2, \ldots, v_r$ of $\mho$ such that $v_1 = u, v_r = u$. Such a directed cycle can be denoted briefly as $(v_1, v_2, \ldots, v_{r-1}, v_1)$.*

Handling feedback is one of the most important capabilities of FCNs. Feedback enables the system to adjust (adapt) itself in response to the changing environment and to the information about the given goals and actual outcomes. Now we introduce the concept of extended feedback.

Definition 10.5.6 *Let $\mho$ be an FCN, let $S(t)$ be an EDDS of $\mho$, and let $P = (v_1, v_2, \ldots, v_r)$ be a directed path in $\mho$. Then P is called an extended feedback of $\mho$ if and only if P satisfies that $v_1, v_r \in S(t)$ and $v_i \in V - S(t)$ for each $i = 2, 3, \ldots, r - 1$. When P only contains two vertices, the extended feedback is reduced to an edge of $S(t)$.*

We can see the difference between feedback and extended feedback by the same FCN $\mho$ shown in Figure 6. In this example, $S(t) = \{v_2, v_4, v_6\}$ is an EDDS of $\mho$ at t. (v_2, v_7, v_5, v_2), $(v_2, v_7, v_6, v_5, v_2)$, (v_4, v_6, v_3, v_4), $(v_4, v_6, v_8, v_3, v_4)$, $(v_4, v_6, v_5, v_2, v_1, v_4)$ are five feedbacks contained in $S(t)$, where each feedback is a directed cycle from a vertex of $S(t)$ to the same vertex. (v_2, v_1, v_4), (v_2, v_7, v_6), (v_4, v_6), (v_6, v_5, v_2), (v_6, v_3, v_2), (v_6, v_3, v_4), (v_6, v_8, v_3, v_2), (v_6, v_8, v_3, v_4) are eight extended feedbacks contained in $S(t)$, where each extended feedback is a directed path from a vertex of $S(t)$ to another vertex of $S(t)$.

The concept of extended feedback presented in this section is another important feature of FCNs, which makes FCNs more powerful and more flexible due to the following reason. When one vertex in an EDDS dominates other vertices, another vertex or other vertices in this subset may receive extended feedback originated from the vertex. In this way, the decision makers are able to obtain necessary information no matter which vertex receives such extended feedback. For instance, in the Department of Computer Science at a university, it is assumed that some leading experts in the department form a dynamic dominating set at t. The staff in this subset are responsible for collecting feedback and extended feedback from each individual staff. Therefore, the department can make decisions based on the feedback and extended feedback that receive from this subset.

10.6 Simulation Results

In this section, we apply the mechanism presented in this article to analyse a simple, real-world application, where we regard the Department of Computer Science at a university as an FCN $\mho$. We would like to confirm that the new inference procedure discussed in Section 10.4 should obtain more reliable inference pattern than the conventional inference procedure (Kosko 1988, Kosko 1993, Liu and Zhang 2001, Miao and Liu 2000, Zhang, Liu and Zhou 2001). In this simulation, we assume an imaginary causal network of the department, as shown in Figure 7.

The department would like to retain excellent teaching/research staff and to admit best students. To accomplish this, the decision makers have to develop policies and have to modify or adjust their policies from time to time based on the feedback and extended feedback collected from the staff. All vertices are connected, which means that one staff member's response to the department's policies may dominate staff members in the department to some degree. For simplicity of calculation, we assume that the department has 12 staff members with one leading expert in each of the following areas, computer networks, databases, and computer vision. It is assumed that in the FCN, the strengths of all edges are -1, 1 or 0, meaning that a staff may have negative, positive, or no influence to other staff members. Every vertex has a value 0 or 1, indicating the staff member has

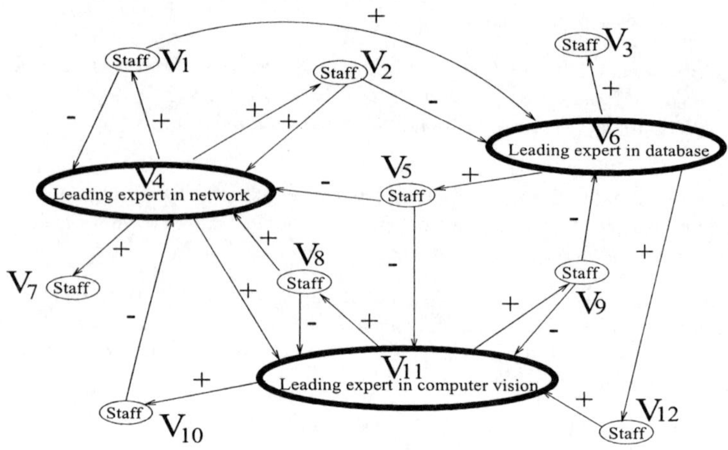

Figure 7. An imaginary personnel affiliation network in an FCN

a response or has no response to the department's policies. In the following two schemes, for simplicity, we set the thresholds as $T_i = 1$ $(i = 1, \ldots, 12)$ for all 12 vertices involved. The adjacency matrix of the FCN is

$$W_\upsilon = \begin{pmatrix} 0 & 0 & 0 & -1 & 0 & 1 & 0 & 0 & 0 & 0 & 0 & 0 \\ 0 & 0 & 0 & 1 & 0 & -1 & 0 & 0 & 0 & 0 & 0 & 0 \\ 0 & 0 & 0 & 0 & 0 & 0 & 0 & 0 & 0 & 0 & 0 & 0 \\ 1 & 1 & 0 & 0 & 0 & 0 & 1 & 0 & 0 & 0 & 1 & 0 \\ 0 & 0 & 0 & -1 & 0 & 0 & 0 & 0 & 0 & 0 & -1 & 0 \\ 0 & 0 & 1 & 0 & 1 & 0 & 0 & 0 & 0 & 0 & 0 & 1 \\ 0 & 0 & 0 & 0 & 0 & 0 & 0 & 0 & 0 & 0 & 0 & 0 \\ 0 & 0 & 0 & 1 & 0 & 0 & 0 & 0 & 0 & 0 & -1 & 0 \\ 0 & 0 & 0 & 0 & 0 & -1 & 0 & 0 & 0 & 0 & -1 & 0 \\ 0 & 0 & 0 & -1 & 0 & 0 & 0 & 0 & 0 & 0 & 0 & 0 \\ 0 & 0 & 0 & 0 & 0 & 0 & 0 & 1 & 1 & 1 & 0 & 0 \\ 0 & 0 & 0 & 0 & 0 & 0 & 0 & 0 & 0 & 0 & 1 & 0 \end{pmatrix}. \tag{10.5}$$

10.6.1   Scheme I: Set One Random Vertex Active at t as The Initial Condition

We would like to estimate the impact an initial condition has on the whole FCN by calculating its causal inference pattern. We simply keep v_6 (an expert) active during the inference cycle and indicate this as $\boxed{1}$. Now it starts with the expert, which implies that only the expert receives an external input from the department, and we would like to see what will happen:

$$\phi_\upsilon(0) = (0\ 0\ 0\ 0\ 0\ \boxed{1}\ 0\ 0\ 0\ 0\ 0\ 0),$$

then

$$\phi_\upsilon(0) \times W_\upsilon = (0\ 0\ 1\ 0\ 1\ 0\ 0\ 0\ 0\ 0\ 0\ 1)$$

$$\phi_\upsilon(1) = f_T(\phi_\upsilon(0) \times W_\upsilon) = (0\ 0\ 1\ 0\ 1\ \boxed{1}\ 0\ 0\ 0\ 0\ 0\ 1)$$

$$\phi_{\mho}(1) \times W_{\mho} = (0\,0\,1\,-1\,1\,0\,0\,0\,0\,0\,0\,1)$$

$$\phi_{\mho}(2) = f_T(\phi_{\mho}(1) \times W_{\mho}) = (0\,0\,1\,0\,1\,\boxed{1}\,0\,0\,0\,0\,0\,1) = \phi_{\mho}(1).$$

We have reached the final stable state. $\phi_{\mho}(1)$ represents $x_3 = x_5 = x_{12} = 1$, corresponding to the following set of staff being activated:

$$\{v_3, v_5, v_{12}\};$$

that is, the activation of v_6 will result in v_3, v_5, v_{12} (three remaining staff members) being activated by the department's policies.

10.6.2　Scheme II: Set all Vertices in Dynamic Dominating Set at t as The Initial Condition

When we calculate causal inference pattern for the same FCN, we first look for a minimal dynamic dominating set of $\mho$ at t, and then set all active vertices in such a subset as the initial condition. From Figure 7, we can see that $S(t) = \{v_4, v_6, v_{11}\}$ is a minimal dynamic dominating set at t. We simply keep v_4, v_6, v_{11} active during the inference cycle and indicate these as $\boxed{1}$, which means that the three leading experts all receive the external input at t from the department. Here is what will happen:

$$\phi_{\mho}(0) = (0\,0\,0\,\boxed{1}\,0\,\boxed{1}\,0\,0\,0\,0\,\boxed{1}\,0),$$

then

$$\phi_{\mho}(0) \times W_{\mho} = (1\,1\,1\,0\,1\,0\,1\,1\,1\,1\,1\,1)$$

$$\phi_{\mho}(1) = f_T(\phi_{\mho}(0) \times W_{\mho}) = (1\,1\,1\,\boxed{1}\,1\,\boxed{1}\,1\,1\,1\,1\,\boxed{1}\,1)$$

$$\phi_{\mho}(1) \times W_{\mho} = (1\,1\,1\,-1\,1\,-1\,1\,1\,1\,1\,-1\,1)$$

$$\phi_{\mho}(2) = f_T(\phi_{\mho}(1) \times W_{\mho}) = (1\,1\,1\,\boxed{1}\,1\,\boxed{1}\,1\,1\,1\,1\,\boxed{1}\,1) = \phi_{\mho}(1).$$

$\phi_{\mho}(1)$ represents $x_i = 1$ $(i = 1, 2, \ldots, 12)$; all staff in the department have been activated:

$$\{v_1, v_2, \ldots, v_{12}\}.$$

It says that the activation of the three experts will result in all remaining staff members being activated directly or indirectly.

10.6.3　Comparison between Case I and Case II

From the inference pattern obtained in Case I, we can see that when v_6 receives an external impact at t, v_3, v_5, v_{12} (three remaining staff members) are activated by the department's policies. However, the expert did not receive any feedback from the three staff members. The reasons for this phenomenon are explained as follows. In the final stable state, except for the three vertices activated by the initial condition, all other vertices were still inactive. As a result, there was no active directed path to transport the responses from the three staff members. Therefore, the decision makers could not receive any feedback or extended feedback from individual staff members. In this case, the conventional inference procedure makes little sense, because it cannot take all or most staff members' responses into consideration, which is obviously undesirable in any decision-making process.

In contrast, Case II is able to take all members' concerns into account. Let's take a closer look at this case. We can see that $S(t) = \{v_4, v_6, v_{11}\}$ exactly satisfies the two conditions of Definition 10.5.2 and is hence an EDDS of the FCN at t. Firstly, we notice that every vertex in $S(t)$ receives feedback. Table 1 summarizes all feedback received by the vertices of $S(t)$ and related information and we

Table 1. Feedback P contained in $S(t)$ and related information

P	$I_P(t)$	Who receives P		
		v_4	v_6	v_{11}
(v_4, v_1, v_4)	-	*		
(v_4, v_2, v_4)	+	*		
$(v_4, v_1, v_6, v_5, v_4)$	-	*		
$(v_4, v_2, v_6, v_5, v_4)$	+	*		
(v_4, v_{11}, v_8, v_4)	+	*		
$(v_4, v_{11}, v_{10}, v_4)$	-	*		
$(v_4, v_{11}, v_9, v_6, v_5, v_4)$	+	*		
$(v_4, v_1, v_6, v_5, v_{11}, v_8, v_4)$	-	*		
$(v_4, v_1, v_6, v_5, v_{11}, v_{10}, v_4)$	+	*		
$(v_4, v_2, v_6, v_5, v_{11}, v_8, v_4)$	+	*		
$(v_4, v_2, v_6, v_5, v_{11}, v_{10}, v_4)$	-	*		
$(v_6, v_5, v_4, v_1, v_6)$	-		•	
$(v_6, v_5, v_4, v_2, v_6)$	+		•	
$(v_6, v_{12}, v_{11}, v_9, v_6)$	-		•	
$(v_6, v_{12}, v_{11}, v_{10}, v_4, v_1, v_6)$	-		•	
$(v_6, v_{12}, v_{11}, v_{10}, v_4, v_2, v_6)$	+		•	
$(v_6, v_{12}, v_{11}, v_8, v_4, v_1, v_6)$	+		•	
$(v_6, v_{12}, v_{11}, v_8, v_4, v_2, v_6)$	-		•	
(v_{11}, v_8, v_{11})	-			⋆
(v_{11}, v_9, v_{11})	-			⋆
$(v_{11}, v_8, v_4, v_{11})$	+			⋆
$(v_{11}, v_{10}, v_4, v_{11})$	-			⋆
$(v_{11}, v_9, v_6, v_{12}, v_{11})$	-			⋆
$(v_{11}, v_9, v_6, v_5, v_{11})$	+			⋆
$(v_{11}, v_9, v_6, v_5, v_4, v_{11})$	+			⋆
$(v_{11}, v_8, v_4, v_1, v_6, v_{12}, v_{11})$	+			⋆
$(v_{11}, v_{10}, v_4, v_1, v_6, v_{12}, v_{11})$	-			⋆
$(v_{11}, v_{10}, v_4, v_2, v_6, v_{12}, v_{11})$	+			⋆

explain all information contained in Table 1 as follows [2].

- Three vertices in $S(t)$ have received 28 pieces of feedback (14 positives and 14 negatives with corresponding to the effects on policies).

- (v_4, v_2, v_4), $(v_4, v_2, v_6, v_5, v_4)$, (v_4, v_{11}, v_8, v_4), $(v_4, v_{11}, v_9, v_6, v_5, v_4)$, $(v_4, v_1, v_6, v_5, v_{11}, v_{10}, v_4)$, $(v_4, v_2, v_6, v_5, v_{11}, v_8, v_4)$ are six pieces of positive feedback received by v_4. (v_4, v_1, v_4), $(v_4, v_1, v_6, v_5, v_4)$, $(v_4, v_{11}, v_{10}, v_4)$, $(v_4, v_1, v_6, v_5, v_{11}, v_8, v_4)$, $(v_4, v_2, v_6, v_5, v_{11}, v_{10}, v_4)$ are five pieces of negative feedback received by v_4.

- $(v_6, v_5, v_4, v_2, v_6)$, $(v_6, v_{12}, v_{11}, v_{10}, v_4, v_2, v_6)$, $(v_6, v_{12}, v_{11}, v_8, v_4, v_1, v_6)$ are three pieces of positive feedback received by v_6. $(v_6, v_5, v_4, v_1, v_6)$, $(v_6, v_{12}, v_{11}, v_9, v_6)$, $(v_6, v_{12}, v_{11}, v_{10}, v_4, v_1, v_6)$, $(v_6, v_{1e2}, v_{11}, v_8, v_4, v_2, v_6)$ are four pieces of negative feedback received by v_6.

- $(v_{11}, v_8, v_4, v_{11})$, $(v_{11}, v_9, v_6, v_5, v_{11})$, $(v_{11}, v_9, v_6, v_5, v_4, v_{11})$, $(v_{11}, v_8, v_4, v_1, v_6, v_{12}, v_{11})$, $(v_{11}, v_{10}, v_4, v_2, v_6, v_{12}, v_{11})$ are five pieces of positive feedback received by v_{11}. (v_{11}, v_8, v_{11}), (v_{11}, v_9, v_{11}), $(v_{11}, v_{10}, v_4, v_{11})$, $(v_{11}, v_9, v_6, v_{12}, v_{11})$, $(v_{11}, v_{10}, v_4, v_1, v_6, v_{12}, v_{11})$ are five pieces of negative feedback received by v_{11}.

---

[2] In Tables 1 and 2, + and - are the values of $I_P(t)$: + stands for a positive effect on the department's policies, - stands for a negative effect on the department's policies; * stands for feedback P received by v_4, • by v_6, and ⋆ by v_{11}

Next, we notice that except for the feedback above, each vertex in $S(t)$ receives extended feedback. Table 2 summarizes all extended feedbacks received by the vertices in $S(t)$ and related information.

Table 2. Extended feedback P contained in $S(t)$ and related information

P	$I_P(t)$	Who receives P		
		v_4	v_6	v_{11}
(v_4, v_{11})	+			$\star$
(v_4, v_1, v_6)	+		$\bullet$	
(v_4, v_2, v_6)	-		$\bullet$	
(v_6, v_5, v_4)	-	$*$		
(v_6, v_5, v_{11})	-			$\star$
(v_6, v_{12}, v_{11})	+			$\star$
(v_{11}, v_8, v_4)	+	$*$		
(v_{11}, v_{10}, v_4)	-	$*$		
(v_{11}, v_9, v_6)	-		$\bullet$	

The following explains the information contained in Table 2.

- Three vertices in $S(t)$ have received nine pieces of extended feedback (four positives, five negatives with corresponding effects on the policies).
- (v_{11}, v_8, v_4) is one positive extended feedback received by v_4. (v_6, v_5, v_4) and (v_{11}, v_{10}, v_4) are two pieces of negative extended feedback received by v_4.
- (v_4, v_1, v_6) is one positive extended feedback received by v_6. (v_4, v_2, v_6) and (v_{11}, v_9, v_6) are two pieces of negative extended feedback received by v_6.
- (v_4, v_{11}) and (v_6, v_{12}, v_{11}) are two pieces of positive extended feedback received by v_{11}. (v_6, v_5, v_{11}) is one negative extended feedback received by v_{11}.

In summary, from Tables 1 and 2 we can see that the three leading experts in the department form an EDDS of $\mho$. If the decision makers give an external input to every leading expert in the EDDS, the remaining staff members will be activated directly or indirectly by the three leading experts. In effect, from the extended feedbacks from this subset, the department is able to receive feedbacks from all staff members. This provides a good basis for the department to make sensible policies. Furthermore, in Case II, the department is only responsible for determining the initial condition, i.e., the EDDS, and concerned only with feedback and extended feedback from the EDDS (Kosko 1986, Dickerson and Kosko 1993)

10.7   Conclusion

In this chapter, we have reported our recent research on the dynamic domination theory for fuzzy causal networks (FCNs). We have provided the definitions of dynamic dominating set and minimal dynamic dominating set in FCNs, investigated their properties and their potential applications, presented an algorithm for finding a minimal dynamic dominating set in FCNs, and gave a brief, intuitive discussion of computational complexity and NP-completeness. We provided a mock-up FCN to demonstrate the inference properties of our theory in modeling real-world applications. We have shown, indeed, the dynamic domination theory enables us to obtain reasonable and reliable inference patterns. We discussed related subsets with a focus on the investigation of an effective dynamic dominating set (EDDS) in FCNs, so that decision makers can make a sensible decision or adjust (adapt) their decision based on both the feedback and the extended feedback from the subset. Finally, we presented a simulation result, which shows that, for the given problem domain, the inference pattern obtained by the new inference procedure is more reliable than that by the conventional inference procedure.

FCN is an effective tool for causal inference, especially, it is able to process feedback, extended feedback and incomplete information, which is most useful in software agents. For instance, with FCN it is possible to develop *super* software agents that supervise other agents, manage information exchange and cooperation between agents, and communicate with the user. In such applications, the feedback mechanisms of FCNs discussed in this paper may play a major role.

With our dynamic domination theory, quotient space theory (Zhang, Liu and Zhou 2001, Zhang and Liu 2001) and dynamic causal algebra (Liu and Zhang 2001), we have established a good theoretical foundation for FCNs. However, our study is still in its early stages. There exist many interesting and challenging problems in FCNs. For instance, in order to estimate accurately the impact of different types of dynamic dominating sets on the whole FCN, further research on their structural properties is imperatively needed.

As a final note, we have to stress that we are still far short of what are available in the Bayesian Causal Networks which started at almost the same period as fuzzy causal networks.

References

Berge, C. and Rao, A.R. (1977), "A combinatorial problem in logic," *Discrete Math*, vol. 17, pp.23-26.

Chen, B. and Zhou, S. (1999), "Domination number and neighborhood conditions," *Discrete Math*, vol. 195, pp.81-89.

Das, B. and Bharghavan, V. (1997), "Routing in ad-hoc networks using minimum connected dominating sets," in *Proc. IEEE Int. Conf. on Communications, ICC'97 Montreal, Towards the knowledge millennium*, vol. 1 pp.376-380.

Dickerson, J.A. and Kosko, B. (1993), "Virtual worlds as fuzzy cognitive maps," in *Proc. IEEE Virtual Reality Annu. Int. Symp,* New York, pp.417-477.

Garey, M.R. and Johnson, D.S. (1979), "Computers and intractability: A guide to the theory of NP-completeness," Freeman, New York.

Gotoh, K. *et al.* (1989), "An application of fuzzy causal networks to supporting plant control," *SICE Joint Symposium of the* 15*th Systems Symposium and the* 10*th Knowledge Engineering Symposium*, pp.99-104.

Haynes, T.W., Hedetniemi, S.T. and Slater, P.J. (1998), "Fundamentals of domination in graph," Marcel Dekker, Inc, New York.

Innocent, P.R. (1999), "Clinical diagnosis using fuzzy causal networks and fuzzy temporal reasoning," in *Conference Proceedings of SCB99 (ICSC)*, Rochester, New York.

Kelleher, L.L. (1985), "Domination in graphs and its application to social network graphs," Ph.D. Thesis, Northeastern University.

Kelleher, L.L. and Cozzens, M.B. (1988), "Domination sets in social network graphs," *Math. Social Sci.*, vol. 16, pp.267-279.

Kosko, B. (1986), "Fuzzy cognitive maps," *International Journal Man-machine Studies*, vol. 24, pp.65-75.

Kosko, B. (1988), "Hidden pattern in combined and adaptive knowledge networks," *International Journal of Approximate Reasoning*, vol. 2, pp.337-393.

Kosko, B. (1993), "Fuzzy thinking – the new science of fuzzy logic," Hyperion, New York, pp.227.

Lee, K.C. *et al.*, (1994), "A fuzzy cognitive map based bidirectional inference mechanism: an application to stock investment analysis," in *Proc. Japan/Korea Joint Conf. on Expert Systems 10(10)*, pp.193-196.

Liu, Z.Q. (2000), "Fuzzy cognitive maps: analysis and extension," in *Soft Computing: Human Centered Machines*, Liu, Z.Q. and Miyamoto, S. Eds, Tokyo, Japan: Springer-Verlag.

Liu, Z.Q. and Zhang, J.Y. (2001) "On dynamic causal algebra for fuzzy cognitive maps," *Soft Computing*, to be published.

Loia, V. and Sessa, S. (2001), "A soft computing framework for adaptive agents," in *Soft computing agents: new trends for designing autonomous systems*, Studies in fuzziness and soft computing, Loia, V. and Sessa, S. Eds, Giugno, Physica-Verlag, Springer, vol. 75.

Loia, V. Ed, (2002), "Soft computing agents: a new perspective for dynamic systems," International Series "Frontiers in Artificial Intelligence and Application", IOS Press.

Miao, C.Y., Liu, Z.Q., Miao, Y. and Goh, A. (2002), "A Dynamic causal multi-agent platform for large decision-support systems," submitted to *Int. J. Fuzzy Systems*.

Miao, Y., Liu, Z.Q., Siew, C.K. and Miao, C.Y. (2001), "Dynamical cognitive network-an extension of fuzzy cognitive map," *IEEE Trans. Fuzzy Syst.*, vol. 8, No.4, pp.760-770.

Miao, Y. and Liu, Z.Q. (2000), "On causal inference in fuzzy cognitive maps," *IEEE Trans. Fuzzy Syst*, vol. 8, No.1, pp.107-119.

Miao, Y. and Liu, Z.Q. (1999), "Dynamical cognitive network – an extension of fuzzy cognitive map," in *Proc. IEEE Int. Conf. Tools Artificial Intell.*, Chicago, pp.43-46.

Ndousse, T.D. and Okuda, T. (1996), "Computational intelligence for distributed fault management in networks using fuzzy cognitive maps," in *Proc. IEEE Int. Conf. Commun. Converging Technol. Tomorrow's Applicat.*, New York, pp.1558-1562.

Neumann, J. V. and Morgenstern, O. (1944), "Theory of games and economic behavior," Princeton University Press, Princeton.

Pelaez, C.E. and Bowles, J.B. (1996), "Using fuzzy cognitive maps system model for failure modes and effects analysis," *Information Science,* vol. 88, pp.177-199.

Perusich, K. (1996), "Fuzzy cognitive maps policy analysis," in *Proc. Int. Symp. Technol. Soc.Tech. Expertise Public Decisions.*, New York, pp.369-373.

Tsadiras, A.K., Margaritis, K.G. and Mertzios, B.G. (1995), "Strategic planning using fuzzy cognitive maps," Studies in Informatics and Control, vol. 4, pp.237-245.

Tsadiras, A.K. and Margaritis, K.G. (1995), "On transition and convergence properties of fuzzy cognitive maps," in *Proc. HERMIS'94, 2th National Conf. in Mathematics and Informatics,* Athens, Greece, pp.917-924.

Tsadiras, A.K. and Margaritis, K.G. (1997), "Experimental study of dynamical behavior of fuzzy cognitive maps for various transfer functions," in *6th Greek National Computer Science Conference(EPY'97)*, Athens, Greece.

Tsai, Y.J. and Mckinley, P.K. (1994), "Broadcast in all-port wormhole-routed 3D mesh networks using extended dominating sets," in *Proc. IEEE Int. Conf. on Parallel and Distributed Systems 1994*, pp.120-127.

Tsai, Y.J. and Mckinley, P.K. (1997), "An extended dominating node approach to broadcast and global combine in multiport wormhole-routed mesh networks," *Parallel and Distributed Systems, IEEE Transactions*, vol. 81, pp.41-58.

Zhang, J.Y., Liu, Z.Q. and Zhou, S. (2001), "Quotient FCMs—A decomposition theory for fuzzy cognitive maps," submitted to *IEEE Trans. Fuzzy Syst.*

Zhang, J.Y. and Liu, Z.Q. (2001), "Quotient Fuzzy Cognitive Maps," in *IEEE Int. Conf. on Fuzzy Syst. 2001*, Melbourne, Australia, vol. 1, pp.170-174.

Zhou, S. (1996), "On f-domination number of a graph," *Czechoslovak Math. Journal*, vol. 46(121), pp.489-499.

Author Index

List of Authors

Dia Ali
Department of Computer Science and
Statistics,
The University of Southern Mississippi,
Hattiesburg, MS 39406-5106, U.S.
dia.ali@usm.edu

Rafik A. Aliev
Dept. of Automatic Control Systems
Azerbaijan State Oil Academy
20 Azadlyg Ave. Baku, Azerbaijan 370601
raliev@iatp.aznet.org

Hamid R. Berenji
Intelligent Inference Systems Corp.
Computational Sciences Division,
MS: 269-2
NASA Ames Research Center
Mountain View, CA 94035
berenji@ptolemy.arc.nasa.gov

Victor Callaghan
Department of Computer Science,
University of Essex,
Wivenhoe Park, Colchester,
CO4 3SQ, UK
vic@essex.ac.uk

Graham Clarke
Department of Computer Science,
University of Essex,
Wivenhoe Park, Colchester,
CO4 3SQ, UK
graham@esex.ac.uk

Maria Cobb
Department of Computer Science and
Statistics,
The University of Southern Mississippi,
Hattiesburg, MS 39406-5106, U.S.A.
maria.cobb@usm.edu

Martin Colley
Department of Computer Science,
University of Essex,
Wivenhoe Park, Colchester,
CO4 3SQ, UK
martin@essex.ac.uk

Hakan Duman
Department of Computer Science,
University of Essex,
Wivenhoe Park, Colchester,
CO4 3SQ, UK
hduman@essex.ac.uk

Bijan Fazlollahi
Dept. of Computer Information Systems
Georgia State University
Atlanta, GA, U.S.A.
DSCBBF@langate.gsu.edu

Hani Hagras
Department of Computer Science,
University of Essex,
Wivenhoe Park, Colchester,
CO4 3SQ, UK
hani@essex.ac.uk

Arran Holmes
Department of Computer Science,
University of Essex,
Wivenhoe Park, Colchester,
CO4 3SQ, UK
acholm@essex.ac.uk

Rajiv Khosla
School of Business
La Trobe University, Melbourne,
Victoria, Australia
R.Khosla@latrobe.edu.au

Zhi-Qiang Liu
School of Creative Media
City University of Hong Kong
Tat Chee Ave., Kowloon
Hong Kong, P.R. CHINA
smzliu@cityu.edu.hk

Vincenzo Loia
Dipartimento di Matematica e Informatica
Università di Salerno
via S. Allende - 84081 Baronissi (SA),
Italy
loia@unisa.it

Witold Pedrycz
Department of Electrical & Computer
Engineering
University of Alberta, Edmonton, Canada
pedrycz@ee.ualberta.ca

Fred Petry
Department of Electrical Engineering and
Computer Science,
Tulane University, New Orleans, LA
70118, U.S.A.
petry@eecs.tulane.edu

Anthony Pounds-Cornish
Department of Computer Science,
University of Essex,
Wivenhoe Park, Colchester,
CO4 3SQ, UK
apound@essex.ac.uk

Shahram Rahimi
Department of Computer Science
Southern Illinois University
Carbondale, IL 62901-4511, U.S.A.
rahimi@cs.siu.edu

Luis M. Rocha
Complex Systems Research
Modeling, Algorithms, and Informatics
Group (CCS-3)
Los Alamos National Laboratory,
MS B256
Los Alamos, NM 87545, U.S.A.
rocha@lanl.gov

Sabrina Senatore
Dipartimento di Matematica e Informatica
Università di Salerno
via S. Allende - 84081 Baronissi (SA),
Italy
ssenatore@unisa.it

Maria I. Sessa
Dipartimento di Matematica e Informatica
Università di Salerno
via S. Allende - 84081 Baronissi (SA),
Italy
misessa@unisa.it

Mihaela Ulieru
Electrical and Computer Engineering
Department
The University of Calgary, Canada
ulieru@ucalgary.ca

Alex Vengerov
School of Administration and Business
Ramapo College of New Jersey
505 Ramapo Valley Rd.
Mahwah, NJ 07430, U.S.A.
abvenger@ramapo.edu

David Vengerov
Intelligent Inference Systems Corp.
Computational Sciences Division,
MS: 269-2
NASA Ames Research Center
Mountain View, CA 94035, U.S.A.
vengerov@stanford.edu

George Vukovich
Canadian Space Agency, Spacecraft
Engineering
6767 Route de l'Aeroport
Saint-Hubert, Quebec J3Y 8Y9, Canada
george.vukovich@space.gc.ca

Jian Ying Zhang
Dep. of Computer Science and Software
Engineering
The University of Melbourne
Victoria, 3010, Australia
jyzhang@.cs.mu.oz.au